LONDON GUIDE

YOUR PASSPORT TO GREAT TRAVEL!

ABOUT THE AUTHORS

Meg Rosoff first moved to London in the late 1970s to study sculpture. After a fleeting ten year interlude in New York City, she returned to London, married an Englishman, and resumed an occasionally glamorous career in advertising and freelance writing.

Caren Acker had her own special events company in New York City until the late 1980s. She subsequently spent three years in Japan documenting traditional festivals before moving to London in 1992 to work as a freelance publicist. Caren currently lives and works in Hong Kong.

HIT THE OPEN ROAD -
WITH OPEN ROAD PUBLISHING!

Open Road Publishing now has guide books to exciting, fun destinations on four continents, but, oddly enough, some people out there still don't know who we are! We're old college pals and veteran travelers who decided to join forces to bring you the best travel guides available anywhere!

No small task, but here's what we offer:

• All Open Road publications are written by authors, authors with a distinct, opinionated point of view – not some sterile committee or team of writers. Our authors are experts in the areas covered and are polished writers.

• Our guides are geared to people who want great vacations, great value, and great tips for both standard tourist sites *and* fun, unique alternatives.

• We're strong on the basics, but we also provide terrific choices for those looking to get off the beaten path and *experience* the country or city – not just *see* it or pass through it.

• We give you the best, but we also tell you about the worst and what to avoid. Nobody should waste their time and money on their hard-earned vacation because of bad or inadequate travel advice.

• Our guides assume nothing. We tell you everything you need to know to have the trip of a lifetime – presented in a fun, literate, no-nonsense style.

• And, above all, we welcome your input, ideas, and suggestions to help us put out the best travel guides possible.

LONDON GUIDE

YOUR PASSPORT TO GREAT TRAVEL!

MEG ROSOFF & CAREN ACKER

OPEN ROAD PUBLISHING

OPEN ROAD PUBLISHING

We offer travel guides to American and foreign locales. Our books tell it like it is, often with an opinionated edge, and our experienced authors always give you all the information you need to have the trip of a lifetime. Write for your free catalog of all our titles, including our golf and restaurant guides.

Catalog Department, P.O. Box 20226,
Columbus Circle Station, New York, NY 10023

First Edition

Cover photographs courtesy of British Tourist Authority, New York. Interior photographs courtesy of British Tourist Authority, New York, except pages 15, 149, & 187, which are courtesy of Nathaniel Stein Graphic Artists, New York & Tucson.

All prices, schedules, and details are subject to change, and we will not be held responsible for any such fluctuations, or other experiences, that travelers may encounter during their visit.

TABLE OF CONTENTS

1. INTRODUCTION   13

2. EXCITING LONDON! - OVERVIEW   14

3. A SHORT HISTORY   19

4. PLANNING YOUR TRIP   32
Airlines   32
Booking Tickets from America   33
Passports & Visas   33
Customs & Immigration   33
Climate & Weather   34
Hotels   36

5. ARRIVALS & DEPARTURES   37
Getting to Town   37
Renting a Car at the Airport   38
Arriving at a Train Station   39
Checking into Your Hotel   39
Hotel Booking Services   39
Jetlag   40
Getting to the Airport   40

6. BASIC INFORMATION   41
Bank Holidays   41
Banking & Money   41
Business Hours   42
Cars & Driving   43
Coin of the Realm   43

Cost of Living   44
Electricity   44
Etiquette   44
Floors   45
Handicapped Travelers   45
Health & Medical Concerns   45
Queues & Zebra Crossings   46
Loos, Lavatories, Toilets & Cloakrooms   47
Lost & Found   47
Newspapers & Magazines   48
Places of Worship   49
Post Offices   49
Precautions   49
Smoking   50
Taxes   50
Taxis   51
Telephones   51
Television & Radio   52
Time   53
Tipping   53
Water   53
Weights & Measures   53

7. GETTING AROUND LONDON   55
Maps   55
Tickets   56
Boats   56
Buses   57
Cars & Driving   59
The Tube   60
Taxis   60
Trains   61
Walking   61

8. WHERE TO STAY   63
Mayfair & St. James   63
Knightsbridge, Chelsea, & South Kensington   69
Bloomsbury, Soho, & Covent Garden   78
Notting Hill   82
North of Oxford Street   85
Hampstead   87

9. WHERE TO EAT 90

Bloomsbury   91
Chinatown   93
Notting Hill Gate   95
Clerkenwell   98
Covent Garden   101
East London   106
Islington, King's Cross, Euston   107
Knightsbridge, South Kensington, & Chelsea   109
Marylebone, Baker Street   117
Mayfair   118
Primrose Hill   120
Soho   121
On or Across the River:
    The Tate, The South Bank, Waterloo & Tower Bridge   129

10. SEEING THE SIGHTS 134

The Must-Sees   134
    The British Museum   134
    The National Gallery   136
    The National Portrait Gallery   140
    The Natural History Museum   141
    Saint Paul's Cathedral   142
    The Science Museum   146
    The Tate Gallery   147
    Tower of London   148
    The Victoria & Albert Museum   152
    Westminster Abbey   155
More Museums & Monuments   159
    The Banqueting House   159
    Bevis Marks Synagogue   160
    The Courtauld Institute   161
    The Design Museum   162
    Dulwich Picture Gallery   163
    The Geffrye Museum   163
    Imperial War Museum   164
    Kenwood House (The Iveagh Bequest)   165
    Leighton House Museum & Art Gallery   166
    The Museum of London   166
    Museum of Mankind   169
    Musuem of the Moving Image   169
    London Transport Museum   170
    The Theatre Museum   171

Sir John Soane's Museum   172
Spencer House   173
St. Bartholomew The Great Church   174
Wallace Collection   175
Art Galleries – Without Permanent Collections   177
The Hayward Gallery   177
The Institute of Contemporary Arts   178
The Royal Academy of Art   178
The Saatchi Gallery   179
The Serpentine Gallery   179
Whitechapel Gallery   180
Entertainment   180
Cabaret Mechanical Theatre   180
Dennis Sever's House   181
Madame Tussaud's   181
London Zoo   183
London Behind the Scenes   184
Cabinet War Rooms   184
The House of Commons & House of Lords
  – The Palace of Westminster   185
The National Theatre Backstage Tour   187
The Old Bailey (Public Gallery)   189
Theatre Royal Drury Lane Backstage Tours   189
Literary Homes   190
Dickens House   190
The Freud Museum   191
Dr. Samuel Johnson's House   191
Keats' House   192
The Sherlock Holmes Museum   193
Royal London   194
Buckingham Palace   194
Kensington Palace   195
The Queen's Gallery   198
The Royal Mews   198
Parks & Gardens   199
Chelsea Physic Garden   199
Hampstead Heath   200
Highgate Cemetery   200
The Royal Botanic Gardens (Kew Gardens)   202
Regent's Park   203
Hyde Park & Kensington Gardens   204
Green Park & St. James Park   205

11. WALKING TOURS OF LONDON 206
Chelsea 206
Fleet Street to Saint Paul's 208
Greenwich 211
Hampstead 214
St. James & Piccadilly 214

12. CULTURE 218
Theater 218
Film 220
Opera, Music, & Dance 221

13. NIGHTLIFE & PUBLIFE 224
Food & Drink 224
Music & Entertainment 225
Pubs 226
    Bloomsbury & Holborn 228
    Chelsea & South Kensington 230
    The City & East London 231
    Covent Garden 233
    Greenwich 234
    Primrose Hill, Hampstead, & Highgate 235
    Islington, Clerkenwell, & King's Cross 238
    Notting Hill 240
    Knightsbridge & Belgravia 240
    Mayfair & St. James 242
    North of Oxford Street 243
    Southwest London (Richmond, Wimbledon, Kew) 244
    Soho 245
    South London 246

14. SHOPPING 247
Big & Classic Stores 249
Very English, Very Quaint 251
Women's Fashions 252
Men's Fashions 254
Shoes 255
Books 256
Antique Markets 257
Miscellaneous 259

15. AFTERNOON TEA   260

Afternoon Tea Classics   260

16. CHILD'S PLAY   263

Babysitting   263
Museums   265
Parks, Playgrounds, & The Zoo   266
Kid-Friendly Restaurants   268
Shopping   270
Children's Theater   272

17. SPORTS & RECREATION   273

Gyms, Spas, & Workout Clubs   273
Horseback Riding   275
Swimming, Tennis, & Golf   275
Snooker   276
Major Sports & Sporting Events   276
   Tennis at Wimbledon   277

18. EXCURSIONS & DAY TRIPS   279

Brighton   279
Hampton Court Palace   281
Oxford & Woodstock   286
Petworth   289
Sandwich   291
Windsor Castle   293

MAPS & SIDEBARS

MAPS

England   12
Central London Hotels   66-67
Central London Restaurants   96-97
Central London   138-139
London Zoo & Regent's Park   183
Theatre District   219
London Excursions   283

SIDEBARS

Car Rental Phone Numbers at the Airports   39
Phoning Home, Quickly & Cheaply   52
Essential Phone Numbers   54
A Couple of Handy Driving Hints   59
Six of the Best Hotels   70
Budget Bests (hotels)   89
Budget Bests (restaurants)   104
Culinary Stars   133
Ravens on Parade   151
Disraeli's Feud   161
The Changing of the Guard   195
The Ladies' Bridge   208
The Thames: From Foul Factories to Fair Fishing   213
Choosing a Pub   229
Pubs to Write Home About   237
Sizes   254
At Last, a Children's Hotel!   264
Divorce English-Style   281
A Collection of Colleges   287
Windsor Info   293
What's in a Name?   294
The Queen's Guards – How Do They Do It?   297

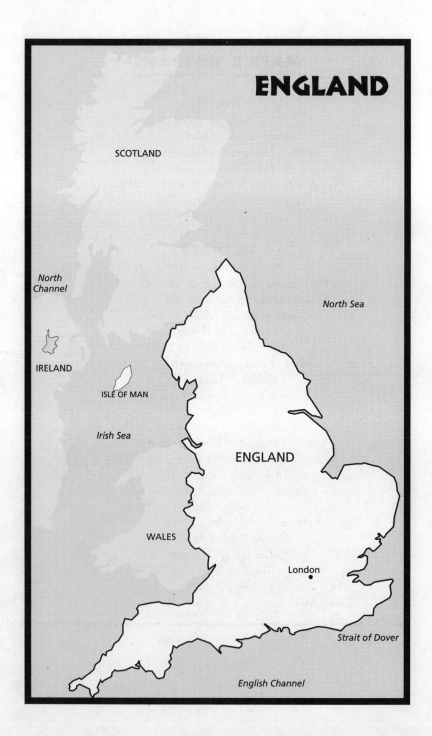

ENGLAND

SCOTLAND

North
Channel

North Sea

IRELAND

ISLE OF MAN

Irish Sea

ENGLAND

WALES

London

Strait of Dover

English Channel

1. INTRODUCTION

Do you know how to convince a London cabbie you're a local? Which common courtesy is completely taboo in pubs? A simple (honest) way to avoid the hefty admission fees many museums charge? How to get into Wimbledon without planning ahead (or mortgaging the house)?

Unless you've lived in London for years, you probably don't. But that's ok, because we do — and we're about to tell you. We'll also tell you how to get tickets to the best shows (and how to choose the best shows), the quickest, easiest way to get around (it's not always taxis), and the best way to avoid dying of starvation and neglect in London restaurants (it's not always easy).

You're about to discover which museum has a lovely (and largely undiscovered) restaurant, where to find the original handwritten manuscripts of early Beatles songs, why your favorite ale tastes different from pub to pub, and where to find the prettiest secret garden in London.

With a tourist's eye and a native's experience, we'll take you through some of the world's biggest and most impressive museums (looking for animatronic dinosaurs? a 1908 Rolls Royce? a frieze that puts the Elgin Marbles to shame?) We'll tell you where Michael Caine buys his groceries, what good quality items are still cheaper in London than the U.S., and who's been poaching Italy's best lingerie designers (Marks & Spencer). Oh yes. We'll also tell you about Christopher Wren churches, the best £60 a night hotel in town, and how to have a really wonderful holiday with kids.

How do we know all this stuff? Simple. We're in love — with London's theater, art, fashion, food and pubs. We wear silly hats to weddings (and know just where to buy them). We'll see anything the Royal Shakespeare Company cares to stage. We love warm beer (you will too, if you follow our pub guide). We dote on the language differences. And best of all, we adore finding a real bargain — and we hate keeping good news to ourselves.

So if you've got a week to spend in London and you're not sure where to start, you've come to the right place. Because we don't just want you to have a good time. We want you to fall in love too.

2. EXCITING LONDON! - OVERVIEW

It's easy to have a miserable time in London. Simply arrive in a downpour on a bleak March day, get lost, get wet, stumble into a wretched, dirty old pub and retire in despair to a ludicrously expensive dinner and a hotel room in which the only object of historical note is the mattress.

This book is dedicated to preventing this from happening. And the good news is, all it takes is a little planning.

The most common stumbling blocks to a successful visit to London are the weather and the scale: the city is huge, and yes, it does it rain.

These problems pale into insignificance, however, as you begin to realize that no matter how gray it is outdoors, London is bursting with color indoors. Museums, antiquities, artworks, theaters and historical houses – the dauntingly large selection of sights in this book represents just a fraction of available options.

When trying to make sense of this wealth of attractions, it's worth remembering one important fact: London is made up of villages, each small and manageable, each filled with historic churches, architectural monuments, eccentric shops and atmospheric pubs – each with its own peculiar charm. As far as possible, we've organized monuments, museums, restaurants and pubs by neighborhood.

You'll find **Bloomsbury** bookish and filled with echoes of literary inhabitants past and present; **Covent Garden** as much a marketplace now as it was in Eliza Doolittle's day; **Mayfair** and **St. James** chock-a-block with the underpinnings of the upper classes – bespoke tailoring, saddlery and soap purveyors to the queen.

And best of all, you'll find that each village contains more than a sufficient number of small museums, ancient pubs and cozy teashops to keep you in rapture through the rainiest week. Explore London one neighborhood at a time and after a while, you'll find the city as a whole beginning to take shape in your head. Don't worry if it doesn't happen all at once – that just gives you an excuse to come back.

And while we're at it, another piece of advice.

Try to familiarize yourself at least marginally with the history of England. Dredge up your memories of Masterpiece Theater and high school Shakespeare – and at least skim our history chapter. Even a cursory familiarity with the characters and events of the last ten centuries will vastly increase your enjoyment of just about everything you experience.

And last, but not least, get a good map. That, a pair of comfortable shoes, a bit of curiosity and a sturdy credit card – and you're on your way.

ORIENTATION

If you want to get a feel for how big London really is, take a taxi from the East End to Chiswick during rush hour. Not only will this cost you about the same as your plane ticket, but you will travel (very slowly, given the usual state of London traffic) through a staggering variety of architectural styles, socioeconomic groups and urban landscapes.

ONE OF THE SPANS AT THE TOWER BRIDGE

There's a good reason for this: today's London, all 50-miles-across of it, is made up of yesterday's villages. This is particularly evident in places like **Highgate** in north London, which was, literally, one of the gates into London – but still half a day's journey away. Similarly, **Islington** was a well-known spa five hundred years ago, where Charles II took his mistress Nell Gwynne for the healing waters. The village feeling in London has not disappeared; each neighborhood still retains its own high street, church, town hall and often its own common and cricket pitch.

The original city of London is what today is known (coincidentally) as **The City of London**. Before the great fire of 1666, this *was* London – with the original Gothic **St. Paul's** cathedral as its centerpiece. Today, The City is London's Wall Street, home to the **Bank of England** and just about every other financial institution. If someone talks about working in **The City** (or the **Square Mile**), they mean the specific area of London, approximately one mile square, about a mile to the east of Covent Garden and Bloomsbury. As London has grown and spread out, it has developed two main centers beyond The City – **The West End** and the **Knightsbridge/ South Kensington** area.

THE WEST END

Technically speaking, the **West End** includes the entire area west of The City, east of Park Lane and north of the Thames, but in the vernacular, it refers to the **Covent Garden/Soho/Bloomsbury** area which contains thousands of restaurants, reasonably priced trendy boutiques, antiquarian bookstores, the theater district, **The British Museum** and **The National Gallery**.

The West End is busy, gritty, noisy, full of publishing houses, advertising agencies, film companies, pretty squares – and people. This is the part of town you're most likely to run into Alan Rickman or Paul McCartney sipping cappuccino at an outdoor cafe.

KNIGHTSBRIDGE/SOUTH KENSINGTON

For all you visiting New Yorkers, **Knightsbridge/South Kensington** is London's Upper East Side. Low on bookstores, artists and pizza joints; big on posh shops and restaurants full of expensively coiffed men and women calling each other darling.

If you're a fan of Absolutely Fabulous, you'll feel right at home with **Harvey Nichols** and **Harrods** so close at hand – if culture is more your forte, the **Victoria and Albert Museum** is just up the road, as are the **Science** and **Natural History Museums**.

This part of town is where you're likely to catch a glimpse of the Duke of Westminster stocking up on smoked salmon or Princess Di shopping for hats; it's packed with charming, exclusive squares, excellent restaurants and double lines of six year olds in elegant school uniforms. On its edges are **Chelsea**, **Kensington**, **Fulham**, **Notting Hill** and **Bayswater**.

MAYFAIR

In the middle is **Mayfair** which is technically, but not psychologically, part of the West End. Mayfair is where young women in Edith Wharton novels settled into charming townhouses on leafy squares after they were married.

Today the main inhabitants are very rich Europeans, very rich Arabs, embassies, private galleries, **The Royal Academy**, expensive restaurants and expensive call girls. As it's walking distance from the theater district to the east and Harrods to the west, Mayfair is understandably the posh hotel center of London.

OUT FROM THE CITY CENTER

Further out from the center you might have reason to visit **Hampstead** or **Highgate** (charming villages on either side of Hampstead Heath) to the north; **Chiswick** and **Richmond** (more charming villages, Kew Gardens, and Richmond deer park) to the west; the **East End** (run-down streets, huge outdoor markets, bagel shops and Indian restaurants) and **Greenwich** (with its lovely park, observatory, museums and antique shops) to the east and south east; and **Dulwich** (home of Dulwich Picture Gallery) to the south. The more distance you stray, the more charming, authentic and village-y London looks.

MANAGING LONDON

A basic rule of thumb is to try and master a small piece at a time. London can feel huge, chaotic and overwhelming, but if you get to know it village by village it will seem much more manageable. And if you like to walk, we offer our favorite walking tours of London, featuring great architecture, great history, great food, and great beer.

ROOM & BOARD FIT FOR KINGS & QUEENS

London is home to some of the finest hotels in the world; you probably already know that. But what you may not know is that London is also home to some of the finest restaurants in the world too. While traditional English fare may not be everybody's cup of tea, you'll find a fantastic variety of world-class cuisine in all price ranges.

EXCURSIONS

When you're ready to spend a day or more outside London, we've got the perfect escapes for you:

A day in **Brighton** will allow you to get acquainted with that strange atmosphere of faded grandeur that permeates English seaside towns.

Hampton Court is one of England's grandest royal and historical sites, where you can visit the country home and hunting grounds for generations of British monarchs since Henry VIII.

The university town of **Oxford**, with itscenturies-old college buildings, cloisters, and gardens, is where you canabsorb all that erudition or simply rent a punt on the River Cherwell.

Woodstock, not far from Oxford, a village that somehow manages to retain its unspoiled, low-key charm, is where you can visit **Blenheim Palace**, the enormous Italianate residence of the current Duke of Marlborough and birthplace of Winston Churchill.

Petworth is where you can wander through a 2,000 acre Capability Brown park, a magnificent stately home filled with the world's largest private collection of Turners, and a pretty country village packed with antique shops.

There's also great antiquing in **Sandwich**, which has retained virtually all of its medieval charm, most of its medieval buildings, and remains unruined by tourism or development.

And finally, the huge, fairytale castle of **Windsor**. Wth its medieval tower rising majestically above the busy little town, its priceless works of art, and 900 years of royal history, it welcomes visitors to the weekend home of the queen.

3. A SHORT HISTORY

BRITONS, CELTS & ROMANS: THE FOUNDING OF LONDINIUM

Although any British schoolboy will tell you that the Romans founded Londinium in 43AD, the first inhabitants of the Thames Valley were tribes of huntergatherers who roamed the region as long as half a million years ago. During the **bronze age** (around 2000 BC), northern European tribes migrated south, settling in the fertile lands of Britain and leaving their mark on the landscape in the form of burial mounds and stone circles such as **Stonehenge**.

The **Celtic** invaders of 600 BC brought with them agricultural, weapon and tool-making skills; so much more sophisticated were they than the local tribes that they became by far the dominant culture for the next five hundred years.

In 54-55 BC, **Julius Caesar** made the first Roman forays across the channel from France. But it wasn't until nearly a century later that the **Emperor Claudius** led his 40,000 Roman soldiers across the Thames. Staking claims to vast tracts of fertile land and mineral wealth, the Romans incurred the wrath of local tribes, especially the Iceni, whose queen **Boadicea** led the first sacking and burning of **Londinium** 17 years after the city was established by **Claudius** in 43AD.

Not easily deterred, the Romans rebuilt Londinium into a grand walled city complete with roads, forts, governor's palace, public baths, a marble basilica and a huge forum. For the next four centuries, the wealthy port prospered under Roman rule, its inhabitants an international mix of Gauls, Britons and Romans, its common language Latin. Christianity was introduced by **Emperor Constantine** in the third century.

THE DARK AGES

From the fourth to the ninth centuries, Danes, Vikings, Picts (from Scotland), Scots (from Ireland) and Saxons and Angles (from Germany) fought for rule of the city; eventually the Romans deserted Londinium altogether, leaving it to the domination of **Anglo-Saxon** rule. The legends of **King Arthur** date from this period, and chronicle the battles between native Britons and the invading Saxons. London's surviving street patterns of ancient times are Saxon as are a majority of the place names in Britain; the graceful logic of Roman city-building was entirely extinguished by the invading force. The eight and ninth centuries saw repeated invasion by **Danish** and **Viking** armies, who sailed their war fleets up the Thames.

Savage battles for the throne amongst Danes, Vikings and Saxons characterized the period from 800 to 1042; an ever-changing succession of kings included Egbert, Ethelwulf, Ethelbad, Ethelbert, Ethelred, Alfred of Wessex and Edward the Elder, Athelstan, Edmund, Eadred, Eadwig, Edgar, Edward the Martyr, Ethelred the Unready, Edmund II, Cnut, Harold and Harthacnut.

Edward the Confessor, a Saxon, became king in 1042. A pious, celibate Christian, he dedicated one tenth of his wealth to construction of the first Westminster Cathedral and was buried in it ten days after its completion when he died, leaving no heir, in 1065. Edward was subsequently sainted.

THE NORMAN CONQUEST

William of Normandy (more familiarly known as **William the Conqueror**) took advantage of the death of Edward to invade England – via the **Battle of Hastings** – in 1066. He defeated **King Harold** (who had reigned only a few months), had himself crowned in Westminster Cathedral, and began immediately to consolidate his military strength – building forts, castles and emplacements around the city, the grandest of which (built on the site of an earlier Roman tower) was the **Tower of London**.

William was also responsible for the **Domesday Book**, the comprehensive census of people, lands and cities that provided the king with a basis for taxation, judicial order and land division. Norman rule continued under William II, Henry I and Stephen; it was a time of prosperity that took in huge building projects (more than 100 churches and monasteries) and endless tribal battles.

THE MIDDLE AGES

In 1154, **Henry II** succeeded Stephen. Henry II is perhaps best known for his attempts to appropriate the power and authority of the church, which led him to clash with and finally order the murder of the loyal friend and wise advisor who refused to condone his actions, **Thomas a Beckett**, Archbishop of Canterbury. Henry married **Eleanor of Aquitaine**, thus gaining a huge French empire, which was lost a few years later by his son, **King Richard the Lionhearted**, who spent innumerable years and vast amounts of the royal purse on his crusades abroad. Richard's brother, **King John**, inherited a massive power struggle between the monarchy and England's land barons; he was forced to sign the **Magna Carta** in 1215 guaranteeing their rights and setting limits on the power of the monarchy.

As London grew and prospered, its Jews were subjected to severe social and financial restrictions; they were forbidden to own land, which led to their amassing great quantities of "movable wealth" such as gold and jewels. The crown took advantage of this vast wealth, imposing taxes and penalty fines at every opportunity until the entire population was banished to Flanders by Edward I in 1290, who subsequently gained great financial advantage by confiscating the businesses left behind.

As fighting for land and rule continued between England and Scotland, Wales and France (the **Hundred Years War** with France began in 1337), the population of London soared to 80,000 – only to be reduced by more than 30,000 as the **black death** swept the land. Imagine London at that time as a crowded maze of squalid settlements of mud and thatch reaching from the Tower of London to (the original) St. Paul's Cathedral; only a few years earlier, a law preventing the obstruction of public roads by pigstys had been passed. The density of London contributed to the huge number of fatalities it suffered during the black death. In all, a third of England's population was wiped out, while the figure in London was probably closer to one half.

The severe shortage of labor that ensued from the black death gave the peasants a taste of market power for the first time in history. After the boy-king **Richard II** imposed a poll tax on the populace, the riots, looting and angry marches of the **Peasants Revolt** began. The 14-year old king bravely marched to meet with the revolutionaries, promised reform, had the ringleader murdered, and in one of the strangest turnarounds in history and with the words "I will be your chief and captain!", took over the leadership of the revolt. The riots dispersed, the king reneged on his promises – but the poll tax was revoked.

THE LANCASTERS, THE YORKS, & THE RISE OF TUDOR ENGLAND

The ineffectual rule of Richard II came to an end when Richard himself crowned **Henry IV**, Duke of Lancaster, king in 1399. His son, **Henry V** (the much-loved reprobate Prince Hal in Shakespeare's Henry IV), took the crown fourteen years later, defeated the French at **Agincourt** (remember the Hundred Years War?) and laid claim to the French throne. The rallying of the French under **Joan of Arc**, however, reversed the accession rights and pushed the English back to England by 1454.

The unstable rule of **Henry VI** (Duke of Lancaster) was challenged by Richard, Duke of York, sparking off the **War of the Roses** in 1455 between the Lancastrians (symbolized by a red rose) and the Yorks (symbolized by a white rose). This resulted in the death of Richard and the subsequent defeat of King Henry VI (and his powerful, ambitious wife, Margaret of Anjou) by Richard's son, who became **King Edward IV** of York in 1461. Edward's son **Edward V** succeeded to the throne at the age of twelve, but was shortly thereafter incarcerated and murdered in the Tower of London, along with his younger brother, by their ruthlessly ambitious uncle, **Richard III**.

Back in London, **William Caxton** had established England's first printing press, the various craftsmen's guilds (ironmongers, vintners, haberdashers, mercers, grocers, drapers, fishmongers) were thriving and gaining power, and almshouses and schools were established for the first time. Lawyers were gaining in prominence and disputes of property and inheritance were increasingly resolved in courts of law rather than on battlefields.

THE TUDORS: HENRY VIII & ELIZABETH I

Henry VII (Lancashire) put an end to the War of the Roses by marrying a York queen, daughter of Edward IV. So the stage of peace and prosperity was set when **Henry VIII** took the throne in 1509. As nearly everyone with even the faintest interest in history knows, Henry's marriage to **Catherine of Aragon** failed to produce a male heir, whereupon Henry, a staunch Catholic, appealed to the pope for marital annulment and permission to marry **Anne Boleyn**.

When the annulment failed to materialize, Henry broke away from the Catholic church in protest, dissolved the monasteries (and claimed their substantial wealth), and formed the **Church of England**, declaring himself its head. Both physically and historically, Henry was a big man – famed for the establishment of the Church of England, the royal navy, the building of Hampton Court Palace, and the founding of St. Bartholomew's Hospital as well as for a lifetime of orgies of hunting (in Hyde Park, Greenwich Park and Hampton Court Park), eating, and drinking.

In all, Henry went through six wives in search of male heirs, attaining satisfaction only with **Jane Seymour**, whose son **Edward VI** succeeded Henry to the throne in 1547 at the age of nine. He died young and was succeeded by Catherine of Aragon's daughter Mary, who restored Catholicism to England in another bloody torrent of religious persecution.

Throughout her reign, **Mary Tudor** prayed for an heir (with her husband King Philip I of Spain) to prevent the succession moving to her half-sister Elizabeth, a non-Catholic. At last in her forties, thinking her dream was realized, she died of a stomach tumor mistaken for pregnancy and was succeeded by **Elizabeth I**. Once again the country swung back to the Church of England. The bloody religious extremes of Tudor times made public burnings, torture and execution a common (and popular) sight at Hyde Park Corner and Newgate Prison.

Elizabeth I's reign was a golden era for England, and saw the glorious defeat of the **Spanish Armada** (1588) and the emergence of men of great talent and vision such as **William Shakespeare**, **Sir Francis Drake**, and **Sir Walter Raleigh** (who brought potatoes and tobacco back from his explorations of America). The **Globe** and a number of other popular theaters were built, each seating as many as a thousand and playing host to bear baiting and cock fighting as well as the plays of Shakespeare, Marlowe, and Jonson. (It helps to remember that the high Renaissance was in full swing in Italy at this time.)

During Elizabeth's reign, London prospered and quadrupled in size to 200,000, despite waves of plague and pestilence. The populace had long since strained past the limits of the City of London, and could now be found setting up house and shop as far west as the Strand, where conditions were less crowded and filthy than in the hopelessly squalid City.

The religious debate had stabilized but not gone away, and great public sympathy for Elizabeth's Catholic cousin **Mary Queen of Scots** was truncated by her execution in 1587.

THE STUARTS, CROMWELL, THE PLAGUE & THE GREAT FIRE

When Elizabeth died in 1603, unmarried and without heir, she was succeeded by Mary Queen of Scots' son **James VI of Scotland**, who became England's **James I**. Due to a quirk of heredity (James was related to Henry VII via his great-grandmother), centuries of English-Scottish conflict were brought to a close. A great believer in the divine right of kings, he was also a spendthrift and conspicuous homosexual who entered into serious conflict with the Puritan Parliament over his policy of imposing heavy taxes to support his extravagant foreign policy. Given the Puritan tone of the country, James I could safely be considered the wrong king at the wrong time.

Compared to Elizabeth's more or less peaceful rule, these were troubled times. The conflict between the King and Parliament led to the rise of the Parliamentarians; simultaneously, Catholic resentment emerged once more in the form of the **Gunpowder Plot**, masterminded by **Guy Fawkes**, to blow up Parliament and overthrow the government.

Meanwhile, London continued to expand. It's sheer size led to a vast increase of carriage traffic, while transport on the Thames suffered gridlock. Massive, festive Frost Fairs were held on the Thames courtesy of the river's extraordinarily dense garbage content which caused it to freeze over, a phenomenon impossible in the ecologically conscientious conditions of the present day.

Charles I took over the throne in 1625 and by 1642 the trouble between king and parliament had erupted into civil war – Royalists versus the Parliamentarian army under the leadership of **Oliver Cromwell**. The result was the execution of the King and the transformation of England into a republic, with Oliver Cromwell at the helm in the role of Protector of the **Commonwealth**.

Perhaps the most important subsidiary character in the reign of King Charles I was **Inigo Jones**, the first great Renaissance architect to work in London. After training in Italy, he set about transforming Henry VIII's Tudor court of timber and thatch to one of great classical monuments built in stone and brick (see the Banqueting House; the piazza and St. Paul's Church, Covent Garden; and The Queen's House, Greenwich). Ironically, it was in front of Jones' greatest commission by Charles I, Whitehall's **Banqueting House** with its magnificent Rubens ceiling, that King Charles was hanged by the Cromwellians for treason.

Cromwell's rule was short. Backed by the army, he defied parliament and became as much a despotic ruler as any king, though with a more republican outlook. He sold off the royal parks to tenant farmers, turned Inigo Jones' Queen's House into a biscuit factory, invited the Jews to return to England, imprisoned political dissenters with impunity and levied heavy taxes on the people to pay for his anti-royalist reforms. Within two years of his death in 1658, parliamentary elections had voted to return the monarchy to power, and **Charles II** was recalled from exile in France.

The reign of Charles II was not without event. In April 1665, five years after Charles returned to England, the **plague** swept England, killing off 100,000 in London alone; by September the dead were piling up at the rate of 12,000 per week. A fatal error of scientific judgment called for the extermination of all dogs and cats, thus wiping out the sole possibility of keeping the rats that spread the plague in check.

In February 1666, the court of Charles II finally deemed it safe to return from the countryside to London, and six months later (after a long hot summer), catastrophe struck again. A fire started in a royal bakery on Pudding Lane, and due to unusually dry conditions and strong winds, swept through the predominantly wood and thatch houses of London like, well, like wildfire. The **Great Fire of London** raged for three days, destroying eighty percent of London – including 13,000 houses, 87 churches, and 450 densely populated acres. Yet in terms of human life, the fire proved a godsend: miraculously only a handful were killed, and many thousands were saved in future years as it became apparent that the fire had banished plague from London permanently.

Christopher Wren was a man perfectly suited to the rebuilding of London. His great energy and aesthetic gifts landed him the job as principal architect of the rebuilding, beginning with **St. Paul's Cathedral** and 51 churches. Wren's **Monument**, located in the City, commemorates the fire; if laid on its side, it would reach 202 feet to the exact spot on Pudding Lane where the fire started.

Another result of the fire was the development of the **West End** of London. Driven from their homes, merchants and wealthy guildsmen moved west and built handsome new houses in the areas we now recognize as Bloomsbury, Soho, St. James and Mayfair.

The Stuarts continued after Charles II with James II. A convert to Catholicism, he soon fled to France amidst religious hostility, and was replaced by James' Protestant daughter Mary and her husband William, offered the crown by the Protestant parliament. After **William and Mary** came **Queen Anne**, whose greatest achievement was the unification of Scottish and English parliaments in the 1707 **Act of Union**. She was the last of the Stuart monarchs; although she bore 16 children, none survived to rule.

THE 18TH CENTURY & GEORGIAN ENGLAND

The Hanoverian **George I** succeeded Queen Anne to the throne by virtue of being great grandson of James I, but he was always a German king and totally German in outlook. Unable and unwilling to deal directly with parliament, he established a minister, **Robert Walpole**, to be his intermediary. Thus the powerful role of prime minister was born.

Great prosperity and relative peace reigned in England until 1749, when **Bonnie Prince Charlie** invaded from Scotland as part of the anti-English Jacobite rebellions; his defeat led to **The Clearance**, a technically precise term for the wholesale massacre by the English of the Scottish tribes. Traditional battles with France culminated in the defeat of Napoleon by the **Duke of Wellington** at Waterloo in 1815.

In the meantime, British interests abroad were expanding at a phenomenal rate; it was during the 18th century that India, Canada, Australia and New Zealand were added to the ever-expanding pink map of the **British Empire**. Expansion continued without hitch until **George III** imposed a tea tax on his American colonies. The **Revolutionary War** ensued (1776-1783, in case you've forgotten), providing a shocking defeat for the British army and a shocking blow to the king's coffers. The concurrent bout of madness suffered by George III caused his wildly extravagant grandson to be named **Prince Regent**.

The 18th century was a period of unprecedented artistic, architectural, and industrial growth in England, much of it centered on London. Canals brought resources from all over the country to fuel the building trade, the invention of the steam engine began a radical new era of industrial development, coffee houses opened, slavery was abolished, hospitals and schools were established, the **Royal Academy of Arts** was founded, Handel composed music, Hogarth and Stubbs painted while Johnson, Boswell, and Fielding wrote.

It was a time of religious tolerance which led to a great influx of foreigners – during the reign of George III, the population of England doubled to 14 million. Throughout all this social and industrial change, the gap between rich and poor widened substantially, setting the stage for the misery, squalor and injustice suffered by the poor in the century to come, as famously documented by **Charles Dickens**.

THE 19TH CENTURY & VICTORIAN ENGLAND

It was during the 19th century that London as we know it today really began to take shape. Manufacturing grew at unprecedented rates, as did trade and transport, causing a greater percentage of the population to migrate towards London. London's first Underground lines were opened, **Tower Bridge** and the **British Museum** were built, railroads and highways covered the country, and the emerging middle class gained prominence and began to thrive. In contrast, the agricultural class was moving into the cities where it was processed and transformed into a new industrial working class, with no noticeable improvement in the wretched conditions of life.

The term **Victorian** conjures up two conflicting images. Banking, insurance, retail and industry guaranteed a thriving middle class, yet child labor was rampant, poor sanitation meant that cholera deaths swept the slums, the Thames stank from sewage, and London was blinded by choking fogs of coal smoke. It was a time of great prosperity and gross poverty. Between 1800 and 1900, the population of London grew from 1 to 4.5 million.

During the long years of **Victoria's reign** (1837-1901), Britain was at the top of its form as an imperial power and an industrial one, a state that culminated symbolically in **The Great Exhibition** of 1851. The Exhibition, Prince Albert's grand celebration of technology and industry, attracted two million visitors to a grand show of everything from utopian housing to unpickable locks to the sort of bizarre inventions for which the Victorians were famous. It was all exhibited in a crystal palace made from 900,000 square feet of glass covering 19 acres of Hyde Park (later moved to north London, **Crystal Palace** burned to the ground in the 1930s).

The expansion of the railroads had a number of interesting knock-on effects. Timetables called for the establishment of standardized time throughout the nation (1852) and in 1884 the **zero meridian** was established in Greenwich, making London the center of world time. The erection of railroad stations caused large slum areas of London to be razed. And new telegraph lines allowed the simultaneous transport of information and manufacturing goods to and from London, establishing it as the largest center of trade in Europe.

Great political conflict arose throughout the century as the **Whigs** and **Tories** fought over free trade versus protectionist policies. The maintenance of manufacturing profits depended on cheap labor, which in turn depended on cheap bread for the workers and the free importation of grain (outlawed by the **Corn Laws** of 1815).

When, in 1834, the Houses of Parliament burned down, Charles Barry and Augustus Pugin were commissioned to rebuild it. A budget of £25,000 and a timescale of six years was proposed; in the event, it took £200,000 and 25 years to finish the Gothic "palace of Westminster", complete with **Big Ben**. Pugin died before the project was completed, in a madhouse.

Abroad, the massive, ever-expanding empire now comprised 500 million people and a quarter of the world's land mass. Two major wars and two ignominious defeats were suffered during this century: defending the Turks against the Russians in the **Crimean War** of 1854 and in South Africa's **Boer War** against the Dutch in 1899.

By the end of the century at home, life was a jolly affair for those with the social status to enjoy it. Oscar Wilde, Gilbert and Sullivan, Sarah Bernhardt, Henry James and George Bernard Shaw were just a few of the literary and stage luminaries setting London society alight. More than thirty grand theaters were built and opened, and in 1878, the Strand was lit for the first time by electric lights.

THE 20TH CENTURY

Edward VII became King in 1901, succeeding his mother Victoria at her death. The early years of the 20th century were distinguished by the emergence of the **suffragettes**, a radical band of middle class ladies led by **Emmeline Pankhurst**, who chained themselves to the railings of Downing Street, went on hunger strike, smashed windows at Parliament and even slashed Velazquez's Rokeby Venus in the National Gallery to gain attention for their crusade for voting rights.

On August 4, 1914, in a home atmosphere of trade union tensions and the threat of a general strike, Britain declared war on Germany. The invention of the airplane and the use of zeppelins meant that for the first time in centuries, London was under siege by a foreign power. Six hundred and fifty bombing deaths resulted. The total carnage from **World War I** was terrible. Half a generation of young men (750,000) were killed, an additional 2-1/2 million wounded and disabled. Class resentments exploded as thousands upon thousands of foot soldiers were used as cannon fodder by upper class officers inadequately prepared for a land war on this scale.

Ironically, women were the victors. Huge shortages of labor at home led to the employment of women as bus conductors, in munitions factory workers, as clerical staff and in banks. On the war front, women toiled alongside men as ambulance drivers and field hospital staff. Thus, it seemed inevitable that in 1918 women over 30 (and in 1928 all women over 21) won the right to vote.

The post war years struggled with a huge national war debt, a subsequent decline in manufacturing and mass unemployment, all of which set the scene for the nine-day **general strike** of 1926, during which the army was called in to subdue half a million striking workers. In London, the largest category of employment was the domestic sector with an astonishing 418,000 men women and children employed as servants.

The post-war period was a fertile one for the arts: D.H. Lawrence, T.S. Eliot, E.M. Forster, society's darling Noel Coward, and in Bloomsbury Virginia Woolf, Roger Fry, Lytton Strachey, Duncan Grant and Vanessa Bell thrived on the social and sexual freedoms of the twenties and thirties.

The breakdown of the power of the monarchy began with the **Imperial Conference** of 1931, which granted the countries of the British Empire commonwealth status with only nominal subordination to the crown. Further erosion of traditional power came with the **abdication of Edward VIII** to marry twice-divorced American Wallace Simpson. Although this liaison has been romanticized across the generations, it may be closer to fact to point out that Mrs. Simpson was a status-seeking social climber with one eye ever on the throne, and Edward VIII a weak, susceptible man who, throughout the war, exhibited enormous sympathy for the Nazis.

With the outbreak of **World War II**, 600,000 children, pregnant women, the elderly and the disabled were evacuated from London and taken into the homes of country folk throughout England. For London, the most significant event of the war was the **Blitz**. It began in September 1940 with 57 nights consecutive nights of intensive bombing by the Germans, and continued more or less continuously until May 1941. Despite masses of citizens seeking refuge in backyard Anderson shelters, the basements of posh hotels and Underground stations, a total of 60,000 civilians were killed in London during the Blitz.

The war ended in 1945, and London's inspiration, prime minister **Winston Churchill** was replaced by Labour's Clement Attlee. During these post-war years, the severely damaged economy maintained food rationing, instituted the National Health Service and nationalized industry and transport.

The resulting welfare state lasted intact into the 1980s, when its demise began with the free market economic policies of **Margaret Thatcher**.

In the postwar years, **India** gained independence (1947), the North Atlantic Treaty was signed (1949), **Elizabeth II** succeeded Edward VIII (1952), Britain's first highway, the M1 opened (1959) and **Beatlemania** swept the world (1963). In 1964, Harold Wilson became the first Labour prime minister since Attlee; in 1973 Edward Heath's conservative government joined the European Economic Community (the Common Market).

The 1974 miners' strike put Britain on a three-day work week to save fuel in 1974; Margaret Thatcher became the first female prime minister in 1979 and declared war on the Falkland Islands off Argentina in 1982. The year 1991 saw British involvement in the Gulf War; **John Major** became prime minister in 1992, and 1994 marked the beginning of the historic ceasefire with **Northern Ireland**.

THE KINGS & QUEENS OF ENGLAND

The House of Wessex

Egbert	802-839
Ethelwulf	839-855
Ethelbad	855-860
Ethelbert	860-866
Ethelred	866-871
Alfred the Great	871-899
Edward	899-924
Athelstan	924-939
Edmund I	939-946
Eadred	946-955
Eadwig	955-959
Edgar	959-975
Edward the Martyr	975-979
Ethelred the Unready	979-1016

The House of Skjoldung

Cnut	1016-1035
Harold I	1035-1040
Harthacnut	1040-1042

The House of Wessex (restored)

Edward the Confessor	1042-1066
Harold II	1066

The House of Normandy
William I
    (William the Conqueror)   1066-1087
William II   1087-1100
Henry I   1100-1135

The House of Plantagenet
Henry II   1154-1189
Richard I
    (Richard the Lionheart)   1189-1199
John   1199-1216
Henry III   1216-1272
Edward I   1272-1307
Edward II   1307-1327
Edward III   1327-1377
Richard II   1377-1399

The House of Lancaster
Henry IV   1399-1413
Henry V   1413-1422
Henry VI   1422-1461

The House of York
Edward IV   1461-1483
Edward V   1483
Richard III   1483-85

The House of Tudor
Henry VII   1485-1509
Henry VIII   1509-1547
Edward VI   1547-1553
Mary *(Mary Tudor)*   1553-1558
Elizabeth I   1558-1603

The House of Stuart
James I   1603-1625
Charles I   1625-1649

The Commonwealth
Oliver Cromwell   1649-1658
Richard Cromwell   1658-1659

The House of Stuart (restored)
Charles II	1660-1685
James II	1685-1688
William and Mary	1688-94
William	1694-1702
Anne	1702-1714

The House of Hanover
George I	1714-27
George II	1727-1760
George III	1760-1820
George IV *(Prince Regent, 1811-1820)*	1820-1830
William IV	1830-1837

The House of Saxe-Coburg
Victoria	1837-1901
Edward VII	1901-1910

The House of Windsor
George V	1910-1936
Edward VIII	1936
George VI	1936-1952
Elizabeth II	1952-

4. PLANNING YOUR TRIP

With low airfares and international travel getting more and more routine, it's easy to grab your passport and a change of clothes and jump on a plane for a weekend in London. Planning ahead, however, guarantees that you'll arrive in the season that appeals to you most, stay in a neighborhood that suits you perfectly, and end up fifth row center at the best play of the season.

AIRLINES

About fourteen major airlines fly direct from the U.S. to London, landing either at **Gatwick** or **Heathrow** airports (Heathrow is somewhat closer to London and connected by tube direct to the center of town; Gatwick is connected by frequent trains; see Arrivals & Departures for more information). Major carriers like **British Airways**, **Virgin**, **American**, **United** and **Northwest** have lowered their fares so much in recent years that they've had to resort to cramming extra seats onto every flight. So if you feel as if you're horribly crammed in, you're not imagining it.

Our airline of choice? **Virgin** has the advantage of individual videos to take your mind off the painful contortions of your body. They also do things like serve Dove Bars during the movies which costs them little but makes passengers feel infinitesimally more pampered. As of this writing, the upstairs on **British Airways 747s** have been converted to economy class – it's quieter and a bit roomier up there so worth requesting. **Kuwait Air** and **Air India** offer more leg room and usually the cheapest fares, but strictly no booze; we've had good experiences with both of them. There never seems to be much to differentiate the big American carriers; choose a fare, a frequent flyer plan, and a time of departure that suits you.

Average travel time is approximately 6 hours from the East Coast (seven on the return flight due to tailwinds) and approximately 11 from California. Nearly all airlines travel overnight and deposit you, disoriented and exhausted, the following morning.

Keep in mind that fares are ludicrously low when no one wants to travel: November through till the third week in December and all of

January, February and March. These are all good times to come to London so keep an eye out for travel bargains.

BOOKING TICKETS FROM AMERICA

If you're planning to travel in **high tourist season** (April to October and Christmas week), we highly recommend booking hotels and theater tickets in advance. If you're not used to phoning abroad, don't worry – it's cheap (about 70 cents a minute) easy, and will save you untold hassle once you arrive.

For **theater**, the best way to find out what shows are on in advance is to phone booking agents **Edwards and Edwards** (*in the U.S. phone 1-800-223-6108*) or write to the **London Theatre Guide** (*London Theatre Guide, SWET, Bedford Chambers, The Piazza, Covent Garden, London WC2E 8HQ or call 0171 836 0971*) requesting their current broadsheet and future booking information. The broadsheet is free, and while it doesn't offer recommendations or reviews, it will usually include the playwright and major members of the cast as well as phone numbers for booking. Edwards and Edwards takes a commission on all tickets sold. In either case, phone for tickets as soon as you know your travel dates to avoid disappointment.

For more general information about festivals, cricket matches, and the like, we recommend you contact your local **British Tourist Authority** head office. They'll send you useful things like maps and calendars of events. *Write or phone: BTA, World Trade Center, Suite 450, 350 South Figueroa Street, Los Angeles, California (tel: 213-628-3525) or BTA, 551 Fifth Avenue, Suite 701, New York, New York 10176 (tel: 212-986-2200).*

PASSPORTS & VISAS

Before you go, check to make sure your passport is up to date. If you're a citizen of the U.S. or Canada, you don't need a visa to enter Britain for up to six months. If you don't hold an American, Canadian or European passport, check with the British Consulate for visa regulations.

CUSTOMS & IMMIGRATION

A few helpful hints on entering Britain: Have a valid passport. Know your hotel name and address. Don't smuggle drugs or stolen goods into the country.

On returning to the U.S., you are allowed one liter of liquor, 200 cigarettes and $400 worth of purchases. Up to an additional $1000 of purchases, you will be charged 10% duty, though we have been waved through by friendly customs officials when declaring an extra pair of shoes or bottle of Scotch.

CLIMATE & WEATHER

The good news is that there's nearly always something blooming in London. We've admired roses in December, crocuses and snowdrops in January, and daffodils, apple and cherry blossoms in February. Winters tend to be fairly mild (35-50 degrees), and you almost never need a really heavy coat. By April, the temperature should have settled into the 50s and 60s and will probably stay thereabouts until October, with the occasional "scorcher" (75-80 degrees) sometime in May through August.

But let's face it, you're probably not coming here to get a tan. The two main things to keep in mind are that yes, it rains a lot of the time in London, and that London is further north than you might imagine, which means summer days are blissfully long – you're likely to get woken by the dawn chorus at 4am, and in May and June the sun won't set until 10:30pm. Sadly, this means that winter days are short, brutish and cruelly bleak. Most Britons suffer from Seasonal Affect Disorder for most of the year, but as they don't believe in such hocus pocus, they just appear to be grumpy.

The best time to come for daylight, flowers and mild weather is May; April through October is the season. Rain is always a gamble and you'll have to trust to chance. Check a national newspaper for up-to-date temperature advice before you come.

What to Wear

The answer comes in two parts, and you've probably heard both before. Be prepared for just about anything and think layers. Even in summer you are likely to find a wool sweater useful. It may not be freezing but it does get raw and damp; Californians will certainly find their year-round cotton knits insufficiently warm in an English winter. At the opposite extreme, furs are generally frowned upon (and sometimes worse). A raincoat with a zip-out lining, or a light wool coat will get you through all but a freak winter freeze, and anything remotely waterproof will be of help.

Just about every man, woman and child in the British Isles owns a green waxed cotton garment lined with flannel called a Barbour that's waterproof and warmish and the butt of thousands of jokes. The rather chic individuals in Knightsbridge sporting brand new Barbours are inevitably French and Italian tourists – Barbours have become fashion trophies in Paris and Milan (if you want to jump on the bandwagon, the department store John Lewis has the best prices). Summers can occasionally get pretty hot, but generally call for a jacket or sweater in the evening. Shorts have become acceptable and, if they're huge and ugly enough, chic.

The great and liberating thing about London is that the English are not known for their fabulous dress sense, so if you are considered reasonably natty in your home town, you will probably look fine in London (if your hometown is New York, you will probably look fabulous). People rarely dress up in any serious way, and you'll see jeans and sweaters even at the theater and at everything but really nice restaurantìs. The opera is one exception; £150 a seat tends to inspire operagoers to make an effort.

A few words of advice: If you don't want to look like a tourist, try not to wear big white sneakers with your best Chanel suit. And if you've been invited to a wedding, see *Four Weddings and a Funeral*, go out and buy a silly hat, and don't be afraid to wear black (promise).

And one last word of advice. Bring a pair of shoes that will splash happily through puddles. Chances are you'll get a lot of use out of them.

Visiting April through October

If you come to London between April and October you will benefit from long days, mild weather and exquisite gardens in full bloom. You will take long, lazy boat rides to **Greenwich** or **Kew Gardens** on the shimmering **Thames**. You will spend charmed hours in the wisteria-draped garden of your local pub, drinking delightful ale and remembering why you fell in love. You will take day trips to **Blenheim** and **Petworth** and, if it only rains a little, think you have died and gone to a heaven generally reserved for 19th century romantic poets.

Visiting November through March

If, however, you decide to be extremely unfashionable and come between November and March, you will glide into the **Tower of London** without waiting in line. You will manage to get last minute reservations at the unbelievably popular restaurant of your choice, and, once there, you will note that your fellow diners all speak with rather attractive English accents and seem to be ordering from the special off-season three-courses for £15 menu.

If you come in December, you will experience the *Messiah* by candlelight in the church of **St. Martin-in-the-Fields**, and **Fortnum & Mason's** wonderful Christmas windows. If you travel in January, you will pick up astonishing bargains at the **Liberty** sale, like hand-painted Italian dishes marked down 80%.

You will find similarly amazing bargains at the **Harrods** sale, which contrary to popular belief, will not be unbearably crowded on, say, the Tuesday morning after the sale has begun. At the **National Gallery** you will find yourself in a peaceful tete-a-tete with the Caravaggio of your dreams, undisturbed by jostling teenagers from Des Moines. On one particularly miserable rainy day you will have the entire **Wallace Collection** to yourself. You will have no trouble picking up tickets to the new

Tom Stoppard play. And ... you will be offered great special deals on plane tickets, rental cars, and hotels.

In short, there are advantages and disadvantages to both choices. We'd have to recommend May or October for a first visit, with an off-season December or February theater tour as a follow-up. So much of what makes London wonderful has to do with its unbelievably beautiful gardens and it's endless summer days. But London without tourists, with roaring fires to keep out the damp, museums without a billion other people, and long winter evenings of theater, opera and nightcaps in wood-panelled bars has its undeniable charms.

HOTELS

Even if you book ahead (and you should), the misery of landing in London dishevelled and crabby at 6am is that your hotel room may not be ready until 1pm. Off-season, early check-in may not be a problem if you inform the hotel of your requirements beforehand; most say they will try their best to accommodate (but promise nothing).

In high season we recommend that you talk to the hotel well in advance – but in fact, in most cases the only way to guarantee a room first thing in the morning is to pay for it from the night before. Off-season, you can often negotiate a special rate for this partial usage.

5. ARRIVALS & DEPARTURES

This is always the most anxiety-provoking part of the journey. But the good news is that everyone speaks your language, there are good, fast **Bureaux de Change** at the arrivals area of the airports, the transport to your hotel should only require a short cab ride from easy tube and train connections, everything is clearly marked – and (best of all) the luggage carts at the airport are free.

GETTING TO TOWN

London has two major and three minor airports: **Heathrow**, **Gatwick**, **Stanstead**, **Luton** and **London City Airport**. Unless you're flying in from Europe, you'll arrive at either Heathrow or Gatwick.

If you're arriving at Heathrow or Gatwick, you have a number of options:

By Taxi

Taxi is the most obvious and the most expensive; from Gatwick it will cost you at least £40 to a central London hotel; from Heathrow, £25-30. At anything like rush hour, that figure will go up significantly.

By the Gatwick Express Train & Flightline Bus

From Gatwick, most travelers opt for the **Gatwick Express** train to cover the 30 miles from Gatwick to the center of London. Although the cost keeps rising, it's currently £8.70 per person, leaves about every 10-15 minutes (every hour between 2am and 5am), takes under half an hour and deposits you at Victoria Station, where you can easily get a cab to your hotel.

In addition, there's a **Flightline 777** *(0181 668 7261)* bus from the Gatwick terminals to Victoria every hour, but as it's slower, less frequent and only marginally less expensive, the only reason we can think to recommend it is that they take credit cards and dollars in payment.

By Tube

From Heathrow, 15 miles west of London, the **tube** is a dream. You can take your (free) luggage cart right up to the platform and buy a ticket for central London (via the Piccadilly line, £3.10 at this writing; if it's after 9:30am and you plan to do any more traveling that day, buy a **one-day travelcard**, zones 1-6 for £3.80). This train takes between 30 and 45 minutes and stops at South Kensington, Knightsbridge, Green Park, Hyde Park Corner, Piccadilly Circus, Leicester Square, Covent Garden, and Russell Square — so there's bound to be one near your hotel or a short cab ride away.

By London Transport Airbus

Two **London Transport Airbuses** also provide transport from Heathrow into central London. For Earl's Court, South Kensington, Knightsbridge and Victoria take Airbus A1; for Notting Hill Gate, Paddington, Lancaster Gate, Marble Arch, Baker Street, Euston and Russell Square take Airbus A2. Airbuses depart daily from terminals 1 to 4 every twenty minutes from 5:20am (5:50am Saturdays and Sundays) till 8:30pm.

They cost £5 (children £4) and can take anything from an hour to 90 minutes, depending on traffic and your destination. *For times and pick-up points for your return trip to the airport, phone London Transport on 0171 222 1234.*

By Airport Transfer

Our favorite in-between option is **Airport Transfers** *(0171 403 2228)*. They offer a flat rate £15 charge from the West End or Knightsbridge/ South Kensington to Heathrow (£5 more from the City or further out); £30 to Gatwick; and £35 to Stanstead Airport, regardless of the number of passengers. Additional pick-up or drop-off points cost an extra £5.

The cars are big and comfortable and the service very reliable. They will also meet your flight from the States for the above fee plus an additional £5, which includes waiting 40 minutes for you to clear customs and all car parking fees. They'll meet you at arrivals with a sign (what could be nicer?) and tipping is optional. If you want to be met at the airport, give them a call from the States a day or two in advance to reserve.

RENTING A CAR AT THE AIRPORT

Due to parking and traffic problems, cost, and the fact that they drive on the wrong side of the car and the road, hiring a rental car for your visit to London borders on the criminally insane.

If, however, you have good reasons for doing so, the major airport rental car phone numbers are listed in the following chart:

CAR RENTAL PHONE NUMBERS AT THE AIRPORTS

Heathrow	Gatwick
• **Avis**, *0181 897 9321*	• **Avis**, *01293 547671*
• **Budget**, *0181 759 2216*	• **Budget**, *012913 540141*
• **Eurodollar**, *0181 897 0811*	• **Eurodollar**, *01293 513031*
• **Europcar**, *0181 897 0811*	• **Europcar**, *01293 531062*
• **Hertz**, *0181 897 3344*	• **Hertz**, *01293 530555*

ARRIVING AT A TRAIN STATION

If you are entering London from Europe or another part of Britain, you will likely come by train. This is not as simple as it sounds: there are eight main train stations spread throughout London (and myriad smaller ones): **Charing Cross** and **Waterloo** to the south; **King's Cross**, **St. Pancras**, **Euston** and **Liverpool Street** to the east; and **Paddington** and **Victoria** to the west.

From the Gatwick Express train you will arrive at Victoria. From the Eurostar train service to Paris, you will arrive at Waterloo East. Every station is well-connected to London's extensive Underground system, buses, and there will be a taxi stand outside as well.

CHECKING INTO YOUR HOTEL

If you are arriving at the crack of dawn, contact your hotel in advance about early check-in (see *Planning Your Trip*). If this is not possible, leave your luggage at the hotel and head instantly for the nearest park if it's a nice day; the nearest street market if it's a Saturday and not raining; or the nearest museum if it's pouring (nearly every museum has a pleasant restaurant where you can sit over coffee and a sandwich until your room is ready).

If you can bear the touristy stigma of a good old-fashioned bus tour, it's not a bad way to kill a couple of hours and will give you a good basic overview of London without taxing your brain too badly.

HOTEL BOOKING SERVICES

Every airport and train station has a gratis hotel booking service which will fix you up with a room in your price range and preferred neighborhood. While they are very efficient, they are not overly concerned with charm. If you are, we suggest you do your research and book ahead.

JETLAG

If you're a world traveler you can skip this bit. If you're an ordinary mortal, we have a few words of advice, based on about a million trips. First the obvious: try not to get sloshed on the plane, you don't need jetlag and a hangover. Don't eat too much airline food, we're convinced it can cause the symptoms of severe jetlag in your own time zone. Try to sleep on the plane. On arrival, drink the awful coffee they bring you, stare at bright light sources, and pretend you've had a good night's sleep.

Here's the important part: If you arrive first thing in the morning, do not give in to the temptation to go to bed. Walk around briskly, have some breakfast and a few cups of good strong tea or coffee, see some stimulating sights. You're allowed an hour or two rest in the late afternoon but no more. Do not decide that your first meal in England should be fish and chips or pub food. Eat lightly and healthily. Don't go to bed before 10pm. You may feel spacy and peculiar for one day, but you're likely to wake up at a pretty normal time feeling pretty normal.

GETTING TO THE AIRPORT

On your way back to the airport, the first morning tube leaves Piccadilly Circus at 5:46am Monday to Saturday; 7:04am Sunday. The last tube at night from Piccadilly to Heathrow leaves Piccadilly at 12:21am Monday to Saturday; 11:27pm Sundays. Figure on an average to-airport traveling time of about 45 minutes.

Any further questions, phone the seven-day, 24-hour London Transport Information line on 0171 222 1234.

6. BASIC INFORMATION

Banks, post offices, doctors and crossing the street — all the practical information you need to know for London living.

BANK HOLIDAYS

Nowadays bank holidays almost always fall on a Monday and virtually everything closes. Don't confuse these days with the American equivalent complete with sale frenzies — most shops and restaurants will shut, as will many museums.

The basic dates to watch out for are: New Year's day, Good Friday, Easter Monday, the first and last Mondays in May, the last Monday in August, Christmas day and Boxing Day (December 26). If Christmas day, Boxing Day or New Year's day falls on a weekend, Monday becomes a holiday too.

BANKING & MONEY

Most banks have recently joined the twentieth century and remain open Monday to Friday, 9am to 5pm. As of this writing, the best place to change travelers checks is at an **American Express** office (you must be a cardholder to take advantage of their services), which charges no commission for their checks. Cardholders can also cash a personal check from a bank in the States free of charge at any American Express office (up to $1,000 for green card holders; $5,000 for gold; $10,000 for platinum). All branches offer the same services and are open Monday to Friday 9am to 5:30pm (Wednesday, 9:30am); Saturday 9am to 4pm.

The American Express offices in London are at the following addresses:
- *78 Brompton Road (across the street from Harrods), tel: 0171 584 6182*
- *6 Haymarket (near Piccadilly Circus), tel: 0171 930 4411*
- *89 Mount Street (near Green Park tube), tel: 0171 499 4436*
- *40 Great Russell Street near the British Museum), tel: 0171 637 0019.*

In addition, a 24 hour help line offers **emergency American Express travel services**, *tel: 0171 930 6554.*

The next best place to change money or travelers checks is at any **National Westminster** bank, where you'll get the standard bank exchange rate with the lowest fee. To change money outside of banking hours, try **Thomas Cook** as a second resort and the neighborhood **Bureau de Change** or your hotel as a last resort (most expensive).

It is, incidentally, a lot easier and usually cheaper to get your initial supply of sterling from the Bureau de Change at the airport when you arrive than to order it from your bank before you go. And don't worry about being tired and disoriented; the whole transaction usually takes under a minute and there's rarely a line.

Credit Cards

Most restaurants, hotels, and shops take major credit cards (Visa, Mastercard, American Express), though they're less useful in rural areas, smaller inns, and bed and breakfasts. (Marks & Spencer, strangely, doesn't accept any credit cards.)

Before you go, check whether you are a member of the **Cirrus Network**. If so, you can withdraw money at selected **Barclays**, **National Westminster**, **Lloyds** and **Midland** cash machines (this service is either free, or comes with a small per-use charge; check with your bank). Simply use your bankcard and PIN number as you would at your branch in the States. This is one of the easiest ways to get money and means you don't have to carry large amounts of cash or bother with travelers checks.

BUSINESS HOURS

Dining

Most things in London happen a little later than in the States, except for theater, which happens earlier. Lunch is at 1pm, which is when most restaurants get crowded and when any English person will arrange to meet you.

Dinner reservations are usually made for 8pm or 8:30pm; though 9pm is not unusual. If you plan to dine at 7pm you will likely find the restaurant nearly empty; the exception is restaurants anywhere near the theaters, which usually start with a moderate crowd as early as 6pm.

So with all this delayed dining, you'd expect restaurants to be open late, right? Wrong. Although they are slowly getting the idea, the majority of restaurants still open from 12:30-2:30pm for lunch and 6:30-10:30pm or 11pm for dinner, so if you're dining after the theater, check closing times carefully.

Showtimes

Standard curtain time for plays is 7:30pm, but 7, 7:15, 7:45 and 8pm are reasonably common. Be sure to check your tickets carefully, or phone the box office if you're collecting them there.

Shopping

Most shops keep very conservative hours. For drug stores, department stores and small shops, 9:30am to 5-6pm Monday to Saturday is standard with no closure for lunch. Because of Sunday trading laws, many shops and department stores are closed on Sundays (except before Christmas).

Newsagents (i.e., news-stands) open early (usually 8am) and close at 5-6pm. Bookstores sometimes stay open late. In some neighborhoods, some smaller shops (and post offices) still close at 1pm on Wednesdays and/or Saturdays.

In general, Sunday is a bad day to try and buy anything.

Pub Hours

By the time this book is published, pubs will open 11am to 11pm Monday through Saturday and noon to 10:30pm on Sundays, though daily summer openings till midnight are being discussed. Liquor stores (called *Off Licences*) tend to follow pub opening hours but close earlier (10pm weekdays, much earlier on Sundays).

Cosmopolitan Americans beware (and entrepreneurs take note): The seven day, 24-hour drugstore, shopping mall, bar, supermarket, restaurant and dry cleaner have not yet been dreamed of here.

CARS & DRIVING

When it comes to driving in London, the simple advice is try not to. Even people born here consider driving in London hell: it's unbearably slow, parking is next to impossible, gas is outrageously expensive, and worst of all, everyone drives on the wrong side of the road — which can be remarkably awkward even if you're the sort of person who's good at those things. (See also *Arrivals & Departures* and *Getting Around Town* chapters.)

COIN OF THE REALM

British currency is pretty easy for Americans. It's based on the **pound sterling**, with one hundred **pence** to the pound. Conveniently, these pence are called **pennies**. There are one penny, two pence, five pence, ten pence, twenty pence, fifty pence and one pound coins; £5, £10, £20 and £50 notes.

The small heavy gold-colored coins are pounds; there is no longer a pound note. There happen to be a lot of fake pound coins in circulation at any one time, so if a tube ticket machine or ticket-taker rejects your coin, you'll know why. Technically you're supposed to turn these coins in at a bank; if you just use them next time we won't tell anyone.

And by the way, shopkeepers aren't constantly holding your notes up to the light to annoy you. They're checking to make sure the silver strip runs through the bill and isn't just painted on (i.e., counterfeit).

COST OF LIVING

If you've recently moved to London from Switzerland or Japan it will seem cheap. Otherwise — assuming exchange rates remain reasonably stable — hold onto your wallets. Transport and hotels are the most expensive in Europe. Restaurant and clothing prices will strike you as exorbitant. Theater tickets are among the few things that will seem cheap, and once you get the hang of it, there are tricks like travel cards and good cheap ethnic restaurants if you're on a budget.

The best way to understand and deal with London's prices is to accept that what costs $10 in America will cost £10 in London (never mind that the £10 you just spent will have cost you $15 or $18 to buy). For masochists, the quickest currency calculation is based on a very approximate $1.50 to the pound, so just multiply those £36 Gap jeans by 1.5. Then buy them at home.

ELECTRICITY

People who care about such things tell us that the electrical current in England is **240 volts AC** — which is more than twice American power. The short answer is: all plugs here are massive three prong affairs, making sockets utterly incompatible with your hairdryer and powerbook. Buy a converter at the airport. And by the way, every plug contains its very own fuse. So if your reading lamp blows and a new bulb doesn't help, inform your concierge sagely that you need a new fuse.

If you happen to fall in love with an antique lamp or chandelier, it can fairly easily be converted to American wiring. However, this does not apply to radios, food processors, televisions, power drills or computers. And if you're travelling through Europe, the hairdryer you cleverly purchased in London won't be compatible there either.

ETIQUETTE

This is a tough one, but a few suggestions might help. Excessive politeness, though usually excessively insincere, is the norm. "I'm awfully sorry" is the phrase most frequently paired with "but your umbrella is buried in my solar plexus." "Thank you so much for your kind assistance" is a perfectly ordinary response to "bugger off." And "if you're sure it won't be too much bother" often precedes the request for a bus ticket. It may help to understand that manners are all that is left of the great British Empire, and its denizens cling to politeness as drowning men to a bobbing plank.

That said, excessive politeness tends to work better than a demand to see the manager, and once you get the hang of it, can be injected with the same covert rage. "Sorry" is one of our favorites, often accompanied by a viciously aimed elbow in the ribs.

In general, the English are excessively charming and helpful as well as exceedingly polite, though you will undoubtedly notice that service is much more grudgingly dispensed than in America. A lot of this has to do with the complex class system and its attendant resentments — when in doubt, behave like a native: smile politely, say "sorry" a few times, and don't budge till you get your way.

Decibel level, by the way, is one place Americans tend to reveal themselves — it's simply not polite to talk loudly enough to be overheard.

FLOORS

In elevators ("lifts") and common parlance, the (American) first floor is the (British) ground floor. Subsequent floors follow from there — so the (American) second floor is the (British) first floor, and so on.

HANDICAPPED TRAVELERS

England is making progress on issues like wheelchair access, but there's still a long way to go. One organization worth contacting if you're handicapped and planning a trip to London is **Holiday Care Service** — a charity organization that offers free information, suggestions and advice on hotels, restaurants, transport and special services available to handicapped and elderly people travelling in Britain.

Write or fax them with a description of your needs, your approximate itinerary (if you have one) and your budget at: *Holiday Care Service, 2 Old Bank Chambers, Station Road, Surrey. Fax: 01293 784647; tel: 01293 774535.*

HEALTH & MEDICAL CONCERNS

You probably know this by now, but AIDs is a serious health problem in the UK, as in most places in the world. Gay or straight, if you have sex with a new acquaintance, use a condom.

For medical problems, consult the concierge at your hotel about locating a private doctor, or phone **Medical Express** (see next page). Emergencies (broken bones, heart attack) should be dealt with at the nearest hospital's accident and emergency unit. In extreme emergencies (medical, police, fire), *dial 999.* National Health treatment at accident and emergency units is not expensive by American standards, but be warned that if you are not actually in mortal danger, you can spend hours waiting to be seen.

Make sure your U.S. medical insurance covers emergencies abroad. In addition, your American prescriptions will not be honored at U.K. pharmacies (most of which close at 6pm), so if you need pills, remember to bring them with you.

For sick children, flu, prescription problems and other general worries, phone Medical Express *(117a Harley Street, London W1. Tel: 0171 499 1991, Monday to Friday 9am to 6pm; Saturday 9:30am to 2:30pm).* Staffed by a rotation of local doctors, they charge £65 (credit cards accepted) for a consultation with a GP (tests are extra), and have x-ray and lab facilities in the building as well as an On-Call housecall service for out-of-hours illness *(24-hour tel: 0181 840 7000).*

A few useful phone numbers:
- **Bliss Chemist**, *5 Marble Arch, London W1. Tel: 0171 723 6116. Open daily 9am to midnight. Marble Arch tube.*
- **Zafash Pharmacy**, *233-235 Old Brompton Road, London SW5. Tel: 0171 373 2798. Monday to Saturday 9am to midnight; Sunday 10am to midnight.*
- **Dental Emergency Service** (central London), *25 Devonshire Place, London W1N 1PD. Tel: 0171 935 9320. Regents Park tube.*

QUEUES & ZEBRA CROSSINGS

There's nothing the British like more than a good **queue** (that's a line to you and me). But customs are changing and today the average bus arrival causes something reminiscent of a rugby scrum — though you'll still hear plenty of tut-tutting if you push onto an empty bus ahead of someone waiting a nanosecond longer than you. When in doubt, go native: get in line, adopt an expression of long-suffering piety, and occasionally mutter "well, really" under your breath.

Another piece of valuable information for tourists is to be ever-aware of **zebra crossings** (Brits will pronounce them *zeh-bra*). They're the crosswalks with the wide white stripes, and once you step into a zebra crossing, no one is allowed to mow you down. This will frustrate drivers, but in the end they will abide by the rules. In fact, if you hover at the edge of a zebra crossing, traffic will usually screech to a halt in anticipation of your intent. Outside of zebra crossings you are fair game, and should be really, really careful crossing roads. Taxis especially have no regard for human life, and if you are uncertain about which way to look while crossing, they will teach you a lesson by running you over.

LOOS, LAVATORIES, TOILETS & CLOAKROOMS

The three year old daughter of a friend tells her very proper grandma she has to go to the lavatory, her mother she has to go to the loo, and her nursery school teacher she has to go to the toilet. This just about sums up the reigning confusion. Luckily, you can always ask for the ladies or the men's room and get directed properly. Confusion, however, may prevail when you follow signs to the Cloaks or the Cloakroom, only to find that half the time it indicates a place to relieve yourself, and the rest of the time it indicates a place to relieve yourself of your cloak.

Once you've mastered the terminology, the question of course is where. Department stores and museums are always dependable. When neither is available, hotel lobbies nearly always have facilities; stride through as if you belong. Train stations all have pay toilets. McDonald's, Pizzaland and other fast food chains are great places to keep in mind when all else fails; the toilets are usually downstairs, clean and no one will glare at you on the way in. Every pub has men's and ladies' rooms — in an emergency, choose the nicest looking one within dashing distance and look for the toilets sign. When in doubt, ask: we've never been humiliated or thrown out of a pub for using the toilet without buying a drink.

Do be warned that pub toilets tend to be unheated and not always up to one's preferred standard of hygiene — however in an emergency they'll do. All restaurants (but not all cafes) also have toilets. And remember: although the British have learned from movies to speak near-fluent American, a bathroom is still thought to be a room containing a bathtub.

LOST & FOUND

There are three places you're likely to leave your wallet, your camera or your umbrella — in a taxi, a tube, or a bus. For the former, there's the **Black Cab Lost and Found** (*0171 833 0996 – open 9am to 4pm Monday to Friday, 15 Penton Street, Islington, London N1*); for **London Transport**, there's a lost property office (*0171 486 2496 – open 9:30am to 2pm Monday to Friday, 200 Baker Street, London NW1*) *near the Baker Street tube*. You'll probably have to allow two working days for the lost item to be turned in.

In addition, each train station has its own lost property office as follows:

• **Charing Cross** – *0171 922 6061*
• **Euston** – *0171 922 6477*
• **King's Cross** – *0171 922 9081*
• **Liverpool Street** – *0171 922 9189*
• **Paddington** – *0171 922 6773*
• **St. Pancras** – *0171 922 6478*
• **Victoria** – *0171 922 6216*
• **Waterloo** – *0171 922 6135*

NEWSPAPERS & MAGAZINES

You can instantly pigeonhole a Londoner by the newspaper he or she reads. Thanks to its purchase by Rupert Murdoch, the once venerable *Times* has been transformed into a tabloid rag masquerading as a quality broadsheet. Skip it, except for amusement value. *The Telegraph* has taken its place as the right-of-center quality newspaper, and lots of otherwise liberal types buy it on Saturday for the very good arts and sports reporting. *The Independent* aims for the middle-of-the-road intelligentsia (but often misses out on basics like news) and *The Guardian* aims left-of-center with a dose of social conscience.

The tabloids are even more confusing, with the *Sun* (right-wing, fanatically royalist and famous for its nude page-3 girl) and the *Mirror* (the traditional Labour-voting working man's tabloid) at opposite ends of the spectrum, with various sex scandal rags in between. *The Evening Standard* is best noted for its good, jazzy Friday magazine (great for listings, special events, restaurant news and reviews, etc.) which comes free with the Friday edition.

The Sunday Sport is a good purchase for a rainy Sunday, as its lead articles usually run something along the lines of "Elvis Spotted on Mars" and "Heaven: Exclusive Photographs Reveal All." And oh yes, the *International Herald Tribune* is available at most newsagents.

When it comes to magazines there's just one mandatory purchase — *Time Out*, the weekly with every imaginable listing from theater to gay cabaret to galleries to sales and bargains to movies to children's events to television. It comes out on Wednesday and is extremely reliable where theater recommendations are concerned (we nearly always agree with their assessments); less so with movie reviews.

For a sense of the local London "scene" (fashion, culture and clubs), *Arena* is a good, fairly intelligent, hip read. If you're interested in how the upper classes party, play and wed (the photos are priceless), *Tatler* and *Harpers & Queen* are fun, if somewhat lacking in even token depth. There's an inexplicable dearth of good news magazines in Britain (possibly due to the excess of newspapers). *The Economist*, however, is far more comprehensive than the international editions of *Time* or *Newsweek*. For the up-to-date modern arts scene, *Frieze* is erudite and beautifully art-directed.

The English versions of *GQ* and *Esquire* make decent reading; *Marie Claire* combines glossy fashion and sex with fairly intelligent, international reporting of women's issues. Depending on your outlook, *Country Life* will either set you swooning with unreconstructed Anglophilia or cause you to start giggling uncontrollably.

PLACES OF WORSHIP

A little something for everyone:

- **Hinde Street Methodist Chapel**, *19 Thayer Street, London W1M 5LJ. Tel: 0171 935 6179. Oxford Street tube.*
- **Baptist Central Church**, *235 Shaftesbury Avenue, London WC2H 8EL. Tel: 0171 836 6843. Tottenham Court Road tube.*
- **Our Lady of Victories**, *235a Kensington High Street, London W8. Tel: 0171 937 4778. High Street Kenisington tube*
- **St. Brides Church**, *Fleet Street, London EC4Y 8AU. Tel: 0171 353 1301. Blackfriars tube.*
- **St. James Piccadilly**, *197 Piccadilly, London W1V 9LF. Tel: 0171 734 4511. Piccadilly Circus tube.*
- **St. Martin in the Fields**, *6 St. Martin Place, London WC2N 4JJ. Tel: 0171 723 7246. Charing Cross tube.*
- **West End Great Synagogue**, *21 Dean Street, London W1V 6NE. Tel: 0171 437 1873. Tottenham Court Road tube.*
- **Chelsea Affiliated Synagogue**, *Smith Terrace, Smith Street, London SW3 4EA. Tel: 0171 836 7204. Leicester Square tube.*
- **Westminster Friends Meeting House**, *52 St. Martin's Lane, London WC2N 4EA. Tel: 0171 435 9473. Leicester Square tube.*

POST OFFICES

Post offices generally open 9am to 5pm Monday to Friday and are recognizable by their huge queues. The larger ones will also open Saturday 9am till about 12:30pm, the smaller ones might still close Wednesday afternoons.

If you can't be bothered to find a post office and spend hours in line, we recommend buying a book of first or second class stamps at any ordinary newsagent (you can buy as few as four at a time) and slapping two second class stamps on your postcard to the U.S. or two first class stamps on your one-page letter to the U.S. It costs a few pence more than the actual rate but is worth it in terms of simplicity and time saved. Cards or letters to Europe take a single first class stamp. And if you have occasion to send a thank-you note, receive tickets or request information by post while you're here, you'll be reassured and amazed to know that next day delivery for first class letters is the absolute norm. Astonishing.

The **main London post office** *is open 8am to 8pm every day except Sunday, and is located just northeast of Trafalgar Square at 24 William IV Street.*

PRECAUTIONS

Most of our friends from big American cities remark on how safe London feels. Don't get too complacent, though. It's a big city complete with pickpockets (remember Oliver?), thugs and muggers. But if you stay away from Hell's Angels and National Front (fascist) pubs and exercise reasonable caution with your person and belongings, you should experience little or no trouble, even late at night.

A few sensible suggestions: lock your tiara in the hotel safe when you're not wearing it, avoid the 11:30pm tube on a Saturday night if you have a low tolerance for happy pub-goers (i.e., drunks), and if you rent a car, don't leave expensive hi-fi equipment, gold bullion (or anything, for that matter) visible on the back seat. Soho and Leicester Square in the early hours of the morning tend to be full of characters you wouldn't want to marry, but the worst you're likely to experience is annoyance.

On the positive side, it's worth mentioning that London's parks are heartbreakingly beautiful at twilight on pretty summer evenings — we've never felt threatened at that hour and you shouldn't either.

SMOKING

Although lots of people even in London have given up smoking, you wouldn't know it from the gray clouds that still fill restaurants and bars all over town. When making reservations, request a table in the no-smoking section (if they have one), otherwise we're afraid you'll have to grin as politely as you can and bear it.

If you happen to be one of the last of the smoking Americans, remember that smoking is strictly outlawed in many public buildings, on all buses, and in tubes and tube stations.

TAXES

In Britain, **VAT** (value added tax) at 17.5% is automatically included in the ticket price of most items (including restaurant meals), which explains why Scotch whisky costs more in Scotland than in Los Angeles, and why local designers like Paul Smith and Nicole Farhi are no cheaper in London than in New York. As a tourist, you are technically exempt from this tax on all items you export (although this tends to work better in theory than in practice).

Tourists can not claim tax back on hotels or other services or on any purchase below a certain minimum (usually £100, set by the individual retailer), but can claim VAT back on any single or multiple purchase of goods from one store totalling more than the minimum. **VAT 707** forms will be provided by the store (don't forget to ask for them), and should be filled in and filed at the VAT refund booth at customs (you will likely be asked to produce the goods in question, so make sure not to check them through with the rest of your luggage). Customs will stamp your form, which you then mail back to the shop.

A check will be sent to you, usually within four to eight weeks. It will be in sterling; sign it and stick it in your bank account and your bank will convert it to dollars (and charge you for the honor). In case you were wondering, you will not get rich by claiming back VAT.

TAXIS

Drivers of **black cabs** have to pass an incredibly gruelling two-year course known as *The Knowledge* before they qualify, and the wonderful benefit to you is that they almost invariably know exactly where you want to go. They will certainly know museums, major restaurants, department stores, hotels and theaters by name alone (but best to have the address anyway) and many will also know banks, office buildings, and more obscure shops as well.

Look for the amber light that indicates an available cab. Always state your destination before you get in (they'll open the window to talk to you as they pull up) and it is customary to get out of the cab to pay (unless it's raining or you have a million packages). Cabbies are legendarily chatty, and if you don't want to get into an elaborate conversation about politics or your cabbie's holiday in Orlando, feign an Estonian accent. They're great sources of knowledge, however, and we've spent hours in traffic blabbing away happily, so don't be shy. A ten percent tip is standard and will be met with appreciation.

Late at night in the center of town, an ordinary-looking car might pull up and offer to take you where you're going. This will be a **minicab** (or a kidnapper), who will charge an approximate fare (usually less than black cabs but not always) for the journey. Minicabs are pretty much unregulated and we don't recommend them except as a last resort. **Dial-a-cab** is a good alternative — its metered black cabs can be ordered by telephone 24 hours a day *(0171 253 5000)*.

TELEPHONES

London is divided into two zones — **0171** and **0181**. Think of them as area codes, and drop them most of the time; they are always followed by a seven digit number. Most of inner London uses the prefix 0171; outer London is 0181. If you are phoning locally in London, skip the 0171 prefix and dial the usual seven digits. If dialing London from anywhere else in Britain, use the 0171 or 0181 code, then add the seven digits. To phone London from the U.S., dial 011 44 followed by 171 or 181 (drop the zero) and then the standard seven-digit number. Clear as mud?

Dialing the U.S. from a London phone requires the prefix 001 followed by the American area code and number (i.e., 001 212 555 1212). Phone numbers for the rest of England can be very confusing, as not all have seven digits and it's often hard to figure out how many numbers to drop when dialing from abroad, London, or locally. Consult your operator.

A local operator can be reached by dialing 100; the international operator by dialing 155. The number for directory assistance in Britain is 192; for directory inquiries abroad (including the U.S.) it's 153. Emergency is 999. All of the preceding numbers are free from a phone booth (or **phone box** as they're called).

In London most phone booths come in pairs — one will say **Phone Card** and the other **Telephone**. The former requires a card, the latter, coins. Phone cards can be bought at any post office or newsagent in various denominations beginning with £2. If you're using coins, the minimum call requires 10 pence, but have plenty of change ready; you get surprisingly little time even for local calls. A beep-beep-beep-beep sound tells you to put more money in instantly or get cut off.

PHONING HOME, QUICKLY & CHEAPLY

Remarkably, 10 pence is all you need for a brief phone call from a phone booth to the States – you can often leave a quick message on someone's answering machine before it cuts off.

Finding a phone can be an arduous task. In an emergency, nearly every pub has one; just ask at the bar and a small payphone will usually be produced. Some of these require you to insert money after you have dialled and some require that you push a button after your party answers. Read the directions.

And by the way, those cards in the phonebox that read "Naughty schoolgirl needs firm hand with cane" are not advertising for elementary school teachers.

TELEVISION & RADIO

Nearly all hotel televisions offer the wonder of cable so you can watch CNN to your heart's content. The four network stations are BBC1, BBC2, ITV and Channel 4. Neither BBC channel has commercials so they're great for movies and historical costume dramas.

For radio, we're partial to **BBC Radio 4** *(93.5 FM)*, which is about as venerable an English institution as you can imagine and has excellent news coverage, not to mention loopy high-brow game shows, afternoon plays, gardening shows, the shipping forecast, and what must be the world's longest running soap opera (since the 1940s), *The Archers*, every day at 7:05pm. And culturally inquisitive insomniacs will simply adore

Farming Today (at 6am).

Daily newspapers (and *Time Out*) provide complete TV and radio listings.

TIME

London is five hours ahead of New York, eight hours ahead of California, and one hour behind most of Europe. There are slight variations in these time differences based on the clock moving forward and backward for spring and fall. When in doubt for telephoning, call the international operator on 155.

TIPPING

Never in pubs. Rarely, or small change, in cafes where you've just ordered a coffee, a cup of tea, or a sandwich. In basic no-frills restaurants, about 10%. In nicer restaurants, 10-15%. Taxis, 10%. Always check the menu or bill to see whether service is included in the total — about half the time it is.

WATER

It's perfectly safe to drink straight from the tap (or so the government insists), but most restaurants encourage you to order the mineral sort (still or fizzy). If you cannot see the necessity in this, you are perfectly within your rights to ask for a glass of tap water, though don't expect ice and lemon. Water is not automatically offered in restaurants, but is brought ungrudgingly on request.

WEIGHTS & MEASURES

Distance and speed are measured in miles and miles per hour, not kilometers. Weight, however, is measured metrically in **grams** and **kilograms**, except for bodyweight which, believe it or not, is measured in **stones** (14 pounds to a stone).

People and rooms are measured in **centimeters** and **meters**, though inches and feet are still pretty much understood. Gas (petrol) is measured in **imperial gallons**, which bear no relation to American gallons, so don't even try to figure out what it costs. Weather is measured in degrees **centigrade**. Remembering that 16 centigrade is 61 fahrenheit sometimes helps; so does sticking your head out the window.

ESSENTIAL PHONE NUMBERS

- *Medical Emergency:* 999
- *Police Emergency:* 999
- *Fire Emergency:* 999
- *Private Medical Clinic (Medical Express):* 0171 499 1991
- *24-Hour House Calls:* 0181 840 7000
- *Pharmacy (daily until midnight):* 0171 723 6116 or 0171 373 2798
- *Dental Emergency Service:* 0171 935 9320
- *American Embassy:* 0171 499 9000
- *American Express (for stolen or lost cards or travelers checks):* 0 800 521 313
- *Visa (for stolen or lost cards or travelers checks):* 0 800 212 615
- *Mastercard (for stolen or lost cards or travelers checks):* 01268 298 168
- *Telephone Information:* 192
- *International Information:* 153
- *Operator:* 100
- *International Operator:* 155

7. GETTING AROUND LONDON

> *"London excited Frederica. She knew little of it and could not connect the parts she knew into a coherent map in her head. What she liked, being young and strong and curious and greedy, was the anonymity and variety of possible journeys from territory to territory. She liked hurling in bright boxes amongst endlessly various strangers from Camden Town to Oxford Circus, from Liverpool Street to Leicester Square ... Differences delighted her."*
>
> From *Still Life* by A.S. Byatt
>
> We couldn't have said it better ourselves.

MAPS

The following is probably the most important piece of advice you'll find in this guidebook (so pay attention): don't try to negotiate London without a good map. Any tourist information center will give you one that has been handily marked with all the big sights on it. But even better, do what every Londoner does and get yourself an *A to Z* (pronounced *zed*).

They're available at every newsagent in about 10 versions and sizes for about £5, and contain a complete index and map reference of every street in London. They are every real Londoner's bible, so you can pull out your trusty *A to Z* on any bus, in any taxi, or on any street corner and not feel like a dork.

You will notice, in fact, that all taxi drivers carry one, which gives you an idea of how necessary (and cool) they are. The necessity for this is simple: London evolved over a couple of thousand years, and it evolved with thousands of tiny lanes, muses, squares, closes and gardens – which hellishly complicates most addresses. The index of the *A to Z* lists a Cleveland Gardens, Cleveland Grove, Cleveland Muse, Cleveland Place,

Cleveland Row, Cleveland Square, Cleveland Street, Cleveland Terrace and Cleveland Way. Try to sort that out with a general tourist map!

The disadvantage of the *A to Z* is that you don't get the whole picture at once. So use your tourist map for getting from your hotel to the British Museum, but use your *A to Z* for finding out how to get back when you find yourself horribly lost. Which, if you're having a good time, is pretty much mandatory.

By the way, ask at any tube station for a good (free) bus, tube, and central London map.

TICKETS

Public transport in London is the most expensive in Europe. The best way to make it less so is to buy a **one-day travelcard** that permits unlimited travel on all buses and tubes in the zones specified – for a single reasonable price. Most of the places you'll want to go are in zones one and two, but if you're straying as far as Kew Gardens or Greenwich, ask the ticketseller which zones you'll need. Generally, if you're going to be taking more than three tubes or buses in one day, the travelcard will save you money. And besides, you can jump on and off buses without shelling out 80 pence each time, which is always nice. Travelcards, by the way, are only available after 9:30am and are not valid on night buses.

Weekly and monthly travelcards can also be purchased at any tube station. You must provide two photo-booth size photographs.

If you're doing without a travelcard, you'll need to buy a single ticket (for your tube journey) from the **tube** station machines or the ticket window. Just state your destination (or press "adult single" and then your destination on the automatic machines). Be sure to get the amount right; if you end up at your destination with an undervalued ticket, the turnstiles won't let you out and the guards will charge you an extra £10. Hang onto your ticket, you'll need it to get out of the station. If you have a travelcard, the machine will return it to you after it goes through.

If you're traveling by **bus**, there are two main types, both double-decker – the old fashioned open-backed buses that you can just jump on and off, and the newer closed-door buses. On the open buses, a ticket conductor will come around and collect your money. State your destination and he or she will tell you the cost. Most journeys in central London cost 80 pence. On the closed buses, state your destination and pay (or show your travelcard) as you get on. You can pay with £5, £10 and in an emergency £20 notes, but they won't be terribly happy about it. Try to have change.

Single-level buses have become an increasingly familiar sight as private bus companies take over city bus routes.

BOATS

If you get lucky and happen upon a gorgeous spring day, run instantly down to the Westminster or Charing Cross Pier and jump on a boat to The Tower of London, Greenwich or the Thames barrier to the east, Kew Gardens or Hampton Court to the west. The eastern trip takes you past the South Bank, St. Paul's cathedral, past the Tower of London, under the utterly delightful Tower Bridge, and gives a great view of one of the world's largest, most expensive follies: Docklands. Docklands is a huge, expensive 1980s city that never caught on – vast office buildings and luxury apartment complexes built during the boom frenzy of the Thatcher years. To the west, you'll pass through some truly splendid scenery of a rather more bucolic nature, recalling the Thames of the last century. In either direction, we guarantee a very pleasant day. The eastbound boats travel all year round; the westbound boats run Easter to October.

Boat trips do not have to be reserved in advance, but because schedules change seasonally, it's best to phone and check on times. The **London Tourist Board River Trips Phoneline** *(01839 123 432)* offers a plethora of information very quickly, so have a pencil poised. In season (Easter to October), you can just show up at Westminster Pier and get on the next available boat to the Tower of London, Greenwich, the Thames Barrier, Kew Gardens or Hampton Court. Boats tend to go every 30-45 minutes, starting about 10am. Last returning boats are at about 4pm; the round-trip tickets (return) at around £6 are nearly as cheap as a one-way.

There are a number of seasonal special cruises including a 2-hour Sunday lunch or supper cruise from Charing Cross pier for about £20; one hour circular cruises from Westminster pier *(phone Catamaran cruises on 0171 839 3572)*; luxury lunch, afternoon tea, and dinner and dance cruises for £20-49 *(phone 0171 925 2215)*; and disco cruises *(phone Tidal Cruises on 0171 928 9009)*.

London Waterbus offers tours of London's historic waterway canals between Camden Lock and Little Venice (Maida Vale), with a stop at London Zoo. On a nice day it makes a wonderfully pleasant, leisurely trip; perfect with kids. April to October, daily on the hour 10am to 5pm. Adults: £3.30 (round trip £4.40), children: £2 (round trip £2.60). *Contact London Waterbus, Camden Lock, London NW1. Tel: 0171 482 2550.*

BUSES

Buses are tricky in foreign cities, but in London they're absolutely mandatory. After years of living here, we still love sitting in the front seat at the top of a double-decker bus and getting the best view in town.

Every bus shelter has a sign with a list of the buses that stop there, and most have a printed schedule of destinations to help you navigate. Study it for the destination of your choice, or better yet, phone **transport**

information *at 0171 222 1234* before you go out and ask which bus takes you where you're going. They're great about plotting routes; in addition, bus drivers and conductors are remarkably good at telling you where to get off (and we mean that in the nice way – usually).

If you're one of only a few people at the bus stop, stick your arm out in plenty of time to stop the bus you want; when getting off, don't forget to ring the bell. If it looks as if no one's interested, the bus driver will often zoom past a stop, especially if there's a **red request sign** (which means the bus stops there by request only).

Everyone's favorite bus for practical purposes is the **number 19**, a hop-on-hop-off green and yellow double decker that runs from Sloane Square to Knightsbridge to Hyde Park to Piccadilly to Soho/Chinatown to the British Museum and beyond. It's a good beginner's route. For scenic routes, it has to be the **number 11** which hits a myriad of tourist hot spots: Sloane Square, Victoria, Westminster Abbey, Trafalgar Square, Fleet Street and St. Paul's. The **53** (Oxford Circus, Regent Street, Trafalgar Square, Whitehall and Westminster, the Imperial War Museum), and the **15** (London Bridge, St. Paul's, Trafalgar Square, Piccadilly) are also good routes.

A warning – buses can be slow. Sometimes excruciatingly so, especially at rush hour or through the parts of town where roadworks are in full swing. But the views are fabulous, they're far friendlier than the tube, and it's the cheapest way we know to make kids happy. Be careful jumping on and off. And don't forget to sit upstairs.

... And Bus Tours

The basic tour bus experience can be had courtesy of **The Original Round London Sightseeing Tour**, which offers a taped commentary on a double decker red bus (with the top chopped off to catch the – we hope – sun). You can pick one of these up daily, every half hour starting at 10am (last bus 5pm; 4pm during the winter), from Piccadilly Circus (Leicester Square side), Baker Street (in front of the tube stop), Victoria Station (Victoria Street) or Marble Arch (Park Lane).

They cost £10 (£5 for children) and last an hour and a half. They actually do offer a really good geographical overview of London, picking out the tourist highlights, and are a wonderful mindless way to kill the couple of hours between arriving in London and being allowed to check into your room.

For a classier experience, we recommend the **Harrods tours**. They leave daily from door 8 of Harrods at 10:30am, 1:30pm and 4pm, include refreshments, come with a taped commentary and cost £18 (adults, £10 children). Harrods also runs all day tours to Stratford-on-Avon and Blenheim Palace for £56, which include a three course lunch with wine and coffee. *Phone 0171 581 3603 for more details.*

CARS & DRIVING

We've said it before and we'll say it again: only masochists and lunatics rent a car for a stay in London. If you're going out of London for a few days or a few weeks, however, make sure you have an up-to-date American license, and nerves of steel to navigate your way out of the city.

For car rentals, we generally go with **Budget** *(0 800 626 063)* which tends to be convenient and cheapest, but you can also try:
- **Avis** *(0181 848 8733)*
- **Eurodollar** *(01895 233 300)*
- **Europcar** *(01345 222 525)*
- **Hertz** *(0181 679 1799)*.

Don't forget, your car will be standard transmission unless you request automatic. You can expect to pay at least £35 per day, so try to arrange a better deal from the States if you can. Figure about £15-20 to fill a compact car with gas. Off season special deals as low as £25 per day with unlimited mileage are often available. Check with your credit card service or American car insurance as to whether you're covered for theft and collision; there's no point paying for it twice. And if you can't find information under Automobile Rental in the yellow pages, that's because it's listed under *Car Hire*.

A COUPLE OF HANDY DRIVING HINTS

Remember to drive on the left. This may sound obvious, but you'd be amazed at how easy it is to forget when you're the only car on a quiet road. Be very aware of two important road markings in particular: a double white line painted at the end of a road at a junction, and the thick white stripes and flashing beacon of a **zebra crossing***. The first indicates a full stop and is easy (and quite dangerous) to miss. The second demands constant awareness, as pedestrians have unequivocal right of way on a zebra crossing. This means that the car in front of you might suddenly stop, or that a person might suddenly step out in front of you.*

If you see a person approaching or standing at the edge of a zebra crossing, you must stop. In addition, cars on a **rotary** *(roundabout) have right-of-way, so enter with extreme caution.*

Double yellow (or worse, red) lines by the side of a road mean you are never allowed to park there. Single yellow lines indicate restricted parking, usually after 8pm and on Sundays. No one really understands the parking regulations in England; look for signs or traffic wardens if you're in doubt, and don't assume it's okay because everyone else is parked there.

As for navigation, the best rule is to invest £5 in a good road atlas (most rental car places and gas stations sell them). Then ask your rental car agent for the best route. London's signage was created by a man fondly known as Harry the Bastard, and is completely impossible to fathom. According to his system, perfectly simple routes remain unmarked, while sadistically labyrinthine roads leading nowhere are plastered with signs saying "To Oxford."

And finally, do check to make sure there isn't a nice little train going your way. You'll miss the traffic and the angst – and the English countryside looks much prettier when you're not trying to figure out how to squeeze past a tractor on a single track road.

THE TUBE

The **tube** (or **underground**) is the quickest way to get around town; far quicker than taxi or bus if you're going any distance. There are eleven lines and each is color-coded (as seen on the famed, much celebrated tube map). By American standards tube trains' frequent service and padded seats make them seem pretty luxurious; at rush hour you probably won't get anywhere near a seat anyway. Take note: Sunday trains are fewer and farther between so leave extra time.

Make sure you have a tube map, or consult the map at the station; you'll need to know the last stop on your chosen line and the general direction (north, south east or west) you're traveling to figure out which train to take. Tubes run from 5am till midnight. They're well-marked, easy to follow, not dangerous – though we don't recommend them on a Saturday night after the pubs close if you're not fond of drunks. And remember to hang onto your ticket, you need it to get out or pay a £10 fine.

TAXIS

Taxis are comfortable, roomy, safe, and fairly expensive. The average short ride from the West End to Knightsbridge costs about £5 with tip. Don't bother trying to figure out what all those extras are on the meter – there are supplements for two people, after 8pm, on Sundays and bank holidays, for luggage, etc.

The great thing about taxis is that they always know where they're going, and will often take you on an unbelievable tour of London's back streets. They're not trying to cheat you, just avoiding traffic or one-way systems. Look for the amber light which tells you it's for hire, state your destination before you get in, get out to pay, and tip 10%.

Parents take note: black cabs are big enough to take an uncollapsed stroller and child. As a general rule we don't recommend the unregulated, unmetered mini-cabs.

TRAINS

Aside from transporting passengers away from London through Britain, a number of **British Rail** routes whisk commuters around London and its suburbs as well. British Rail commuter lines come in very handy for suburban destinations like Hampton Court, Windsor, and Greenwich. British Rail information is roughly divided by the direction you're traveling, although any of the numbers listed below will be able to offer general station, scheduling, and price information to any destination in Britain:

• **North**: *0171 278 2477 (Kings Cross)*
• **South**: *0171 928 5100 (Waterloo)*
• **East**: *0171 387 7070 (Euston)*
• **West**: *0171 262 6767 (Paddington)*
• **International destinations**: *0171 834 2345.*

Eurostar Information

The exciting nwe channel tunnel train will take you direct to **Paris** (three hours), **Brussels**, and 150 other connecting destinations.

For information and tickets, call 01233 617 575.

WALKING & WALKING TOURS

There's no possible way to escape walking around London. Which is good, given that it's one of the city's greatest pleasures. London is huge, however, so make sure you're prepared with comfortable shoes. It rains a lot, so a collapsible umbrella is mandatory. The amount of traffic in central London means the air quality gets pretty unpleasant, especially in the summer, so plot your routes through parks and off main thoroughfares – you'll make all sorts of wonderful discoveries that way in any case.

If you get lost and even your trusty *A to Z* isn't helping, ask directions. English people love directing unfortunate foreigners; something about a flashback to the days of the empire. And please, please, please look everywhere before you cross a street. Knocking pedestrians over is kind of a hobby in London.

Walking tours are a great way to see some of London's obvious and more offbeat neighborhoods, and pick up some real insight, lore, and history on the way. We like *The Original London Walks*, whose distinctive black and white brochures can be found in most hotel and theater lobbies *(or phone 0171 624 3978 and they'll mail a copy to your hotel)*.

Their offerings include The London of Shakespeare and Dickens, The Old Jewish Quarter, a Knightsbridge pub walk, a Thames walk, London by Gaslight, Regent's Canal, Legal London, Doctor's London, Samuel Pepys' London and many, many more.

Most walks meet outside tube stations at a specified hour (no reservations necessary), take place rain or shine, cost £4 (accompanied children under 15 free) and last about two hours. The guides are usually knowledgeable and enthusiastic. There are also guided walks at Hampton Court and Oxford, as well as really special treats like a Christmas Day Dickens walk, a Children's Mystery Walk, and a Jack the Ripper walk. Check the Around Town/Visitors section of *Time Out* for more listings.

For self-guided walks, turn to Chapter 11, *Walking Tours of London*, for our recommendaations on the best walks in town.

8. WHERE TO STAY

London is not an inexpensive holiday destination; the tiny, attractive £30 a night "find" you can still hope for in France or Italy barely exists. There is, however, a quite dazzling array of good, charming hotels in London – some will set you back a small fortune, but others are quite reasonably priced. We've offered as wide a price range as possible without dipping into the down-and-dirty, and haven't listed any hotels we wouldn't stay in ourselves, though one or two of the least expensive would involve a bit of practical compromise.

Even if you're the sort of free-spirit who likes to make your own reservations, we suggest that where possible, you book hotels through your travel agent. Over the past few years, London tourism has suffered from the unfavorable exchange rate, and many hotels are willing to offer significant reductions to travel agents.

Please keep in mind that amenities that Americans take for granted (like orthopedic mattresses and good showers) can be rare as hen's teeth, especially in the lower price ranges. Fortunately, warmth and charm can be had across the board. This section is divided into neighborhoods; choose the area that's closest to your travelling spirit and style.

And as a final note: for some reason, hotels are among the very few products or services in London that don't automatically include VAT. If the price quoted is exclusive of VAT, add an additional 17.5%. VAT on hotels is not refundable.

MAYFAIR & ST. JAMES

Probably the most expensive part of town, and the most centrally located, **Mayfair** is equidistant from the West End and Knightsbridge, is bordered by Park Lane on the west and Regent Street on the east. For the purposes of easy categorization we've included **St. James** to the south and the area around Wigmore street just north of Oxford Street in this grouping.

Mayfair's squares are leafy and elegant, its restaurants expensive and swish, but there's nothing to stop you wandering over to Chinatown if you've had your fill of chateaubriand.

1. THE ASCOTT, *49 Hill Street, London W1X 7FQ. Tel: 0171 499 6868; fax: 0171 499 0705. Rates (exclusive of VAT): £135 studio; £175 one bedroom; £275 two bedroom. Rates include continental breakfast Monday through Friday. Major credit cards. Hyde Park Corner tube.*

Why didn't anyone think of this before? All the services of a luxury hotel combined with all the convenience of your own private apartment. We can't think of a nicer way to spend a week. The Ascott is one of London's newest hotels, well-located just across Park Lane from Hyde Park in the heart of Mayfair. Every apartment comes completely equipped with a coffee-maker, microwave, pots and pans, glasses, cutlery, fine bone china, washing machine and tumble dryer. Groceries can be ordered and are delivered free of charge from local shops – though in this part of town, basics obviously won't come cheap.

The rooms are well-designed and handsomely furnished with simple modern furniture and a choice of queen or king-size beds; the counters are topped with marble, the bathrooms spacious and tastefully outfitted. For business guests (and anyone else requiring such services), voice mail and fax machines are standard. The breakfast room overlooks a small outdoor patio with a pretty fountain. Other in-house facilities include a health club, sauna and steam room. Weekly and monthly rates are available.

2. BROWN'S HOTEL, *Albemarle and Dover Streets (off Piccadilly), London W1A 4SW. Tel: 0171 493 6020; fax: 0171 493 9381. Rates (exclusive of VAT): £175-195 single and superior singles (with separate sitting area and desk); £185-235 double; £255 family room; £295-525 suites. Major credit cards. Green Park tube.*

Brown's was established in 1837, the year Victoria became queen, and it retains the reserved elegance of a 19th century men's club. With its softly carpeted hallways, wood panelling and chintz-covered chairs, the hotel is quintessentially English – unassuming and underplayed – which causes most visitors to love Browns (though some do find all that exquisite restraint and those manly hunting prints just a touch irritating).

It can't, however, be faulted where comfort is concerned. The bedroom walls are covered in deep blue wallpaper; the windows look out over Mayfair and are draped in chintz that matches the bedspreads; the handsome wardrobes are rosewood; and the bathrooms impressively grand with old-fashioned double sinks and enormous bathtubs (with shower). Worth considering if you're traveling with children are the family rooms made up of a double room, a twin bedded room and two bathrooms. For history buffs, it's worth noting that Napoleon III stayed here after the Franco-Prussian war; Theodore Roosevelt was married here; Franklin and Eleanor Roosevelt honeymooned here; Kipling wrote here. Brown's serves a famous (and famously artery-clogging) afternoon tea in its very pleasant tea rooms.

3. DUKES HOTEL, *St. James Place, London SW1A 1NY. Tel: 0171 491 4840; fax: 0171 493 1264; U.S. toll free: 1 800 381 4702. Rates (exclusive of VAT): £125-145, single; £160-185 double; £210-250 suites. Major credit cards. Green Park tube.*

Nestled in a quiet cul-de-sac off St. James Street, this hotel offers a remarkably secluded location two minutes walk from Buckingham Palace and four minutes from Piccadilly. Each evening, the gas lamps outside your door are lit by hand, and each morning you'll awake to the sound of cooing pigeons. The beautifully preserved Edwardian building is extremely attractive, and offers a private, clubby retreat. Rich wood panelling, dark green walls, paisley carpets and leather chairs create an atmosphere of privilege and calm in the sitting room – and throughout.

You can choose a standard double room with king or queen-size bed; unless you're planning to smuggle in legions of friends, we recommend the queen – the rooms with king-size beds feel squeezed. Each room is attractively decorated with antique furniture and floral chintz fabrics. The small bathrooms are generously outfitted with good quality toiletries.

4. 22 JERMYN STREET, *22 Jermyn Street, London SW1Y 6HL. Tel: 0171 734 2353; fax: 0171 734 0750; U.S. toll free: 1 800 682 7808. Rates (exclusive of VAT) £170 studio; £220-250 suites. Major credit cards. Green Park or Piccadilly Circus tube.*

Parallel to Piccadilly, nearly across from the Royal Academy, you'll find Jermyn (pronounced *German*) Street, famed for its handmade suits, custom-tailored shirts and upmarket clientele. Appropriately, the small (18 room) hotel that shares the Jermyn Street address has the same luxurious custom-tailored feel. It's intimate and doesn't stint on detail: can you think of another hotel where you'll find an umbrella in your closet? The furniture is a mix of contemporary and antique and some rooms have fireplaces; ceramics, potted plants, framed prints, fresh flowers and fruit bowls in every room complete the atmosphere of grace and care.

Concierge, valet, business and secretarial service are available, the room service is 24 hour (continental breakfast can be served in your room), every room has satellite TV and a fax machine, and exercise equipment can be provided in the suites. Temporary membership to the exclusive Champney's Health Club can also be arranged, though at £20 per visit (classes and massage extra) you might find it just as satisfying to get your exercise walking around London. If it's available, request Suite Two.

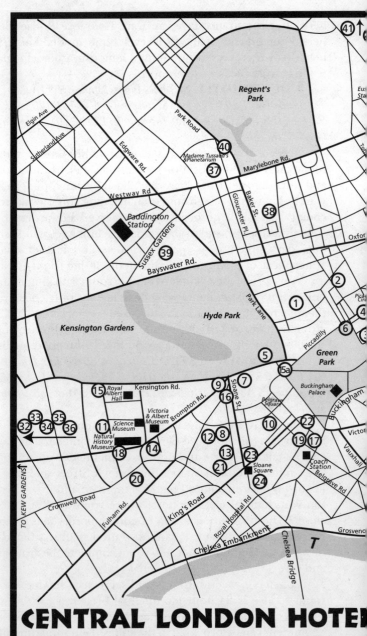

CENTRAL LONDON HOTE[

1. The Ascott
2. Brown's Hotel
3. Duke's Hotel
4. 22 Jermyn St
5. The Lanesborough
6. The Stafford
7. The Basil Street Hotel
8. The Cadogan
9. The Capital
10. The Diplomat
11. Embassy House Hotel
12. The Executive
13. The Penja
14. The Franklin Hotel
15. The Gore
15a. The Halkin
16. L'Hotel
17. James House
18. John Howard
19. Lime Tree Hote
20. Number Sixte
21. The Sloane Ho
22. Tophams Ebur
23. The Wilbrahan

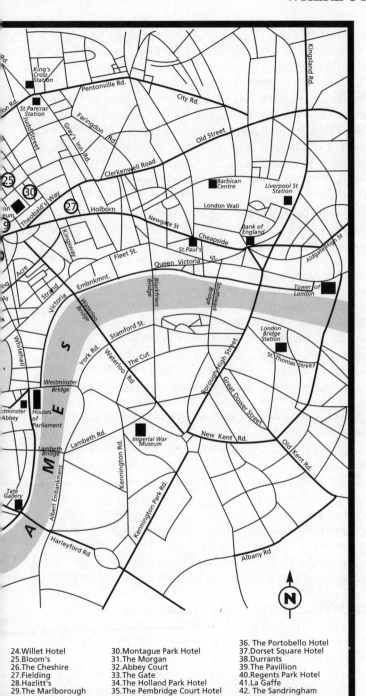

24.	Willet Hotel	30.	Montague Park Hotel	36.	The Portobello Hotel
25.	Bloom's	31.	The Morgan	37.	Dorset Square Hotel
26.	The Cheshire	32.	Abbey Court	38.	Durrants
27.	Fielding	33.	The Gate	39.	The Pavillion
28.	Hazlitt's	34.	The Holland Park Hotel	40.	Regents Park Hotel
29.	The Marlborough	35.	The Pembridge Court Hotel	41.	La Gaffe
				42.	The Sandringham

5. THE LANESBOROUGH, *Hyde Park Corner, London SW1X 7TA.*
Tel: 0171 259 5606. U.S. toll free: 1 800 999 1828; toll free fax: 1 800 937 8278.
Rates (exclusive of VAT): £170-195 single; £230-295 double; £375-475 junior
suite; £610-£720 suites. Major credit cards. Hyde Park Corner tube.

On the border of Knightsbridge and Mayfair, the Lanesborough is
pretty much universally considered London's finest hotel. With spectacular views of Hyde Park and Buckingham Palace, it captures all the refined,
restrained grandeur of a Georgian manor house; it's probably as close as
any of us will ever get to experiencing "Remains of the Day"-style living.
A roaring wood fire greets you on winter evenings as you enter the marble-
floored, wood-panelled lobby; twelve foot windows are swagged in heavy
silk, the furnishings are early 19th century. From the 24-hour butler, ready
to assist with unpacking or to iron your jetlagged suit (no extra charge),
to the personalized business cards waiting in your room on arrival, The
Lanesborough is all about service in the way of the old British Empire —
lavish, discreet, exquisitely polite.

Every room is furnished in full Regency glory: canopied beds, dark
wood panelling, satin cushions, gilt-framed paintings. On a more modern
note, fax machines, compact disc stereo systems and videocassette players
are standard equipment. A personal direct-dial telephone number is
reserved for each guest, so your callers can avoid the dreadful inconve-
nience of the Lanesborough's (predictably perfect) switchboard. Whatever could be next ? A fresh bowl of fruit appears in your room daily. Wake
up calls are accompanied by tea or coffee. Bathrooms that could almost
qualify as billiards rooms are fitted with jacuzzi-spray tubs, heat framed
mirrors (to prevent unsightly steaming), bidets and terrycloth robes.
Breakfast, lunch, afternoon tea, dinner and after theater supper are all
available in the Conservatory, the hotel's glass-domed restaurant.

The interior of the Conservatory pays homage to the Royal Pavilion
— the Regent King's sumptuous pleasure palace in Brighton. The decor
is Oriental: giant urns of potted ginger plants and ceiling-high palms greet
you at the door. For those poor folk not willing to mortgage the yacht for
a week here, a visit to the dining room for afternoon tea or a drink offers
a fleeting glimpse of the lifestyles of the rich and famous. As for those
who've recently made a killing in the stockmarket — get on that phone.
You only live once.

6. THE STAFFORD HOTEL, *St. James Place, London SW1A 1NJ. Tel:*
0171 493 0111; fax: 0171 493 7121; U.S. toll free: 1 800 525 4800. Rates
(exclusive of VAT): £157 single; £170-208 double; £247-366 junior suites.
Major credit cards. Green Park tube.

Tucked quietly behind Green Park in St. James Place, this elegantly
understated hotel has a great sense of neighborhood — you feel transported back to the 19th century when London was a series of country

villages. The hotel is distinguished by its discreet atmosphere, attractive English decor and personal service; it feels more like a refined house than a big hotel. The sitting room offers a comfortable arrangement of sofas, Chesterfield chairs, small tables and fresh flowers — all terribly intimate and civilized — while the American Bar boasts a variety of American University paraphernalia.

The newest addition to the original 74 room hotel is also its nicest: the 18th century stable, once used by coachmen and grooms, has been converted into 12 rooms and junior suites. Separate from the main hotel, the coach house offers greater privacy and feels rather like a group of well-appointed country bungalows.

All rooms come with television and CD/stereo systems; the junior suites in the stable feature king size beds, and pleasant sitting areas in addition to exposed wooden beams and beautifully restored wooden doors. One of the hotel's original (1741) wine cellars has been converted into an atmospheric subterranean dining room; the other stores the hotel's impressive cache of 20,000 bottles of wine.

KNIGHTSBRIDGE, CHELSEA, & SOUTH KENSINGTON

The combination of these three neighborhoods includes some of London's loveliest and most exclusive shops (**Harrods** and **Harvey Nichols** among them), hotels, squares, pubs and three of its best museums: **The Science Museum**, **The Natural History Museum**, and **The Victorian & Albert**. Ten minutes by bus or cab takes you to the theaters of the West End.

7. THE BASIL STREET HOTEL, *8 Basil Street, London SW3 1AH. Tel: 0171 581 3311; fax: 0171 581 3693; U.S. toll free: 1 800 448 8355. Rates (including VAT): £125 single; £175 double/twin. Major credit cards. Knightsbridge tube.*

There was a time, over a decade ago, when the Basil Street Hotel had a reputation as one of the most charming hotels in Knightsbridge. Since then, it has developed a slightly down at heel air – though remnants of its former glory remain, mainly in the form of the Edwardian-style dining and sitting rooms which are nicely decorated with antiques and oriental rugs. The rooms are all of a comfortable size, clean and well-kept, but without remarkable details.

But there are actually three good reasons to stay at the Basil Street Hotel. One is its location, which for lovers of Knightsbridge, shopping and museums, is perfect. Two is the bargain weekend package — for a minimum stay of two nights (Friday, Saturday or Sunday) a double/twin is £149 per night (£135 off season) and a single £105 per night (£95 off season). Reason three is the Parrot Club – a ladies only retreat with separate dining room/lounge facilities where you (assuming you are female) can write a letter, use a phone or fax, receive messages or just borrow an umbrella. It's a popular haunt of the county ladies who shop – just right for relaxing with your hatboxes while awaiting a lift home to Surrey with darling George. All female hotel guests receive free membership privileges.

Request a quiet room. The local fire station is just down the road.

SIX OF THE BEST HOTELS

There are more expensive hotels in London, and more luxurious, and hotels that have been around for a few hundred more years. But when it comes to charm, comfort and that individual something that makes a hotel stay memorable, these are our favorites.

BLOOM'S HOTEL, *7 Montague Street, London WC1 5BP. Tel: 0171 323 1717; fax: 0171 636 6498. Rates (including VAT and breakfast): £95-110 single; £140-170 double/twin. Major credit cards. Goodge Street, Russell Square, or Tottenham Court Road tube.*

THE GORE, *189 Queens Gate, London SW7 5EX. Tel: 0171 584 6601; fax: 0171 589 8127. Rates (including VAT): £105-117 single; £148-160 double/twin; £208 deluxe room; £235 Tudor room. Major credit cards. Gloucester Road or South Kensington tube.*

THE HALKIN, *5 Halkin Street (off Belgrave Square), London, SW1X 7DJ. Tel: 0171 333 1000; fax: 0171 333 1100; U.S. toll free: 1 800 637 7200. Rates (exclusive of VAT): £200-250 single/double; £325-375 suites. Ask about special weekend rates. Major credit cards. Hyde Park Corner or Knightsbridge tube.*

HAZLITT'S, *6 Frith Street, London W1V 5TZ. Tel: 0171 434 1771; fax: 0171 439 1524. Rates (excluding VAT): £105 single; £130 double/twin; £170 suite. Major credit cards. Leicester Square or Tottenham Court Road tube.*

THE PORTOBELLO HOTEL, *22 Stanley Gardens, London W11 2NG. Tel: 0171 727 2777; fax: 0171 792 9341. Rates (including VAT and English or Continental breakfast): £75 single cabin; £99 single; £110-130 double/twin; £150-195 special rooms. Major credit cards. Notting Hill Gate tube.*

THE SLOANE HOTEL, *29 Draycott Place, London SW3 2SH. Tel: 0171 581 5757; fax: 0171 584 1348; U.S. toll free: 1 800 324 9960. Rates (exclusive of VAT): £120 double; £175 deluxe double/twin; £225 Gallery Suite. Major credit cards. Sloane Square tube.*

8. THE CADOGAN, *75 Sloane Street, London SW1X 9SG. Tel: 0171 235 7141; fax: 0171 245 0994. U.S. toll free: 1 800 448 8344. Rates (including VAT): £125 single; £145-165 double/twin; £275 suites. Major credit cards. Knightsbridge tube.*

The Cadogan (pronounced *cuh-DUG-in*) sits on a small, busy street connecting Knightsbridge, Belgravia and Chelsea which makes it an ideal location for shopping at Harrods and museum-going. Historically its roots are in the theater – the hotel was once the home of actress Lilly Langtry, and Oscar Wilde was a regular guest of the turret room that now bears his name. The atmosphere is quiet and unpretentious; the staff friendly and helpful.

The 65 cozy, simply furnished rooms and five suites vary considerably in size (to avoid a particularly small one, try telling them you're a basketball player or need space for your St. Bernard). Floral patterns dominate in all the rooms, with the ubiquitous matching curtains and bedspreads. A common drawing room offers the privacy of a study with lots of comfortable chairs and sofas; it's a lovely place to read the paper, meet friends or partake of afternoon tea (3-6pm). It's worth asking about their theatre, off-season and weekend packages – in other words, try a bit of bargaining.

9. THE CAPITAL HOTEL, *22 Basil Street, London SW3 1AT. Tel: 0171 589 5171; fax: 0171 225 0011. U.S. toll free: 1 800 926 3199. Rates (including VAT): £187 double/twin; £250 deluxe double. Major credit cards. Knightsbridge tube).*

Discreetly hidden away on Basil Street, just around the corner from the two great meeting and shopping places in Knightsbridge (Harrods and Harvey Nichols) you'll find The Capital Hotel. But only if you're really looking. The top-hatted doorman discreetly positioned by the front door is the only hint that this is something other than a luxurious Knightsbridge residence – which is, of course, exactly the effect the management has spent a great deal of time and effort achieving. The hotel itself has 48 rooms, lots of wood panelling, handsome wallpaper and artwork – all aimed at the discerning male.

In fact just about everything at The Capital is aimed at the discerning male, which gives it a slightly studied, formal air the average discerning female might find off-putting. That said, The Capital is classy and comfortable and fabulously positioned. The rooms (with king-size beds) are not enormous, but the fabrics and fixtures are all carefully chosen and good-quality – when making a reservation you can even request your favorite color scheme (green, blue or beige – though we can't imagine who would actually go out of his or her way to choose beige). The toiletries are particularly good quality and include toothbrushes; robes are provided in every room.

We happily recommend The Capital to tourists of all sorts, though it is the Platonic ideal of a hotel for the discriminating businessman. Which is a bit of a shame given all the great shopping time likely to be wasted in meetings. The Capital restaurant has justifiably received a great deal of attention lately (see *Where to Eat chapter*).

10. THE DIPLOMAT HOTEL, *2 Chesham Street, London SW1X 8DT. Tel: 0171 235 1544; fax: 0171 259 6153. Rates (including VAT and breakfast): £70 single; £105 double/twin; £120 executive double. Major credit cards. Sloane Square tube.*

The Diplomat is one of those rare finds, a comfortable, pretty hotel in a great neighborhood that doesn't cost a fortune. The lobby has a magnificent staircase that rises through the center of this former family residence; the staff is friendly, unpretentious and helpful, and the location couldn't be better. The 27 rooms are spacious, nicely furnished and retain lots of original architectural details from the original house – the Lyall or Belgravia rooms are particularly worth requesting. A substantial buffet breakfast, light lunch, and afternoon tea are served in the cheery dining room; massage can be arranged on request, and a portable exercise bike will be provided in your room for £10 per hour.

11. EMBASSY HOUSE HOTEL, *31-33 Queen's Gate, London SW7 5JA. Tel: 0171 584 7222; U.S. toll-free: 1 800 247 3643; fax: 0171 589 3910. Rates (including VAT and continental breakfast): £89 single; £99 double/twin. Major credit cards. Gloucester Road or South Kensington tube.*

Modern comfort combines with Victorian design in this late 19th century ex-private residence located an easy walk from the Albert Hall, Hyde Park, Harrods and the Victoria & Albert Museum. During the past year, the hotel has been carefully restored to its former glory – elaborate plaster ceilings, decorative cornices, a grand staircase and mirrored doors were all included in the original grand house and today look fresh and new.

You'll find comfortable reproduction-antique furniture, vases of fresh flowers and Victorian paintings in the public rooms; the decor of the seventy guest rooms is neutral and somewhat characterless (though the rooms are comfortable and spacious). Cable TV, hairdryers, trouser press, room service, and tea and coffee-making facilities are all standard. The hotel also has a restaurant, bar and fully equipped conference center. The Embassy House is owned by Jarvis Hotels which offer substantially discounted packages, special weekend rates and children's rates; check with your travel agent.

12. THE EXECUTIVE, *57 Pont Street, London SW1X OBD. Tel: 0171 581 2424; fax: 0171 589 9456. Rates (including VAT and buffet breakfast): £55-70 single; £75-99 double; £110 suite. Major credit cards. Knightsbridge or Sloane Square tube.*

For fabulous location and great value, you can't really beat The Executive. This recently renovated red brick Victorian town house has "listed" status with National Heritage, which simply means it's a building of genuine architectural importance. The dark mahogany door opens into a beautifully restored early 19th century lobby with carved stairway and detailed wall carvings.

Rooms are well-lit and cheery; the bathrooms small but spotless. Television, complimentary newspapers, and bathrobes come with each room; the staff is friendly and helpful; the hotel is just around the corner from Harrods and an easy walk to the Victoria & Albert, Science and Natural History museums. A block or two away, Pont Street turns into Beauchamps (inexplicably pronounced *Beechams*) Place where the likes of Princess Di shop and dine. In this toney neighborhood, The Executive represents very good value indeed.

13. THE FENJA, *69 Cadogan Gardens, London SW3 2RB. Tel: 0171 589 7333; fax: 0171 581 4958. Rates (inclusive of VAT): £130 standard double/ twin; £195 superior double/twin. Major credit cards. Sloane Square tube.*

The discreet, twelve room Fenja is another of Chelsea's charming private residence-turned-hotels. The tidy, neatly appointed rooms are all named for writers and painters from the neighborhood (Jane Austen, Swinburne and John Singer Sargent, to name a few); high ceilings throughout create a feeling of spaciousness. The furnishings are unre-markable, but the location is central to major museums and Knightsbridge shopping, and guests are given access keys to Cadogan Gardens, the lovely, private neighborhood retreat across the street from the hotel entrance. Breakfast and light meals can be ordered from the room service menu. There is also a pleasant ground floor sitting room in which to relax with a book, receive guests or enjoy evening cocktails.

14. THE FRANKLIN HOTEL, *28 Egerton Gardens, London SW3, 2DB. Tel: 0171 584 5533; fax: 0171 584 5449; U.S. Toll free: 1 800 473 9487. Rates (exclusive of VAT): £120 single; £145-180 double/twin; £180-210 garden rooms and suites. Major credit cards. Knightsbridge tube.*

Luxurious and romantic, The Franklin backs onto one of the loveliest secluded tree-lined garden squares in Knightsbridge. The rooms are spacious, air-conditioned and furnished with antiques, English porcelain, oil paintings, pillows trimmed with lace, and chintz bedspreads and curtains. The bathrooms are marble and roomy; every room has a direct dial telephone, satellite television and bar.

The hotel offers 24 hour room service, though we would prefer tea or an after dinner drink in the charming drawing room with its working fireplace and inviting sofas – it opens directly onto the pretty garden for strolling in mild weather, which in London could as easily be March as July. Room number 12 features a large canopy bed and a curved wall of glass doors overlooking the garden. Though London's reputation as a city of romance has a long way to go, The Franklin is making inroads.

15. THE GORE, *189 Queens Gate, London SW7 5EX. Tel: 0171 584 6601; fax: 0171 589 8127. Rates (including VAT): £105-117 single; £148-160 double/twin; £208 deluxe room; £235 Tudor room. Major credit cards. Gloucester Road or South Kensington tube.*

The Gore is an unforgettable hotel. Throughout, it's densely decorated and crowded with curiosities – paying homage to the eccentric, inventive, collector mentality of the Victorians. Take a minute to apprceiate the sumptuous lobby, with its mosaic tiled floor, Turkish rugs, potted palms in Chinese porcelain urns and, behind the reception desk, a shrine to Queen Victoria made up of photographs, paintings and drawings. More paintings line the reception area and lead into a luminous emerald green sitting room filled with comfortable sofas and chairs.

The thirty large guest rooms are nothing short of magnificent with their mahogany four-poster beds, rich textured fabrics and beautifully tiled dark wood bathrooms with original turn-of-the-century fixtures. Request the Venus room with its huge, painted reclining nude over the brocade sofa and gilded bed that once belonged to Judy Garland. In the marbled bathroom, there's a painted mural of Zeus driving his chariot over the bathtub.

All rooms come with cable TV, direct dial telephone and hairdryers; for business guests, the friendly professional staff will arrange fax, photocopy and messenger services. Bistrot 190, the adjoining ground floor restaurant is open all day and features modern British/Mediterranean cuisine. The hotel is convenient to lots of good restaurants, Harrods, Hyde Park and the museums of South Kensington, but we'd stay here even if it weren't.

15A. THE HALKIN, *5 Halkin Street (off Belgrave Square), London, SW1X 7DJ. Tel: 0171 333 1000; fax: 0171 333 1100; U.S. toll free: 1 800 637 7200. Rates (exclusive of VAT): £200-250 single/double; £325-375 suites. Ask about special weekend rates. Major credit cards. Hyde Park Corner or Knightsbridge tube.*

Slipping into the Halkin after a long transatlantic journey is like easing into an Armani suit – it's contemporary, understated, elegant, and very, very beautiful. Located in the opulent heart of Belgravia, it eschews all the horrid sentimentality of ye olde England, and relies instead on simple shapes and neutral colors — gray carpets, cream furnishings, and rosewood.

The brightly-lit lobby is elegant and uncluttered; polished marble and granite dominate and there's not a trace of swagged curtains, trimmed lightshades and moire curtains. A large wall painting leads you into the lounge which is simply furnished with lapis blue leather chairs, round glass tables and sleek modern sofas. The forty-one rooms have an almost Japanese feel to them; each is uncluttered, elegant and practical and features warm rosewood-panelled walls, marble bathrooms and silky Egyptian cotton sheets. Other standard features include queen-size beds (with oversize headboard, great for reading in bed), a compact desk, private fax machine, videocassette player, two telephone lines, and 24-hour room service.

Egon Ronay named the Halkin hotel of the year for 1995, and it's easy to see why — staying at the Halkin is a truly remarkable experience. (Dining at the Halkin is another remarkable experience – see *Where to Eat*.)

16. L'HOTEL, *28 Basil Street, London SW3 1AS. Tel: 0171 589 6286; fax: 0171 225 0011. Rates (including continental breakfast and VAT): £145 twin; £165 The Suite (double bed). Major credit cards. Knightsbridge tube.*

This small, 12 room hotel feels more like a house in the country than a hotel just a hundred yards from Harrods and two minutes from Hyde Park. Although it shares ownership, a fax number and prepping kitchen with The Capital next door, the atmosphere is altogether different — warmer and more inviting than The Capital, and a bit less imposing. Both the lobby and the rooms of l'Hotel are decorated with whimsical English primitive paintings; the twin-bedded rooms are done in French country-style antique pine furniture. Each has television, a spacious bathroom and feels crisp, fresh and airy.

Room 302, with its own fireplace, feels somewhat larger than average. In the basement of l'Hotel is le Metro — a trendy wine bar/restaurant that starts with good coffee and croissants in the morning and continues all the way through to late supper. L'Hotel's welcoming intimacy and charm make it a perfect base for a woman travelling on her own.

17. JAMES HOUSE, *108 Ebury Street, London SW1W 9QD. Tel: 0171 730 6176. Rates (including VAT and breakfast): £48 single; £60 double/twin; £80-90 family room. Major credit cards. Victoria tube.*

Not long on charm, James House is nonetheless a neat, no-frills bed and breakfast establishment with spotless, well-lit rooms complete with tea and coffee-making facilities and TV. Breakfast is served in a wood-panelled basement dining room dotted with the owner's family photos and personal mementos. If what you seek is a reasonably priced place to lay your head, this is basic and comfortable and about a fifteen minute walk from all the big sights: Buckingham Palace, Westminster Abbey and Harrods.

18. JOHN HOWARD HOTEL, *4 Queens Gate, London SW7 5EH. Tel: 0171 581 3011; U.S. toll free: 1 800 448 8355; fax: 0171 589 8403. Rates (including VAT): £79 single; £89-99 double; £119 suite. Major credit cards. Gloucester Road tube.*

If the marble floors and contemporary furniture of the John Howard lobby somehow remind you of an American Best Western Hotel, you get an "A" for atmosphere-detection. The John Howard is owned by Best Western, and this accounts for the spacious rooms, the rather bland color schemes and the modern hotel-style furnishings. Don't write it off yet, though, because it's set in a converted regency townhouse on a wide, tree-lined boulevard minutes from the Royal Albert Hall, the Victoria & Albert Museum, Hyde Park, and lots of great restaurants. In addition, it boasts American-quality king-size beds, mini-bars, hairdryers, air conditioning, 24-hour room service and conference facilities. All of which makes it a real London bargain.

For longer stays, the hotel offers studio and one and two bedroom apartments with fully-equipped kitchens and maid service (the full two bedroom apartment costs £225 per night). In short, while not exactly loaded with charm, the John Howard offers an immaculate, comfortable, reasonably-priced night's sleep in an elegant neighborhood. Which might be just the sort of trade-off you can live with.

19. LIME TREE HOTEL, *135/137 Ebury Street, London SW1W 9RA. Tel: 0171 730 8191; fax: 0171 730 7865. Rates (including VAT and breakfast): £60 single; £65-75 double; £90 triple. Major credit cards. Victoria tube.*

This bed and breakfast-style hotel is owned by an outgoing Welsh/English couple, who have created a homey, casual atmosphere and address all their guests by their first names. The rooms vary in size, but the doubles feel surprisingly spacious, aided by high ceilings and large windows. The decorations are simple and pleasant; each room comes with a TV, hairdryer, direct dial telephone and a bathroom with bathtub and shower. Rooms on the first floor have tiny balconies overlooking the street. Buckingham Palace, Westminster Abbey, Harrods and Victoria Station are all within walking distance.

20. NUMBER SIXTEEN, *16 Sumner Place, London SW7 3EG. Tel: 0171 589 5232; fax: 0171 584 8615. Rates (including VAT and continental breakfast): £78-99 single; £130-155 double; £180 triple. Major credit cards. South Kensington tube.*

Set in a row of white, early Victorian houses just minutes from Knightsbridge and Chelsea, Number Sixteen is stylish, secluded and elegant. The blend of formality and friendliness is always a tricky one, but the management achieves exactly the right balance with perfect grace. The drawing room has floor to ceiling windows, vases of fresh flowers and attractive antiques. Before dinner or theater (or before breakfast if you're so inclined), you can pour yourself a drink from the honor bar in the library. The lovely glass conservatory opens onto a delightful award-winning garden which is simply gorgeous in summer. Each room is individually decorated with antiques and traditional furnishings and comes with cable TV, direct-dial telephone, mini-bar, complimentary soft drinks, terry-cloth robes and a wonderful collection of English soaps and creams.

The high-end prices refer to ground floor rooms with terraces opening onto the garden; no one makes more sumptuous gardens than the English, so in the warmer months, splash out if you can afford to. Guests order breakfast the previous evening and can have it served in the bedroom, the drawing room, the conservatory or in the garden among the roses. Arrangements to use a gym and health club can be made for an additional fee.

21. THE SLOANE HOTEL, *29 Draycott Place, London SW3 2SH. Tel: 0171 581 5757; fax: 0171 584 1348; U.S. toll free: 1 800 324 9960. Rates (exclusive of VAT): £120 double; £175 deluxe double/twin; £225 Gallery Suite. Major credit cards. Sloane Square tube.*

This quiet, intimate 19th century Chelsea townhouse (near Sloane Square and the King's Road for shopping; within easy reach of Harrods and the Victoria & Albert Museum) is one of our very favorite places to stay in London. The owner is an antiques collector and furnishes each of the twelve (air conditioned) rooms – from beds and dressers to lace bedspreads and tapestry cushions – with antiques and objects d'art she has gathered over the years (and still can't resist buying). This gives the Sloane Hotel a most un-hotel-like ambience; the unique size and decor of each room combine to give the sense that you are visiting the home of some distant (and wealthy) relative. Best of all, if you fall in love with a picture on the wall, an exotic vase, a quilt, or even your very own four-poster bed, you can take it home — everything in the hotel is for sale. Shipping costs are added to the price; packing and mailing arrangements can be made by the hotel.

Every room has VCR, satellite TV, and direct dial telephone; a secretarial business center is available if you find yourself missing the office. The 24-hour room service specializes in light, well-prepared pastas, salads and fish dishes; the a la carte menu includes organic produce and health foods. Meals can be served in your room, or in the pretty roof-top terrace. The hotel is affiliated with a nearby health club, offering a fully equipped gym, swimming pool and massage. This is a particularly welcoming environment for single women. We especially like rooms 101, 301 and 302.

22. TOPHAMS EBURY COURT, *28 Ebury Street, London SW1W 0LU. Tel: 0171 730 8147; fax: 0171 823 5966. Rates (including VAT and breakfast): £70-75 single; £115-135 double/twin; £150 triple. Major credit cards. Victoria tube.*

This small, family-run hotel is loaded with charm. Located in the heart of Belgravia it boasts distinguished neighbors like Baroness Thatcher,

Andrew Lloyd Webber and Sean Connery. The layout of rooms is maze-like, with some tucked away in curious corners, which contributes to the sense of privacy and a very un-hotel-like atmosphere. The rooms are pastel-painted, furnished with antique reproduction furniture, and decorated in traditional Laura Ashley English Heritage style. If you're feeling particularly romantic, request the four-poster canopied bed. A comfortable sitting room provides a nice spot for afternoon tea, while a tiny restaurant adjoining the hotel offers reasonably-priced traditional English and continental food.

23. THE WILBRAHAM HOTEL, *Wilbraham Place, London SW1X 9AE. Tel: 0171 730 8296; fax: 0171 730 6815. No credit cards, but checks are accepted from American banks. Rates (exclusive of VAT): £39 single without private bath; £54 double with bath; £78 for deluxe twin with bath. Sloane Square tube.*

Three Victorian townhouses (until recently, privately owned) were put together to form this modest, 52 room hotel. Spartan but friendly, convenient and clean, the Wilbraham is a bargain in Chelsea's high-priced neighborhood and just a three minute walk to the Sloane Square tube (or ten minutes to Harrods). A small restaurant serves inexpensive breakfast, lunch and dinner.

24. WILLET HOTEL, *32 Sloane Gardens, London SW1W 8DJ. Tel: 0171 824 8415; fax: 0171 730 4830. Rates (including breakfast but not VAT): £70 double (or single occupancy); £85 large double/twin. Major credit cards. Sloane Square tube.*

This restored Victorian townhouse is conveniently located in a quiet residential side street off Sloane Square about a minute's walk from the tube. The 18 modest-sized rooms are simply and comfortably decorated and come with cable TV, hairdryers, coffee and tea-making facilities and ensuite bathrooms. An extensive buffet breakfast is served each morning in the well-lit, cheerful dining room. There is no elevator.

BLOOMSBURY, SOHO, & COVENT GARDEN

Artists, writers, film makers, restaurants, theaters, boutiques – and of course the Royal Opera and the British Museum – all coexist in this, the hub of London. **Bloomsbury** is quiet, leafy and literary; **Covent Garden** is full of bustling shops and restaurants; and **Soho** is where film directors, actors, London's gay population and advertising commandos meet to edit films, share power lunches, and sip cappuccino.

25. BLOOM'S HOTEL, *7 Montague Street, London WC1 5BP. Tel: 0171 323 1717; fax: 0171 636 6498. Rates (including VAT and breakfast): £95-110 single; £140-170 double/twin. Major credit cards. Goodge Street, Russell Square or Tottenham Court Road tube.*

This elegant 18th century townhouse sits on the grounds of what used to be Montague House and is now the British Museum; its original owner was Richard Penn, a Whig member of Parliament from Liverpool. From the decanter of sherry at reception to the hotel's extensive library, Bloom's is a wonderfully welcoming hotel of great literary and historical charm in the heart of Bloomsbury. Regency portraits and equestrian paintings decorate the walls, and the brocade sofas in the sitting room create an inviting atmosphere. The rooms (27 in total) vary in size but are all nicely furnished and come complete with refreshment tray, trouser press, TV/radio and 24-hour room service.

If you're a light sleeper, request a room that faces the garden; the street gets a bit of traffic noise at rush hour. Bloom's library is large and comfortable with magazines and newspapers as well as books. A small walled garden overlooking the British Museum makes a nice place for summer coffee, afternoon tea and light meals. Downstairs is a cocktail bar, a cluster of sofas for reading, and a dining room which serves breakfast and dinner.

26. THE CHESHIRE, *110 Great Russell Street, London WC1B 3NA. Tel: 0171 637 7777; fax: 0171 436 1142; U.S. toll free: 1 800 447 7011. Rates (including VAT) £91-99 single; £125 double/twin. Major credit cards. Tottenham Court Road tube.*

Everything about this modest 38 room hotel, located on a quiet street in Bloomsbury nearly across from the British Museum, is small, pleasant and compact. The lounge is the size of a comfortable living room; the rooms, neatly decorated with pastel floral bedspreads and curtains, are small but cozy. There's 24-hour room service, and breakfast and dinner are available at the hotel's own restaurant.

The location is perfect for easy walking to West End theaters, Covent Garden, and restaurants; ten minutes strolling though Soho will take you to Liberty where you can spend what's left of your holiday budget. Except for the location, there's nothing spectacular about The Cheshire, but the price isn't bad and the casual, unassuming, friendly atmosphere is a plus.

27. FIELDING, *4 Broad Court, London WC2B 5QZ. Tel: 0171 836 8305; fax: 0171 497 0064. Rates (inclusive of VAT): £60, single; £78 single suite; £78 double/twin; £125 four-bedded family suite. Continental and English breakfast served in the dining room £2.50-£4.00. Major credit cards. Covent Garden tube.*

Now here is an unusual find: a small, inexpensive, fabulously situated London hotel that even manages to dredge up a fair bit of charm. Admittedly, it's more charming on the outside than the inside, but it's clean, and just the ticket for budget-minded theatergoers who'd prefer to spend their money on something other than an expensive hotel.

The vine-covered converted Georgian building is located on a quiet pedestrian walk just across from the Royal Opera House in the heart of

Covent Garden. The rooms are small, the halls narrow and there's no elevator and little in the way of luxury, but carefully preserved 19th century gas lamps illuminate the hotel at night, and the whole mad glory of the Covent Garden market awaits just outside your door for shopping and unlimited free entertainment on those long summer evenings. The eponymous Henry Fielding, author of Tom Jones, was a magistrate at next door's Bow Street Magistrates Court, site of the first police station in the world.

28. HAZLITT'S, *6 Frith Street, London W1V 5TZ. Tel: 0171 434 1771; fax: 0171 439 1524. Rates (excluding VAT): £105 single; £130 double/twin; £170 suite. Major credit cards. Leicester Square or Tottenham Court Road tube.*

In about a million trips up and down Frith Street, we never noticed the entrance to Hazlitt's, so don't walk too fast or you'll pass it by – which would be a terrible mistake. Named for essayist William Hazlitt, this very attractive, intimate, twenty-three room hotel occupies three 1718 townhouses just off leafy Soho Square. Espresso cafes, restaurants and London's advertising and film industry call Soho home, and you'll find more than thirty theaters, twenty cinemas, two opera houses and about a billion restaurants and bars all within easy walking distance.

Curious portraits, paintings and prints crowd the walls of every room (including most of the bathrooms) and add to the eccentric but very real charm of the place — all 23 bedrooms are named for famous former occupants of the building (Baron Willoughby, the Duke of Portland, poet Mary Barker...ok, not wildly famous) and are decorated with antiques; many have oak or mahogany four-poster beds. Except for modern plumbing, the bathrooms are vintage 19th century, complete with deep clawfooted tubs, brass fixtures and wooden toilet seats. Showers rely on a handheld hose.

The Baron Willoughby is a particularly nice spacious double with ornamental fireplace, four-poster bed and handsome armoire. All rooms include television and direct dial telephone; room service delivers coffee or tea and hairdryers are available on request. The reception desk closes from 11:30pm to 7:30am; front door keys are given out along with room keys. For an extra £6.25, a continental breakfast is served in your room. This is not your typical London hotel. Perhaps that's why we love it.

29. THE MARLBOROUGH, *Bloomsbury Street, London WC1B 3QD. Tel: 0171 636 5601; fax: 0171 636 0532; U.S. toll free: 1 800 333 3333. Rates (including VAT): £125 single; £167-197 double. Major credit cards. Tottenham Court Road tube.*

This grand, impressive-looking Edwardian-period hotel just around the corner from the British Museum has an impressively restored lobby with floral papered walls, period furniture and an elegant staircase; it's an inviting place to sit and recover from a long trek round the British

Museum. Two restaurants and a dark wood-panelled bar make this large hotel feel quite cozy; wooden arched corridors provide nice architectural detail.

The bedrooms are not as charming as the public spaces, but the rooms are spacious with modern facilities (trouser press, hairdryer, cable TV and 24 hour room service), the beds comfortable (with chintz spreads), and the good-sized bathrooms have proper American-style showers. For a novel experience request a turret room. The location couldn't be more perfect for all the restaurants, bars and shops of Bloomsbury, Covent Garden and Soho.

30. MONTAGUE PARK HOTEL, *12-20 Montague Street, London WC1B 5BJ. Tel: 0171 637 1001; fax: 0171 637 2506; U.S. toll free: 1 800 448 8355. Rates (including VAT and buffet breakfast): £99-125 single; £135-170 double. Major credit cards. Tottenham Court Road, Goodge Street or Russell Square tubes.*

In the road behind the British Museum, nine Georgian townhouses have been combined to form this attractive 109 bedroom hotel. The sitting rooms are spacious, comfortable and pleasant, the bar has a small terrace, and the breakfast room overlooks a Bloomsbury garden.

Although the rooms are small, most have recently been given a face-lift with new furnishings and wallpaper; all are well-equipped with hairdryers, trouser press, TV, and tea and coffee-making facilities. The bathrooms are sparkling clean and come with good-quality bath gel and soaps; request a room at the back for a quiet garden view. A restaurant annexed to the hotel serves lunch and dinner, and room service is available. The Montague Park Hotel welcomes families and will arrange for babysitting in the room (£4 per hour) if required.

31. THE MORGAN, *21 Bloomsbury Street, London WC1B 3QJ. Tel: 0171 636 3735. No fax. Rates (including VAT and full English breakfast): £45 single; £68 twin; £85 suite with twin beds. No credit cards. (Reservations must be confirmed with a dollar check which is held and returned to you on arrival. Payment in travellers checks or cash only.) Tottenham Court Road tube.*

This Regency brick bed and breakfast hotel in the heart of Bloomsbury has been owned and managed by the same family for almost twenty years. It's their home too, and it shows in the overflowing window boxes and the effort they make to extend every comfort to their guests.

The twenty well-cared-for rooms are furnished with single or twin beds, night tables, and floral bedspreads; old framed photographs of London add a homey touch and the windows overlook the inner court of the British Museum. Suites include a separate bedroom and a living room outfitted with antique desk and Chesterfield sofa. Full English breakfast is served in the oak-panelled dining room which has been fitted with booths and decorated with the owner's collection of blue and white china and Toby jugs. The Morgan is close to the British Museum, Covent Garden, Soho and the theater district and is an excellent choice for the budget-conscious.

NOTTING HILL

Of all the neighborhoods listed in this section, **Notting Hill** is likely to be the least-known to tourists – it's also the farthest west of center and lacks the proximity to museums, theaters and central London shopping that most visitors desire. However. As a neighborhood, Notting Hill is beautiful, loaded with character, charm, good shopping, great restaurants and a general buzz of lively excitement. Margaret Drabble lives here, so do actor John Cleese and author Martin Amis.

For a third or fourth-time visitor to London, the abundance of chic cafes and the proximity of the huge Portobello Road Market might provide irresistible lures. For a first time visitor seeking excellent accommodation at less than exorbitant prices, it's ideal. Tube connections, by the way, are quick and easy.

Only one caveat: beware the last weekend in August. That's when the largest street festival in Europe (**The Notting Hill Carnival**) takes place in the neighborhood. And while we love a couple hours of the huge crowds and screaming steel band and reggae music, basing a holiday in the middle of it could be sheer hell.

32. ABBEY COURT, *20 Pembridge Gardens, London W2 4DU. Tel: 0171 221 7518; Fax: 0171 792 0858. Rates including VAT & breakfast: £80 Single; £120 - £130 Double; £160 Four-poster room. Major credit cards. Notting Hill Gate tube.*

Guests receive a warm welcome at the lovely Abbey Court, starting with the huge vase of fresh flowers in the foyer and the subtle aroma of Victorian potpourri. Light from a crystal chandelier illuminates walls lined with framed 19th century cartoons; the furniture is antique, the staff charming and helpful. The 24 guest rooms in this pretty Victorian hotel are bright, comfortable, spacious and filled with yards of soft chintz; the comfortable reading chairs are covered in the same fabric, as are the curtains at the large windows. Italian marble bathrooms are spacious and equipped with whirlpool baths, showers and heated towel-rails; the oversized sinks are fitted with old-fashioned fixtures, and even the ceiling light is adorned with a lovely Victorian cut-glass shade.

Standard amenities include 24-hour room service, color TV, direct dial telephone, hairdryer, trouser press and terrycloth robes; a selection of magazines, books and a tin of homemade shortbread in every room help you to feel at home (only nicer). Even the continental breakfast (served in the room) is better than usual. You can choose a bowl of homemade muesli, good croissants and brioche, coffee or tea. For no extra charge, a full English breakfast, served buffet style, can be had in the downstairs breakfast room. If you're in the market for antiques, Abbey Court is located just around the corner from the world famous Portobello Road Market, with its myriad antique, curio and junk dealers. This Saturday morning market attracts browsers and collectors from all over London (and Europe) and injects the entire neighborhood with a festive, party atmosphere.

33. THE GATE HOTEL, *6 Portobello Road, London W11 3DG. Tel: 0171 221 2403; fax: 0171 221 9128. Rates (including VAT and continental breakfast): £36 single (with private bath and shower down the hall); £60 double; lower rates off-season. Major credit cards (with 4% surcharge). Notting Hill Gate tube.*

With daffodils overflowing the windowbox and another dozen planted in a wooden wash tub by the door, this tiny six-room hotel would make a perfect postcard to send home from a village in Cornwall. The quaint and charming Gate Hotel, however, is located in a bustling west London neighborhood with a small pub down the road, lots of family-owned shops nearby and all the pleasures and madness of Portobello Market practically at the doorstep. It's also within walking distance of Kensington Gardens and close to the Central Line which will whisk you to Oxford Circus in five stops.

On checking in, guests receive a key to the front door which contributes to the feeling of visiting a private home. The rooms are white, small, fresh, clean and simply decorated, with windows that overlook the street. Each has color TV, refrigerator and tea and coffee-making facilities. A continental breakfast of croissant, juice, jam and instant coffee or tea is served in the room; complete English breakfast (eggs, potatoes, sausages, grilled tomatoes, mushrooms, juice and coffee) is served in the owner's breakfast room for an extra £5. This is a popular place and tends to fill quickly so try to book two to three months in advance. Request the double room with a small table and settee; it offers a bit more space for the same price.

34. THE HOLLAND PARK HOTEL, *6 Ladbroke Terrace, London W11 3PG. Tel: 0171 792 0216 or 0171 727 5815; fax: 0171 727 8166. Rates (including VAT and continental breakfast): £37-49 single; £66 double/twin; £10 for an extra bed. Major credit cards. Notting Hill Gate tube.*

A pretty front garden frames the steps leading to the bright green door of this converted Victorian townhouse. Located on a quiet, tree-lined street minutes from Holland Park, Kensington Gardens, the Victoria & Albert Museum and the Portobello Road antique market, The Holland Park has twenty-three rooms varying in size from a cozy single to a three-bedded family room. All the rooms have been recently refurbished and decorated with comfortable, simple pine furniture, pretty framed prints and newly tiled modern bathrooms; each is equipped with TV, direct dial telephone and coffee and tea-making facilities.

The extremely pleasant staff contribute to the hotel's homey, friendly atmosphere; making you feel welcome seems to be part of their job description. In warm weather, guests can use a small garden, and year round there's a shared sitting room with nice red sofas, desk, working fireplace and large bay windows. Guests can request private use of the room for parties or reserve it for meetings. Continental breakfast is served in a basement room with linen tablecloths and fresh flowers. For budget-conscious travellers, this gracious hotel in its unhurried residential neighborhood makes a very good choice.

35. THE PEMBRIDGE COURT HOTEL, *34 Pembridge Gardens, London W2 4DX. Tel: 0171 229 9977; fax: 0171 7287 4982; U.S. toll free: 1 800 709 9882. Rates (including VAT and English breakfast): £95-120 single; £145-155 double. Major credit cards. Notting Hill Gate tube.*

Churchill and Spencer, the ginger-colored cats-in-residence, greet you at the door of this homey, inviting 20-room Victorian townhouse in the heart of Notting Hill Gate. The hotel is situated on a quiet, tree-lined street in this lively, colorful west London neighborhood that's home to Tina Turner, John Cleese, Martin Amis and the world-famous Portobello Road antiques market. Furnished with miscellaneous Victoriana and framed 19th century fans, it's an antiques lover's dream. Coordinated chintz fabrics and furnishings decorate the stylish, comfortable rooms, which come with cable TV, direct-dial telephones and 24 hour room service. Health club facilities are available at a discounted rate (£15/day) at an exclusive neighborhood club, including gym, swimming pool, steam room and spa.

The owner's wife Merete is responsible for all the hotel's wonderful antiques; she is more than happy to share her encyclopedic knowledge of the local market shops and stalls, and will even act as a market guide for serious antique hunters on special arrangement. Breakfast is served in Caps Restaurant, a cozy, attractive, basement bistro that adjoins the hotel (the caps in question are cricket caps). After a day of shopping, it's the perfect place to celebrate your priceless find or mourn your empty wallet with a drink or quiet supper.

36. THE PORTOBELLO HOTEL, *22 Stanley Gardens, London W11 2NG. Tel: 0171 727 2777; fax: 0171 792 9341. Rates (including VAT and English or Continental breakfast): £75 single cabin; £99 single; £110-130 double/twin; £150-195 special rooms. Major credit cards. Notting Hill Gate tube.*

Famous people who could afford to stay just about anywhere choose to stay at the Portobello Hotel, and we don't blame them – this is indeed a small gem of a hotel. It overlooks a quiet private garden on an elegant street near the Portobello Road antique market and somehow manages to combine state-of-the-art facilities with the character and eccentric charm of a private Victorian club, *and* exceedingly reasonable prices. Antique chairs and rich, comfortable paisley-covered sofas invite you to curl up in the lovely sitting room with its big arched windows, central fireplace, oriental rugs, lush plants and flower arrangements. Each guest room is a treat and a delight, decorated with its own touch of wit and whimsy.

For a romantic holiday, request room 16, a round room with a round bed draped in white and square windows overlooking the garden. The bathtub is a collector's item and stands on a tiled platform in the same room as the bed. In true Victorian style, it includes brass pipes that curve around the tub and gently spray jets of water, surrounding you in mist. Antiques and goose down duvets are standard in every room. Single "cabins" on the upper floors are tiny and not for the claustrophobic, but still charming.

The hotel has a 24 hour restaurant and bar, laundry and valet service, cable TV and complete business services. Health club facilities can be had nearby for £15 a day (swimming pool, sauna, steam room, Nautilus equipment, massage and hairdressing). Lots of fashion people stay here, including Kate Moss and Naomi Campbell. Try not to stare.

NORTH OF OXFORD STREET

Including Regent's Park, Baker Street, & Paddington

Though not as central as Mayfair, as exciting as Soho or as elegant as Knightsbridge, this area of London is quiet, pretty, close to the center and has superb connections (two to four stops by tube) to the majority of important museums and attractions.

For hotels near Baker Street tube, the best thing about the area is **Regent's Park**, which our committee of two considers London's most beautiful. From April through October it's an explosion of color. For families with young children, Regent's Park offers ducks to feed, the **London Zoo**, a good playground, and a boating lake; for teenagers there's the massive chaos of **Camden Market** across the park; and for everyone there's **summer Shakespeare** in the Park and the lovely rose gardens.

37. DORSET SQUARE HOTEL, *39/40 Dorset Square, London NW1 6QN. Tel: 0171 723 7848; fax: 0171 724 3328. Rates (excluding VAT): £85 single; £110-150 double/twin; £160 and up, junior suite. Major credit cards. Baker Street tube.*

The Dorset Square Hotel is steeped in the atmosphere of that most singular of English passions (spying? kinky sex?): cricket. And it's not just a gimmick. Dorset Square was the original site of Thomas Lord's first cricket ground, and ghosts of that quality don't fade with time. Look first for the pretty leafy square. Then for the polished brass plaque, the overflowing window boxes, and finally, the porter in white cable knit V-neck vest – you guessed it, traditional cricket wear. Inside, the sitting room boasts floor to ceiling windows, warm red walls, soft chintz sofas with needlepoint cushions, and antiques (including a cricket bat stand now filled with umbrellas).

The bedrooms are graceful, full of character, and are furnished with antique armoires, linen presses and 19th century landscapes. All the first floor bedrooms have balconies and views overlooking the square. Room 406 with its warm yellow walls and angled ceiling eaves is particularly lovely; the marble and mahogany bathroom has a large window so you can soak in the tub while gazing out onto Dorset Square. The restaurant and bar is open all day. Cable TV, direct-dial telephones, hairdryers, laundry, dry cleaning, and 24-hour room service are all standard.

38. DURRANTS HOTEL, *George Street, London W1H 6BJ. Tel: 0171 935 8131; fax: 0171 487 3510. Rates (including VAT): £85 single (£62 without bath); £100 double (£90 without bath); £104 twin; £143 family room; £195 suite. Major credit cards. Bond Street tube.*

Durrants remains one of the really good hotel values in London. Located in a pretty street a few blocks north of Bond Street, it's just around the corner from the sublime Wallace Collection, surrounded by some of London's best shopping, and a short walk to (or jog) to Hyde Park. The attractive Georgian building has been a hotel for more than 200 years, and has been owned by the same family since 1921.

Inside, the atmosphere is congenial and clubby; dark wood, Chesterfield-style leather banquettes and comfortable, padded chairs prevail. The 96 pretty, predominantly cream and pink rooms are of good size, clean, comfortable and attractively decorated with old prints and reproduction antiques; the carpets are good quality and big windows insure lots of light. The modern bathrooms include hairdryers, bidets, and big mirrors. There's nothing frilly about Durrants and nothing sagging or dusty either.

Drinks are available in The George, a rather masculine bar that keeps regular pub hours; an attractive, wood-panelled restaurant serves continental breakfast (£5.95) and full English breakfast (£8.95), and has a good quality lunch and dinner menu. Room service is available for light meals and breakfast.

39. THE PAVILION HOTEL, *34-36 Sussex Gardens, London W2. Tel: 0171 262 0905; fax: 0171 262 1324. Rates (including VAT and continental breakfast): £25-35 single; £55 double. Major credit cards. Edgware Road tube.*

We can't help but like this tiny, inexpensive hotel. It's a bit like finding a Calvin Klein jacket for $50 at a discount boutique, so bargain-lovers take note. Set in an historically listed Victorian townhouse, and conveniently located to Hyde Park and Oxford Street, the hotel is full of character and has thirty rooms with all the original architectural features. Elaborate cornices, cartouches and scrolling iron railings, in addition to potted palms, oriental rugs, oil paintings and eccentric framed prints all contribute to its cluttered Victorian charm.

Most rooms are furnished with antiques, polycotton quilted floral bedspreads and matching curtains; cable TV and coffee and tea-making facilities are standard. Room 8B, with its dark green wallpaper, antique wardrobe, large oval mirror and mahogany four-poster bed with antique cushions, seems to have remained most true to the hotel's Victorian tradition. The smallish bathrooms are newly tiled and have showers. All the rooms on the "B" side of the hotel are larger and more authentic, so make sure to specify when you reserve. Croissants, tea or coffee, cereal and orange juice are served in your room.

40. REGENTS PARK HOTEL, *156 Gloucester Place, London NW1 6DT. Tel: 0171 258 1911; fax: 0171 258 0288. Rates (including VAT and continental breakfast): £50 single; £70 double/twin; £85 triple/family. Major credit cards. Baker Street tube.*

The Regent's Park Hotel feels a bit like an American motel, and like an American motel, it's neat, tidy, efficient and inexpensive. Newly renovated in a residential neighborhood, the white stone building is framed with an iron fence hung with pretty flower boxes. The reception room is bright and clean, and each of the twenty-nine rooms has high-ceilings, beige walls, floral drapes, desk and a good-sized closet. The bathrooms are fitted with showers, no baths; all rooms have cable TV, coffee and tea making facilities and direct dial telephone. Hairdryers, irons, fax, photocopy, laundry and dry cleaning services are also available.

The hotel is conveniently located for Regent's Park, Oxford Street and major public transportation, and adjoins with Singapore Garden, one of London's best Singaporean/Malaysian restaurants. Breakfast is served in the bright attractive restaurant under a glass atrium roof.

HAMPSTEAD

Most tourists never make it to **Hampstead**. Which is a shame, because Hampstead is one of London's most attractive villages. The **West End** (theater district, Soho and Covent Garden) is a short, direct trip on the Northern line tube, about 15 minutes (cab addicts take note: at about £8-10 a trip, the fares can add up).

Still, with its wild, magnificent expanse of green (**Hampstead Heath**), Freud's House, Keats' House, the wonderful paintings at Kenwood House, historic pubs and excellent shopping all within an easy walk, we'd understand if you never bothered to go into central London at all. You'll hear a lot of foreign accents in Hampstead, but in general they don't belong to tourists. With an eye for London's prettiest, most livable neighborhood, lots of Americans and Japanese have settled here permanently.

41. LA GAFFE, *107-111 Heath Street, London NW3. Tel: 0171 435 4941 or 0171 435 8965; fax: 0171 794 7592. Rates (including VAT and continental breakfast): £42.50 single; £50-65 double/twin; £95 honeymoon suite. Major credit cards. Hampstead tube.*

In London slang, your gaffe is your home. And if you fancy making your vacation home an 18-room ex-shepherd's cottage on Hampstead Heath, we've got just the place. The original building dates from 1734, and today is owned and run by an Italian poet and playwright whose neatly typed work is framed and displayed (along with an interesting collection of antique deeds and contracts) throughout the hotel's maze of corridors.

You enter the hotel through the adjoining Italian restaurant of the same name. Once inside, informality is the watchword: the guest book sits on a wooden shelf and room keys hang on nails by the door. The single rooms are tiny but neat and tidy and equipped with canopy bed, night table and TV. The doubles are better, and the honeymoon suite best of all with its jacuzzi, four-poster bed and steam shower. The overall friendliness (and the bargain price) more than compensates for any shortfall in space, and the huge rambling expanse of Hampstead Heath is right outside your door in case you should ever feel claustrophobic.

The restaurant serves hearty homemade Italian food, and is a favorite spot with Hampstead's large population of successful actors – Peter O'Toole is a Sunday lunchtime regular. Coffee-lovers note: breakfast includes good Italian espresso or cappuccino.

42. THE SANDRINGHAM HOTEL, *3 Holford Road, London NW3 1AD. Tel: 0171 435 1569; fax: 0171 431 5932. Rates (including VAT and full English breakfast): £54-68 single; £74-85 double; £97 deluxe triple. Major credit cards. Hampstead tube.*

The Sandringham's brochure calls itself "England's Finest Small Hotel" and they might just be right. A four minute walk from the tube station through lilac and wisteria-lined cobbled village streets, the Sandringham occupies a large Victorian house with spectacular views over London and the Thames valley. Everything about this small hotel is attractive, welcoming, beautifully appointed and clean. The sunny breakfast room (where they serve fresh squeezed orange juice and homemade bread with your bacon and eggs) overlooks a pretty, flower-filled walled garden with fountain in which afternoon tea is served in summer.

Each of the nineteen rooms has been decorated with great individual style – yours might have dark red walls, Hogarth prints, a working fireplace, a heavy striped silk canopy, and/or a wonderful view. The deluxe doubles are particularly roomy and worth the extra £10 if you can manage it. Every room has a good solid bed and clean modern bathroom with shower. The beautiful expanse of Hampstead Heath is only 100 yards from the front door (joggers take note) and all the charming cafes, restaurants, and excellent shopping of Hampstead Village are just around the corner.

BUDGET BESTS

You don't have to be rich to stay in a hotel that's memorable for its charm, warmth and that certain attractive je ne sais quoi. Herewith, our budget favorites.

THE EXECUTIVE, *57 Pont Street, London SW1. Tel: 0171 581 2424; fax: 0171 589 9456. Rates (including VAT and buffet breakfast): £55-70 single; £75-99 double; £110 suite. Major credit cards. Knightsbridge or Sloane Square tube.*

LA GAFFE, *107-111 Heath Street, London NW3. Tel: 0171 435 4941 or 0171 435 8965; fax: 0171 794 7592. Rates (including VAT and continental breakfast): £42.50 single; £50-65 double/twin; £95 honeymoon suite. Major credit cards. Hampstead tube.*

THE GATE HOTEL, *6 Portobello Road, London W11 3DG. Tel: 0171 221 2403; fax: 0171 221 9128. Rates (including VAT and continental breakfast): £36 single (with private bath & shower down the hall); £60 double; lower rates off-season. Major credit cards (with 4% surcharge). Notting Hill Gate tube.*

THE HOLLAND PARK HOTEL, *6 Ladbroke Terrace, London W11 3PG. Tel: 0171 792 0216 or 0171 727 5815; fax: 0171 727 8166. Rates (including VAT and continental breakfast): £37-49 single; £66 double/twin; £10 for an extra bed. Major credit cards. Notting Hill Gate tube.*

THE SANDRINGHAM HOTEL, *3 Holford Road, London NW3 1AD. Tel: 0171 435 1569; fax: 0171 431 5932. Rates (including VAT and full English breakfast): £54-68 single; £74-85 double; £97 deluxe triple. Major credit cards. Hampstead tube.*

9. WHERE TO EAT

The days when visitors were consigned to potted hare, fish and chips or malnutrition in London are finally gone. Astonishingly, Michelin recently rated England ahead of Italy in the distribution of stars, and although this probably says most about the top end of the dining scale, lesser restaurants are scrambling to follow suit. You still have to choose carefully when dining out in London, but there's nothing to stop your visit being a fine culinary experience. And if you're willing to experiment with the various good-quality ethnic restaurants, you can manage to dine well without spending a fortune either.

A few helpful guidelines are worth noting.

We've listed restaurants by neighborhood. You can waste lots of time and money travelling when what you really feel like is a good local meal. London offers a range of cuisines and prices in just about every part of town, and on the nights you feel like a new neighborhood you can always jump in a cab (or on a bus).

Eat more or less when the locals eat; there's nothing more depressing than being the only 6:30 reservation in a restaurant known for its buzzy atmosphere after eight.

Although we've only listed a few here, one of the best sources of good cheap food is the new wave of pizza restaurants scattered throughout the city. And while you haven't come all this way for pizza, there are times when you've had enough nouvelle British at £50 a head, and simply crave a snack, a beer, and a reasonable bill.

Good curry houses perform the same function and every neighborhood has one; a lively crowd is the surest indication of quality.

Although we're not suggesting you avoid it, be wary of pub food. It ranges wildly in quality from the truly bad to the really-quite-edible. In the center of town, however, you're usually better off with a good Dim Sum in Chinatown or a sandwich at one of London's ubiquitous Italian-owned sandwich bars. And if you come across a good, pretty local pub (or follow one of our suggestions), by all means try their bangers and mash.

Prices here represent a serious meal for two with two or three courses, a bottle of wine, and coffee, though we can't imagine you'll want to eat like that twice a day. Most of the places listed (including many of the upmarket ones) will run much less than the estimated price if you're sticking to a single course and a glass of wine, so adjust your expectations accordingly.

And please don't forget to make reservations. It's worth the price of the phone call to make sure you're not wasting a trip.

BLOOMSBURY

Close to the **West End** theaters, **Covent Garden Opera**, and the **British Museum**, Bloomsbury has recently made great strides in the new British cuisine stakes.

1. ALFRED *(modern British, moderate), 245 Shaftesbury Avenue, London W1. Tel: 0171 240 2566. Daily, noon to 4pm and 6pm to 11:45pm. Major credit cards. Tottenham Court Road tube.*

As of this writing, Alfred is one of the newer and more popular restaurants in town. Just around the corner from the British Museum and cabbing distance to the City, it has already made a surprising number of serious diners' list of top faves. It's nicer for dinner than for lunch; at 1pm, the rather stark enamelled robin's egg blue and yellow decor becomes cluttered with city types wearing dark suits and conspicuous expense accounts. It's a little too post-modern designy to be really romantic, or even particularly comfortable, but the food is splendid – modern and creative with enough of a twist on the traditional so it doesn't clash with the decor.

The menu changes to accommodate seasonal specialties and fresh market ingredients – a typical winter day offered starters like steamed mussels in stilton cream, salad of wood pigeon, wild mushrooms, bacon and potatoes, and crab soup. Main courses (£8-12) in winter lean towards old fashioned comfort food like calves liver, bacon, bubble and squeak; rabbit in beer and sage sauce; braised knuckle of bacon with pickled cabbage and pease pudding; cod and herb fish cakes; wild boar sausages with colcannon potatoes.

Desserts manage to combine the traditional with the odd: gingerbread with lavender custard, Trinity college burnt cream, prune ice cream. Breads are all baked on the premises; the wine list is English and French; the waiters are decorative and look tormented by over-passionate social lives. Lunch or dinner for two with wine and service will run £55-75.

2. CHIAROSCURO *(modern British, moderate), 24 Coptic Street, London WC1. Tel: 0171 636 2731. Monday to Saturday noon to 3:30pm and 7pm to 11:45pm; Sunday 11am to 4pm and 7pm to 11pm. Major credit cards. Tottenham Court Road tube.*

This pretty, cool, minimalist restaurant is one of the newer additions to the British Museum neighborhood, competing with Alfred for the title of best-in-Bloomsbury. Chiaroscuro wins on intimacy — it's small and narrow — though the hyper-modern lighting, and an entire glass wall of wine keeps it from feeling either cold or claustrophobic. The husband and wife team who run the restaurant have kept the menu small and innovative, and are dedicated to keeping the details and presentation perfect.

The menu changes frequently, but for starters try blackened swordfish cake with cucumber salad or warm salad of skate with roast peppers and potato galette. Steamed mussels, spiced chicken and chorizo with frites and rouille is a house speciality. Roast rack of lamb with fig halves and spicy sausages with baked pumpkin are typically untypical main courses. Vegetarians are well catered for, and the desserts (courtesy of their Swiss-trained pastry chef) are nothing short of amazing. Chiaroscuro mousse combines mocha and white chocolate mousse, piped into a shell of bitter chocolate topped with chocolate and creme Anglaise.

Service is pleasant and responsive; a two-course Sunday brunch at £10 per person is an excellent bargain. Bring along your children (two maximum, under 12 years old) for brunch and they'll be entertained and eat free upstairs with the owners' nine year old daughter who has devised a special children's menu of her favorite dishes, including macaroni and cheese, chicken and French fries and chocolate pudding. Dinner for two with wine and service: £50-60.

3. THE COFFEE GALLERY (*cafe, inexpensive*), *23 Museum Street, London WC1A 1JT. Tel: 0171 436 0455. Monday to Saturday, 8am to 5:30pm. No credit cards. Tottenham Court Road tube.*

This cozy little non-smoking cafe a stone's throw from the British Museum is handy for continental breakfast, a light lunch, or an afternoon remedy for museum fatigue. The espresso and cappuccino are good; there's also juice and twenty varieties of tea. Sandwiches, croissants or quiche and salad do nicely at lunchtime; lemon cheesecake and chocolate tart will revive flagging blood sugar at teatime. This is a good place to take a book, write a postcard or read a newspaper. Then once your caffeine and sugar hit takes hold, head for the good antiquarian book and print shops on Museum Street.

4. PIZZA EXPRESS (*pizza, inexpensive*), *30 Coptic Street, London WC1. Tel: 0171 636 3232. Daily 11:30am to midnight. Major credit cards. Tottenham Court Road tube.*

One of the first branches of this successful chain, attractively situated in a lovely old brick and tile dairy around the corner from the British Museum, Pizza Express serves up the usual variety of good pizzas and salad nicoise, accompanied by Italian wine or Peroni beer. Always full and buzzing; lunch or dinner with all the usuals will cost £10-15 per person.

5. WAGAMAMA (*Japanese noodle bar, inexpensive*), *4 Streatham Street, London WC1. Tel: 0171 727 3184. Monday to Saturday noon to 3pm and 6:30pm to 11:45pm; Sunday noon to 3:30pm and 6:30pm to 10:15pm. No credit cards. Tottenham Court Road tube.*

Wagamama was one of the first of the Japanese noodle bars to open in central London, and the competition still can't really measure up. The stark, modern underground restaurant just around the corner from the British Museum is always packed with students and real people who come for the very good, very cheap, very filling fare. Don't be put off by the long line, it moves quickly and most waits are under 20 minutes.

Once inside the busy buzzy dining room, you're seated at long communal tables where a waiter with electronic notepad takes your order: huge bowls of noodles and vegetables, fragrant with coriander; delicious fried dumplings; stir fried bean sprout and noodle chow mein – it's almost impossible to choose badly. With beer, green tea, or mineral water the bill will barely hit £10 per person.

CHINATOWN

Chinatown is Chinatown the world over. In London, it's very centrally located (a stone's throw from all the theater, museums and movies of **Soho**, **Leicester Square**, **Trafalgar Square**, **Covent Garden** and **Bloomsbury**). You'll eat good Cantonese cooking (you'll rarely find Szechuan) at great prices.

6. CHINA CHINA (Chinese, inexpensive to moderate), *3 Gerrard Street, London W1. Tel: 0171 439 7502. Daily noon to 11:45pm (12:45am Friday and Saturday). Major credit cards (£15 minimum). Leicester Square tube.*

This big, bustling four-story Chinese restaurant in the heart of Chinatown offers a good compromise between the down and dirty Chinese canteens along Newport and Lisle Streets, and the more expensive, upmarket choices like Fung Shing. It's open late, the service is good (if not exactly cheerful), and for the price, the Cantonese food is terrific.

Try the hot pots, the fried noodle dishes (with seafood) or the barbecued pork on rice for really cheap one-meal dishes. The Peking duck with pancakes is excellent, although every once in a while it turns up on the dry side. Hot and sour soup, a barometer of any Chinese restaurant, is dependably good. And the four floors means there's always a seat — even if you have to do some climbing to get one.

7. CHUEN CHENG KU (*Chinese, inexpensive*), *17 Wardour Street, London W1. Tel: 0171 437 1398. Daily 11am to midnight. Dim sum daily 11am to 5:45pm. Major credit cards. Leicester Square tube; and*

8. NEW WORLD (*Chinese, inexpensive*), *1 Gerrard Place, London W1. Tel: 0171 734 0677. Daily 11am to midnight; Sunday 10:45am to 10:45pm. Dim sum daily 11am to 6pm. Major credit cards. Leicester Square tube.*

Dim sum has to be one of London's cheapest epicurean thrills: inscrutable Oriental trolley maidens seduce us willingly into one unpronounceable dish after another. A little of this, a little of that – the method of ordering celebrates the culinary promiscuity in us all. For the inexperienced, let us clarify that dim sum consists of a wide variety of dumplings and other bite-sized snacks steered around the room in metal steam trolleys. When a trolley arrives at your table, lids are lifted off individual dishes (usually consisting of 2-4 items) for your perusal. Just say no to things that look like chicken feet or squid beaks; say yes to fluffy white pork buns, prawns wrapped in paper, vegetarian peanut dumplings, stuffed mushrooms, prawn and pork dumplings, and whatever else takes your fancy.

Although all the dishes have proper names, not knowing them doesn't seem to get in the way; it's all incredibly simple and satisfying. A tally of your meal is kept on a scorecard on the table; two really hungry people would have a hard time spending more than £20 between them. Although most Chinatown restaurants offer dim sum at lunchtime, these two are our favorites; both also serve complete menus throughout the day and at night. New World seats 500 on two huge floors, giving some idea of how many people keep coming back for more. Cheun Cheng Ku is of the old-fashioned, red and gold dragon school. Both restaurants tend to get very busy by 1pm; try to get there earlier (or later in the afternoon), or be prepared to wait — usually no more than ten minutes.

9. FUNG SHING (*Chinese, moderate*), *15 Lisle Street, London WC2. Tel: 0171 437 1539. Daily, noon to 11:30pm. Closed, December 24, 25, 26. Major credit cards. Reservations recommended. Leicester Square or Piccadilly Circus tube.*

Having spent our formative years in New York City where fabulous cheap Chinese food is a constitutional right, we remain skeptical about paying serious food prices in London's Chinatown. But we may as well jump on the bandwagon for Fung Shing, which even the terrifyingly snobby Gault Millault has plastered with stars. Fung Shing's main virtue is its really interesting menu – spicy jelly fish with chicken and pickles, braised whole abalone (£55) and double boiled fluffy supreme sharks fin (£50) spring to mind. For the adventurous but less extravagant, there are delicious soft shell crabs with chili and salt (in season), stuffed fish maw with prawn and crabmeat sauce, stewed eel with roast pork, and broccoli with dried scallops.

Crispy spicy eel sounds awful but tastes wonderful. And in case you're thinking you'll just wait till you get home, remember that you're unlikely to find grilled minced pork with salted fish or stir fried milk at your local Columbus Avenue Lucky Garden. For the faint of heart, there are plenty of good choices that won't stretch your imagination – like salt-baked chicken or sizzling spicy prawns. There's also a good, extensive wine list, if you happen to like fine wine with your Cantonese food. The restaurant is casual and bustling; prices are higher than at most of the surrounding Chinatown joints, but not massively so. About £20 per person will get you all the preserved eel, jelly fish, rice, and beer your heart desires.

10 & 11. IKKYU *(Japanese, inexpensive), 7-9 Newport Place, London WC2. Tel: 0171 439 3554. Open Sunday to Thursday noon to 10:30pm; Friday and Saturday noon to 11:30pm. Major credit cards. Leicester Square tube. And 67a Tottenham Court Road, London W1. Tel: 0171 436 6169. Goodge Street tube.*

Although London can't begin to compare with New York or California for sushi, we've always been fond of Ikkyu on Tottenham Court Road (by Goodge Street tube) for decent cheap Japanese food (sushi, teriyaki and tempura) and a refuge from meat pies and fish and chips. The newer Ikkyu — more conveniently located in the heart of Chinatown — has a longer menu and works even harder to assuage the desperately homesick or desperately overfed. There are two tatami rooms, mainly for groups, but this is primarily a bustlingly busy, clean, unglamorous place for a good light lunch of Teriyaki, tempura, dumplings or sushi by the piece or by the roll.

The noodles passed the test of our resident Japanese expert who declared them above average; udon, soba or ramen are available with a selection of vegetables, seafood or meat. The set meals are good and reasonably priced (£6-12). Lunch or dinner with sushi, beer or wine and service (included) should run about £15 per person; at least a third less for noodles or dumplings.

NOTTING HILL GATE

Not every tourist makes it to **Notting Hill**, which is a shame given the wealth of streetlife, good shops, and interesting restaurants. The lively Portobello Road **market** on Saturday gives you an excuse to visit.

12. KENSINGTON PLACE *(modern British, moderate to expensive), 201-207 Kensington Church Street, London W8. Tel: 0171 727 3184. Daily noon to 3pm (3:30pm Saturday and Sunday) and 6:30 to 11:30pm (10pm Sunday). Major credit cards. Notting Hill Gate tube.*

Kensington Place was one of the first of the California/New York style London restaurants, by which we mean it was designed by a hot young architect, is always full of actors and models (and lots of locals), and the food includes everything from couscous to duck breast, with lamb shank in-between. But what the restaurant is really known for is its noise level. Due to its reasonable prices, terrific food, and great people-watching, the exuberant customers have been streaming in since the day it opened, and although a quiet tete a tete would be impossible here, the

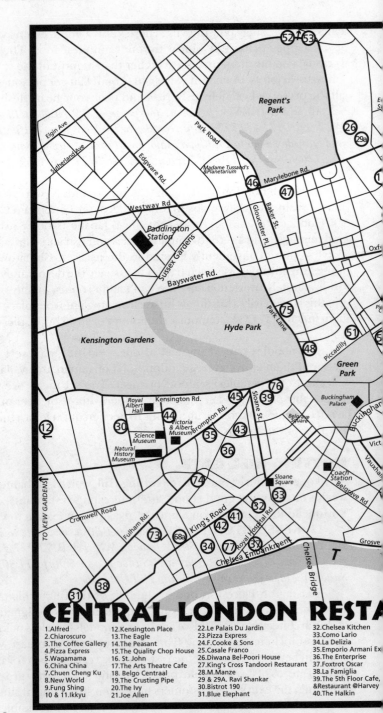

CENTRAL LONDON RESTA

1. Alfred
2. Chiaroscuro
3. The Coffee Gallery
4. Pizza Express
5. Wagamama
6. China China
7. Chuen Cheng Ku
8. New World
9. Fung Shing
10 & 11. Ikkyu

12. Kensington Place
13. The Eagle
14. The Peasant
15. The Quality Chop House
16. St. John
17. The Arts Theatre Cafe
18. Belgo Centraal
19. The Crusting Pipe
20. The Ivy
21. Joe Allen

22. Le Palais Du Jardin
23. Pizza Express
24. F.Cooke & Sons
25. Casale Franco
26. Diwana Bel-Poori House
27. King's Cross Tandoori Restaurant
28. M.Manze
29 & 29A. Ravi Shankar
30. Bistrot 190
31. Blue Elephant

32. Chelsea Kitchen
33. Como Lario
34. La Delizia
35. Emporio Armani Ex
36. The Enterprise
37. Foxtrot Oscar
38. La Famiglia
39. The 5th Floor Cafe,
   &Restaurant @Harvey
40. The Halkin

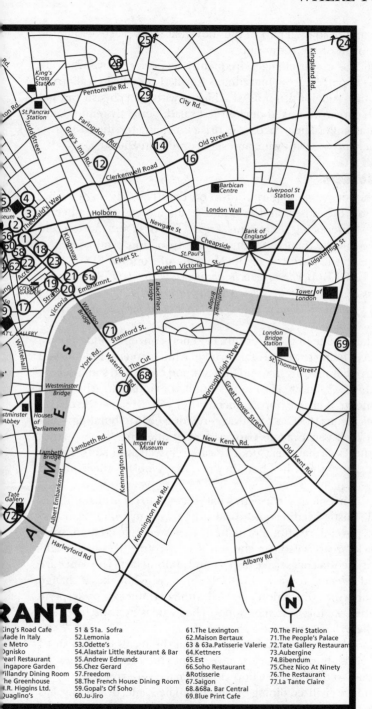

RANTS

King's Road Cafe	51 & 51a. Sofra	61.The Lexington	70.The Fire Station
Made In Italy	52.Lemonia	62.Maison Bertaux	71.The People's Palace
e Metro	53.Odette's	63 & 63a.Patisserie Valerie	72.Tate Gallery Restaurant
Ognisko	54.Alastair Little Restaurant & Bar	64.Kettners	73.Aubergine
earl Restaurant	55.Andrew Edmunds	65.Est	74.Bibendum
ingapore Garden	56.Chez Gerard	66.Soho Restaurant	75.Chez Nico At Ninety
illandry Dining Room	57.Freedom	&Rotisserie	76.The Restaurant
he Greenhouse	58.The French House Dining Room	67.Saigon	77.La Tante Claire
.R. Higgins Ltd.	59.Gopal's Of Soho	68.&68a. Bar Central	
Quaglino's	60.Ju-Jiro	69.Blue Print Cafe	

razzle-dazzle and flash is all part of the show that takes place behind the 50 foot glass front of the restaurant.

Although the menu changes frequently, expect creative, delicate combinations of perfect fresh ingredients – grilled swordfish, scallops or skate, a beautiful tricolor fish mousse, chicken with goat cheese, braised calamari with chorizo, smoked duck breast salad, perfectly tender lamb steak with ratatouille. The weekday set price lunch is a terrific bargain at £13.50; dinner for two with wine and service will run £50-60.

CLERKENWELL

This authentic, very old part of town borders The City on one side, Bloomsbury on the other, and is home to an increasing number of London's most interesting restaurants. Expect less flash and more eccentric, pared-down style than you'll find in West London. And keep it in mind for visits to the **Barbican** or the **Museum of London**.

13. THE EAGLE *(Mediterranean, inexpensive to moderate) 159 Farringdon Road, London EC1. Restaurant open Monday to Friday 12:30-2:30pm and 6:30-10:30pm; pub open Monday to Friday, 11am to 11 pm. No credit cards. Farringdon tube.*

The Eagle was one of the forerunners in new-concept London pubs, the new-concept being to get rid of the fruit machines and the hideous red patterned carpets and bring in wood floors, wood tables and some decent food. We know, we know, it sounds stupidly obvious and why hasn't everyone done it? Well, we hope someday they will. Because the dearth of such places means the Eagle is always crowded near to bursting – but don't let that keep you away. Its patrons are a motley mix of newspaper types from the Guardian next door, local architects and suits who've strayed over from the City, but they're always noisy, cheerful and attractive.

The food, conveniently, is exactly what you want to eat in an upmarket pub – simple rustic Mediterranean nosh like Tuscan white bean and bacon soup, porcini risotto, Portuguese fish stew, Neapolitan spicy sausages, duck breast salad, or chicken liver crostini. Desserts might include lemon ricotta cheesecake or pear and almond tart. The wines are drinkable and selected to go well with the food, which makes a change from most pub wines which don't go well with anything except desperation. And in case we forgot to mention it, The Eagle is first and foremost a pub – the beers are authentic and varied.

If you find the crowd a bit much, do what the locals do: just sit (if you're lucky enough to find a seat), have a pint and a chat, and then go across the street to the Quality Chop House (make sure you reserve) for a marginally more civilized dining experience. The Eagle, by the way, has an art gallery upstairs that features good contemporary English artists.

14. THE PEASANT (*rustic Italian, moderate*), *240 St. John Street, London EC1. Tel: 0171 336 7726. Monday to Saturday 12:30pm-2:30pm and 6:30pm-10:30pm. Closed bank holidays and December 23 to January 5. Farringdon or Barbican tube.*

Unless you're going to the Barbican or Sadler's Wells, The Peasant is somewhat off the beaten track, but it's worth the detour for the good food and charming atmosphere. From its massive old-fashioned horseshoe bar (it used to be the George and Dragon pub) to the dramatic mosaics, tile floors and huge gilt mirrors, it's the kind of place locals take for granted but any of us would be overjoyed to stumble across in a foreign country. Happily, it hasn't completely rejected its humble pub origins, and the interesting mixed crowd that fills it nightly obviously approves of the unadorned wooden tables, mismatched pottery plates and the congenial buzz.

The food would best be described as nouvelle Italian peasant – the short menu might start with pappardelle with mascarpone, peas and bacon; purple artichokes with mozzarella, Parmesan and anchovies; or a spicy vegetable soup. Four main courses are usually on offer, and might include cured salmon, cod with green lentils, seabass with garlic saffron mayonnaise, or a grilled veal chop with potatoes, lemon and garlic. The desserts are delicious (split lemon pudding, pear and chocolate custard) and while the Peasant isn't pitching for Michelin stars, it's a really comfortable, happy place to spend an evening. Entrees run about £7-10, and dinner for two with wine and service will come to a reasonable £40-50.

15. THE QUALITY CHOP HOUSE (English, moderate), *94 Farringdon Road, London EC1R 3EA. Tel: 0171 837 5093. Open daily except Saturday (noon to 3pm and 6:30pm to 11pm). Reservations recommended. No credit cards. Farringdon tube.*

The subhead on the Quality Chop House menu reads "progressive working class caterer," and indeed, the modest exterior with etched glass panels remains virtually unchanged from its days as a traditional London working man's cafe. The spirit of simple food in unpretentious (some would say uncomfortable) surroundings lives on – only now the chef cooking all these traditional English meals is French, ex-of le Caprice, and the working men in attendance are likely to be journalists from across the street at the Guardian, or city stockbrokers who know they're on to a winner.

At first glance you'd figure the restaurant seats about 20, in fact it somehow manages to stuff in closer to 50 on narrow wooden pews; couples or groups of four will usually find themselves sharing one of the longish tables. Start with one of their eccentric selection of beers – usually strong, usually unusual. The starters might include fresh anchovies, a very good fish soup with rouille, roast vegetables and goat's cheese salad, and raclette cheese and Parma ham. Main courses range from egg, bacon and chips (homage to the restaurant's humble beginnings) or steak and kidney pie, through to Toulouse sausages with mashed potatoes, perfectly grilled lamb or veal chops, confit of duck, or corned beef hash served with a fried egg. Add a rocket and Parmesan salad, a huge plate of chips and a treacle pudding for dessert and you'll have had a great lesson in how really good simple English food can be. Taught by a Frenchman, naturally. The average bill runs about £25 per person with wine and service, a little less for lunch and teetotallers.

One of the best things about The Quality Chop House is that it's a stone's throw from two of London's best pubs – the crowded, artsy Eagle across the street; and O'Hanlons (reputedly the best Guinness in town) further up Rosebery Avenue. By the way, don't forget to bring cash; the restaurant doesn't take credit cards.

16. ST. JOHN *(English, moderate), 26 St. John Street, London EC1M 4AY. Tel: 0171 251 0848; fax: 0171 251 4090. Monday to Saturday, bar 11am to 11pm; restaurant, noon till 3pm and 6pm to 11:30pm. Sunday, bar noon to 3pm; restaurant, noon to 3:30pm. Major credit cards. Farringdon or Barbican tube.*

This new restaurant made everyone's ten best list this year – which, given that it specializes in offal ("nose to tail eating" is their motto) is pretty impressive. Not to mention wholly deserved. The unprepossessing entrance is just north of Smithfield market (London's soon-to-be-defunct hundred year old meat market) and marked with their trademark pig. You pass first into a massively high-ceilinged, white and zinc bar, which was once a Smithfield smoke house and still retains the huge fireplaces and chimney chutes. Then up a few steps to the restaurant (once a meat storage room) which is equally unadorned, with high white walls and white tablecloths. The kitchen is open to the room; it is the only design element in this aggressively undesign-y restaurant.

The people, however, are another story, a wonderfully eclectic mix of high-art and high-commerce, often at the same table, sometimes even in the same couple. Women with severely fashionable haircuts converse intently with men in Savile Row suits. Artists and their dealers? Company execs and their daughters? Go figure. The end result is a kind of bare, casual elegance we associate more with Milan than London but which is, in fact, wholly original.

Ditto the food. Though clearly not for vegetarians (there are vegetarian selections, but the atmosphere is resolutely carnivorous) or the overly squeamish, it is very very good. Whole crab and mayonnaise to start, or duck terrine, or deep fried salsify and aioli, or fried fresh cods roe and sorrel, or oysters. Followed by cod, parsnip and green sauce; Lambs kidneys, spicy sausage and butter beans; ox tongue; grilled mackerel and rocket; duck leg confit, or boiled beef and pickled walnuts. The portions are hearty and perfectly prepared and the menu changes daily, but don't expect California cooking – there isn't a raspberry coulis or a baby vegetable in sight.

Desserts are more conventional, and might include lemon tart or black fruit crumble. A limited range of food is available at the bar – including olives, boiled eggs and celery salt, oysters, and cured salmon (40 pence to £4.50). Dinner with a bottle of wine runs about £30 per person.

COVENT GARDEN

Theater, opera, shopping – **Covent Garden** is where much of London's evening action takes place. It's a nice place to explore before and after your meal, and if your first choice of eatery is booked, there's bound to be another one next door.

17. THE ARTS THEATRE CAFE *(Italian, inexpensive to moderate), 6-7 Newport Street, London WC2. Tel: 0171 497 8014. Monday to Friday, noon to 11 pm; Saturday 6pm to 11pm. Closed bank holidays. Major credit cards. Leicester Square.*

This cozy, basic little basement restaurant in Covent Garden (just around the corner from the Leicester Square tube) is much loved by the sort of people who hang around in the Photographer's Gallery next door, in other words, artsy types with more taste than money and more love for food than for atmosphere. What there is of atmosphere at The Arts Cafe is decidedly unflash and frill-free, with a token attempt at flowers, candles, and an orderliness which never seems to be achieved. Cigarette smoke is a usual affliction; pretend you're in Italy or stay away. The food, however, is delightful and delightfully inexpensive which can be a huge relief towards the end of a high-ticket, high-calorie vacation.

A short, handwritten menu changes daily and offers genuine Italian homecooking — which means simple, earthy ingredients impeccably prepared — and might include mussels in saffron cream; spinach, potato and garlic soup; pan fried snapper with pancetta; or, for the vegetarian crowd, baked radicchio and fennel with smoked mozzarella. Risotto, grilled pigeon and leg of lamb are frequent choices and there's always a good simple pasta on offer.

Desserts are delicious and unusual – to our astonished delight we have never known this establishment to offer anything with bananas and butterscotch sauce. Instead, you might choose from a dense chocolate and orange tart; chilled zabaglione with vin santo and raspberry sauce or ripe pears with talleggio. A two course meal with a bottle of wine can be had here for well under £20 per person. Lunch with a glass of wine will barely set you back £10.

18. BELGO CENTRAAL, *(Belgian, inexpensive to moderate), 50 Earlham Street, London WC2. Tel: 0171 813 2233. Open daily noon to 3pm and 5:30pm to 11:30pm. Major credit cards. Covent Garden tube.*

This new branch of the popular Chalk Farm Belgo hasn't been open long, but already it's one of the area's most popular restaurants. It has the same male waiters dressed as monks, and serves the same good Belgian cuisine as the original, only on a much larger scale. Belgo Centraal accommodates 350 diners in some of the strangest, most stylized dining facilities you're likely to encounter in London – the medieval clatter of the kitchens combined with the roar of the crowd make it feel somewhat like an artist's conception of hell, but a chic hell for all that, where you can throw back all number of exotic Belgian beers and devour massive quantities of mussels and frites for remarkably reasonable prices.

Diners enter on the metal-and-duct-filled ground level that looks like something out of Terry Gilliam's movie *Brazil*. Descending into the steam and clamour of the kitchen via a huge metal lift, you're guided either to one end or another of the basement: the smaller, restaurant end or the cavernous, table-sharing beer-hall end. Kilo buckets of mussels (available 8 ways) and shoestring fries are the most popular menu item, accompanied by mayonnaise and 100 varieties of very strong (and often very strange) Belgian beer. There are other offerings on the menu, like duck breast salad, wild boar sausages, rabbit casserole, and good grilled fish, but most people come for the moules et frites at about £9. A la carte meals with beer and service run about £20 per person, less for lunch (there's a £5 daily special of a kilo of mussels and a beer) and mussel specials.

If you're ever in Chalk Farm, try the original Belgo *at 72 Chalk Farm Road (0171 267 0718).*

19. THE CRUSTING PIPE *(pub, inexpensive), 27 The Market, Covent Garden, London WC2. Tel: 0171 836 1415. Lunch daily noon to 3pm; dinner 5:30pm to 10pm; bar snacks available all day, 11am to 10pm; closed Sunday night. Major credit cards. Covent Garden tube.*

The Covent Garden area is loaded with restaurants. But if you're in the neighborhood and fancy a glass of wine and some traditional British pub food, head for The Crusting Pipe located in the lower level (south east corner) of Covent Garden market. It's just the sort of location you'd expect to be touristy, overpriced and unpleasant, but this cozy winebar is none of those things.

In the cave-like interior, you'll find wooden tables, stone floors covered in sawdust, candles stuck in bottles and brick vaulting; you'll also find vintage ports as well as reasonably priced house wines.

Waitress service at meal times offers basic pub food: ham off the bone, fresh salmon, steak, kidney and mushroom pie and sirloin steak (£6.75 to £11.50) with treacle tart and clotted cream or good stilton and crusty bread for afters. For those arriving at one minute past 3 (a pubgoer's nightmare), there are sandwiches, soup, chicken liver pate with brandy, and cheeses – all for less than a fiver. The Crusting Pipe is by no means a memorable culinary experience, but in a pinch it's cozy, nearby and more than adequate for a bit of food and an hour off your feet.

20. THE IVY (*modern English, moderate to expensive*), *1 West Street, London WC2. Tel: 0171 836 4751. Open daily for lunch (12 to 3pm) and dinner (5:30 to midnight). All credit cards. Leicester Square tube.*

We love the Ivy. But then, so does everyone else in London, which explains why you have to book at least a few days (and preferably at least a week) in advance. Here's why we love it:

The atmosphere is perfect, not too formal, not too casual, discreet, pretty, comfortable and buzzy. The menu is perfect (the same for lunch and dinner), offering everything from a hamburger to baked lobster thermidor. The service is perfect, there when you need it, not when you don't. The crowd is a perfect mix of publishing, TV and advertising types, some ordinary human being types, a few very familiar looking actors, some literary luminary types and a smattering of stars. All at a perfectly reasonable price. On our first visit, we thought we'd died and gone to New York.

Oh yes. The food is terrific. Try the crispy duck and watercress salad. The tomato and basil galette. The roast Rosevale potatoes with duck livers, garlic and pancetta. The crab risotto. Or the deep fried lambs brains if you're that way inclined (£5-9). To follow there's beautifully grilled fish (the skate is a must if it's on), or fish and chips or salmon fishcakes or kedgeree. There's calf's liver and bacon. Cumberland sausages. Osso Bucco with Parmesan polenta. Shepherd's pie with mashed neeps. Griddled chicken salad with piquillos and guacamole. Venison artichoke and wild mushroom salad. All simple, fresh ingredients, beautifully, nay impeccably, prepared.

Dare we even mention desserts? Possibly the best bread and butter pudding on earth. Tarte aux pommes Chantilly. Iced Scandinavian berries with white chocolate sauce – so good, you don't care what strange Scandinavian bush they fell off. All this for around £35 per person with wine and service, so the bill comes in about the same or less than at hundreds of inferior London restaurants.

Convinced of your need to go instantly? We hope not. Reservations are hard enough to get already.

BUDGET BESTS

Who says you can't eat wonderfully well in London for peanuts? Here's how to get two weeks of London dining for the price of one.

17. THE ARTS THEATRE CAFE *(Italian, inexpensive to moderate), 6-7 Newport Street, London WC2. Tel: 0171 497 8014. Monday to Friday, noon to 11 pm; Saturday 6pm to 11pm. Closed bank holidays. Major credit cards. Leicester Square.* Really good food in Covent Garden with a fun, artsy (ok, crowded and chaotic) atmosphere.

26. DIWANA BEL-POORI HOUSE *(Indian, inexpensive), 121 Drummond Street, London NW1. Tel: 0171 387 5556. Open daily noon to 11:30 pm. Major credit cards. Euston tube.* Southern Indian vegetarian delight. We eat at Diwana as often as possible.

24. F. COOKE & SONS *(traditional British, inexpensive), 41 Kingsland High Street, London E8. Tel: 0171 254 2878. Monday to Wednesday, 10am to 7pm; Thursday 11am to 8pm; Friday and Saturday 10am to 10pm. Closed Sunday. No credit cards. By bus: 22A, 22B, 38, 67, 149, 243.* The most traditional London meal you'll ever eat. And you'll never know if you like jellied eels until you try them (we're still wondering)

8. NEW WORLD *(Chinese, inexpensive), 1 Gerrard Place, London W1. Tel: 0171 734 0677. Daily 11am to midnight; Sunday 10:45am to 10:45pm. Dim sum daily 11am to 6pm. Major credit cards. Leicester Square tube.* Dim sum for lunch is the best cheap meal in London – and you don't have to eat anything you haven't had a good look at first.

44. OGNISKO *(Polish, inexpensive to moderate), 55 Exhibition Road, London SW7. Tel: 0171 589 4635. Open daily, noon to 3pm and 6:30pm to 11pm. Closed Easter Sunday and Monday, December 25 and 26. Major credit cards. South Kensington tube.* The most odd, interesting, delicious, £7.50 fix priced lunch west of Warsaw.

46. SINGAPORE GARDEN *(Malaysian, inexpensive), 154-156 Gloucester Place, London NW1 6DT. Tel: 0171 723 8233. Daily noon to 2:45pm and 6pm to 10:45pm (11:15 Friday and Saturday). Major credit cards. Baker Street tube.* Superb heaps of Singapore noodles, given an enthusiastic thumbs-up by our resident noodle expert.

51 & 51A. SOFRA *(Turkish, inexpensive to moderate), 18 Shepherd Street, London W1. Tel: 0171 493 3320. Daily, noon to midnight. Green Park tube. And 36 Tavistock Street, London WC1. Tel: 0171 240 3773. Major credit cards (no Amex). Covent Garden tube.* Healthy salads, grilled meat and assorted mezes with a lot more atmosphere than the prices would suggest.

5. WAGAMAMA *(Japanese noodle bar, inexpensive) 4 Streatham Street, London WC1. Tel: 0171 727 3184. Monday to Saturday noon to 3pm and 6:30pm to 11:45pm; Sunday noon to 3:30pm and 6:30pm to 10:15pm. No credit cards. Tottenham Court Road tube.* Bustling, crowded and fun. London's ultimate Japanese noodle bar, just around the corner from the British Museum.

21. JOE ALLEN (*American, moderate*), *13 Exeter Street, London WC2. Tel: 0171 836 0651. Daily noon to 12:45am (last orders). No credit cards. Covent Garden tube.*

Back in the early days of the original Joe Allen in New York City, we spent many happy hours with their good, off-the-menu burger in one hand and a beer in the other. The burger still isn't on the menu, but 15 years and 3,000 miles later, the burgers are still good, the walls still brick, the after-theater crowd still buoyant, and Joe Allen still makes for a lively night out. If the burgers don't tempt you, try some of the other American specialities – barbecued ribs with black-eyed peas, grilled swordfish with roasted peppers, smoked chicken quesadilla or lamb steak with mint pesto. Desserts run to brownie, cheesecake and pecan pie. And don't look for a neon sign. Like the burger, the entrance isn't broadcast.

22. LE PALAIS DU JARDIN (*French, moderate*), *136 Longacre, London WC2. Tel: 0171 379 5353. Daily, noon to midnight. Major credit cards. Reservations suggested. Covent Garden or Leicester Square tube.*

Think of Le Palais du Jardin as Quaglino's French cousin – big, buzzy, comfortable and fun, with an ambitious menu and a bit of a party atmosphere. It's also right in the middle of Covent Garden so it's perfectly located for theatergoers, and the food's good and reasonably priced. Enter at bar level and you'll be ushered back into a surprisingly large dining room in which lobster-balancing waiters weave expertly between tables.

Lobster is a house favorite due in large part to its confusingly reasonable price of just £9.95. Seafood here is good and copious – Irish or Pacific oysters (£9/dozen), five choices of moules (including Thai and Italian), lobster (four ways including cold, in a salad), and fabulously decorative seafood platters. Other seafood includes pan fried baby scallops with saffron potato cake; grilled shellfish; fricassee of turbot in dill cream; or fish cakes with French fries. Good meats and grills include that well-known French dish bangers and mash; fillet of venison; duck breast; fillet of beef with stilton crust; and veal steak. Smoked chicken and shrimp salad, or parma ham, goats cheese and rocket are among the lighter choices.

Everything is prettily presented and everyone always seems happy to be here, including (oddly, for England) the exuberant staff. And the really good news is that the bill always seems to be less than you expected – £25 per head for a full meal with wine and service. We don't know how this happens, but no doubt someone will rectify the situation sooner or later. Get in there while you can.

23. PIZZA EXPRESS (*pizza, inexpensive*), *9-12 Bow Street, Covent Garden, London WC2E 7AH. Tel: 0171 240 3443. Daily 11:30am to midnight. Major credit cards. Covent Garden tube.*

Don't be misled by the name, this is not a fast food joint. It is, however, a pizza joint, and a particularly nice one, a few doors up from the Royal Opera. The dramatic decor of this new branch of Pizza Express seems almost too hip for the prices, but we're not complaining. It's a nice way to have a good cheap dining encounter without feeling all tawdry and sad afterwards.

First, a word about the jazzy decor: Greek-style columns, some half buried in brick walls, some "supporting" thick Tudor-style wooden ceiling beams, white plaster, black tables and spot lighting. Next, a word about the menu: good-sized, well-made, authentic pizzas, one or two pastas, a decent salad nicoise, bottles of Italian red or white and Peroni beer. There's not much else to say about the place except that the location is great, the crowd buzzy, the light flattering, and the bill reasonable (£15 per person with wine and service).

EAST LONDON

Remember Fagin and Bill Sykes? And all those scheming Dickens heros? The east end is where they (still) hang out.

24. F. COOKE & SONS *(traditional British, inexpensive), 41 Kingsland High Street, London E8. Tel: 0171 254 2878. Monday to Wednesday, 10am to 7pm; Thursday 11am to 8pm; Friday and Saturday 10am to 10pm. Closed Sunday. No credit cards. By bus: 22A, 22B, 38, 67, 149, 243.*

Before World War II, family-run pie and mash shops could be found on just about every corner of every street in London. There aren't many of them left, but if you want to experience the very most genuine, the very most traditional British cooking, it's worth going out of your way to find one. "What a lovely idea," we hear you cry, as you dash off, tastebuds akimbo.

Perhaps you'd better slow down and hear what's on the menu first: pie and mash (ground beef and mashed potato), pie and mash with liquor (ground beef and mashed potato covered in green parsley sauce) and the ever-popular jellied eels. Did we mention that the portions are gargantuan (kind of a mixed-blessing, given the menu)? There's also tea, coffee and fruit pie for dessert. We admit to having never tried the jellied eels, but the pie and mash borders on the truly edible and the experience is so authentic it's reminiscent of time travel.

Tiled walls and marble-top picnic tables are the featured decor; the servers tend to be female, motherly, tough as old boots and dressed in starched green aprons, and you don't have to take our word for the quality of the food, there's always a queue for takeout. If only these ancient walls could speak! (If only we could understand the waitress' rhyming slang!)

ISLINGTON, KING'S CROSS, & EUSTON

Not far from **Bloomsbury**, this area has a couple of huge railway stations (**Kings Cross** and **St. Pancras**), some lovely pubs, and one of the best antique markets in London.

25. CASALE FRANCO *(Italian, moderate), 137 Upper Street, London N1. Tel: 0171 226 8994. Tuesday to Saturday 6:30pm to 11:30pm; Sunday 6:30pm to 10:30pm; also Friday to Sunday noon to 3:30pm. Major credit cards. Located equidistant from Angel and Highbury Islington tubes; 19 Bus takes you to the door (ask the conductor for the stop before the Almeida Theatre).*

This "house of Franco" is aptly named. Papa bought the restaurant for his children, two of whom (Mario and the eponymous Franco) can be found in the kitchen. Papa himself is nearly always on the door. "He's a better chef than a business man," confided Franco's dad, though how bad a businessman is questionable considering the place is nearly always packed – with actors, judges, theatergoers and happy locals, and at prime time you can wait up to half an hour. It's a bit hard to find (walk about half a mile north on Upper Street from the Angel or half a mile down from Highbury & Islington tube, across from the big church, look for Vulture Video. Casale Franco is at the end of the little alley).

Don't go expecting haut cuisine, even of the Italian variety; the food is simple and authentic. But within this rustic, bustling restaurant are the sort of Pizzas you'd expect somewhere more like Palermo – a thin hand-thrown base covered with great folds of parma ham, bresaola, rocket and garlic, or heaps of grilled vegetables. The pastas – with mussels, smoked bacon and cream, porcini and cream, or baby cuttlefish in ink – are well-prepared and filling (£5.50-£6.50); other good choices are a whole grilled sea bass, spicy Italian sausages with polenta, or fegato all Veneziana (calves liver in wine and onions). Main courses average £7 to £12.

If you're in the neighborhood for the Camden Passage antique fair on a Saturday, or have ventured to Islington for the (very good) Almeida or Sadler's Wells theaters, Franco's makes a worthwhile detour.

26. DIWANA BEL-POORI HOUSE *(Indian, inexpensive), 121 Drummond Street, London NW1. Tel: 0171 387 5556. Daily noon to 11:30pm. Major credit cards. Euston tube.*

The unusual Indian vegetarian cuisine served by Diwana will delight even experienced Indian food lovers with its fresh flavors and unfamiliar spices – not to mention its ludicrously low prices. As far as we know, bhelpoori hasn't yet made its way across the Atlantic, so take advantage of it while you're here. The style of cooking hails from Gujarat in the West and Madras in the South. Try the *Annapurna thali* – a set meal in Gujarati style served on tin plates and offering a sampler of dishes. *Dosa*, a large crispy rice pancake, comes with a variety of accompaniments including coconut chutney and potato curry. We admit an addiction to the delicious starters: *dahi poori* and *bhel poori* (potatoes, onions, chickpeas and crispy rice with yogurt and a sweet and sour sauce – or any combination thereof) are both wonderful.

A set price all you can eat lunch buffet is offered, where you can sample a wide variety of vegetarian dishes for around £4. It's nearly impossible to spend £10 on the ala carte menu, which makes this food possibly the best value in London.

27. KING'S CROSS TANDOORI RESTAURANT *(Indian, inexpensive), 341 Grays Inn Road, London WC1X 8PX. Tel: 0171 278 0506. Daily noon to midnight. Major credit cards. Kings Cross tube.*

Although it's impossible to list every good local Indian restaurant in London, we've decided to include this one for two reasons: first, because it's located just across from King's Cross Station, which is otherwise a bit of a wasteland for food; and second because it's actually surprisingly good. King's Cross is a notorious hang-out for all sorts of unsavory types but it's also one of London's biggest and busiest train stations, and you might very possibly find yourself in the neighborhood with a couple of hours to kill. And if you like good spicy, generous portions of delicious fragrant nan bread, lamb and spinach curry, and tandoori king prawns, King's Cross Tandoori will pass the time very well indeed.

Don't forget the very popular and very pleasant Waterside Inn just around the corner. The pub is scenic. The Indian food is good. Just don't expect the rest of the neighborhood to measure up.

28. M. MANZE *(traditional British, inexpensive), 74 Chapel Market, London N1. Tel: 0171 837 9690. Tuesday to Thursday 10:30am to 3pm; Friday 10:30am to 5pm; Saturday 10am to 5pm; Sunday 10am to 2pm. No credit cards. Angel tube.*

The sign on the window says "Large Bowl of Jellied Eels, Ideal For Weddings," and whether you agree with them or not, you've got to admit it's original. London used to be riddled with pie and mash restaurants, but few survive intact, and this is one of the great ones. The decor (if you could call it that) consists of wooden booths and white tiles; the menu offers pie and mash, stewed eels and mash, double eels and mash (double eels? your guess is as good as ours) and not a lot more. The bustling vegetable market is fun to browse through; come on a Wednesday or Saturday and you can combine a trip to Manze's with a visit to the Camden Passage antique market around the corner.

29 & 29A. RAVI SHANKAR, *422 St. John Street, London EC1. Daily noon to 11pm. Tel: 0171 833 5849. Major credit cards. Angel tube. And 133-135 Drummond Street, London NW1. Tel: 0171 388 6458. Euston tube.*

Both branches of Ravi Shankar enjoy a certain level of happy notoriety among north Londoners who come again and again for the very good, ludicrously cheap southern Indian vegetarian cuisine in clean, pleasant surroundings. The menu is divided between different varieties of *dosas* (large pancakes often served with a potato and coconut chutney) and the delightful *bhel pooris* – cold starters made with crunchy rice, yogurt, chickpeas, potatoes, coriander and various exotic spices. We're happy with a variety of *bhel pooris*, followed by spicy curried eggplant or okra, or a *dosa*, *dal*, *raita* and *nan* bread.

Bring your own beer or wine; if you can manage to run up a bill of more than £15 for two, we'll be amazed. A daily lunch buffet special offers a choice of about 10 different good vegetarian main courses and desserts for £3.95.

KNIGHTSBRIDGE, SOUTH KENSINGTON, & CHELSEA

Now here's where graceful, upmarket neighborhood dining really comes into its own, with a plethora of attractive restaurants and equally attractive diners.

30. BISTROT 190 *(Mediterranean, moderate), 190 Queen's Gate, London SW7. Tel: 0171 581 5666. No reservations. Daily 7:30am to 12:30am (11:30pm Sunday). Major credit cards. Gloucester Road tube.*

Walls covered in Victorian prints, gilt-framed mirrors and bunches of dried flowers; a ceiling fan turns lazily, lending the lofty dining room the ambience of an old fashioned saloon. Well-used marble tables complete the grab-bag charm of this much-lauded restaurant. The menu – long, eclectic and frequently updated – is dominated by fish, pasta, and grilled southern French, Moroccan and Italian dishes. An average selection might include seared tuna with artichoke, eggplant and wild onion salad; roast cod with tomatoes and spinach; chargrilled baby squid with chili oil; braised lamb with Tuscan beans and grilled eggplant; chargrilled rump steak with gorgonzola butter and pepperonata; spicy Moroccan chermoula fish. An array of pasta dishes featuring chargrilled vegetables, chorizo sausage, fresh tomato and Parmesan (in varying combinations) are reasonably priced at £5-9.

Wine by the glass and bottle are offered, along with more than a dozen unusual bottled beers. A two course dinner for two with wine, coffee and service will come to £40-60. Bistrot 190 is particularly pleasant for breakfast (muesli and fruit, French toast, bacon and eggs, croissants, etc.), *served daily 7:30am to 11am.*

31. BLUE ELEPHANT *(Thai, moderate to expensive), 4-6 Fulham Broadway, London SW6 1AA. Tel: 0171 385 6595 or 381 2896. Fax: 0171 386 7665. Daily noon to 2:30pm and 7pm to 12:30am (10:30pm Sunday). Closed Saturday lunchtime. Major credit cards. Fulham Broadway tube.*

Welcome to Disneyland. This wonderful stage-set of a restaurant takes its cue from The King and I – fishponds (with fish), thatched roofs, tiered terraces, bamboo, waterfalls, palm trees and other tropical foliage set a distinctly Hollywood atmosphere in this incredibly popular 250 seat restaurant. On entering, you are met by hostesses in silk sarongs, palms pressed together and heads bowed for the traditional Thai greeting. The menu is huge; prawn crackers are provided while you try and sort it all out.

For the uninitiated, or those who want a taste of everything, try the 17-dish Royal Thai banquet. The Seven Pearls starter offers dim sum, spring rolls, paper-wrapped prawns, fish cakes, vermicelli noodles, chicken satay, and a variety of dipping sauces. Hot dishes are indicated by little red elephants – chili beef rated a maximum three on the elephant scale, Bangkok fish with red chili and ginger sauce scored two. Lemon grass, mint, and coconut flavor the exotic, rich fish stew; Thai curries served with fragrant sticky rice are unlike any you have tasted. Delicacies such as pea eggplant are flown in weekly from Bangkok, it's this sort of detail that reassures us that the food is as fresh and as authentic as the decor is over-the-top. Though to be honest once the food arrives, no reassurance is necessary.

A vegetarian menu is available, and the Sunday buffet lunch (at £14.50 per person) is highly recommended, as well as being significantly cheaper than the average £35 per person (with service and wine or Thai beer). And kids adore it here (see *Child's Play* chapter).

32. CHELSEA KITCHEN *(inexpensive), 91 King's Road, London SW3. Tel: 0171 589 1330. Daily 8am to 11:45pm; Sunday 9am to 11:30pm. No credit cards. Sloane Square tube.*

Chelsea's most famous cheap and cheerful neighborhood establishment has been going strong since the 60s on a recipe of enormous helpings and simple, straightforward fare. The menu is international, and so are the waitresses — Greek, Italian and Indian specialties are served up by South African, Spanish and Polish employees. Booths are shared, and the menu starts early with traditional English breakfast, scones or toast and coffee, moving on as the day progresses to spaghetti marinara, curried chicken with rice, chicken pot pie, moussaka, salads and omelettes. Homemade apple crumble is served (English-style) floating in custard, and once you get used to it it's kind of addictive. Service is fast and friendly; the patrons range from local grannies and shop assistants to European expats and tourists. Lunch or dinner for two: £12-15.

33. COMO LARIO *(Italian, moderate), 22 Holbein Place, London SW1W 8NL. Tel: 0171 730 2954. Monday to Saturday 12:30pm to 2:45pm and 6:30pm to 11:30pm; Sunday 12:30pm to 3:30pm only. Major credit cards. Sloane Square tube.*

This upbeat Italian trattoria is always bustling with a loyal neighborhood crowd chatting happily over generous bowls of pasta and Como Lario's good Italian specialties. The decor is sharp and chic, tables are small and close together, but no one seems to mind, it just adds to the ambience. The large menu offers starters like carpaccio of sturgeon drizzled with lemon juice and olive oil or homemade mushroom pasta with walnut sauce, followed by polenta with mushrooms and sausages, thinly sliced lamb in a rosemary and garlic sauce; breast of chicken in lemon and cream. The specials usually seem to have benefited from more attention by the chef; give them first priority. This isn't the best Italian restaurant you'll ever eat in, but it's convenient, lively and congenial. Two courses with wine and service run about £25-30 per person.

34. LA DELIZIA *(pizza, inexpensive), 63-65 Chelsea Manor Street, London SW3. Tel: 0171 376 4111. Monday to Sunday, noon to 3pm; 6pm to midnight. No reservations or credit cards. Sloane Square tube.*

For delicious, crispy thin-crust pizza, this Chelsea pizzeria is the business. The menu offers 15 combinations that are imaginative without venturing into pineapple and Chinese duck land. All the ingredients are fresh, and many of the customers are French and Italian ex-pats, which gives La Delizia a continental air (and reassures you that the food is good). Fresh pastas and salads are also available, as well as wine, cappuccino and espresso. The tiramisu and homemade gelato taste genuinely Italian. £10 should be more than enough for a pizza and a glass of wine, which makes this a great spot for lunch or a late night snack.

35. EMPORIO ARMANI EXPRESS *(Italian, moderate), 191 Brompton Road, London SW3. Tel: 0171 823 8818. Monday to Saturday 10am to 6pm; Wednesday 10am to 7pm. Major credit cards. Knightsbridge or South Kensington tube.*

Why is it that the instant we start talking about Armani the only adjective that leaps to mind is "elegant"? Why fight it. This low-key, elegant little restaurant on the first floor of the elegant Armani shop (all pale wood and glass) with its elegant waiters (mainly Italian, all dressed in outfits so chic they look like pyjamas) attracts an elegant fellowship of Armani-clad shoppers ranging from the Duchess of Kent to Queen Nôor of Jordan to Simon le Bon to Sting. Ordinary mortals, however, can take advantage of the fashion-victims' love of delicious light modern Italian lunches in the most pleasantly (elegant) atmosphere.

Good pastas, salads and grilled fish can be undone in an instant with chocolate truffle cake for dessert. Pasta with a glass of wine, coffee and service shouldn't run more than £15. It's open for breakfast, lunch and tea, and is the perfect place to stop for cappuccino mid-afternoon; we even brought a rambunctious two-year-old one day and nobody (overtly) glared. Put it on your favorite-lunch-spot list. It's on ours.

36. THE ENTERPRISE *(English, moderate), 35 Walton Street, London SW3. Tel: 0171 584 3148. Daily noon to 3:30pm and 5:30pm to 11pm (food served 12:30pm to 2:30pm and 7:30pm to 10:30pm); Sunday noon to 3pm and*

7pm to 10:30pm (food as above). Closed December 25-26. Major credit cards. No reservations. South Kensington or Knightsbridge tube.

The Enterprise joins The Eagle and The Peasant as one of the new wave of London pubs cum restaurants. It is by far the poshest of the three, with a large gilt mirror, massive flower arrangement, and rather up-market South Kensington crowd all competing for attention in the very pleasant, smallish square room. The long bar along one wall asserts that it is still very much a pub; though perhaps not immediately recognizable as such by east London standards. Drop in for a drink and you'll find yourself in the company of a mostly neighborhood, mostly well-dressed 30-40ish crowd. Huge bowls of kettle chips are free (gasp!) at the bar and the average patron is as likely to be drinking champagne (£24/bottle and up) as beer. There may be a short wait for a table; if possible get there by 8pm before it starts to crowd up. Once seated, you can choose from a menu of nicely ambitious pub food (or rather run-of-the mill restaurant food, depending on your perspective), starting with new potato skins stuffed with sourcream and caviar, warm chicken liver salad with goats cheese, or deep fried feta, brie and mozzarella.

Main courses run to lamb cutlets, Lincolnshire sausages, chargrilled tuna steak and salmon fishcakes, and are mostly competently prepared and well-presented, though any real American should skip the alleged Caesar salad. As the evening progresses, the place gets buzzier and the crowd gets thicker – there's a nice casual enthusiasm about The Enter-prise that makes it feel neighborhoody even though people do drive halfway across London to meet there. Figure about £25 per head for two courses with wine and tip; £30 with champagne.

37. FOXTROT OSCAR *(British, moderate), 79 Royal Hospital Road, London SW3 4HN. Tel: 0171 352 7179. Monday to Friday 12:30pm to 2:30pm and 7:30pm to 11:30pm; Saturday and Sunday 12:30pm to 3:30pm and 7:30pm to 10:30pm. Major credit cards. Sloane Square tube.*

You can always tell the tourists at this popular local bistro – they're the ones the bartender doesn't greet by name. Don't let that make you feel unwelcome however, just sit back and enjoy the comfortably low-key atmosphere while you study the blackboard of updated traditional British fare. An average evening's offerings might include homemade soup, good-quality burgers, cottage pie, Scotch sirloin steak, duck roulade salad and salmon steak with creamed leeks and mashed potatoes. Good desserts include lemon tart, or brandy snaps with brandy cream.

Reservations are recommended unless you want to sit at the bar, which is perfect for solo dining. A two or three course meal for two with wine and service will run £50-60, but you can eat for less. And if you want to know what the cryptic, military slang name means, try figuring it out from the first initials alone.

38. LA FAMIGLIA (*Italian, moderate*), *5-7 Langton Street, London SW10. Tel: 0171 351 0761. Daily noon to 2:45pm and 7pm to 11:45pm. Major credit cards. Sloane Square tube plus number 14, 22 or 31 bus.*

The warm Italian greeting and entrance filled with family photographs set the tone for this attractive, up-beat northern Italian restaurant; La Famiglia is one of those London restaurants that constantly appears on friends' ten-favorites lists. The owners and waiters are Italian, the cooking is simple and honest (in the modern sense of the word): buffalo mozzarella, basil and sun-dried tomato salad, puttanesca pasta, rabbit cooked with rosemary and olive oil. Game features strongly, as do simply grilled meats and fish and seasonal vegetables. Tiramisu and fresh orange tart are among the good desserts, wheeled-around from table to table on a cart.

La Famiglia is popular with families, especially on Sunday, and while not exactly cheap, it's the sort of restaurant in which the whole experience is such a treat, you immediately find yourself planning your return trip. A short but well-chosen list of Italian wines is featured; dinner for two with wine and service will cost £65-70.

39. THE FIFTH FLOOR CAFE, BAR (*inexpensive*) **AND RESTAURANT AT HARVEY NICHOLS** (*modern British, moderate to expensive*), *109-125 Knightsbridge, London SW1. Tel: 0171 235 5250. Monday to Saturday noon to 3pm (3:30pm Saturday) and 6:30pm to 11:30pm; closed Sunday. Major credit cards. Knightsbridge tube.*

Take the express elevator to the fifth floor and you emerge into a light-filled post-modern architectural-award-winning atrium, set on the top of this elegant department store. Along with the attractive food shop, there's an exuberant cafe (filled mainly with ladies and their packages), a designy bar and a quiet, attractive, excellent restaurant.

The cafe is pleasant and fun, and features just what you want to eat at lunchtime – a good smoked chicken or goat cheese salad, a couple of jazzy pastas, gazpacho or white bean soup accompanied by a glass of chardonnay. There's usually a 10-15 minute wait for a table, unless you get there well before 10pm, but lunch won't cost more than £10-15 per person and it's worth the wait. The nearby bar offers 17 varieties of beer, cappuccino and espresso and good elegant open sandwiches – pastrami on rye or smoked chicken and walnut or tuna with mango chutney. With a glass or two of beer or wine, you can perch at the Philippe Starck-style bar or claim a comfortable banquette and deeply padded chair. From 6pm to 1pm, the bar offers sushi by the piece, Thai fish cakes, and tortilla chips with salsa. It's all very attractive, comfortable, and will run about the same as the cafe for a sandwich, a glass or two of wine and service.

The restaurant is a different kettle of bouillabaisse altogether. It's shut off from the main floor by a glass wall, cultivates the same aura of luxurious chic as the department store, and is exceedingly popular with the modern ladies who lunch (Maggie Smith and Miranda Richardson among them) and gentlemen from local ad agencies. At dinner the crowd is more mixed from surrounding Knightsbridge and Chelsea, and at all times the food is that modern British concoction of French, Italian, traditional British and Asian: acorn-fed black pig ham with quince cheese, pan fried scallops with shredded duck confit, roast duck with apple fritters, grilled veal kidneys with aubergine cous cous, rump of lamb with black pepper and roast garlic, oysters with grilled spicy sausages.

As a special incentive, the Fifth Floor has one of the best (and most reasonably priced) wine lists in town. The prix fixe lunch (£17.50 for two courses, £21.50 for three) helps somewhat with the bill, but you still won't escape for much under £30 per person at lunchtime, £40 at night.

40. THE HALKIN (*modern Italian, expensive*), *in The Halkin Hotel, 5-6 Halkin Street, London SW1X 7DJ. Tel: 0171 333 1234. Lunch, Monday to Friday 12:30pm to 2:30pm; dinner Monday to Saturday 7:30pm to 10:30pm; Sunday (dinner only): Sunday 7pm to 10:30pm. Major credit cards. Hyde Park Corner tube.*

The synthesis of great food, seriously elegant surroundings, intelligent service and its first Michelin star makes dining here a real joy. Everything manages to feel calm, uncluttered and opulent – with an almost mathematical aversion to frills. The food is best described as Italian nouvelle, and everything, but everything, is made on the premises. Antipasti and first courses include wonderfully imaginative variations on seafood: a salad of scallops with black truffle; fillet of turbot with artichokes; squid ink tagliolini in celery and sun dried tomato sauce. Other offerings include pasta with rabbit and wild mushrooms, stuffed monkfish with black truffle, and venison with blueberries, polenta, chestnut ravioli and sauteed savoy cabbage. To accompany the main courses, a salad of rocket and dried aubergine with tomato in a sweet and sour sauce is typical.

Among the light and delicate desserts are a ricotta stuffed crepe with raspberry sauce and a tiny scoop of homemade chocolate ice cream; banana cake with coconut tuille; poached pear with panna cotta. Dinner for two, with a selection from the seriously impressive wine list, and service (note: it's included in the final bill), will not come to less than about £50 per person. There's a good £19.50 set price lunch – add wine, and you should escape for about £40. Considering all the mediocre food available in London for that sort of money, it's cheap at the price.

41. KING'S ROAD CAFE (*inexpensive*), *located on the first floor of Habitat, 208 King's Road, London SW3 5XP. Tel: 0171 351 1211. Monday to Saturday, 10am to 5:30pm; Sunday noon to 5:30pm. No credit cards. Sloane Square tube.*

If you find yourself stuck on the King's Road looking for a cheap, child-friendly snack, head for the first floor of the home furnishings store

Habitat. This spacious, airy cafe serves breakfast and light lunches with an Italian flair – pasta, soups, salads and parma ham sandwiches on ciabatta bread. The homemade tarts, cakes and scones are delicious, the espresso and cappuccino are good, and there's also tea, soft drinks and wine. But best of all, the service is cheery, there's room to maneuver strollers and they genuinely like children.

42. MADE IN ITALY *(Italian, inexpensive), 249 King's Road, London SW3 5EL. Tel: 0171 351 5098. Daily noon to 3pm and 6pm to 11:30pm (10:30pm Sunday). No credit cards. Sloane Square tube.*

This simple, casual, no-fuss pizza, pasta and salad restaurant features homemade tagliolini and ravioli with authentic fillings and toppings like parma ham, gorgonzola, ricotta cheese and rocket. Pizzas are thin-crusted and good; a help-yourself antipasto table makes a good buffet, with tiramisu and apple tart for dessert. Dinner for two with wine is a reasonable £25-30.

43. LE METRO *(French bistro, moderate), 28 Basil Street, London SW3 1AS. Tel: 0171 589 6286. Monday to Saturday, 7:30am to 11pm. Closed Sunday, Christmas day and Easter Monday. Major credit cards. Knightsbridge tube.*

This hyper-modern basement bistro around the corner from Harvey Nichols serves good quality food all day long – a rare find in London. Croissants and breads are baked fresh daily; the lunch and dinner menu includes a daily changing vegetarian soup and club sandwich, spinach gnocchi with tomato olives and basil, or an excellent fish stew. Terrine of sole, leek and mint; salmon steak; or duck confit with baby turnips are all good quality and well-prepared. The wine list is extensive, offers a huge variety of quality wines by the glass and is arranged under annoyingly trendy headings like "Clean & Classic" or "Everyday Hedonists."

Sadly, a good number of noisy, smoky everyday hedonists tend to clutter the place up after work. Avoid their prime time (5-8pm) if possible, and opt instead for lunch or late dinner. Le Metro's bright lights and stainless steel decor don't exactly add up to a warm and cozy experience, but the atmosphere is friendly and cheerful and a good time, a good meal, and a good drink are invariably had by all. The average visit will cost about £15 per person with a couple glasses of wine.

44. OGNISKO *(Polish, inexpensive to moderate), 55 Exhibition Road, London SW7. Tel: 0171 589 4635. Open daily, noon to 3pm and 6:30pm to 11pm. Closed Easter Sunday and Monday, December 25 and 26. Major credit cards. South Kensington tube.*

Around the corner from the Victoria & Albert Museum, nearly across from the entrance to the Science Museum, you'll find 55 Exhibition Road. There's no mention of a restaurant, but don't let that stop you. Walk confidently through the bar with the big "Polish Club Members Only" sign over it, and wait for one of the genuine daughters of Poland to seat you in the large pink dining room. We may as well come clean: we love the Polish Club.

If travel is about discovering exotic new places and people and tastes, you've hit the jackpot here. The rather formal, old-fashioned, pretty pink dining room tends to attract what look like ousted members of the Polish aristocracy (a huge moustache and burning gaze seems de rigeur), large tables of Polish businessmen and a few in-the-know Londoners, enjoying the spectacle. Huge portraits of 19th century members of the Polish aristocracy hang on the walls.

There's a wonderful daily three course fixed price lunch, £7.50 at this writing; at a recent trip it consisted of a hot cucumber and potato soup followed by fish cakes with dill and a side dish of leeks in cream and a fine apple tarte. If the prix fixe doesn't appeal, try the riches on the a la carte menu. Start with pickled herring in sour cream, hot Borscht or blinis with smoked salmon, sevruga caviar and cream. For a main course, there's roast goose with gnocchi and red cabbage, knuckle of pork Bavarian style, hunter's stew or pork chop and sauerkraut. But the star of the menu has to be the pierogi dumplings with meat or cheese (ask for half and half). All of this is served with dense, chewy Ukrainian sourdough rye bread and tastes best accompanied by good Polish beer or a bottle of Polish (!) red wine. The bill for two, depending on your stamina and alcohol consumption, can run anywhere from £25 to £45.

45. PEARL RESTAURANT *(Cantonese, inexpensive to expensive)*, 22 *Brompton Road, London SW1. Tel: 0171 225 3888. Open daily noon to 3pm; 6pm-11:30pm. Closed December 25-26. Major credit cards. Knightsbridge tube.*

Pearl is an oasis of undiscovered calm in the hectic rush of Knightsbridge. Its location (nearly across from Harvey Nichols) should mean that it's always bustling and noisy, but due to the fact that it looks expensive and rather formal, it gets overlooked. Which is good for you. Because the best thing about Pearl is the fact that you can sit down at this glitzy, expensive Cantonese restaurant at lunchtime, order the dim sum dumplings or Singapore noodles and a cup of Chinese tea, and find that you've had an exceedingly civilized, comfortable meal — for not much more than £5.

Which isn't to say you can't spend a lot of money at Pearl. There are set price lunches at £8.50, £11 and £12.50, and the set price dinners start at £25 and go up to £55. The fish and vegetarian dishes are excellent; the service unhurried and polite, and the linen always beautifully starched. And if you're homesick for good Cantonese food and don't want to head all the way to Chinatown, Pearl will do nicely. But we'd rather spend the (fairly serious) dinner money somewhere a little more interesting and stick to the wonderful cheap lunch.

MARYLEBONE, BAKER STREET

The reason most tourists end up in this neighborhood is a visit to **Madame Tussaud's**; we'll give you the benefit of the doubt and assume you were at the **Wallace Collection**.

46. SINGAPORE GARDEN *(Malaysian, inexpensive), 154-156 Gloucester Place, London NW1 6DT. Tel: 0171 723 8233. Daily noon to 2:45pm and 6pm to 10:45pm (11:15pm Friday and Saturday). Major credit cards. Baker Street tube.*

About a five minute walk from Baker Street is one of London's best little Singaporean/Malaysian restaurants. We ordered the popular businessman's lunch, Singapore noodles, to test the waters and they turned up perfect – loaded with large shrimp, chicken and crunchy vegetables. The menu is strong on seafood; ginger crab, and sizzling prawns in black bean sauce were both beautifully seasoned and delicious. *Mee goreng* and Malaysian-style curries are also featured, along with *san choy bau* (mixed seafood rolled in lettuce with a chili sauce). Vegetarian dishes will be specially prepared on request. The glass atrium roof contributes to the fresh, sunny atmosphere. Lunch for two with service and beer will cost about £20.

47. VILLANDRY DINING ROOM *(French country, moderate to expensive), 89 Marylebone High Street, London W1. Tel 0171 224 3799. Open Monday to Saturday 12:30-3:00pm for lunch; dinner served third Thursday of every month, 7:30pm-11ish, call to confirm dates. Reservations recommended for lunch and essential at least a few weeks in advance for dinner. Major credit cards. Baker Street or Bond Street tube.*

Only people-in-the-know know about lunch at Villandry, the charming little neighborhood charcuterie a few minutes walk (and a million miles) from the exhausting bustle of Oxford Street. It used to consist of a small dining room in the back of the charcuterie where about eight wooden tables of local well-heeled shoppers and business folk went for good, unpretentious French country cooking. But in this city of glitzy new-concept eateries and darkly panelled, expensive old ones, word started to get out about Villandry and they've gone to the radical step of ... well, of putting a few tables in the front of the shop and opening once a month for dinner. This seeming disregard for the quick buck, combined with the cheeses and huge French sausages swinging over your head go some way to explaining Villandry's charm. The rest of it can be explained by the food, which is seriously unflashy but seriously good.

If you're going to be in town around the third Thursday of any month, by all means phone a few weeks ahead from the U.S. for the actual date and reservations. The monthly dinners are remarkably festive. The restaurant groans with the 90 or so guests (including children), everyone seems peculiarly friendly and happy, the waiters are young, helpful, knowledgeable and charming and it all feels like a group of friends in a small village in France. And the food? Prosciutto with braised endive and shallot, foie gras on frisee with a haricot vert salad, or Arachon moules marinieres to start; all delightful. For the main course, a hearty oxtail stew with brisket of beef, prunes and carrots served with potato croquettes was rich, substantial and delicious; also good were roast partridge stuffed with chicken liver served with celeriac puree, grilled Chateaubriand served on wild mushrooms and baked halibut with smoked haddock brandade and a herb salsa, all £15-16. Desserts are equally fine (average £5); cranberry lattice tart, hot chocolate tart with a milk sorbet and clementine sorbet with a citrus compote.

Lunch offers the same theme, though mercifully lighter – Toulouse sausages with mashed potatoes, soup, a savoury tart. Given the relaxed country atmosphere, you might be a little surprised at the size of the bill; lunch can easily run to £20 per person, dinner (per person) with wine, about £40-45. We don't think you'll mind, though, Villandry is one place you won't find done better back home. Unless of course home is Provence.

MAYFAIR

Mayfair is where we head when we want our food served with a few Michelin stars and a big bill on the side.

48. THE GREENHOUSE (*modern British, expensive*), *27a Hay's Mews, London W1X 7RJ. Tel: 0171 499 3331. Open daily (except Saturday) noon to 2:30pm and 7pm to 11pm; dinner Sunday 7-10pm. Closed Christmas and bank holidays. Major credit cards. Reservations essential. Green Park tube.*

Located in a quiet mews in Mayfair, this much-talked about restaurant has been making nearly everyone's list of ten best for the past two or three years. Chef Gary Rhodes dedicates his considerable talents to a rediscovery of traditional British ingredients and recipes – nearly always with a few surprising twists. For example: fillet of smoked haddock with Welsh rarebit is served on a tomato and chive salad; potato and leek cake comes topped with spinach crumble; a relish of cockles (yes, the alive alive-o) and chili accompanies grilled tuna. Word has it that the menu has been toned down a bit of late, which is probably good news – braised oxtail is something of a house specialty and the simple grilled calf's liver with mashed potatoes is spectacular. Desserts eschew the seriously complicated in favor of chocolate tart, rice pudding and homemade ice cream.

The Greenhouse makes a nice setting for celebrations. Casually elegant, spacious and pretty; votive candles on every table add the requisite romantic twinkle. There's a good wine list, and the service is appropriately discreet and attentive. Dinner for two with wine and cover charge should run at least £80.

49. H.R. HIGGINS LTD. *(coffee bar, inexpensive)*, *79 Duke Street, London W1M 6AS. Tel: 0171 491 8819. Monday to Friday 9:30am to 4:30pm; Saturday 1:30pm to 3:30pm. No credit cards. Bond Street tube.*

No croissants. No scones. No clotted cream. No cucumber sandwiches. This family-owned wholesale and retail shop is coffee and tea purveyor to the queen, and they do coffee and tea, pure and simple. You don't so much enter this shop as find yourself seduced into it – the aromas of fresh ground coffee have a tendency to follow you down the street. Once inside, head downstairs to the lower ground floor coffee room. There, clustered around a large roaster, are several small tables and chairs where you can sip a cup of good coffee or tea served with a selection of biscuits. Hanover blend, Kibo Chaggo, Creole, and Blue Mountain were among one day's offerings. Before you go, spare a moment for the photos upstairs paying homage to the founder, Mr. Higgins himself.

50. QUAGLINO'S *(modern Italian, moderate), 16 Bury Street, London SW1. Tel: 0171 930 6767. Daily noon to 3pm and 5:30pm to midnight. Closed December 25. Major credit cards. Reservations suggested. Green Park tube.*

A friend of ours once saw a couple having sex at a table at Quaglino's. We think this about sums the restaurant up, for better and for worse. For better, it's possibly the only restaurant in England stimulating enough to inspire that sort of behavior (though on numerous repeat visits, there's been no sign of a repeat performance). For worse, Quaglino's tends to suffer from terminal hipdom circa 1988, which often takes the form of county girls and their stockbroker boyfriends hilariously quaffing champagne at the table next to you.

Quaglino's is huge (400 seats), brash, expensively and impressively designed, noisy, and exciting. The food is remarkably good, interesting, and consistent.

And it's an experience lots of people adore. Not least for the ambitious menu. You might start with oysters, Sevruga or Beluga caviar (£20-80), seared squid with Chinese watercress, bresaola with a poached egg, smoked bacon and truffle pate or spicy Malay noodles. Seafood specialties include crab, crawfish, langoustine or lobster mayonnaise (served in the shell), and from the rotisseries and grill you might try shoulder of pork with crackling, peppered rib of beef, or calves liver and bacon. There's also roast pheasant, rabbit with prosciutto and roast pumpkin, seared scallops and, for vegetarians, a spicy potato galette with chick peas and coriander.

For desert, there's the inevitable sticky toffee pudding in addition to prune and armagnac parfait, blackberry crumble and apricot cheesecake. You can also opt for lunch or dinner at the upstairs (ground-level) bar overlooking the dining room, which has a shorter menu featuring cold dishes from the main menu. For a lighter, quieter (at lunchtime at least) meal – dressed crab, perhaps, or Chinese chicken salad, and a glass of wine – the bar is perfect and your bill will remain under £20. Complete dinner with wine and tip (included in the bill) runs about £30-35 per person. Entertainment provided by adjoining tables is free.

51 & 51A. SOFRA *(Turkish, inexpensive to moderate)*, *18 Shepherd Street, London W1. Tel: 0171 493 3320. Daily, noon to midnight. Green Park tube. And 36 Tavistock Street, London WC1. Tel: 0171 240 3773. Major credit cards (no Amex). Covent Garden tube.*

The original Sofra, in the heart of Mayfair's Shepherd's market, and its new clone in Covent Garden are just what the doctor ordered for visitors fed to the gills on English breakfasts and French dinners. Sofra specializes in set-price "Healthy Meals" at £8.45 (lunch) and £9.95 (dinner), consisting of a series of Middle Eastern mezes, or small dishes – humus, broad beans, falafel, taramasalata, tabouleh, baba ganoush (eggplant), and spicy sausage. Everything is fresh and well-prepared and seasoned simply with lemon juice, olive oil and parsley; a la carte choices include very good chicken and lamb kebabs served with rice pilaf.

For such reasonable prices, you wouldn't expect much in the way of location or atmosphere, but both Sofras have both – white tablecloths, well-attired waiters, and an attractive, up-market clientele. Lunch or dinner for two with a bottle of wine and service will cost under £40.

PRIMROSE HILL

A dear friend who lives in this charming north London neighborhood keeps begging us not to mention its pubs or restaurants for fear tourist pilgrimages will begin. When you go, don't mention our names.

52. LEMONIA *(Greek, inexpensive to moderate), 89 Regent's Park Road, London NW1. Tel: 0171 586 7454. Daily noon to 3pm and 6pm to 11:30pm. Closed Saturday lunch and Sunday dinner. Major credit cards. Chalk Farm tube.*

Since it opened in the early 90s, this large, open, attractive Greek restaurant has been booked solid day in and day out. The food is good (not thrilling, just good), but the restaurant has an attractive, buzzy crowd and an attractive buzzy charm, and it all adds up to a really pleasant evening out – especially in summer when the large French (Greek?) doors are thrown open to pretty Primrose Hill village.

Start with a drink down the block at The Queens, then order a mix of starters (taramasalata, deep fried aubergine, tabouleh, fried kalamari, grilled Cypriot cheese, etc.) and a bottle of traditional Retsina wine with its distinctive turpentine bouquet. Good main courses include the many variations on kebabs – grilled fish kebab, lamb shashlik, and sheftalia – casseroles and marinated grilled fish. If you're hungry, the very best meal is the £10.50 meze (a selection of hot and cold starters, salads and main courses) which could feed most of the Greek army and offers small dishes of just about everything on the menu. And don't forget to call before and reserve a table. Lunch or dinner can range from as little as £12 to as much as £20 per person with wine.

53. ODETTE'S (*modern English, moderate to expensive*), *130 Regents Park Road, London NW1. Tel: 0171 586 5486. Open for lunch weekdays only 12:30pm to 2:30pm and dinner Monday to Saturday, 7pm to 11pm. Major credit cards. Chalk Farm tube.*

The word absolutely everyone uses to describe this pretty restaurant is "romantic." Make a late reservation on a long summer evening; wander across Primrose Hill at twilight, then stroll through the lovely Primrose Hill village looking in the windows of all the quaint and pretty shops until it's time to dine. Don't go with someone you're not certain about; you're sure to get carried away and end up proposing marriage (or worse). On the other hand, don't get the idea that it's only for lovers; it's also the perfect place to take parents, visiting VIPs, and old college friends now living in London (yes, us).

But about the restaurant. The walls are covered with mirrors in huge gilt frames, the service is restrained and elegant without being stuffy, and the food – simply delightful. Start with Irish Oysters, red mullet and blood orange terrine, tartare of tuna with pear, ginger and coriander pancake or slow roasted fish soup with fennel risotto. Main courses (which change every few weeks) might include roast suckling pig and plum pickle, fillet of seabass with fennel and burnt butter; or honey-spiced saddle of hare with garlic potato pie. Desserts (like pear and cranberry tarte or white chocolate terrine) are delicious; the wine list imaginative and diverse. Dinner for two with wine (and service) will run about £75-80.

SOHO

London's foremost neighborhood for the working lunch and the after-work dinner (with the six-hour drink in between), Soho has about twenty restaurants per block and enough streetlife to jolt you out of the worst case of jetlag. Restaurants in Soho tend to come and go – we've chosen the ones good enough to stick around for awhile.

54. ALASTAIR LITTLE RESTAURANT (*modern English, expensive*) **AND BAR** (*reasonable*), *49 Frith Street, London W1V 5TE. Tel: 0171 734 5183. Open for lunch Monday to Friday (noon to 3pm); dinner, Monday to Saturday (6pm to 11:30pm). Major credit cards. Closed bank holidays. Tottenham Court Road or Leicester Square tube.*

Alastair Little is known as one of London's best chefs, but somehow this bare, noisy little post-modern restaurant in the heart of Soho just isn't as appealing as it should be. The comment most people have about Alastair Little's is "overpriced." So why are we including it here?

Because it has a secret. The fixed price lunch in the downstairs bar is delightful. For £12.50, you can choose from a menu that changes frequently and might include pappardelle with rabbit sauce, grilled vegetable salad or ribollita to start, followed by a sea-food hot pot, lamb stew with pasta and beans or duck confit with potatoes and salad. Coffee and dessert are extra, but who wants a three course meal at lunchtime anyway? The food, which at £40 a head for lunch isn't always good enough, is a steal at £12.50. The bar is small and very pleasant, right in the heart of Soho, about equidistant from the National Gallery and the British Museum.

55. ANDREW EDMUNDS *(bistro, low moderate), 46 Lexington Street, London, W1. Tel: 0171 437 5708. Open Daily 12:30pm to 3pm and 5:30pm to 11pm. Closed bank holidays. Major credit cards. Piccadilly Circus or Oxford Circus tube.*

Set in the ground and basement floors of a somewhat ramshackle 18th century Soho house, Andrew Edmunds has a rabid local following of artsy publishing types who like the jammed-together tables and the intimate French bistro atmosphere. Not to mention the very nice food and wine. You wouldn't take your parents here, or your children, but a good companion and the newest Martin Amis novel will feel just right in this charming, dark-painted, crowded restaurant. The menu varies daily according to what's in the local market, but might include shellfish soup and rouille, Moroccan butternut squash soup or duck breast terrine to start (£3-6); followed by Italian sausages with cannellini beans, swordfish steak with warm potato salad, and best end of lamb with rosemary mashed potatoes (£5-8). Desserts for around £3 are good, but a second bottle of wine is better. This is the kind of restaurant that makes you feel glad to be alive, on vacation, and drunk.

56. CHEZ GERARD *(French, moderate), 8 Charlotte Street, London W1P 1HE. Tel: 0171 636 4975. Daily noon to 3pm (except Saturday) and 6pm to 11pm. Major credit cards. Tottenham Court Road tube.*

We like Chez Gerard for lots of reasons. It has emerged from last year's renovation fresher and more attractive than ever thanks to cool colors, good lighting and comfortable seating. The food is good, very basic, unfussy and unpretentious, and the crowd (there's always a crowd) is lively, attractive and sophisticated. The booths are just intimate enough, and when the weather warms up, tables spill out onto the sidewalk and the atmosphere turns even happier. The £1 cover charge starts your meal off with French bread and anchovy butter, olives and toasted nuts; you might choose gravadlax; onion, anchovy, olive and tomato tart; fish soup with rouille, or chicken liver pate for a first course.

Chez Gerard's speciality is its very good cote de boeuf (for two) with sauce bearnaise; other main courses include lamb cutlets, seafood or lamb brochette, grilled calf's liver with bacon, duck confit, salad nicoise (with fresh tuna), and escalope of veal – all served with copious dishes of shoestring fries. Vegetarians are catered for, and dessert runs to creme brulee, lemon and fruit tarts and various extremely pleasant concoctions of chocolate. The £15 prix fixe three course menu takes effect every evening after 6pm and during Sunday lunch, and has to be one of the best bargains in town. And the house champagne is delicious. Dinner for two with wine and service: £50-60.

57. FREEDOM (*inexpensive*), *60-66 Wardour Street, London W1V 3HP. Tel: 0171 734 0071. Open daily noon to 7pm. Major credit cards. Leicester Square Tube.*

There are a few good reasons to know about Freedom. Lots of models eat there. So do music biz types. And lesbian couples. The people watching is fab. It's cheap. The food is California style – salads and sandwiches with lots of health drinks (the Fruit Cocktail combines eight different types of fresh juice). And it gives you an excuse to browse in Ally Capellino (well-cut, accessible – which isn't to say cheap – English designer clothes and jewelry) across the street.

The salads are big and varied and include things like avocado, tofu, nuts, sundried tomatoes and fruit; the sandwiches run to honey roast bacon on wholemeal and corned beef on rye. The excellent soups can be ordered with salad, cheese and bread. The entire menu runs between about £3.50 and £7. Leave your big lug of a boyfriend behind (unless you're also a boy, in which case the two of you will feel right at home), and make lunch Freedom with a side order of Ally Capellino jacket and trousers. It works for us.

58. THE FRENCH HOUSE DINING ROOM (*English, moderate*), *49 Dean Street, London W1. Tel: 0171 437 2477. Open Monday to Saturday, 12:30pm to 3pm and 6:30pm to 11:15pm. Major credit cards. Leicester Square tube.*

Don't be fooled by the name. The "French" in French House refers to the original (and legendary) owner of the pub downstairs; this restaurant is delightfully and eccentrically English – and exceedingly reasonably priced. Climb the narrow stairs beside the pub, and enter the elegant small dining room, all windows, dark red wallpaper and gilt mirrors.

The menu makes use of rigorously traditional ingredients – like ox tongue, roast pigeon and lamb's sweetbreads – and prepares them with great flair and confidence. You might have a whole boiled crab with fresh mayonnaise and brown bread or ox tongue served with lentils. The salad will likely be made of something unusual like dandelion leaves. For the faint of heart, there are more familiar dishes like baked hake and celeriac mash, rare beef fillet, or grilled pork chop. And astonishingly, main courses are nearly all under £10.

Desserts are equally simple, unusual and good: black bottom cake, Hokey Pokey or blackberry ice cream, pear and almond tart, terrific ripe English cheeses. It's impossible to oversell the combination of simplicity and assurance that characterizes the menu; there's nothing extra, not a trace of flash or flourish, nothing you've seen elsewhere in London, nothing copied from that little place in Paris, New York or Rome. The clientele is demographically diverse and almost entirely local – movie directors, distinguished looking gentlemen and their youngish girl-friends, women in short fashionable garments, friends in for a gossip. For a sunny Sunday lunch we can't imagine a nicer, less pretentious venue. Or for a rainy Tuesday dinner, now you mention it.

59. GOPAL'S OF SOHO *(Indian, moderate), 12 Bateman Street, London W1V 5TD. Tel: 0171 434 0840. Daily noon to 2:45pm and 6pm to 11:30pm. Closed December 25-26. Major credit cards. Leicester Square or Tottenham Court Road tube.*

Everyone knows you're supposed to eat lots of good cheap Indian food in London. But with neighborhood restaurants often unpredictable and out-of-the-way, Gopal's offers a consistently dependable option. The food is excellent, the restaurant comfortable and pleasant, the Soho location central. And if the bill usually comes to a bit more than you might have expected, well, at least you always get what you pay for.

Gopal's specializes in fish and shrimp dishes from Goa, Malabar, and Hyderabad in southern India. There's little dependence on heaps of chili to disguise dull, undifferentiated cooking; subtle and unusual spices rule. Try the tandoori dishes and anything with coconut; cod with fresh fenugreek, and Malai prawns are particularly nice. The breads are homemade and memorable. For dessert try *kulfi* (pistachio/almond ice) or *gulab jumun* (milk cake stuffed with pistachio) and marsala tea. Skip the house wines in favor of big bottles of Kingfisher beer. And when in doubt, ask for advice – the service is friendly and they've never steered us wrong. Dinner for two with beer and service will cost somewhere around £40.

60. JU-JIRO (Japanese, inexpensive to moderate), *18 Frith Street, London W1. Tel: 0171 494 3878. Daily noon to 3pm and 6pm to 10:30pm (last orders). Closed Saturday lunch and Sunday. Major credit cards. Tottenham Court Road or Leicester Square tube.*

When anyone asks what we miss about home, we get all misty-eyed and think of raw fish. Sadly, the sort of inexpensive, good quality Japanese food available in most American cities is virtually unknown here – with one or two exceptions. Ju-Jiro is a notable one. Low on exotic concoctions (don't bother requesting a dragon roll), elegant design, and expensive lighting, it nonetheless manages to deliver basic, good quality sushi for almost absurd prices by London standards. The lunchtime menu is restricted to bento boxes, each with miso soup, salad, a selection of sushi and tempura or teriyaki; the seafood box is very fresh and very good, and at just £7.50, a remarkable bargain. It's quiet enough at lunchtime to enjoy the overheard conversations about casting, auditions and script development – this is, after all, the heart of the film district. Lunch for two with beer, sake and service will cost between £20 and £35, dinner at least 25% more.

61. THE LEXINGTON *(modern English, moderate), 45 Lexington Street, London W1R 3LG. Tel: 0171 434 3401. Open Monday to Friday, noon to 3pm and 6pm to 11:30pm; closed Saturday lunch and Sunday. Major credit cards. Piccadilly Circus or Oxford Circus tube.*

The Lexington is narrowish, newish, youngish, hippish and fun. With its orange walls, green banquettes and blonde wood tables, you won't be surprised to hear that the food is English by way of California and includes lots of things like sun-dried tomato risotto, chargrilled vegetables and garlic, olive bread crostini and marinated goats cheese. It's all very well prepared and presented and has a strong (unusual for England) emphasis on healthy things like vegetables, salads and simply-grilled chicken, fish and meats. Starters include dishes like smoked chicken with green beans and artichoke, a good Caesar salad (which they'll turn into a main course on request); dill herrings with cucumber and chives; and slow baked peppers with olive bread crostini. The Lexington Paysanne (starter or main course size) is a heap of salad greens with a poached egg and enough smoked chicken and sausage to keep you from feeling worthy and depressed – it's the perfect antidote to fish and chips and a sure-fire cure for homesickness.

Main courses include grilled chicken with chicory, sauteed calves liver, rump of lamb with creamed aubergine, and red mullet. For dessert, vanilla burnt cream, British cheeses with walnut bread, and cappuccino mousse are all good. The menu changes frequently and there's a live pianist every evening; the bill (with a bottle of wine) for two will come to between £40 and £50; a fantastically good value £10 set price evening meal includes two courses and coffee and is highly recommended. Lunchtimes are usually full of Soho trendies, so remember to book ahead. A couple of quieter tables by the bar in front are perfect for latecomers or noshers.

62. MAISON BERTAUX *(cafe, inexpensive), 28 Greek Street, London W1. Tel: 0171 437 6007. Open daily 9am to 8pm; Sunday 9am to 1pm and 3pm to 8pm. No credit cards. Leicester Square tube.*

If you're fed up with London and wished you'd gone to Paris, take an hour out at this tiny charming little French patisserie. With its wonderful homemade croissants, cakes and pastries, French waitresses and tiny cramped tables upstairs and down, it's the next best thing to being there. Don't expect privacy, or any concern for non-smokers, but the atmosphere is unique – to London at least. Word has it the upstairs becomes a very good fringe theatre some evenings, though how actors and an audience fit in the tiny room simultaneously is a mystery to us.

63. PATISSERIE VALERIE *(cafe, inexpensive), 44 Old Compton Street, London W1. Tel: 0171 437 3466. Monday to Friday, 8am to 8pm; Saturday, 9am to 7pm, Sunday 9am to 6pm. Tottenham Court Road or Leicester Square tube. And 215 Brompton Road, London SW3. Tel: 0171 589 4993. Monday to Friday 7:30am to 7:30pm; Saturday 7:30am to 7pm; Sunday 8:30am to 6pm. No credit cards. Knightsbridge tube.*

Patisserie Valerie on Old Compton Street is as much a London landmark as Buckingham Palace. The crowd is a mixture of students from St. Martin's College of Art around the corner, creative directors from local ad agencies, writers (screen and postcard) and just plain cafe aficionados. Depending on one's level of affection, it is either cozy or jam-packed, buzzing or furiously loud, but the one thing everyone agrees on is that the coffee is good, the croissants (left in baskets on every table in the morning) are great, the pastries divine, and the atmosphere pure center-of-the-world.

Don't give up if the place looks totally full, if you're lucky, it just means you'll have to squeeze in next to some rather attractive stranger. There are also delicate toasted sandwiches and a good croque monsieur. And anyway, Ralph Fiennes buys his cakes here, which is all the recommendation we need. The Brompton Road Valerie by Harrods is a bit more glamorous and a bit less bohemian, and the fare is equally good.

64. KETTNERS *(pizza, inexpensive), 29 Romilly Street, London W1. Tel: 0171 734 6112. No reservations. Open daily noon to 1am (last orders midnight). Major credit cards. Leicester Square tube.*

Kettners is a comfortable, nay, elegant branch of Pizza Express in the heart of Soho – with a champagne bar on the side. Don't ask us who comes up with this stuff, but in this case it has its charms.

Fancy a bottle of champagne before your pizza? You have 70 to choose from in the comfortable bar to the left of the entrance. They range from a £23 Irroy Brut to a Pol Roger Balthazar at £539. We'll take the latter, thanks, then move through to the restaurant for a Napoletana with extra chili peppers. In fact, the champagne bar is a good (and popular) place to meet friends; unlike most pubs, it won't make you feel insanely conspicuous as you nurse your scotch (or your Taittinger) and wait for your pals to show. It's also neither posh nor shabby, which makes it quite a find in this alternately posh and shabby part of town.

Moving right along, the pizza restaurant has carpets and linen tablecloths and a grand piano (manned nightly and Thursday to Sunday at lunchtime) and a range of good pizzas (all around £6.50), and average burgers, sandwiches and salads. The wines are seriously ordinary and when we can't afford Pol Roger Balthazar, we stick to the good Italian beer. What else can we tell you. It's close to theaters and cinemas. It's open till 1am. And it'll make you feel less poor than you probably are by this point in your vacation.

65. EST *(Italian, inexpensive/moderate), 54 Frith Street, London W1. Tel: 0171 437 0666. Weekdays noon to 3pm and 6pm to 11pm; Saturday 7pm to 11pm; closed Sunday. Major credit cards. Tottenham Court Road or Leicester Square tube.*

It's hard to say why so many people like this sliver of a Soho restaurant. The food sometimes misses rather badly. The tables are arranged close together which makes for good eavesdropping but bad privacy. And the bar can get pretty manic of a Friday or Saturday evening. But we count ourselves among its fans, and here's why. The location is great, right at the crossroads of civilization as we know it, ie, Soho. The pizzas are excellent. The simpler dishes on the menu (like rocket radicchio and Parmesan salad, ravioli in porcini cream, or lamb shank with mashed and potato) are often surprisingly good, and the clean, pale wood decor is friendly and pleasant. You can spend anywhere from a few pounds for a salad and a glass of wine, to £25 for a meal and a bottle.

Est is a great place to sit at the crowded bar, order the focaccia with sun dried tomatoes and mozzarella, drink a few beers and catch up on the local gossip. If that doesn't make you feel like a local, nothing will.

66. SOHO SOHO RESTAURANT AND ROTISSERIE *(French, low moderate to high moderate), 11-13 Frith Street, London W1. Tel: 0171 494 3491. Monday to Saturday, noon to 3pm and 6pm to midnight (restaurant), noon to 12:45am (rotisserie). Major credit cards. Tottenham Court Road or Leicester Square tube.*

The rotisserie at Soho Soho is a fun, crowded, noisy, happening kind of place. If this description strikes fear and loathing in your heart, skip this paragraph and go directly to paragraph two. The cheerful, attractive ground floor always seems to be full of people stopping at other tables to exchange greetings and gossip on the way in – you, the tourist, will have the advantage of knowing nobody and thus achieving a quick entrance.

Once seated, you'll notice the colorful painted wall murals, the huge open grill, the frantic young (mainly French) waiters, and the at-times deafening noise. On the plus side, there's the reasonably priced, well-prepared Provencale food and the fact that you've probably been married long enough to eschew conversation anyway.

There's something for everyone here, from a salade nicoise or salade du Maquis (smoked loin of pork, ewe's milk cheese and walnuts) and mushroom tortellini with sage cream and Parmesan, to fillet of cod baked with olive paste, chicken brochette, terrine of rabbit with bacon and hazelnuts, fresh sardines, baby guinea fowl roasted with juniper berries or steak and chips. Starters include a really good Marseillaise fish and shellfish soup; desserts run to tarte au citron with creme fraiche. About £25 per person with wine; considerably less for a single course lunch or lighter meal.

Upstairs, the restaurant returns to civilized living. It's quiet, discreet and pretty, with low lighting and nice views of Soho through the big windows. You can start with carpaccio of beef, canelloni stuffed with fresh crab meat and seaweed (better than it sounds), or bouillabaisse; followed by grilled tuna steak with fresh lemongrass sauce, roasted calf's liver, skewers of Barbary duck on wild mushroom polenta or wild boar served with fresh noodles and chestnuts. Desserts are rich and, amazingly, don't include Britain's ubiquitous sticky toffee pudding. Two or three course lunch or dinner for two with wine and service: £60 plus.

66. SAIGON *(Vietnamese, moderate), 45 Frith Street, London W1. Tel: 0171 437 7109. Open Monday to Saturday, noon to 11:30pm. Closed Sundays and bank holidays. Major credit cards. Leicester Square or Tottenham Court Road tubes.*

It's amazing how quickly you can get fed up with all the bruschetta and polenta in Soho. If this is the case, or threatens to become the case shortly, head instantly to Saigon. The restaurant is comfortable and attractive, spread over two floors decorated with ceiling fans, bamboo and lovely Vietnamese waitresses. And the food is exceedingly agreeable – though Americans used to wheelbarrows full of Oriental food may be somewhat unnerved by the dainty portions.

The menu is heavy on all those wonderful flavor standards like coriander, lemongrass and peanut sauces, but pushes the envelope with lily flower, Ban Hai herbs, sugar cane and peppermint. Many of the dishes come with rice paper wrappers that you dunk in hot water to render flexible; others rely on lettuce wrappings which is especially enjoyable if you like to combine eating with arts and crafts.

With such an extensive and extensively praiseworthy selection, it seems futile to single out one or two recommendations, but the green papaya salad and mixed wind dry duck sausage are both worth remembering; as is aromatic duck with rice paper wrappers; stir fried prawn and pork with bamboo shoot, roast peanut and mint; chicken with coconut curry; and stuffed squid with pork, Chinese mushroom, lily flower and etc (their words).

As of this writing, there's a very good value £14 set lunch and dinner. Dinner for two with Vietnamese beer or sake should come to about £40-45.

ON OR ACROSS THE RIVER: THE TATE, THE SOUTH BANK, WATERLOO & TOWER BRIDGE

The **Thames** is London's most underused resource, and lots of Londoners consider dining south of the river tantamount to foreign travel. Given how convenient these restaurants are to the center of town (and how lovely the views are once you get there) we think they're barmy.

68 & 68A. BAR CENTRAL *(moderate), 131 Waterloo Road, London SE1. Tel: 0171 928 5086. Daily noon to 11:30pm. Major credit cards. Waterloo tube. And 316 King's Road, London SW3. Tel: 0171 352 0025. Monday to Friday noon to midnight; weekends 11am to midnight. Sloane Square tube.*

Where once there was a restaurant desert, there are now two decent alternatives. So if you find yourself at the Old Vic theater, stuck at Waterloo Station or on the way home from the South Bank (and you don't fancy the crowd and noise of the Fire Station bar across the road) stop in at Bar Central. It's a pretty, pale blue and yellow restaurant with a big open kitchen and jazz on the sound system; just a few months old as of this writing and gaining popularity all the time. The menu is appealing and the food above average for this sort of bruschetta and shaved Parmesan joint; there's a warm salad of oyster mushrooms with black olives and croutons; arugula, baby spinach and Parmesan salad; and pumpkin soup with sour cream (£3.50-£5) for starters; cassoulet of pork with boudin noir; chicken with pancetta and caponata, and lamb shank with lentils and yogurt (all around £8) for mains. (The King's Road branch is even newer and more popular, with the same menu.)

Dinner for two with wine and service will run a moderate £40-50 and reservations are a must – though if you happen to be in the neighborhood for a matinee or just passing through mid-afternoon, it's a lovely place to stop for a cappuccino and an apple and blueberry crumble.

69. BLUE PRINT CAFE *(modern British, moderate), at The Design Museum, Shad Thames, Butler's Wharf, London SE1 2YD. Tel: 0171 378 7031; fax: 0171 386 7665. Daily noon to 3pm (Sunday 3:30pm) and 7pm to 11pm. Closed Sunday dinner. Major credit cards. Tower Hill tube.*

Sir Terence Conran strikes again. The design store mogul, inventor of Habitat, restaurateur (Bibendum and La Pont de la Tour) and star of his own American Express commercial probably deserves his knighthood for sheer style and energy. In the case of the Blue Print Cafe, we'd knight him ourselves for the view.

Set atop the Bauhaus-influenced Design Museum, the dining room evokes the spirit of le Courbusier, Philip Johnson (pre-Chippendale), and Mondrian in its stark purity with accents of primary colors – even the tulips look more like design elements than flowers. But this is not criticism, mere admiration, because the Blue Print Cafe is not only a delightful restaurant, but offers truly delightful views of Tower Bridge through the one wall of the restaurant entirely constructed of glass. If you can tear your eyes off the view long enough to look at the menu, you'll find an eclectic mix of California, Italy and Asia. Roast tomato and red pepper soup, Caesar salad (amazingly, a delicious one) and timbale of prawns and lemongrass wrapped in bok choy were featured starters, though the menu changes daily.

Main courses might include roast duck breast with black pepper, pan-fried calf's liver with caramelized onions; linguine with clams, mussels, squid and saffron sauce; or spicy steamed pink bream with black bean and ginger sauce. The servings are generous, but the superb desserts include an unusual selection of sorbets (grapefruit, passionfruit and rhubarb), homemade ice creams and tarts (lemon curd, ginger and pear) so pace yourself.

The excellent wine list includes a dozen by the glass and half-bottle. Dinner for two with wine and service will cost about £60. The restaurant is popular with pinstriped denizens of the nearby City, so reserve early, especially if you want a front row river view. In the summer, seats on the terrace are spectacular; although they won't guarantee them, make your request with your reservation.

And don't just leap in a cab and flee after dinner. Follow the river esplanade to the foot of the deliciously eccentric Victorian creation that is Tower Bridge, walk across, and hop on the number 15 bus on the other side. For 80 pence, it will return you to central London via a most spectacular (and totally unofficial), tour of London by Night – past the Tower of London, Monument (to the Great Fire), St. Paul's Cathedral, Fleet Street, the Strand, the law courts, through Trafalgar Square and up Pall Mall to Piccadilly Circus. Grab front row seats upstairs and you can practically hear the overture begin as you pull away and architectural treasure after treasure slips past in a spotlit dazzle. Pure magic.

70. THE FIRE STATION *(Mediterranean, inexpensive to moderate), 150 Waterloo Road, London SE1. Tel: 0171 620 2226. Open Monday to Saturday, noon to 11pm. Major credit cards. Waterloo tube.*

There are three reasons you might find yourself in the Waterloo area: Waterloo Station (terminal for the new Eurostar train to Paris), the Old Vic theater across the road, and the South Bank arts complex very nearby. Otherwise, the area isn't particularly savory, nor particularly convenient, but thanks to the Fire Station (and the newer Bar Central across the road), at least once you get there you can have a decent meal and a pint of beer at a congenial bar.

This converted (you guessed it) fire station is generally filled with a noisy and animated under-40 crowd which turns into an intolerably noisy and smoky crowd around 6pm on weeknights. But it's all in good fun, and though you'll probably spend a lot of time shouting over the din, it's quieter at lunchtime and positively civilized on weekends. The cavernous space has been filled with an eccentric collection of mismatched pine tables and chairs; the menu (which changes daily and sometimes hourly) is a kind of South-of-the-River-Nouvelle-British-Mediterranean-Melange: bruschetta, grilled vegetables, mussels with leeks, goat cheese and artichoke heart salad (£4-7) to start or for a light meal; lamb shank, beef and Guinness stew or broiled fish (£6-9) for something more substantial.

For dessert you might find apple tart Normandie with clotted cream – if you do, order it instantly. Pints come from the bar in front; wine is also available. If you see yourself as more the sedate civilized sort of person, cross the street, and try Bar Central.

71. THE PEOPLE'S PALACE *(modern British, moderate), Royal Festival Hall, South Bank, London SE1. Tel: 0171 928 9999. Daily noon to 3pm and 5:45pm to 11pm. Major credit cards and foreign currency accepted. Waterloo or Embankment tube.*

It takes a bit of hunting to find this restaurant, hidden away on the second floor of the Festival Hall, but once you find it, you won't forget it in a hurry. Which has less to do with the food (though it's good) than the 80 foot glass window that runs the entire length of the restaurant and offers stunning views of the Thames – preferably as twilight falls. The restaurant has a slightly strange air to it, as if it's been built in a walled-off length of lobby, but it's comfortable, hushed and very attractive nonetheless. And the views! Or did we mention them already?

Gary Rhodes (of the Greenhouse) oversees the kitchen, and the menu includes a number of dishes which bear the mark of his modern eclectic British cooking. The menu has a pre- and post-theater feel to it – specialties like grilled skate with lime hollandaise, open peppered beef sandwich with fried eggs and capers, and leek and gruyere flan feature. There are two prix fixe menus at £10.50 (two courses) and £13.50 (three courses); the service is very friendly and attentive; the desserts are simple and delicious (cappuccino brulee, pear apricot, prune and almond tart); and those views! Dinner for two with wine and service runs about £30 per person (a la carte); less for the fixed price meals.

72. TATE GALLERY RESTAURANT *(British, moderate to expensive), in the Tate Gallery, Millbank, London SW2P 4RG. Tel: 0171 887 8877. Monday to Saturday noon to 3pm. Major credit cards. Reservations suggested. Pimlico tube.*

You've been tramping around London for days now, devouring art, history and the occasional ham and tomato sandwich. It's obviously time for a bottle of wine and a good old-fashioned two hour lunch ... followed by a little more culture, preferably only a short stagger away. Well this is your lucky day. In the basement of the Tate Gallery lurks a hidden gem of a restaurant serving good modern British cuisine in hushed attractive surroundings. The first thing you'll notice are the very pretty Rex Whistler murals on every wall – aptly titled The Expedition on Pursuit of Rare Meats. The meats on our particular expedition ranged from a smoked venison salad to roast beef sirloin with Yorkshire pudding. For those less inclined to the hunt, there's skate with capers and black butter, roast Greshingham Duck with spiced apricots, smoked halibut and grilled fillet of pork with caramelised apple and calvados.

If it all sounds a bit heavy for lunch, fear not. There are lighter offerings (like pasta, seafood crepes or an omelette), and the chef resists ye olde British tradition of cooking it to death and piling it high. In fact the food is remarkably good and the atmosphere remarkably pleasant. Which may account for the fact that the regular clientele is reputed to include senior ranking spies from the huge new MI5 (British Intelligence) building just across the river and MPs who've wandered down the Embankment from the Houses of Parliament.

Personally, we were more encouraged by the number of well-heeled French and Italian tourists in fur coats, assuming that they cared more about the food. In any case, you can sneak in for an omelette, a glass of wine and a lot of great ambience for under £10, or go the whole hog with three courses, wine and dessert (all of the good, very English desserts come with a complimentary glass of champagne) and spend up to £30 each. Rather depends whether you want to save room for the Turners.

CULINARY STARS

There are a number of restaurants in and around London — most with Michelin stars and/or celebrity chefs – expensive enough to make your head spin. If you're a serious gourmet, and unworried by prices that can soar upward of £100 per person, read on.

73. AUBERGINE, *11 Park Walk, London SW10. Tel: 0171 352 3449.* Poor Aubergine has only one star, but at this writing it's booked weeks, if not months in advance. The £19.50 fixed price lunch is highly recommended (and still works out to well over £40 per person).

74. BIBENDUM, *Michelin House, 81 Fulham Road, London SW3. Tel: 0171 581 5817.* The best wine list in town and the trendiest dining room. Don't get carried away and you might escape for £75 a head. If that seems steep, opt for the small, attractive oyster bar downstairs.

75. CHEZ NICO AT NINETY, *90 Park Lane, London W1. Tel: 0171 409 1290.* The number refers to the address, not the chef's age. Chez Nico appeared on the coveted Michelin three star list for the first time this year.

76. THE RESTAURANT, *Hyde Park Hotel; Knightsbridge, SW1. Tel: 0171 259 5380.* The young, handsome Marco Pierre White has been known to physically attack insufficiently appreciative diners. His three Michelin stars justify the means.

77. LA TANTE CLAIRE, *68-69 Royal Hospital Road, London SW3. Tel: 0171 352 6045.* Very conservative, beautiful, elegant — and famous for its £25 fixed price lunch. Michelin three star.

And if you're willing to leave London:

LE MANOIR AUX QUAT'SAISONS, *Church Road, Great Milton, Oxfordshire OX44 7PD. Tel: 0184 427 8881.* Raymond Blanc is the superstar chef of this very well-known restaurant about an hour's drive from London. Very pretty, very expensive.

10. SEEING THE SIGHTS

We start off with the major museums and monuments that should be included on every visitor's list ... even if it takes a few trips. You'll also find plenty of other attractions in this chapter, including famous homes and churches, art galleries, zoos and other entertaining diversions, the Houses of Parliament, Buckingham Palace, and some of the most beuaiful parks and gardensin the world.

THE MUST-SEES

THE BRITISH MUSEUM

Great Russell Street, London WC1. Tel: 0171 636 1555 (recorded information 0171 580 1788). Monday to Saturday 10am to 5pm, Sunday 2:30pm-6pm. Free. Tottenham Court Road tube.

Thirteen and a half acres of antiquities, four million objects, ten million books, 1200 staff. Sounds kind of overwhelming, doesn't it? So maybe you could get away with just nipping in for ten minutes or so, or even skipping the British Museum altogether, after all, antiquities can be really dull.

Don't even think about it.

Aside from being one of the world's greatest museums, the British Museum happens to be one of the world's nicest. Meticulous intelligence and great passion (not to mention plenty of grand larceny) have gone into choosing and assembling this extraordinary collection, and it shows, even in so-called secondary matters like the floor plan and the labelling of exhibitions. Every exhibit is marked so interestingly and so well, you won't succumb to the museum daze that comes from hours of too many undifferentiated artifacts.

And anyway, you'll have to tell your friends you've seen the Parthenon friezes, or as they're commonly known, the **Elgin marbles** (try to imagine them as they originally were, vividly painted with a brilliant blue background, the horses in bridles and saddles of gold). Don't miss the pediment sculptures at each end of the giant room; the roughly triangular arrangement of figures on the right hand end illustrate the birth of Athena from Zeus' head. Although this is probably the museum's most famous acquisition, it isn't necessarily its best – so move on, even bigger treats await you.

Backtrack to **room 17**, where you'll find a series of indescribably beautiful **Assyrian reliefs** representing various stages of the king's lion and wild horse hunts. You'd have to have a heart of stone to remain unmoved by these magnificently rendered lions, pierced through with arrows, twisted and writhing and vomiting blood; the exquisite grace of the wild horses; the determined violence of the hunters. The stories can be read almost like comic strips – the king on his horse, attacked by lions and achieving triumph in the end (of course). In another frieze, captured lions emerge from cages into an arena – it wasn't always convenient for the king to ride far afield in search of beasts to kill. These friezes date from the 7th century BC. Not much in the intervening 2600 years has managed to eclipse them.

From there, head for the **Rosetta Stone**. It's only when you see for yourself the juxtaposition of identical Greek and Hieroglyphic texts that you begin to appreciate the enormity of its importance in cracking the Egyptian code.

While you're on the ground floor, make your next stop the **manuscripts**. You'll find them just to the right of the main entrance – you'll also find them utterly irresistible. Look for the manuscript of James Joyce's *Finnegans Wake*, with everything (yes, every line) crossed out in red. Dickens' handwritten draft of *Nicholas Nickelby* is nearby, as is a handwritten *Alice's Adventures Underground*, with Lewis Carroll's own drawings. Original manuscripts of the Beatles' *Help* and *I Wanna Hold Your Hand* are there, with the line "and please, say to me you'll let me hold your thing." We don't remember the song going quite that way, but perhaps memory fails us.

What else? Handel's *Messiah*, a letter from Henry VIII to Oliver Cromwell, the **Magna Carta** (1215), manuscripts from Keats, Shelley, Marvel, Donne and Milton; 15th century editions of *Sir Gawain* and Chaucer's *Canterbury Tales*; a map of Britain circa 1215, showing castles as the only landmarks, and a 16th century letter from then-Princess Elizabeth (later Queen Elizabeth I) to her brother Edward VI (who, dying, had refused her an audience) that starts: "Like a shipman in stormy wether pluks downe the sailes, so did I, most noble Kinge, pluk downe the hie sails of my joy...." History comes alive in that sentence with an almost stunning poignancy.

Of course there's also a wonderful selection of bibles (including the famed **Gutenberg Bible** of 1455), Shakespeare's first folio, and on and on and on. Give yourself enough time here, it's not an easy place from which to tear yourself away.

Next stop? Try the **mummies**. You probably haven't been to see them in years, and may have forgotten how great they are. There's also an extraordinary collection of mummified animals – a bull, an ape, a gazelle, a crocodile, a duck, two falcons and a fish. Companions in the afterlife, no doubt, but a motley crew nonetheless. Accompanying x-rays reveal all sorts of strange contents and treasures.

On the same floor, don't miss the bizarre and discomfiting **Lindow man** in his dual incarnation as hologram and eerily preserved corpse.

If you're still going strong, try **room 68** with its collection of small Roman bronzes, including a wonderfully frumpy Aphrodite with big hips and a sad face, and Mercury as a charmingly odd child. Or **room 56**, early Mesopotamian sculpture, with its Picasso-esque copper bull dated an incredible 2500 BC. Or the huge laughing Ming Dynasty monk in the Oriental galleries. Or the Aztec skull mask of turquoise mosaic in the new Mexican gallery. The recently installed Japanese galleries on the top floor are softly lit, uncrowded and peaceful for solitude-seekers. And if we've failed to mention the Greeks and the world's largest collection of Egyptian antiquities (outside Egypt) it's merely because that's probably what you'd expected to find here.

Had enough? There's a pleasant, child-friendly cafe serving sandwiches and teas on the ground floor past the bookshop, and a restaurant with reasonably priced (£5-7) hot meals and salads just above. There are also a number of decent sandwich bars on Museum Street, hot food available at the Museum pub across the street, and **Wagamama** – a terrific cheap Japanese noodle bar nearby (see *Where to Eat*).

THE NATIONAL GALLERY

Trafalgar Square, London WC2N 5BN. Tel: 0171 839 3321, recorded information, 0171 839 3526. Open Daily 10am to 6 pm, Sunday, 2pm to 6pm. Free. Charing Cross tube.

The National Gallery, squatting majestically on the entire north side of Trafalgar Square, is quite simply one of the finest museums of (predominantly) European art in the world, so perhaps the most compelling thing we can say about it is: go.

The National Gallery's collection spans the history of art from the 12th to the 20th Century, hitting every high-point in between, and remaining remarkably uncluttered in the process. If you haven't visited London recently, the new **Sainsbury Wing** (designed by Robert Venturi and opened in 1990) offers fresh delights – quite literally fresh, in fact, due to the blazing lights and the fashion for scrubbing every trace of varnish (and occasionally paint as well) off old paintings. If you're used to peering at dark old masters, you may suffer an eerie feeling that these paintings (dating from about 1200 to 1500) are as new as the building itself.

Even with the addition of the Sainsbury Wing – named for the family of grocery store magnates who bankrolled it – one of the best things about the National Gallery is its size: it's not too big. Unlike the Met or the Louvre, this comprehensive collection entrances and stimulates without leaving you limping, panting, exhausted and dazed. The other best thing about it is that it's free. So you can nip in the front entrance, sigh over a couple of Sargents, Titians, or Cezannes, and slip out the back exit to Chinatown and Soho on your way to lunch. Art as aperitif – what could be finer?

Are any of you still dragging your feet? If so, here are one or two lures. A roomful of Rubens. Nearly a roomful of Rembrandts, including four stunning portraits – of his wife, his mistress Hendrickje Stoffels (heart-breakingly beautiful) and two of himself, at age 34 and age 63. If you ever had questions about youth and age, man and woman, love, marriage, wisdom, beauty and sadness, the answers are in these portraits. In another room, Van Dyck's massive equestrian portrait of Charles I competes with a 1663 Rembrandt equestrian portrait across the room. There is an unreasonable number of wonderful Titians, including the tragic *Death of Acteon* (having chanced on the goddess Diana bathing, Acteon is trans-formed into a stag and devoured by his own hounds) and the wonderfully bonkers *Bacchus and Ariadne*. There are two unfinished Michelangelo paintings.

A whole roomful of Raphaels, with the breathtaking crucifixion as a centerpiece. The *Rokeby Venus* (named for its previous home in Rokeby Hall, Yorkshire), Velasquez's only surviving female nude and the inspira-tion for Goya's majas in the Prado. Holbein's *Ambassadors*. Constable's *The Hay Wain* (probably the most famous English painting in history). Van Eyk's *Arnolfini Wedding* (remember the so-called pregnant bride?). Vermeer's *Woman Standing at a Virginal*. Piero della Francesca's eerie *Baptism of Christ* (ethereally calm with an almost palpable undertone of anxiety). And the perfect and perfectly moving Leonardo cartoon, Virgin and Child with St. John the Baptist and Saint Anne, immaculately displayed behind bullet-proof glass in its own small room.

For lovers of impressionism and post-impressionism the gallery's impressive collection (one of four Van Gogh *Sunflowers*, Degas' *After the Bath*, Seurat's pre-pointilist *Bathers*) has been fleshed out by paintings and drawings from the **Berggruen collection** (including a large Monet *Waterlilies* and Picasso's *Child With A Dove*), on loan to the National for 15 years.

The **Brasserie** restaurant on the first floor of the Sainsbury wing deserves special mention for its Italian-style coffee bar and reasonably priced meals in the kind of stylish atmosphere you'd expect to find in

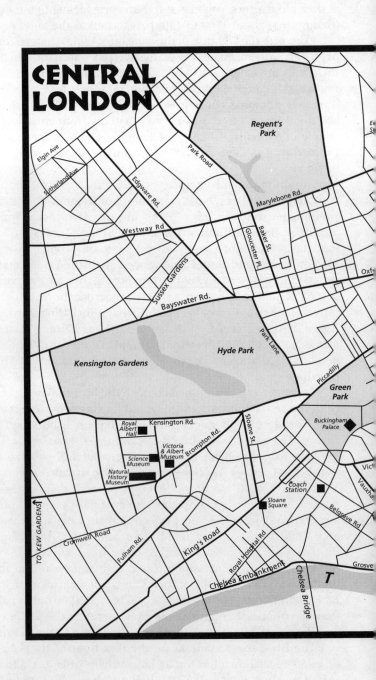

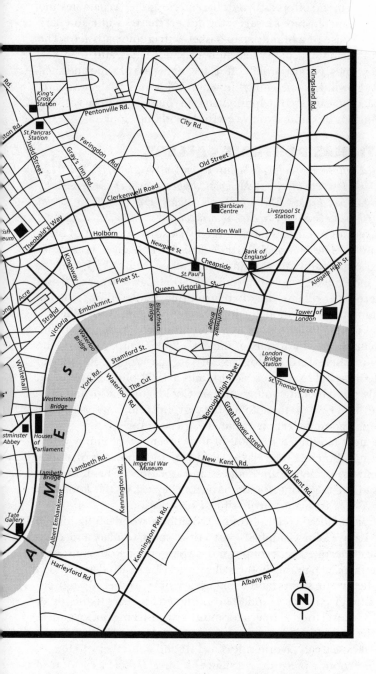

Soho. The lunch menu offers assorted charcuterie, grilled vegetables and hot dishes like Lincolnshire sausages; for dessert there's white and dark chocolate dacquoise or a brandy snap basket with creme patissiere. The all-day menu includes a good selection of sandwiches and teacakes, pastries and scones. Or just order coffee, tea, or a glass of wine and sit at one of the huge windows watching the action below in Trafalgar Square. It's a great place to eat lunch at 4pm, when everyone else in town is giving you that "lunch at this hour? you've got to be kidding" look.

THE NATIONAL PORTRAIT GALLERY

St. Martin's Place (by Trafalgar Square), London WC2H OHE. Tel: 0171 306 0055. Daily 10am to 6pm, Sunday noon to 6pm. Closed December 24, 25, 26, January 1, Good Friday, May Day bank holiday. Free (except for special exhibitions). Charing Cross or Leicester Square tube.

There are a lot of famous faces in English history and most of them can be found in The National Portrait Gallery. This gives visitors an unparalleled opportunity to gaze into the eyes of Henry VIII, wink at Princess Di and exchange mournful looks with D.H. Lawrence. You'll find that your heroes (or villains) are often beautifully rendered by someone at least as famous as the model – John Singer Sargent, Andy Warhol, Holbein and Joshua Reynolds are all well-represented in the collection. Some particularly good portraits of the early 20th Century include the famous George Beresford photograph of Virginia Woolf, a wonderful painting of Churchill by Walter Sickert, and a 1932 photograph of an astonishingly good-looking young Alistair Cook. You'll also find P.G. Wodehouse, the rest of the Bloomsbury group (either as artists or subjects), and a good collection of Punch caricatures.

On the next landing, a roomful of the current royal family offers inadvertent insight: even the relaxed, informal 1980 portrait of Prince Charles seems to prefigure the sadness and isolation of his miserable marriage and life-in-waiting for the crown. The rest of the family, in various degrees of formality, invite similar observations.

On the next floor, you'll encounter Boldini's wonderfully louche portrait of Lady Colin Campbell ("art critic, sportswoman and dilettante") in black decolletage, a couple of so-so Sargents, a Rodin bust, and perhaps our favorite painting in the gallery, a terribly scarred and folded portrait of the Bronte sisters (and their barely visible brother, Brangwen) painted by Brangwen himself and then consigned for years to the top of a cupboard. On level four, a superb roomful of English kings are grouped, painted in the early 16th century on board in the style of Holbein. Look for your Shakespearean favorites: Richard III and a number of Henrys, including the room's piece de resistance, a huge Holbein cartoon of

Henry VIII. Staggering ever upward to level 5, you'll be rewarded with some lovely Reynolds and Gainsboroughs.

Sound great? It is, mostly. Unfortunately, to reach the Sargents, Holbeins, Warhols and Gainsboroughs, you have to plod through about a million and a half truly execrable paintings of literary and historical figures, some of whose names don't ring even the vaguest of bells. If these men and women could speak, they would no doubt have many fascinating stories to tell, but the gallery hasn't helped in the telling by labelling the pictures. As there's no admission charge, and the location is so convenient (right next door to the National Gallery), we find the best way to avoid exhaustion and irritation is to visit in short bursts, taking in a few rooms or half a century at a time.

The National Portrait Gallery has a good gift shop, excellent special exhibitions and an extensive free lecture series (pick up a current list at the information desk).

THE NATURAL HISTORY MUSEUM

Cromwell Road, London SW7 5BD. Tel: 0171 938 9123. Monday to Saturday, 10am to 5:30pm, Sunday 11am to 5:30pm. Closed December 23 to 26. Adults: £5, children (5-17): £2.50. Free, Monday to Friday after 4:30pm and Saturday, Sunday and bank holidays after 5pm. South Kensington tube.

Enter this massive, imposing, Victorian cathedral of natural history and you instantly find yourself nose to nose with an 80 foot, 150 million year old Diplodocus dinosaur – just the first of many big surprises to come. Accompanying the Diplodocus in the grand entrance lobby are large cases of fossils recalling a time when elephants, lions, bears and even the occasional hippopotamus roamed London. These are some of the few elements of the museum to have been left untouched in its recent dramatic overhaul. With its huge banks of video monitors, animatronic dinosaurs and futuristic walkways, the new Natural History Museum does, amazingly, manage to live up to its own press as one of the finest museums of its kind in the world.

The biggest problem you'll encounter at the museum is where to start – but even that problem has been addressed in the form of guides positioned throughout the museum, each trained in detecting a puzzled look at 10 paces. We decided to start, quite sensibly, at the beginning – with the **dinosaurs**. And even without a child for a chaperone, we had a great time. We saw bones, eggs, fossils and models; Japanese-built animatronic Demonychus dinosaurs feeding on a (nearly) dead Tenontosaurus; a nest with 18 eggs and hatching dinosaur babies; and video monitors illustrating a variety of dinosaur gaits (including one with a fabulously casual saunter). Best of all, were the amazing screeches and crunches and other dinosaur-like noises, all of which contributed to the general sense of having been transported back to another world. These high-tech exhibitions have been suspended on futuristic walkways within the old building, leaving the original Victorian splendor unharmed, and often sensitively highlighted. Look for relief portraits of fantastical beasts and plants on the terracotta facings throughout the interior of the building.

The **Ecosystem exhibition** follows the same glamourous high-tech approach as the dinosaurs, again offering beautifully presented information, wonderful sound-effects, and answers to questions like "why are flamingos pink?" and "why are there so many kinds of living things?" The general creativity of the approach pays off – genetics explained via dog breeding proved a lot clearer and more compelling than the peas we studied in school.

There's also a renowned Creepy Crawlies exhibition featuring bugs of all nations, but we went through with our eyes closed, so we will leave you to judge.

As of this writing, the **Earth Sciences exhibition** was still under construction, due to be finished for the fall of 1995. In the meantime, we entered **Human Biology**; a hands-on maze featuring hundreds of cheery high-tech interactive monitors, display cases and do-it-yourself tests. They range from the terrific (an interactive video of a robbery, after which you try to provide details to the police) to the ridiculous (a keep-your-body-alive machine that kept flashing up a "Sorry, you have just died" sign), but all in all, they kept us occupied for well over an hour. We suspect the 6 to 15 year old contingent would have a particularly wonderful time here.

Vestiges of the old Natural History Museum live on in the deserted calm of the mineral gallery (worth a visit for its massive collection of minerals, crystals, precious and semi-precious gemstones and meteorites), and with a few old-fashioned (but still very effective) dioramas of Giraffes and Kudu by a watering hole.

There's a large bookshop and a museum shop; heavy on plastic dinosaurs and trays of minerals.

The modern, tastefully designed restaurant serves lunch from 11:30am to 2:30pm and snacks from 10am to 5pm. You'll find good pastas for about £4, soup at £2.50, a children's menu for under £2 and vegetarian meals. Beer, coffee and wine by the bottle or glass are also available.

SAINT PAUL'S CATHEDRAL

St. Paul's Churchyard, London EC4. TEL: 0171 248 2705. Open daily 8:45am to 4:15pm (cathedral), 10am to 4:15pm (galleries and crypt). Adults: £3 (cathedral only), £5 (cathedral, galleries and crypt). St. Paul's tube.

Your first glimpse of St. Paul's should be from the top of a bus, preferably at night, preferably traveling east along Fleet Street from the

Strand (numbers 11, 15 or 23). Although the new Thameslink station (one of Prince Charles' pet "carbuncles" on the London landscape) obstructs the vista somewhat, St. Paul's still bursts into view in a blaze of spotlit glory, giving you a pretty good idea of how it has dominated the London cityscape for the past three centuries.

Alternately, you might approach it on foot – despite the surrounding office towers built on World War II bomb sites, it's easy to imagine how a humble 17th century parishioner would have felt as he walked along Fleet Street toward this extraordinarily grand Cathedral Church of the Diocese of London. Awed, probably, as we still are today. Towering in front of you, and mysteriously disappearing from view as you reach the portico on the west front, is one of the largest church domes in the world. Yet for all it's magnificence (365 feet to the top of the dome), St. Paul's is not a humbling cathedral. It is a place to worship – the power of god, or if you prefer, the prowess of man – on a human, earthly scale.

ONE OF THE MAGNIFICENT CHAPELS INSIDE ST. PAUL'S

There can be no doubt that St. Paul's is a work of genius, and the genius is **Christopher Wren**. The Great Fire of London (1666) burnt most of London to the ground (including the original St. Paul's cathedral – huge, wooden, and Gothic), giving Wren a blank check with which to rebuild. So seriously did he take this sacred 35-year task, that he purchased and lived in a house across the river in Southwark (still standing and inhabited) in order to keep on eye on the proceedings 24 hours a day. And despite meddling committees, public outcry, and the mandatory revisions of Wren's original plans (see the models in the crypt), the "compromised" design that was finally built gained the immediate affection and admiration of its parish: London.

To enter, walk up the steps on either side of the portico with its six pairs of huge columns supporting four smaller pairs. If you are in relatively good shape, and don't suffer from claustrophobia or vertigo, buy a ticket for both the cathedral and the galleries above. We recommend the recorded tour, but St. Paul's is one place where part of the pleasure is just wandering, so we'll understand if you set out on your own.

Walk to the center of the cathedral, stand under the dome and look up. The segmented arches not only keep the dome aloft, but define the spiritual heart of the building. It's worth a stiff neck to study the beautiful gilded mosaics, which lead the eye up the inside of the dome, past the Whispering Gallery, past the Golden Gallery and onward to heaven. The stairway to heaven (or at least to the Golden Gallery) has 627 steps. But don't attempt the 300 foot climb just yet.

Look at the **choir**. Its richly carved panels and stalls are the work of the celebrated woodcarver to the Royal Court of Charles II, Grinling Gibbons. Beyond the choir is the high altar, its spiral columns reminiscent of Michelangelo's black marble altar at St. Peter's, Rome. This one, however, dates largely from the late 1940s; it was rebuilt based on Wren's original drawings after suffering bomb damage during the war.

Which brings us to one of the reasons St. Paul's is so loved by Londoners: its miraculous survival during the Blitz. Surrounded by hundreds of fires and dramatically backlit by searchlight beams, the dome's silhouette became a symbol of dignified defiance against the Germans. Night after night it survived brutal bombing raids that virtually decimated the surrounding city, with only a minimum of damage. A target of that size? To this day, no one knows by what miracle it survived (though perhaps the Germans had the same orders as the allies – to avoid cathedrals if at all possible). St. Paul's played it's part in the war effort as well; from the top of the dome, aircraft spotters gave warning of impending attack.

Look for the monument to **Wellington**. It's massive, about 35 feet high, but then the Iron Duke was a popular man, and not just for his boots:

it was he who defeated Napoleon at Waterloo. His tomb is downstairs in the crypt, as is that of **Horatio Nelson**. Nelson, who defeated Napoleon's admirals, also has a memorial, near the entrance to the crypt. It's much smaller than Wellington's, but then Wellington doesn't have a column in Trafalgar Square. You'll probably have noticed by now that St. Paul's puts paid to the idea that old soldiers never die. For it is here that so many of them rest, and so many others are remembered. Britain's artists and kings are buried in Westminster Abbey, its soldiers lie here.

And now, to the **crypt**. Perhaps the most important memorial here is to Christopher Wren himself; he lies beneath his own work of art with a simple, eloquent Latin inscription translated as: "If you seek his monument, look around you." Although the majority of the tombs and memorials will mean little to the casual visitor, there are many small discoveries to be made. The memorial to "The Special Correspondents Who Fell in the Soudan, 1883-85" is probably the first memorial to journalist war dead; in addition, it boasts exceptionally beautiful typography. There is a monument to **John Donne**, the great English poet and Dean of (the earlier) St. Paul's, who died in 1631. Unlike his wooden cathedral with its 555 foot spire, Donne's life-like, shrouded monument survived the Great Fire.

There are monuments to **Florence Nightingale**, **Alexander Fleming** (discoverer of penicillin) and **Edwin Lutyens**, architect. But the majority of the dead remembered in this crypt are the soldiers from the myriad wars fought in the name of the British Empire – most recently in 1984, when 250 young British soldiers died defending the 15,400 inhabitants of the Falkland Islands.

In a simple glass cabinet, you will find the felt cap belonging to an anonymous 17th century workman. It was discovered in the roof space in 1928, and is a tangible reminder that this massive feat of masonry was carved and erected by men using nothing but handtools, rope and wood. No steam power, or gas or electric light, no metal scaffolding or pneumatic drills or tower cranes. Suddenly, the 35 years it took to build seems miraculously quick.

And finally, the galleries. Take a deep breath and climb the steps to the **Whispering Gallery**. When you arrive, you'll notice people standing, faces close to the wall of the dome, listening to messages from their friends on the opposite side. Thanks to the dome's acoustical properties, a whispered message is perfectly audible across the diameter of the dome.

Whisper sweet nothings at a perfect stranger for a minute or two, then head onward and upward to the **Golden Gallery**. When you emerge into daylight, all London is before you. Recover your breath and look out over the panoramic history of two thousand years. From here you can see where Roman troops under Julius Caesar first crossed the Thames.

Eleven hundred years later, William the Conqueror built his fortress in the Tower of London, on the same site. Everything else for miles in each direction – churches, hospitals, houses and roads – is testament to what happened next. The rest, as they say, is history.

After all this, you might just feel like a beer. Walk back up Fleet Street and keep a lookout for the **Punch Tavern** and the **Old Bell**, each with its claims on the distant past. Both are dark and woody and offer real ale. Further along on the other side of Fleet Street, is **Ye Olde Cheshire Cheese** – famed as a journalist's hangout since Dr. Johnson's day.

THE SCIENCE MUSEUM

Exhibition Road, London SW7 2DD. Tel: 0171 938 8008. Monday to Saturday 10am to 6pm, Sunday 11am to 6pm. Adults: £5; children £2.60; 4:30-6pm, free. Closed Christmas day. South Kensington tube.

After a visit to The Natural History Museum next door, The Science Museum – sans special effects and starship lighting effects – might at first seem a little tame. It's remarkably child-friendly and loaded with hidden treasures, however, so don't be tempted to give it short shrift.

If the grown-ups outnumber the minors, head straight through the somewhat disappointing **Exploration of Space exhibition** (the Brits aren't really serious about space, after all), leaving the kids to gawp at the genuine Apollo 10 space capsule if need be, and continue on to **Land Transport**. The trains! And the cars! And the buses, bicycles, and motorcycles! The centerpiece of the room is a massive, genuine 1923 Express locomotive that just glows with the pride of industrial Britain. A 1910 horsedrawn coal trolley still smells so strongly of coal it's hard to imagine it's been out of use for more than half a century, and you can almost imagine a smart team of bays hitched to the elegant yellow phaeton carriage of 1760. Even those more or less indifferent to cars (us) will want to linger over the lovely 1909 Silver Ghost Rolls Royce, the 1924 Bentley, and an 1897 Daimler. Great stuff indeed.

Take the space-age elevator up to the first floor for plastics, agriculture, telecommunications and **The Launch Pad**. If you have younger kids, this place is hands-on heaven. In a large room filled with school groups and happy shrieking, kids can try computerized finger painting, shake hands with their own hologram, experiment with rising bubbles, watch lightning generated in a plastic dome, demonstrate centrifugal force on a human spinner – and experiment with all sorts of other fantastically entertaining applied principles of science.

Level two offers **Computing Now and Then**; **Ships**; and **Nuclear Physics and Chemistry**, so unless your heart beats faster at the thought, go through at a trot to level three where the wonderful **Flight Gallery** is packed full of early airplanes. The **Flight Lab** offers aspiring pilots lots of hands-on exploration of the principles of flight, and the chance to sit in the cockpit of a plane. And whatever you do, don't miss the **History of Medicine exhibition**, which makes us appreciate even the limited technology offered on **National Health**.

Just beyond is a pretty cafe serving full meals from noon to 3pm, with kid-friendly food like macaroni and cheese and sausage and beans. Children's portions are £2.10; there are reasonably priced sandwiches, hot meals and cakes for grown-ups, and cream teas from 3pm onwards. A new 180 seat cafe is due to open in late 1995.

The shop, by the way, is terrific, crammed with good quality scientific games, toys, kits and puzzles. The equally good bookshop is a branch of Dillons, and full of science and science-related reading. Access to the museum shop can be had without paying admission.

THE TATE GALLERY

Millbank, London SW1P 4RG. Tel: 0171 887 8752. Monday to Saturday 10am to 5:30pm; Sunday 2pm to 5:50pm (last admission 5:15pm). Admission free except special exhibitions. Pimlico tube or 88, 77a, C10 buses.

Although mainly known as London's modern art museum, the Tate Gallery is actually the keeper of the flame of British art from the 16th century to the present day. Under the superb, creative curatorship of Nicholas Serota, it accomplishes this gargantuan task with a kind of joie de vivre that would horrify most curators. For one thing, Serota refuses to let the museum turn into, well, a museum. Every autumn heralds a fresh rehang of the collection which pulls paintings out of storage, rethinks juxtapositions, and completely refashions the central sculpture hall. This active intellect operating behind the scenes results in a museum that is nothing short of thrilling.

Because of the frequent rehangs, there's no point in suggesting a particular route. But keep an eye out for some of the Tate's more magnificent highlights. Picasso's *Three Dancers*. John Singer Sargent's paintings of Ena and Betty Wertheimer in red velvet and white damask, and the misses Hunter dressed in black and white to match their dog, Crack (named in a more innocent time). The strange and intriguing Tudor painting of the Cholmondeley ladies – identical twin sisters, each with a baby identical in every detail except eye color. Gainsborough's exuberant portrait of ballerina Giovanna Baccelli in costume (you'll recognize it). A roomful of Constable landscapes. Monet's *Poplars on the Epte*. Stubb's loving portrait of two foxhounds. David Hockney's *Bigger Splash* from 1967. Carl Andre's *14 Magnesium Squares* (don't be shy, you're supposed to walk on it). Warhol's *Marilyn*. Some glorious late Rothkos. And, as they say in the shopping mall biz, much much more.

Take some time to look at the English paintings that never make it to America – the shamelessly sentimental Victorian paintings of which Frederic Lord Leighton is king and the now out-of-fashion Pre-Raphaelites, one of which, when exhibited at the Royal Academy in 1852, was deemed "exceptionable, simply on the score of the absurdity of the situation."

And of course the Turners. Enter the **Clore Gallery** (entrance around the back of the gift shop), and you enter a room of such luminous beauty it will literally take your breath away (though on a really crowded day, your first impression will be of people standing in front of paintings, so in the height of the season get there early). As you walk through the gallery, don't miss the room dedicated solely to Turner's Canalletti paintings and oil sketches of Venice (based on Canalletto), or the less familiar classical subjects: Leander delivered by Hero to the stormy sea; Apollo with a massive gory python.

If you've seen enough, and have worked up an appetite, you have two choices. Downstairs there's a cafe with cakes, croissants, sandwiches, salads and savory pies, beer, wine, coffee and tea, all at reasonable prices. Across from the cafe, you'll find a hidden gem, **The Tate Gallery Restaurant**: a good, peaceful, rather elegant dining room, beautifully decorated with 1926 Rex Whistler murals (see *Where to Eat – it's open Monday to Saturday, noon to 3pm (reservations 0171 887 8877)* and features an updated British menu that changes seasonally.

TOWER OF LONDON

Tower Hill, London EC3N 4AB. Tel: 0171 709 0765. Open daily 9am to 6pm (March to October), 9am to 5pm (November to February); Sunday, 10am to 5pm (year round). Jewel House closed during January or February for cleaning; phone before you visit. Adults: £8.30, children £5.50. Tower Hill tube.

The Tower of London (officially known as **Her Majesty's Royal Palace and Fortress of the Tower of London**) has served as a palace, fortress, armory, treasury and menagerie, but is probably best known as a prison. Anne Boleyn, Sir Walter Raleigh, Sir Thomas More, Lady Jane Gray, Catherine Howard and the two little princes (Edward V and the Duke of York) are among the thousands who spent their final miserable days locked in the tower. A lesser known fact is that spies and traitors were executed here throughout World Wars I and II.

For your visit, we suggest you get up early (to beat the crowds), put on a pair of comfortable shoes, pay your entrance fee and join one of the free guided tours led by the **yeoman warders** – honorary members of the Queen's bodyguard of the Yeomen of the Guard (**Beefeaters** to you). Established in service by Henry VIII and nicknamed (some say) after the main ingredient of their rations – or is it a French corruption of "buffetieres"? depends who you ask – each of these 42 men has served as

WITHIN THE GROUNDS OF THE TOWER OF LONDON

a non-commissioned officer in the British army for a minimum 22 years. They live with their families in apartments within the tower walls, know the history of the tower inside out, and just in case you were wondering, those distinctive uniforms date from 1858. Most importantly, they make superb tour guides, giving abundant texture to history with their gleefully gory accounts of political in-fighting, illicit liaisons (and the resulting bastards), torture and beheadings. The kids will love it.

A bit of history to start you off: Two months after the Battle of Hastings, **William the Conqueror** was crowned king and began erecting fortifications, as kings were wont to do. Thus, the Tower began life in 1066 as a mud and wood structure at the southeast corner of the Roman city walls. Construction of the tower itself began in 1078 and was finished by his son William II. It stands 90 feet tall with 15 foot thick walls at the bottom. As the rest of the castle grew up around the tower, the entire fortress became known as the Tower of London and the great central tower was dubbed the White Tower.

In the 13th century, **Henry III** spent lavishly to improve the Tower as a royal residence. As a palace amusement, he established a **royal menagerie**, begun with a gift of leopards from Frederick of Hohenstaufen in Germany. The collection grew in 1255 with an elephant from Louis IX of

France, and a polar bear from the king of Norway (pause for an instant, as we did, and consider the logistics of transporting leopards, elephants and polar bears thousands of miles in the dark ages....) This menagerie eventually formed the nucleus of today's London Zoo.

Between 1275 and 1285, **Edward I** completed the medieval castle, excavated a 120 foot moat, built a new curtain wall around the moat and along the riverfront (containing new royal apartments) and constructed the drawbridge that's still in use today. At this time, the Tower contained the royal mint, treasury and the main arsenal for the royal army and fleet. (In 1843, after several outbreaks of cholera in the Tower, the moat was drained and filled; today Tower residents make use of the tennis court, playground and bowling green built thereon.

It was during the reign of Henry VIII that the Tower became known chiefly as a prison of state. The King's enemies, religious dissidents, traitors and petty thieves were all held captive, awaiting execution; they were soon joined by a legion of ex-wives. Then Whitehall took over as the preferred royal residence, and the Tower's defenses were allowed to decay, leaving only the **Royal Mint** and the **arsenal**. But following the restoration of the monarchy in 1660 and the return of **Charles II**, a permanent garrison was housed in the Tower, the arsenal was expanded, guns were set in place along the walls, and coronation regalia, historic armor and arms were displayed to impress the first sightseers.

When the Duke of Wellington became Constable in 1826, he believed England to be on the brink of revolution and set out to restore the Tower's military importance. The Royal Mint was moved out, the menagerie closed, and public records removed. A fire in 1841 destroyed the **Grand Storehouse**, ending the Tower's 500 year history as an arsenal. In its place, the **Waterloo Block** with accommodation for a thousand men was built in neo-Gothic style, complete with battlements and gargoyles. Since 1967, the Crown Jewels have been housed in this building.

By 1852, the fear of revolution gone, the Tower was no longer seen as having military significance. Queen Victoria and Prince Albert moved to convert the Tower to a national monument. Medieval towers were restored or recreated and by 1901, half a million people were visiting the Tower each year, drawn by its dark romantic and macabre appeal.

And so to the **Crown Jewels**, the most popular attraction within the Tower grounds, as anyone who has waited in line for hours will have noticed. A newly opened presentation area features three screens with film footage from the 1953 coronation of Queen Elizabeth II, with Prince Charles as a child sweetly waving from the royal box. And finally, the jewels, glittering away like, well, like the massive diamonds they are. The wealth displayed in these super-high-security cases is nothing short of mind-boggling, though the wealth of history is somewhat limited by the fact that nearly all the crown jewels were melted down by Cromwell after the civil war as symbols of the corrupt monarchy, and had to be recreated when the monarchy was restored in 1660. St. Edward's crown, part of which survived Cromwell's attack on all things royal, is thought to be Edward the Confessor's original 11th century crown; it was remade for Charles II and has been used to crown every king of England since.

The **Imperial Crown**, made for Queen Victoria in 1837, holds 3,737 precious stones and 2,800 diamonds, including the astonishing 317 carat **Second Star of Africa**, the **Stuart Diamond**, and the **Black Prince's Ruby**. But that's not all! The **Sceptre With the Cross** was remade in 1910 to hold the **First Star of Africa**, the largest cut diamond in the world weighing 530 carats. Hide your engagement ring, it'll only feel embarrassed. Then there's the exquisite **Koh-i-noor** (mountain of light) **diamond**, a gift to Queen Victoria from the East India Company in 1850 – set in the Queen Mother's crown. And look for the little **"Bun Crown"** made for Queen Victoria who, in later life, suffered from migraines and found the Imperial Crown uncomfortably heavy.

On with the show. Explore the **White Tower** and the **Royal Armories** – a collection of European armor and arms from the Saxons and Vikings to modern times. Hunting, tournament and ceremonial armor shares the stage with fearsome weapons and graceful rapiers. In addition there's armor for a giant, a child, an elephant, and Henry VIII – with its 52 inch girth and (speaking of fearsome weapons) enormous codpiece. According to legend, women of the 17th century stuck pins in that codpiece to bring about conception. Close inspection of the armor reveals that these aren't just glorified tin cans – the finely etched patterns, design and detail were created by master metalsmiths who worked metal the way tailors work fabric.

In the basement there's a collection of instruments of torture that's always crowded with pain enthusiasts; on the second floor, **St. John's Chapel** is the only surviving example of intact Norman architecture in London. The stark symmetry of the chapel inspires spiritual contemplation that huge cathedrals tend to crush; Prince Charles came here to celebrate communion on his twenty-first birthday.

RAVENS ON PARADE

*The huge ravens that strut round the Tower are fed a weekly horseflesh allowance and are the focus of great superstition: legend says that when they leave the Tower it (and England) will fall. Charles II took this threat seriously, and decreed that their wings be clipped and that they should be kept by a **Raven Master** and locked every night in a cage near Wakefield Tower. Which is how they live to this day.*

Near the White Tower is the **Chapel of St. Peter ad Vincula** which became official chapel of the Tower after Henry III's expansion brought it within the fortress' boundaries. It has been fully restored to its Tudor glory and can only be entered as part of the yeoman tours. The beautiful Spanish chestnut wood ceiling and delicate windows house funerary monuments to two of Henry VIII's six wives; Anne Boleyn and Catherine Howard are buried here, along with three saints (including Henry VIII's beloved friend, Sir Thomas More, who would not sanction his divorce). Just outside the Chapel, there is **Tower Green**, part of the old Tower burial ground and "the saddest spot on earth" (Lord Macaulay). It is marked with a granite square showing the location of the scaffold which dispatched Anne Boleyn, Lady Jane Grey, and Catherine Howard.

Pomp and ceremony still play a big role in the daily function of the tower – every day at 11:30am in summer (alternate days in winter) there is a changing of the guard on Tower Green. The **Ceremony of the Keys**, dating back 700 years, is part of the Tower's nightly ritual. At 9:40pm, a sentry is challenged at the gate, followed by identification of the keys and the presenting of arms. It's an ancient, evocative ritual and well worth observing. *Tickets are free, but limited to 70 per night; they can be obtained by writing in advance to the Resident Governor, The Queen's House, Tower of London, London EC3N 4AB.*

And finally, two gift shops supply Tower of London postcards, books, videos, toys, cassettes and chocolate. A snack bar and vendors outside the grounds sell ice cream, sodas, fruit and sandwiches.

THE VICTORIA & ALBERT MUSEUM

Brompton Road, South Kensington, London SW7 2RL. Tel: 0171 938 8500. Open Tuesday to Sunday 10am to 6pm; Monday noon to 5:30pm. Admission £4.50 (suggested donation); children under 12 free. South Kensington tube.

Welcome, as the brochure says, to the world's greatest museum of decorative arts. Take this as a warning as well as a boast. The V&A can truly claim to have something for everyone – art lovers, history buffs, followers of fashion, students of wrought iron – you name it, they seem to have it. And if you're planning to be in London for more than a few days, you might even want to consider visiting twice. To try and see the V&A in one fell swoop is risking certain exhaustion, and perhaps permanent addling of the mind.

The collection is divided into **Art and Design Galleries** and **Materials and Techniques Galleries**. The former tend to be organized by region (Japan, China, India) and the latter by materials (glass, jewelry, porcelain). Huge banners attempt to put order into the massive collection, but the best thing to do is pick up a map at the information desk, and plot out a few things you must see. If you don't have a particular reason to race straight to the 18th century interiors (for example) we have some helpful suggestions regarding the highlights of the highlights.

The first has to be the **cast room**, past the Chinese imperial dragon robes to the right of the main entrance. Walk through room 50 instead of following the hallway; among other treasures, look for a beautiful Bernini sculpture of Neptune and Triton once owned by Joshua Reynolds, and two lovely enamelled terracotta heads of Tiberius and Caligula attributed to Minghetti. At the end, turn left and then right – you can't miss it, as your first thought will probably be, "but I could have sworn Michelangelo's David was in Florence." Well, right you are, this is a plaster copy. A life-size one too. And unlike the one in Italy, the V&A's David has been conveniently placed on a six foot platform, which offers a unique opportunity to view David's finest assets from a most dramatic angle.

If you wonder what copies of David (and all his slave friends) are doing in the V&A, the answer is simple: the 19th century zeal for antiquarian and Renaissance art, combined with the difficulty and expense of travel, inspired casts to be made and returned to the Royal College of Art, then located on the premises of the V&A, for study. The collection has remained intact, and is today the largest cast collection in the world (for what that's worth!) It includes the obvious and reasonably straightforward (Donatello's lovely, louche David is also here) and the ludicrously huge and complex (Trajan's column in massive continuous low relief dating from 113 AD – it must have taken some barmy Victorian years to cast). At best, these rooms will save you a trip to Italy and Northern Europe. At the very least, they provide a delightfully spooky half-hour Best Hits of the Classical and Renaissance Worlds experience.

Return to the front entrance, and this time turn left. Walk past the **Islamic galleries** (stop to gape at the massive 34 foot silk Persian carpets), have a quick turn around the **India galleries** (don't miss the ravishing Rajasthan paintings and 17th and 18th century silk floorspreads and Mughal fabrics), nip into the **Japan gallery** (the 16th to 19th century armour of woven metal and lacquered leather is not to be missed) then turn right into the **Dress gallery**. This is an easy place to lose an entire day. And don't let the men in your entourage slink off to look at boy stuff like guns and swords; this huge exhibition must be seen by all persuasions of gender and fashion.

It covers everything from 17th century gold embroidered velvet shoes (in perfect condition) to an 1815 black and white polka dot men's silk dressing gown to a display of 19th century undergarments to Mary Quant and Biba fashion from the 60s. In between there are treasures too numerous to catalog here – highlights include an English figured silk dress from 1790 with the front cut down so far as to render the wearer virtually topless; corsets of unbelievable construction and size; an English day dress from 1870 made of innumerable yards of fragile white gauze; an 1860 court dress with 10 foot hand-embroidered train; a huge selection of hats through the ages; a collection of 1950s tweed day suits from France (fantastically elegant) and England (spectacularly dowdy); Balmain, Balenciaga and Shiaparelli ball gowns also from the 50s; and a 1993 Christian Lacroix black gold and pink gypsy wedding dress. Not to mention the famous 12 inch platform shoes from which Naomi Campbell took a tumble on a Paris catwalk.

If all this sounds a little trivial, well, it's just not. Nothing gives you a better sense of women's (and men's) place in society than these extraordinary garments and shoes – some constricting, some virtually obscene, flamboyant, elegant, formidable. And the body parts come and go like commuter trains over the centuries: breasts are in, then out, then in again; hip bones appear and disappear; waists are tiny, hats massive, cod pieces and tights are in (or should we say out?), waists disappear. All pretty similar to the average 12 months of contemporary haute couture, come to think of it. The gaggle of 16 year old girls giggling at the silliness of '60s fashion (long before they were born), left us feeling prematurely elderly.

If you can tear yourself away from the clothes, make a quick turn of the musical instruments (up the stairs in the center of the room).

Head back to the museum entrance, and this time walk straight through the **Medieval treasury** to **Europe** (1100 to 1600). Our favorite here is a tiny, exquisite wax study for one of Michelangelo's slave sculptures; amazing to think it survived. Continue around the center courtyard in the Italy halls until you come to the magnificent **Raphael Cartoons** – studies for tapestries.

Upstairs on the first floor you'll find a series of rooms, removed intact from their original buildings – the oak panelled tower room from a 16th century castle, the music room from the 9th Duke of Norfolk's residence of 1756, and an early 18th century drawing room from a rather grand London residence. There's also the massive eight by eight foot Great Bed of Ware from 1590 (mentioned in Shakespeare); an entire corridor of wrought iron through the ages (the massive keys are strangely evocative); stained glass, textiles (including damask linen with scenes of London before the great fire), and the fantastic **Devonshire Hunt Tapestries** (75 feet long and 15 feet high with scenes of otter, boar and bear hunts, falconry and games) dating from the early 1400s.

Do not under any circumstances miss the **jewelry room** – it's tucked away but well worth finding. Passing through a high security turnstile (fatties beware), you find yourself in a series of small rooms crammed full of diamonds as big as the Ritz (and smaller), Colombian gold, massive papal rings, gold crowns, girdles, scarabs, seals, semi-precious rings the size of golf balls, Roman earrings, enamelled boxes and art deco pave diamond watches. There are royal jewels dating from the first century BC to the present day, stones inscribed with magic spells, cameos and the gold whistle Henry VIII gave to Anne Boleyn. Pick up a catalog as you go in; they're not individually labelled.

Continue up to Level C for the **glass gallery**. Even on a gray day it seems flooded with light and sparkles magnificently. The glitter emanates from such treasures as Mycaenean pendants (1550 BC), 17th century wine bottles, and modern glass sculpture. The whole room is dominated by a dramatic green glass staircase.

You'll be relieved to know there is a restaurant, brand new and modern, though lacking the charm of the V&A restaurant you may remember from your last visit. There's alot of blonde wood and an atmosphere of genteel chaos; take our advice and jump the queue waiting for hot food (chicken supreme or roast beef and two veg), pick up a pre-made sandwich on French bread and a cup of tea or a beer and collapse with a newspaper (provided). They also serve salads, quiches and savory pies and tarts, and have an afternoon cream tea for under £5. The restaurant is open noon to 5pm Mondays, 10am to 5pm Tuesday through Sunday. A jazz brunch is served 11am to 3pm on Sundays and includes a full English breakfast priced at £8.

WESTMINSTER ABBEY

Parliament Square, London SW1. Tel: 0171 222 7110. Monday to Friday 9am to 4:45pm (last admission 4pm); Saturday, 9am to 2:45pm (last admission 2pm) and 3:45pm to 5:45pm (last admission 5pm). Open Sunday for services only. Admission: Adults £4, children £1 (adults and children free to nave and cloisters). St. James Park, Victoria or Westminster tube.

Guided Super Tours leave the enquiry desk in the Nave at the following times: April to October, weekdays: 10am, 10:30, 11, 2pm, 2:30, 3 (except Friday). Saturdays: 10am, 11 and 12:30pm. November to March, weekdays: 10am, 11, 2pm and 3 (except Friday). Saturdays: 10am, 11 and 12:30pm.

Historically speaking, this is the place. Just about anyone who's anyone is buried here, and every important chunk of English history is represented. Coronations, burials, kings, queens, poets, musicians, scandals, coups and, oh yes, religion – Westminster Abbey is simply loaded with the stuff. Which makes it one of the most visited sites in Britain and the perfect place to start any trip. A sense of who did what in English history is a big help in deriving pleasure from the Abbey, so even if history isn't your long suit, it's worth doing a bit of prep for your visit. All you need is a bit of guidance to figure out the main cast of characters and how they all fit together, so do some reading, or once you get there rent the tape or take the Super Tour. Aside from detailing some utterly riveting scenes from history, they'll give you the structure to understand Westminster Abbey and provide a start on English history and culture as well.

The history of the Abbey starts in the 8th century, with the first church to stand on this site. In 1065 a Norman church was consecrated on the site by **King Edward the Confessor** (the only English King to become a saint); and finally in 1245, **Henry III** commissioned the current abbey (in honor of King Edward). The construction continued into the 1500s, which explains the sometimes uneasy mix of architectural detail. Imagine the interiors as they would originally have looked, painted in dazzlingly bright colors. The towers, by the way, were an 18th century addition, designed by Wren and Hawksmoor.

The abbey was built attendant to a Catholic Benedictine monastery; the monks were ruthlessly dispersed when Henry VIII, in an attempt to sort out his marital difficulties, dissolved the Catholic church and founded the **Church of England**. After Henry's death (and the premature death of his only son Edward VI), his first daughter, Mary Tudor, restored Catholicism, the monastery, and the monks during her reign as queen, but, as she could produce no heir, this restoration of Catholicism was short-lived. Knowing Elizabeth (her half-sister and next in line to the throne) was a devout Protestant, Mary prayed for a son – and in her mid-forties it seemed her prayers had been answered. Her pregnancy however, turned out to be a stomach tumor and she died 18 months later in 1558. Elizabeth I took the throne, reinstated the Church of England and once again expelled the monks.

The first king to be crowned here was **Edward I** in 1272; the present Queen Elizabeth II was the most recent in 1953. In the intervening 700 or so years, the only monarch not to be crowned here was Edward VIII, who gave up the throne before his coronation took place (for Wallace Simpson, but that's another story). The throne in the center of the altar is where the big event happens.

For those not thoroughly au fait with the structure of the Church of England, it's worth mentioning that Westminster Abbey is an Abbey by virtue of its connection with a monastery (it has no presiding bishop or archbishop, which would make it a cathedral). It is, in addition, a *royal peculiar*, which means that it is presided over by a dean who answers solely to the queen in her capacity as head of the Church of England. There are only a handful of royal peculiars in England (the chapel at Windsor Castle is another).

Once you enter the Abbey, you're faced with a bewildering density of people – all, except the tourists, long dead. We can't begin to do justice to the architecture and this extraordinary jumble of the royal, civil and artistic departed, but we do suggest that you take at least a few minutes to admire the Abbey itself before you get involved in the celebrity hunting. Look up (it's remarkably easy to forget to) and admire its delicate, sweeping gold and white lines; observe the light filtering through the windows. Then set off on your tour. One of the first celebrities you'll encounter (left of the entrance, look for an inscribed two by two foot stone on the floor) is **Ben Jonson**, buried standing up at his own request (so as not to take up too much space) with the somewhat mystifying inscription "O rare Ben Jonson." Continuing along the north aisle you'll need to pay a £3 entrance fee before entering the **Musician's Aisle** where you'll find Vaughn Williams, Elgar and Henry Purcell (organist at the Abbey in the mid 17th century) among others.

The **choir**, on your right, dates only from the 19th century; it is the official chapel of the exclusive Westminster School which is attached to the Abbey. Look for the royal coat of arms indicating the queen's seat; when she is not in attendance, the Dean of Westminster has sole authority to occupy it.

Walk beyond the choir and if you're lucky, you'll get a look at the **Great Pavement**. Usually covered with carpets, this extraordinary 13th century mosaic is only occasionally unveiled to the public. It is thought that the pope donated the money for it to be designed and constructed in the elaborate Roman Cosmati style of 1270. Sadly, the intervening seven hundred years of traffic has taken its toll, and an oddly awkward replacement of the central design hasn't helped either. But it's still an amazing piece of work, and if it's not on view, you can hunt down a representation of it in Holbein's painting *The Ambassadors* at the National Gallery.

Continue past the statuary (look for the statue of **Bobby Peel**, founder of the British police force and after whom London "bobbies" were named) and you'll come to the simple black stone tomb of **Edward I** (he died in 1307), known as "longshanks" due to his great height.

At the rear of the Abbey are the royal chapels – **Henry VII** lies in a large black marble sarcophagus; the chapel housing the tombs of his granddaughters, half-sister queens **Elizabeth I** and **Mary Tudor**, bears an inscription that is both poignant and rich in irony, given their bitter battles over religion: "Partners in rule, here us two sisters sleep in hope of resurrection."

The gorgeous **Henry VII Chapel** has been newly restored, its wonderful vaulted ceiling strengthened and repaired. Built in 1519, the chapel illustrates the glorious height of English Gothic architecture combined with the first rich hints of the Renaissance. The chapel has served the Order of the Bath since 1725; each banner and crest represents one of its knights.

For fans of Shakespeare's (not to mention Laurence Olivier's and Kenneth Brannagh's) Prince Hal, the tomb of **King Henry V** is a holy pilgrimage indeed – over a little bridge to the entrance of the **Chapel of Edward the Confessor**. The effigy's original solid silver head was melted down by Cromwell and not replaced until 1971, but that's merely a detail. Listen for the echoes of Shakespeare's Henry at Agincourt:

And Gentlemen in England now a-bed/Shall think themselves accursed they were not here/And hold their manhoods cheap while any speaks/That fought with us upon Saint Crispin's day.

Henry III dedicated the Abbey to Edward the Confessor, whose tomb (originally covered in elaborate gold mosaic, looted during the Reformation) is considered its holiest spot, imbued with mysterious powers of healing. The recesses in the side of the tomb are for kneeling Catholic pilgrims to pray for cures. Near to Edward's tomb is the dramatic bronze effigy of **Queen Eleanor of Castile**. Her massive funeral procession from Lincoln (where she died) to London was marked at every stop by the construction of an "Eleanor Cross." On the other side of the chapel look for Edward I's coronation chair dating from 1300. Edward stole the chair and the Stone of Scone under its seat from Scotland in 1297; legend says it is mentioned in the book of Genesis.

Continuing on to the south transept, you find yourself in **Poet's Corner**. The great poet **Geoffrey Chaucer** began the tradition: he was buried in the Abbey in 1400 less because of his profession than because he was in service to the king and lived on the Abbey grounds. His grave is marked by an eroded stone monument, which was augmented in 1556 by a much grander tomb. Notwithstanding his large memorial, Shakespeare is in fact buried in Stratford.

Browning, Tennyson, Henry James, Edward Lear, D.H. Lawrence, Trollope, Gerard Manley Hopkins and Edward Lear as well as the Eliots – T.S. and George – Laurence Olivier and Lewis Carroll all have memorials here, though again, not all are actually buried in the Abbey. Byron was not accepted for memorial here until 1969 because he was considered too controversial, and Oscar Wilde (imprisoned for homosexuality) finally gained a place in 1994. Dylan Thomas' very moving inscription reads: *Time held me green and dying though I sang in my chains like the sea*; Charles Dickens' stark stone records only his date of birth and death. Across the way, the grand monument to George Frederick Handel portrays him holding a music scroll printed with an air from the Messiah.

As you leave Poets' Corner, look on the floor for the white marble stone of Old Parr, Thomas Parr, who "lived in the reignes of ten princes" and died aged 152 in 1635.

Head through the lovely **Little Cloister** with its wonderful view of the Houses of Parliament tower, and you come to the **College Garden** (*open Tuesdays and Thursdays, 10am to 6pm*) – an acre oasis of flowers and rare trees which has been continuously cultivated for 900 years. Originally, this garden supplied medicinal herbs to the Abbey's Infirmarer, the medieval version of a general practitioner; a reconstructed garden based on the original is in the process of being planted. Peek through the doorway to the courtyard beyond, for a glimpse of Westminster School students in their black school uniforms.

And even if your strength is flagging, don't miss the superb octagonal **Chapter House**, with its stained glass walls and 14th century frescoes of scenes from the life of St. John the Divine. Parliament met here until 1547; over the years it housed Henry VIII's Great Council and provided a meeting room for kings, feudal lords and knights. Today, the Abbey's monks meet here daily for a reading from the *Book of Martyrs*. The benches around the perimeter seat 80, and the stone and glass octagon produces some rather stunning acoustics. You'll also find the *Golden Book* and the *Book or Remembrance* here, containing the names of every soldier who died in World War I and II; relatives only are allowed to turn the pages.

The **Abbey Museum** is worth a visit for its bizarre collection of royal death masks and wax effigies; the 11th century **Pyx chamber**, once the sacristy of Edward the Confessor's church, then home to the treasury "standard" (the gold and silver coins used for annual coinage testing) now contains the gold and silver Abbey plate. There is a small additional admission charge to the Chapter House, Pyx Chamber and Museum.

A couple of final notes: the **Super Tours** are conducted by the Abbey's **Vergers**, who are extremely knowledgeable about all aspects (history, architecture and legend) of the Abbey. The volunteers around the Abbey, many ex-army, are also wonderfully well-informed and a delightful source of fact and anecdote. If you have a question, ask – they're perfectly patient with even the most extreme cases of historical ignorance.

As a last point, try to visit the Abbey for **evensong**, which is held at 5pm weekdays and 3pm weekends. It's magic.

MORE MUSEUMS & MONUMENTS

London has hundreds of small museums dedicated to subjects as esoteric as the canals and the postage stamp. These are some of our favorites.

THE BANQUETING HOUSE

Whitehall, London SW1A 2ER. Tel: 0171 930 4179. Adults: £3, children: £2. Monday to Saturday 10am to 5pm. Closed Sundays and bank holidays. Charing Cross Tube.

The Banqueting House (diagonally north across Whitehall from Downing Street) is famous for two reasons: its grand classical Renaissance architectural style and its spectacular **Rubens** ceiling. Commissioned by

James I on the site of Henry VIII's palace (a largely unplanned Tudor brick and timber affair), **Inigo Jones'** gleaming stone monument to symmetry and reason was something of a one-building architectural revolution. Previously, state banquets would have been held in temporary timber banqueting halls, each specially (and hastily) constructed for the grand event.

Imagine, then, how Jones' creation must have appeared upon completion in 1621, towering over the crowded, chaotic sprawl of Elizabethan London; playing host to visiting royalty with elaborate dinners and masques featuring grandiose themes like *The Temple of Love* and *The Triumph of Peace*. When Charles I took over the throne, he commissioned the **grand ceiling** from Rubens to celebrate the reign of his father (James I), the unification of England and Scotland, and the divine right of kings – a subject which, in this period of struggle between the monarchy and parliament, eventually led to his execution. Ironically, or perhaps appropriately, the execution took place on a scaffold erected just outside the banqueting house.

For Rubens fans, the majestic ceiling is a must. Sadly, the relatively new (and relatively steep) admission fee is likely to discourage those desiring a quick stop and just a peek at the paintings. What can we say? It's a lovely, peaceful place to stop, sit and contemplate history and art after the hubbub of Westminster Abbey or a long haul round the National Gallery – both of which are a short walk (in opposite directions) away. So stop. You won't regret it.

BEVIS MARKS SYNAGOGUE

Bevis Marks, London EC3. Telephone: 0171 626 1274. Sunday to Wednesday 11:30am to 1pm; Friday 11:30am to 12:30pm. Closed Thursday. Tours for groups of ten or more can be arranged by appointment. Services held on Saturday. Contribution: £1. Aldgate tube.

A pair of wrought-iron gates mark the entrance to the stone courtyard of Britain's oldest synagogue. The cornerstone was laid in 1701 by a congregation that emigrated from Amsterdam in 1656, and a plaque on the corner of Creechurch Lane and Bury Street marks the site of the house first used as a synagogue after the readmission of Jews to England during Cromwell's Commonwealth years. Cromwell believed in the teachings of the Old Testament and wanted to increase the coffers of government, so he allowed Jews to settle in London – 350 years after their expulsion. Permits for building were granted only to Christians, however, and it was a sympathetic Quaker who actually obtained permission to build the synagogue.

The building itself is brick with two huge walls of windows, very much in the classic Christopher Wren style so popular in the post-Great Fire decades. We were welcomed by the caretaker, who paused in the lighting of the synagogue's 160 candles to greet us, and explained that the seven large candelabras represent the seven days of the week; ten candles burn for the ten commandments; and the twelve pillars that support the women's gallery recall the twelve tribes of Israel.

At its peak, the congregation numbered 400, but changing demographics have reduced the residential population of this part of London and attendance has dwindled to thirty, though it is still a popular venue for weddings and bar mitzvahs. In the 1993 IRA bombing of the City, most of the synagogue's glass windows were shattered and the roof actually lifted off – anchored by its huge Dutch brass chandeliers, it then fell neatly back into place.

DISRAELI'S FEUD

*Isaac Disraeli was a respected member of the congregation of the Great Synagogue. When he declined to become a synagogue elder, however, he was fined £40. Instead of paying up, he left the congregation. When it came time for his son's bar mitzvah, he was invited to return for the cherished ceremony only if he paid the fine. As a matter of principle he refused, and in 1817 his son was baptized in a nearby church. Which is how **Benjamin Disraeli**, the great English statesman (twice prime minister) came to describe himself as the "blank page between the Old and the New Testament," and though a Jew, was allowed (twice) to hold the highest public office in the land.*

THE COURTAULD INSTITUTE

Somerset House, The Strand, London WC2. Tel: 0171 873 2526. Monday to Saturday 10am to 6pm, Sunday 2pm to 6pm.

Prints and Drawings Study Room open Tuesday and Thursday afternoons. Adults: £3,; children £1.50. Charing Cross tube.

Remember the wonderful intimacy and superb paintings at The Frick in New York? The (old) Jeu de Paume in Paris? Well, add this to your memories. The extraordinary Courtauld Institute on the Strand will make you forget, for an hour at least, every museum (and possibly every Playboy centerfold) you ever loved.

The museum's setting, in Sir William Chambers' elegant neoclassical building, encourages the peaceful contemplation of Manet's *Bar at the Folies-Bergere* and the lovely sketch of *Dejeuner Sur l'Herbe*, a roomful of Rubens, Van Gogh's *Self-portrait* with bandaged ear, a beautiful series of Tahitian-period Gauguins, Degas' *Woman Drying Herself After the Bath*, Cranach's *Adam and Eve*, and Fra Angelico's simple, lovely *Christ* flanked by six saints – to name but a few. You'll also find 12 pretty Tiepolo oil sketches, a bunch of Monets, Turners, and Cezannes, a beautiful Parmigianino *Virgin and Child* and a wild, ghostly monochrome Bruegel.

Furniture aficionados will find some lovely pieces, including two very grand gilded, painted and carved Italian wedding chests from 1472.

The Institute, founded on Samuel Courtauld's 1913 gift to London University, unites teaching, research and conservation under the same roof (access to the extensive research libraries is free to interested members of the public). The gallery is usually uncrowded, the guards are charming, there's a branch of London's best art bookshop at the entrance and there's even a little studenty cafe in the basement. The Courtauld is only a short walk from Covent Garden and Trafalgar Square. Don't forget to make it.

THE DESIGN MUSEUM

Butler's Wharf, Shad Thames, London SE1 2YD. Tel: 0171 403 6933. Monday to Friday, 11:30am to 6pm; Saturday and Sunday, Noon to 6pm. Adults: £4.50, students and senior citizens, £3.50. Tower Hill tube, then walk over Tower Bridge.

Part of the fun of the Design Museum is getting there – the journey across Tower Bridge affords excellent views of the Thames and the city skyline, not to mention an intimate perspective on the stunningly whimsical Victorian creation that is Tower Bridge. Apparently the misguided American who bought London Bridge in 1971 and transported it back to Arizona mistakenly imagined that he was getting the much prettier bridge down the river ... or so goes the legend. Don't miss the gargoyles as you pass under the bridge's arches. Turn left over the bridge, past the parade of trendy waterfront shops and restaurants that have cropped up over the past few years, and you arrive at a stark white building converted from a former warehouse.

The Design Museum was inspired and funded by the Conran Foundation as a showcase for industrial and domestic design. It's a clean, stark, elegant space in which three floors of permanent exhibits share galleries with temporary shows. The permanent collection offers such treats as the history of telephone design (bet that '60s Swedish upright phone will take you back), cars of the past and future (including the tiny Fiat 500), typewriters, vacuum cleaners, furniture and tea kettles. The permanent exhibition of contemporary chairs bears a series of polite little "You May Sit on this Chair" cards so we tried out the Panton – a curving Danish single-molded fiberglass model that looks like a question mark but feels more like an exclamation. The 1957 Superleggera made of wood and wicker is so light you can lift it with one finger (so we did). Special exhibitions might include advertising design, new technologies and applications of plastic, and the annual design time-capsule.

The ground floor coffee bar serves sandwiches, salads, cakes, tea and coffee and has a terrace overlooking the Thames that's lovely in summer.

For something more elaborate and expensive try the popular **Blue Print Cafe** for lunch or dinner (see *Where to Eat*). The small but selective gift shop offers a smart collection of designer teapots, pen and pencil sets, plates, cards, books and magazines.

DULWICH PICTURE GALLERY

College Road, London SE21. Tel: 0181 693 5254 (recorded information 0181 693 8000). Tuesday to Friday 10am to 5pm, Saturday 11am to 5pm, Sunday 2pm to 5pm. Adults: £2, Children under 16: £1. Free Fridays. Dulwich British Rail station.

Take the train from Victoria or Charing Cross to West Dulwich or from London Bridge to North Dulwich, add a 12 minute walk (through the pretty village if you come in at the north) and you come to England's oldest public art gallery set in the middle of a lovely garden. The building was designed and built in 1814 by Sir John Soane, and if you've been to his home in Bloomsbury, you'll recognize a number of trademark elements – particularly the masterful manipulation of natural light.

Although it has been endlessly burgled (thieves have been known to treat those spectacular skylights as alternative entrances), the collection remains breathtakingly beautiful. Gainsborough's well-known portrait of the Linley family is here, as are some wonderful Hogarths, Tiepolos, Rubens, and Rembrandts. The little Raphael panels alone are worth the trip, and the gallery is justly famous for its beautiful Poussins. It is now owned and run by Dulwich College, a boys' school (founded by 17th century Shakespearean actor Edward Alleyn) whose most famous alumnus is Raymond Chandler.

THE GEFFRYE MUSEUM

Kingsland Road, London E2. Tel: 0171 739 9893. Tuesday to Saturday, 10am to 5pm; Sunday (and bank holidays) 2pm to 5pm. Free. Old Street tube (exit 2, then 15 minute walk or take bus 243).

Can you tell the difference between a Regency and a Tudor table? Ever mistake a Windsor for a Chippendale chair? Don't bother registering for a course in the history of English interior design, have a stroll through the delightfully eccentric Geffrye Museum instead.

The museum occupies a semicircle of small almshouses (built in 1715) in the Shoreditch area of east London, which was once the city's center of furniture-making. It takes its name from Sir Robert Geffrye (1613-1704) who bequeathed his estate for the purchase of the site and the building of charity houses for the poor. The almshouses closed in 1908 and five years later opened as a museum.

A series of English domestic interiors from the 1600s to the 1950s have been recreated from historical research, documents and pictures.

Each house represents a different historical style, so visitors follow a chronological progression as they pass from house to house – from the dark carved oak walls of the **Elizabethans**, past the **Georgians** and **Egyptian revival**, to the stylish clutter of a **Victorian parlor**, and finally, to the syncopated boogy-woogy patterns of the 50s. Period music plays in the background to enhance the mood.

One of the best times to visit the Geffrye is December, when the **Christmas Past exhibition** is in full swing. Each room is decked out in the festive finery of the period – ribbons, flowers, candles, angels, chests laden with sweetmeats, garlands of fresh laurel and bowls of oranges. The innocent, non-commercial radiance of the show could restore the true spirit of Christmas to Scrooge.

At the end of your trip through time, stop for tea in the delightful, cozy cafe. Other facilities include a reference library, gift shop and a walled herb garden open from April to October.

IMPERIAL WAR MUSEUM

Lambeth Road, London SE1 6HZ. Tel: 0171 416 5320 (enquiries), 0171 820 1683 (recorded information). Daily 10am to 6pm. Closed December 24, 25, 26. Adults: £3.90; children (5-16): £1.00; 4:30 to 6pm, free. Excellent access for the disabled throughout. Lambeth North tube.

Expecting piped-in military marches and dusty old tanks? Wrong. This award-winning overhaul of the old Bedlam insane asylum won the respect and admiration of even old bleeding-heart liberals like us – it's simply too good to leave to the male contingent while the women do Harrods. And don't forget to bring the kids. The Imperial War Museum is an exciting, child-friendly environment that intelligently and perhaps miraculously avoids glamorizing its subject.

Visitors enter first into an 80 foot high light-flooded atrium filled with all the impressive gear you'd expect in a war museum: a Spitfire, a Polaris missile, part of the Messerschmitt flown by Rudolf Hess, your usual mix of weapons of destruction. Many of these old war horses are displayed with cutaway glass panels, so you can actually see how cramped and frightening the space inside a tank is and imagine what it was like to sit in the gunner's tail of a Lancaster 1. Don't forget to look through the eyepiece of the 80 foot German mast periscope. It was used on the Western Front in 1917 and now, fully extended into the glass dome ceiling, offers an astonishing view of London.

The real stuff of war, however, unfolds on the lower level where hundreds of interactive exhibitions, videos and exhibition cases take you through the two world wars – and then some. German propaganda films of the invasion of Europe offer a most unexpected perspective, a home movie of London during the Blitz gives the kind of domestic detail you never learn in history class, and a film of the liberation of Belsen concentration camp will break your heart and haunt you for days. We loved the plucky WWII posters with messages like "Carrots Keep You Healthy and Help You See in the Blackout," and "Better Pot-luck Than Humble pie – Don't Waste Food."

The star of the museum is the **Blitz Experience**, a dramatic and (nearly) frightening recreation that begins in a cramped bunker bombarded with sound effects. When you hear the "all clear" siren, you emerge to wander around in the rubble of a simulated bombed-out London neighborhood. The **Trench Experience** and **Operation Jericho** (a simulated flight with the RAF over occupied Europe) are similarly low-tech but remarkable. Upstairs again, there are art galleries, a light, pleasant self-service cafe, and an excellent gift shop.

As we left, we noticed for the first time the numbers of elderly men gazing almost tenderly at one or another of the massive war machines. Like everything else in this museum, these men added to a poignant, complex sense of the technological glory and the human cost of doing battle. As a prominently displayed quote from Plato reminds us: *Only the dead have seen the end of war.*

KENWOOD HOUSE (THE IVEAGH BEQUEST)

Hampstead Lane (on Hampstead Heath), London NW3. House: 0181 348 1286, Restaurant: 0181 341 5384, Concerts information: 0171 973 3472. Open April 1 to September 30, 10am to 6pm daily. October 1 to March 31, 10am to 4pm daily. Closed December 24, 25. Admission free. Hampstead tube and walk across the Heath, or Archway or Golders Green tube.

Approach Kenwood House from across Hampstead Heath, and you'll feel as if you've traveled back in time – and fifty miles out of London. It's easy to imagine this grand house with its great sweeping lawns and landscaped grounds buried deep in some rural 18th century dale – rather than a mere five miles from Piccadilly Circus.

The villa was remodelled in neoclassical style by Robert Adam, perhaps the most revered architect of the day, from a simpler brick structure of 1700. It was purchased to house the exceptionally fine collection of paintings that **Edward Cecil Guinness**, **First Earl of Iveagh**, bequeathed the nation in 1927.

For a collection of this size, you'll find an unusual number of very famous, very lovely paintings. A particularly moving Rembrandt self-portrait and a delicate, luminous Vermeer keep company with excellent works by Van Dyck, Reynolds, Gainsborough, Romney, Turner and Franz Hals. Even if you're not a fine art connoisseur, the sheer quality of the house – with its majestic staircase, massive marble fireplaces and impressive library – is reason enough for a visit.

When you've done your tour, retire to the coach house for lunch and a glass of wine or excellent tea and cakes. The very pretty self-service restaurant extends to tables outdoors in the summer, making it a particularly congenial place to recover from your tramp across the Heath.

LEIGHTON HOUSE MUSEUM & ART GALLERY

12 Holland Park Road, London W14. Tel: 0171 602 3316. Open Monday to Saturday, 11am to 5:30pm. Closed Sunday. High Street Kensington tube.

You might never have heard of **Sir Frederic Leighton** (1830-1896) but you should seriously consider visiting his home. Victorian painter and president of the Royal Academy, Leighton commissioned architect George Aitchison to build him a glorious palace of art. And he did.

The centerpiece of the house is **Arab Hall**, based on the 12th century reception hall of an Italian Moorish palace. A dazzling gilt mosaic frieze depicts exotic birds and mythological scenes; turquoise and white Isnik tiles are decorated with tulips, roses and hyacinths. Leighton brought many of the tiles back from North Africa, where he travelled extensively; others came from his friend Richard Burton, the 19th century explorer whose translation of Arabian Nights scandalized Victorian society. Delicate birds have gold slits across their throats – thus conforming (in a somewhat backhanded manner) to Islamic law banning the representation of living things. The bejewelled dome ceiling rises two stories in a crazy quilt of dazzling color and pattern. There's even a screened balcony for the harem in his Oriental fantasy.

Sensuality gives way to Victorian style in the rest of the house. Tobacco brown walls are covered with paintings, cabinets and display cases of his collections. The library and studio are filled with paintings – Leighton's own work is displayed throughout, and deserves a careful look if you haven't seen it before. Although the Victorian stylization of classical subjects sometimes borders on camp, the paintings themselves are wonderfully rich, grand in scale, and reveal much about 19th century society. Don't miss the large bronze (and exquisitely Victorian) Athlete Struggling with a Python in the garden behind the house. And if you decide you rather like his work, head for the Tate where a large number are (usually) on display.

THE MUSEUM OF LONDON

London Wall, London EC2. Tel: 0171 600 3699; 24-hour information line: 0171 600 0807. Tuesday to Sunday: 10am to 6pm, Sunday noon to 5:30pm. Closed Mondays, except bank holiday Mondays. Adults: £3.50; children: £1.75. Barbican, St Paul's, Moorgate or Bank tube.

Buried in that strange no-man's land somewhere between the outer edges of the huge Barbican complex and the City of London (the financial district), you'll find – if you're lucky – the Museum of London. The easiest way to approach it is from the Barbican tube station, and once you get the hang of the tunnels, roads and overhead walkways, you might even realize that it's just a two minute walk away. Arriving at the modern cement and glass building, you enter a world that intriguingly combines antiquities (the real stuff, don't forget London was once Londinium), costumes, coaches, furniture, relics (a remarkable number of which were dredged out of the Thames), biscuit tins, war posters, an entire jail cell and myriad other monuments to cultural history.

If all that sounds a little confusing, that's because, well, it is. But don't be tempted to write it off, the museum is in fact loaded with treasures and delights, which more than make up for its rather confusing personality. A word of warning however: this is one of those museums in which you can spend most of a day dawdling through the ice age, finding yourself with ten minutes to gallop through the next half a million years. Keep moving, especially at the beginning – an enormous lower floor awaits you.

The exhibitions begin with a very good historical dateline (for those a bit shaky on world history, it helps to be reminded thatElizabeth I and the Italian Renaissance were roughly contemporary). This kicks off a fairly extensive section on the **Ice Age**, clearly designed for school children. Breeze through here to **Roman London**, with a glance or two at the woolly mammoth tooth found near Downing Street (120,000 B.C.), the chopping tool discovered near the Bloomsbury YMCA (350,000 B.C.) and a pair of bone tweezers found in the Thames (1,000 B.C.)

Roman London covers a good number of archaeological finds from around the third century AD, when London was a Roman city. A reconstructed Roman kitchen, dining room and dressing table with elaborate jewelry and cosmetics are highlights. In this section, as in the rest of the museum, copious charts help make sense of all the history as you go. Further on, a wonderful Viking battleaxe (looking straight out of a cartoon) reminds us of the invasion of Guthrum and Halfdon from Norway in the 9th Century. It was found in the Thames, the route 300 Viking ships (and just about everyone else) took to invade London.

Displays that follow cover an extraordinary variety of subjects – from the construction technique (in about 1200) of London Bridge, maps of medieval England (royal roads had to be wide enough for 16 knights to ride abreast), the making of a Tudor House, coins, documents, armor, kitchen utensils, Cromwell's death mask, a 17th century rocking horse.

We were stunned by the original Mortality Broadsheet, listing the names of the London plague deaths between November 1602 and November 1603 (there were 37,000). The Fire of London experience (with narrative from Samuel Pepys' diary) is charmingly low-tech and memorably evocative; exhibitions that follow tell us about the lucrative fire insurance business that spread through London in the year following the disaster.

The **Lord Mayor of London's coach** is on display in all its Florentine gilded and painted glory; it takes on an extra gleam when you realize that it is actually still in use – once a year, on Lord Mayor's Day, it leaves the museum drawn by six horses, whose elaborate harnesses are also here.

THE LORD MAYOR'S COACH, OUT FOR A SPIN ON LORD MAYOR'S DAY

There's also an 1890 Hansom Cab (the forerunner of today's black cabs, and not a million miles away in design), a huge 1928 elevator car, in all its art deco glory, from the early days of Selfridges department store, an Anderson shelter used during the Blitz, an 1836 surgeon's kit consisting mostly of saws and huge chopping knives, and an intact prison cell from Wellclose Square prison, complete with 250 year old graffiti. A reconstructed 19th century high street features a barber shop, bank manager's office, tobacconist, pub and grocer.

Those interested in costume and contemporary dress will love, among the many costumes on display, the 19th century dandy's outfit, wedding dress, and evening gown. For some reason, Charles Dickens' chair is also here, rather than in the Dickens museum. There's a complete Stuart interior with elaborate panelling and marble chimney from Poyle Park, in Surrey. And a nursery garden open during the summer with plantings from the middle ages through to the 20th century.

And if you (or the kids) lose strength halfway through, you can always come back another day. As of this writing, the basic entry ticket is good for three months.

The shop stocks some good accessible history books for children, as well as the usual mix of t-shirts, key rings and carrier bags. There's also a modern museum cafe across the walkway.

MUSEUM OF MANKIND

6 Burlington Gardens, London W1X 2EX. Tel: 0171 323 8043. Monday to Saturday 10am to 5pm; Sunday 2:30pm to 6pm. Free. Piccadilly Circus or Green Park tube.

With an hour or two to spare, you can embark upon one of the nicest journeys of (self) discovery in London – via the ethnographic department of the British Museum, the Museum of Mankind. It celebrates mankind – the indigenous cultures of Africa, Asia, Australia, the Pacific Islands, and the Americas – with a remarkable collection of more than 300,000 artifacts and a series of beautifully-curated special exhibitions. Over and over, the power of the hand is demonstrated by means of carved, etched, woven, and stitched objects designed to heal, protect and wage war; the marriage of creativity and catastrophe illustrated time and again by objects of great human interest and beauty – and great destructive power.

An exhibition of African armor and weapons features a helmet of black ostrich plumes and an elegant string of chimes (more appropriate, in its delicacy, to the Royal enclosure at Ascot than a field of battle); Amazonian shrunken heads are displayed, along with a human skull from Borneo incised with abstract designs and cowrie shell eyes; one of the collection of painted wood masks represents Naga Rassa, the snake demon of Sri Lanka with coiled cobras for ears; soul-piercing eyes bring two wood-carved female figures from the Easter Islands to life. Zulu weapons, Eskimo clothing, a Bedouin tent – all set against the wedding-cake plaster cornices of this high Victorian building, without a trace of that dusty, abandoned quality that so often characterizes museums of this sort.

Cafe Columbia offers sophisticated light lunches (couscous salad with goat's cheese, fresh figs, pasta, good desserts and cappuccino). The gift shop features British Museum ethnographies, artifacts and original artwork. All in all, a wonderfully intimate place to seek out a bit of quiet contemplation amid the manic bustle of London.

MUSEUM OF THE MOVING IMAGE

South Bank, London SE2 8XT. Tel: 0171 401 2636. Daily 10am to 6pm (last admission 5pm), closed December 24-26. Accessible to wheelchair users.

Adults: £5.50, children (5-16): £4.00. Family Ticket (up to 2 adults and 4 children): £16.00, under 5: free. Waterloo or Embankment tube.

It's February, you've come to London with the kids, and it's raining cats and dogs. Have we got the place for you. It's lively, it's fun, it's educational, it's interactive, it's got monitors at kid level, it's all about TV and film, and it's indoors. All of which makes it a good place to spend an otherwise miserable day. In fact, the only problem with this massive technodrome (called MOMI for short) is that it's all just a bit too much. There's a bit too much information crammed onto reading boards. A bit too many slightly-off-the-point-gimmicks. All in all, a bit too much razzle dazzle and far too few good, clear, genuinely engaging displays. But there's also a good time to be had – if you pace yourself.

MOMI has a fascinating subject to explore, and it frequently does so in an exciting, innovative way. Kids, for instance, will love the do-it-yourself animation workshop and the chance to get inside a robot and speak with a synthesized voice simulator (we heard a 5 year old repeating "e-rad-i-cate, ex-term-i-nate" gleefully over and over). We particularly liked the **Russian agitprop train** playing Eisenstein films, the **History of Sound** in the Movies exhibition, a behind the scenes look at a projection booth, and a chance to fly over London like Superman. Be sure and check out the **documentary film room** – the ads done for the postal system in the 30s are smashing.

Though we can't give MOMI an unqualified rave, we do suggest that you give it a try, with or without the kids, on that rainy day in February. Just remember – don't try to read everything, don't linger unless you're really interested, don't get too excited about the television section, you won't have heard of most of the shows, do leave a little energy for the gift shop. And even if you're lifelong movie fanatics (as we are), don't skip the British Museum for this one.

LONDON TRANSPORT MUSEUM

The Piazza, Covent Garden, London WC2. Tel: 0171 379 7961. Disabled Access. Daily 10am to 6pm (last admission 5:15pm). Adults: £4.25; children: £2.50; under 5 free. Covent Garden tube.

If you're entertaining children, or have a thing about old buses and trams, you'll love it here. The museum, set in the southeast corner of the old Covent Garden flower market, is full of light and air and has been beautifully designed to allow maximum appreciation with minimum hassle – including wheelchair access and a non-sexist baby-changing room. The exhibits and accompanying newsreels and videos are straightforward and entertaining and there are a wide variety of interactive exhibits, but the stars of the show are, of course, the vehicles themselves. There, in the flesh, is London's first horse-drawn tram circa 1829 (complete with life-size plastic horse), a whole series of enormous double-decker buses, a couple of Underground cars, a train engine, even a set of turnstiles.

Climb aboard the old tram, take a seat, and an actress dressed in period dress will tell you all about London life and transport in the early part of the 19th century. As you continue through the museum, there are all sorts of treats and surprises. A very realistic exhibition on the building of the tube features an actual cross-section of a tunnel complete with taped sound effects and builders' conversations – we stared unabashedly at one of the incredibly lifelike mannequins, when we suddenly realized he was staring back. Your average young person will adore the 1938 train simulator that lets you sit in the conductor's seat and use the real controls to travel through a computer-simulated tunnel. An automatic "safety system" stops the train if the driver makes a mistake. Newsreel footage from the 40s and 50s accompanies the appropriate buses, and gives a really vivid feel for London life after the war.

The Transport Museum has a pleasant, modern cafe with a variety of decent sandwiches and cakes. The shop is a wonderful place to buy souvenirs and to browse through prints of the superb posters London Transport has commissioned over the years, all of which are for sale. Look especially for the Man Ray poster of the Underground symbol spinning in space with Saturn. It has to be one of the best poster designs of all time, and we bet you'll be the only one on your block to have one.

THE THEATRE MUSEUM

(The National Museum of the Performing Arts) Russell Street, Covent Garden, London WC2. Tel: 0171 836 7891. Tuesday to Sunday, 11am to 7pm. Adults: £3.00, children: £1.50. Covent Garden tube.

You've been in London a week, seen six evening shows and two matinees and you're stuck with a couple hours before your flight out. What better place for a theater fanatic to tarry than this rather charming little branch of the Victoria & Albert Museum?

Set just around the corner from the Covent Garden Market and a stone's throw from the Royal Opera, the Theatre Museum boasts the world's largest collection of British stage paraphernalia – including props, costumes, programs and scripts going back to the 17th century. It's a very low-key place with few tourists, and you can spend a peaceful hour studying Italian theater costumes from 1741, drawings for the French Court Ballet (1614-34), or a video of a National Theatre movement director teaching actors to act (very convincingly) like ferrets.

There's usually a live demonstration; when we visited, a make-up artist was transforming kids into Andrew Lloyd Webber-style cats. This museum makes a pleasant footnote to your trip.

SIR JOHN SOANE'S MUSEUM

13 Lincoln's Inn Fields, London WC2 3BP Tel: 0171 430 0175. Tuesday to Saturday, 10am to 5pm; first Tuesday evening of each month, 6pm to 9 pm. Closed Sunday, Monday, Bank Holidays and December 24. Admission free. Holborn Tube.

What an extraordinary gem this small museum is! And what a perfect introduction to that strange and wonderful breed of Englishman, The Collector.

John Soane was born in 1753, the son of a country bricklayer. He moved to London to study architecture, winning a scholarship from the Royal Academy to travel in Europe for three years; a rare opportunity for a young man of such modest means. During these years, his as-yet unrequited passion for antiquities and for collecting was born – and his contacts among the young aristocracy were established. Thanks to these contacts, his architectural practice flourished, and he made enough money to spend the next 60 years of his life in and out of the auction houses of London. The Sir John Soane's Museum, his home for 24 years, is the glorious result, virtually unchanged in any detail from the days of his habitation.

Informative and anecdotal guided tours every Saturday at 2:30pm will add much to your experience. Get there at least 15 minutes early – the tickets are free but limit the group to a maximum 25. On the first Tuesday evening of every month, the house is open late (6-9pm). Visit on a dark, bleak evening for the perfect antidote to winter gloom.

As you enter the **dining room**, look for the wonderfully languid Joshua Reynolds painting *Snake in the Grass*, which portrays Love unloosing the girdle of Beauty, and the portrait of Soane (a very flattering likeness, one suspects, as the sitter was then 75 years old) by Sir Thomas Lawrence. In this room and throughout the house, note the architect's unusual use of mirrors; great planes and slivers of reflected light add to the general sense that things aren't entirely what they seem. Walls are disguised as bookcases, windows are disguised as walls, domes seem to float like canopies – even the ubiquitous golden glow has been carefully orchestrated by the use of tinted glass in the skylights. It adds up to a complete sense of architectural uncertainty, but a delightful one.

Backtrack through to the **breakfast room**. With a bit of experimentation, you'll hear the strange effects of this miniature whispering dome from diagonal corners of the room. Note the prints of the Villa Negroni and compare them to the two rooms you've just left. Any similarity is not coincidental; Roman architecture was the source for many of Soane's ideas and color schemes.

Probably the most important room in the house is the **Picture Room** with the original of William Hogarth's wonderfully picaresque *Rake's*

Progress. The paintings represent the dissolute life and times of the fictional Tom Rakewell as he progresses from perfect respectability to poverty, ignomy, and ruin. We particularly like the wonderfully craven wedding scene, in which Tom pledges his troth to an ugly (but rich) old widow, while the defiled and abandoned Sarah and his bastard son look on.

Don't leave the Picture Room without asking the guards to open the panels for you. They swing back to reveal an entire wall of rare and wonderful Piranesi drawings, an early Turner and a couple of pretty Ruisdaels. On the other side of the room, a double layer of panels reveals first a series of Clerriseau architectural drawings, followed by the rather unexpected appearance of – well, go and see for yourself.

Proceed downstairs to the **Monk's Parlour** and the **Cloister**. Reportedly, Soane would explain to quests (in gentle satire on the prevailing fashion for antiquarianism and Gothic revival) that the room and the cloister behind the house had recently been excavated, uncovering the tomb of Friar Giovanni and the rich, eccentric collection of artifacts displayed in the room itself (not that you'd expect to excavate Egyptian relics in a Bloomsbury back garden). The monk's tomb, by the way, contains the remains of Mrs. Soane's beloved dog Fanny.

The house is literally crammed with art, artifacts and antiquities – from a 13th century B.C. Egyptian alabaster sarcophagus (genuine) to an ever-changing exhibition from Soane's collection of 30,000 drawings. Five years of painstaking renovations have recently been concluded, leaving the museum sparkling like a Faberge egg. Two or three hours passed here will likely be among the most pleasant you spend in London.

SPENCER HOUSE

St. James Place, London SW1. Tel: 0171 499 8620. Sunday, 10:45am to 4:45pm (closed August and January). Admission £6 adults; £5 children under 16. No children under 10 admitted. Green Park tube.

Remember Diana Spencer, shy Di, before she became the Princess of Wales? If you're interested in pursuing the quality of her ancestors, a visit to Spencer House is in order. On the other hand, if you're interested in gaining entree to an extravagant, beautifully restored 18th century residential Palladian-style palace, you might have an even better reason to visit Spencer House.

Built in 1765 by John Vardy (student of William Kent) for the very wealthy **First Earl of Spencer** and his young bride, Spencer House served as their stylish city residence, dedicated to hospitality, love and the arts – in other words, lavish parties and the Earl's extensive collection of painting and sculpture. The first thing you should look at is the lovely facade with its array of neoclassical sculptures, visible through the trees of Green Park. Once inside, visitors join a tour supervised by the J. Rothschild Administration which, since 1985, has leased the house from the Spencer family and taken charge of the extensive (and expensive) renovations.

The house reflects the dual aesthetic of Vardy and James "Athenian" Stuart, who replaced Vardy halfway through the project; the nickname was acquired after publication of The Antiquities of Athens, documenting his survey of ancient monuments in Greece. Stuart incorporated the then-fashionable neoclassical style throughout Spencer House, filling rooms with exact duplicates of Greek and Roman friezes, paintings and temple details.

Vardy's **Palm Room** is the architectural high point of the ground floor – elaborate columns are carved and gilded to resemble palm trees (symbols of marital fertility); the green and gold ceiling is bordered by a frieze of griffins and candelabra copied from a Roman temple. It was in this modest chamber that the Spencer men retired for a manly chat after dinner.

A marble **centaur**, copied in 1736 from the original excavated at Hadrian's Villa, stands with a whimsical smile at the foot of the stairs, gesturing upward like a mute doorman. Following his directions, we ascend the stately staircase to the first floor, where Stuart's influence is felt most vividly. The ceiling of **The Great Room** is covered in hundreds of white, pale green and gold mosaic compartments; the dazzling Painted Room incorporates fresco and canvas panels of Venus and Cupid and elaborate scenes of Roman weddings, in celebration of Lord and Lady Spencer's connubial bliss. Green brocade sofas with gold-winged lions add the final garnish to the room.

In 1942, fearing damage from the Blitz, the Spencers removed everything they could – furniture, paintings, mouldings, fireplaces, doors and railings – to Althorp, the family's country seat. The restoration of the interior, completed in 1989, has been partially financed by letting the house for private functions: Henry Kissinger celebrated his 70th birthday here, the Queen uses it for state dinners. And for a mere £10,000 (without food or flowers), you too can celebrate your nuptials or your child's bar mitzvah in a style to which we would all like to become accustomed.

ST. BARTHOLOMEW THE GREAT CHURCH

Bartholomew Close (off Little Britain), London EC1. Monday to Friday 8:30am to 4:30pm; Saturday 10am to 4:30pm; Sunday noon to 6pm. Barbican, Farringdon or St. Paul's tube.

"Est. 1123," says the sign out front, which makes St. Bartholomew's by Smithfield Market the oldest surviving church in London – and, not surprisingly, one of its most atmospheric. You can combine a trip to St.

Bartholomew's with a visit to St. Paul's, though even better to combine it with a trip to one or two of the many fine traditional pubs and excellent restaurants throughout this rapidly changing area. Enter through the Norman arch, on Little Britain, on which sits a Tudor house which, until WWI, was entirely panelled over. A 1919 German bomb knocked some of the facade free, revealing the old (1559) Tudor Gatehouse, which has since been restored.

The church itself is a historical mish-mash. From the choir east to the high altar is all that remains of the original Norman church, which Henry VIII ordered demolished during the Dissolution of the Monasteries. Local parishioners saved what remains, which over the years served as a blacksmith's works, a stable and a printing house (Benjamin Franklin worked in it for a time). Reconstructed through the centuries, it survived the Great Fire of London when the wind fortuitously shifted; and today has a truly magical aura of serene dignity.

Look for some of the interesting inscriptions on the many tomb-stones and monuments; our favorite (on the monument to John and Margaret Whiting along the north wall) finishes: "Shee first deceased, hee for a litle tryd/to live without her, likd it not & dyd." Other good inscriptions include the one for Captain John Millet, Marriner (1660): "Many a storme & tempest passt, here hee hath quiet anchor cast," and the eloquent title on the stone of Mr. Jonathan Thornell, 1757: Hair Merchant of this Parish.

Frequent lunchtime concerts are held; the 6:30 choral evensong is a treat.

WALLACE COLLECTION

Hertford House, Manchester Square, London W1. Tel: 0171 935 0687. Monday to Saturday 10am to 5pm; Sunday 2pm to 5pm. Free. Guided tours conducted weekdays (usually 1pm, phone to check times). Bond Street tube.

There's a lot of good history and one superbly racy sensibility behind the Wallace Collection, which adds a fillip of intrigue to this magnificent small museum.

The collection was started with six Canalettos by Francis Seymour-Conway (1719-94) First Marquess of Hertford, Tory courtier and am-bassador to Paris. His son purchased Hertford House and added more paintings, including Gainsborough's alluring *Perdita Robinson*, a gift from his friend the Prince of Wales. The third Marquess was the real connoisseur of the family, and a fortunate marriage to an Italian heiress increased his purchasing power considerably. He bought French furni-ture, Sevres porcelain and Titian's sublime *Perseus and Andromeda*.

The **fourth Marquess** (1800-1870) is the really interesting one. He inherited his father's vast fortune and the family taste for art, in particular for lush pink nudes and mythological love stories. One of Europe's richest men, the fourth Marquess bulldozed his way through auction houses, outbidding major national collections to such an extent that potential buyers left in droves if he was spotted among the bidders.

As you walk through the collection his imprint is easy and fascinating to trace – the gorgeous, sexy Bouchers (*The Rape of Europa* should be titled Afternoon Dalliance With a Rather Attractive Bull), the provocative bucolic *Divertissements* of Watteau; even the unaccountably seductive biblical and religious scenes by Murillo. Fragonard's infamous *The Swing*, in which the Baron de Saint Julien (who commissioned the painting) lounges in the lea looking up his mistress' skirt, was meant to include a bishop pushing the lovely lady to new heights. In a fit of (almost) good taste, the bishop was replaced in the composition by an elderly man.

To be fair, only a portion of the Marquess' contributions to the collection involve desirable women. Rembrandt's moving portrait of his son Titus, Franz Hal's *Laughing Cavalier*, and paintings by Velasquez, Rubens, Poussin, Reynolds, Gainsborough, Ruisdael and Van Dyck were among his purchases, and all grace the walls of this extraordinary collection.

The collection, finally, was named for **Richard Wallace**, illegitimate son of the fourth Marquess (who never married). While never acknowledging paternity, the Marquess employed his son as secretary and agent, and when he died, left Wallace his fortune, his chateau in Paris' Bois de Boulogne (delightfully named "Bagatelle"), and his entire art collection. Wallace returned to England and Hertford House with his inheritance, and continued to add to the collection throughout his lifetime, broadening it with medieval and Renaissance art, European armour, illuminated manuscripts and decorative arts. On his death, he left the collection to his wife, with the expressed wish that on her death it should pass to the state. Three years after she died (1900), the great house on Manchester Square opened to the public.

According to the will, nothing may be removed from or added to the collection, even temporarily or on loan. And that is how the Wallace Collection remains today – the result of five generations of connoiseurship – a treasure trove of priceless works or art, one of the world's finest groupings of 18th century French paintings and furniture, and the second largest arms and armory collection in Britain (the first is in the Tower of London).

Aside from the paintings, seek out some of the other treasures. The Deplessis Musical Clock of 1756 (gallery 14) plays a cycle of 13 different tunes (including *Baa baa black sheep*) as it strikes the hours of the day; an 18th century gold and red cornelian snuff box reveals a secret panel with portraits of Voltaire and his mistress, Madame du Chatelet; a group of

15th-7th century Indian and Persian swords are encrusted with diamonds, rubies and emeralds. Look for the black and white Limoges dishes copied from Raphael, Marie Antoinette's marriage coffer, and various astonishingly ornate examples of Louis XV furniture from Versailles. The arms and armor beggar description, but include rare 14th-16th century pieces, and a complete (and completely elegant) set of Gothic armor for man and horse.

As a last note, look for Jan Steen's *Celebrating the Birth* with its jokey food symbolism – cracked eggs everywhere and women gripping sausages; Poussin's *Dance to the Music of Time* featuring Pleasure, Poverty (barefoot), Labor, and Riches dancing out the cycles of life; and Delacroix's strangely composed *Execution of the Doge Marino Faliero*.

With your head full of art, retire to **Villandry** *(89 Marylebone High Street)* for more corporeal pleasures – i.e., lunch.

ART GALLERIES - WITHOUT PERMANENT COLLECTIONS

Although London has hundreds of small private art galleries (mainly grouped around **Cork Street**), the galleries listed here mount significant shows of everything from Dutch Masters to video installations. Check *Time Out* or local papers for a schedule of exhibitions.

THE HAYWARD GALLERY

The South Bank (at Waterloo Bridge), London SE1. Tel: 0171 261 0127. Daily 10am to 6pm; Wednesday and Thursday until 8pm. Adults: £5-6; children £3.50. Waterloo or Embankment tube.

There's almost always something interesting on display at the Hayward Gallery. And although the entry fees are starting to look a little steep, it's one of the best places in London to find large shows of modern and contemporary art – like Bonnard, German Expressionism, Georgia O'Keefe and aboriginal art. The gallery is big enough to do real justice to its subjects, and the recent mixed contemporary shows have been full of strange and wonderful work. There's a good shop, a nice, simple little cafe on the top floor and impressive views of London from the rooftop sculpture areas (if they're open).

It's worth mentioning, as an aside, that it's very fashionable among the chattering classes of London to complain about the Hayward (and the whole South Bank for that matter). So much so, that there are always plans in the works to pull it down. Others believe that the Hayward is a particularly fine example of spare, meticulously-designed 60s architecture – and a great place to look at art. We fall into the latter group and hope they leave it alone.

By the way, if you have trouble finding the gallery, look for artists Vaughan and Daiton's wind-driven multi-colored neon sculpture on top of the building. You can see it from quite a distance away, and it's particularly dramatic in a stiff wind.

THE INSTITUTE OF CONTEMPORARY ARTS (ICA)

Nash House, The Mall, London SW1. Tel: 0171 930 3647. Daily noon to 7:30pm (Friday 9pm). Admission £1.50. Piccadilly or Charing Cross tube.

This hotbed of hyper-contemporary art and cinema is set, rather inappropriately we think, right on the grandest and most formal of London's royal parades. While Queen's guards in silly hats and gold braid trot their horses in strict formation outside, the whole naughty, burblingly subversive world of contemporary art does its gleefully iconoclastic thing inside. Luckily, its thing happens to include some of London's most interesting art shows and some of its best alternative cinema.

There's also a good bookshop, a cafeteria, and a popular bar that stays open every night (except Sunday) until 1am. *Admission to the gallery and bar is by day pass, cinema admission is extra.*

THE ROYAL ACADEMY OF ART

Burlington House, Piccadilly, London W1. Tel: 0171 439 7438. Open daily 10am to 6pm. Admission charged separately to each show. Piccadilly Circus or Green Park tube.

When you first walk through the grand courtyard toward the Palladian mansion that has housed the Royal Academy since 1837, don't forget to peer into the windows to your right and left. The east and west wings of the building house the **Royal Astronomical Society**, the **Antiquaries Society**, and the **Chemical, Geological and Botanical Societies**. Imagine the cross currents of scholarly thought bouncing around in that courtyard! Some of which might even concern art.

All of the British art and architectural establishment are members of The Academy, which many of the younger generation of British artists dismiss as insufferably stuffy. In fact, this opinion is largely irrelevant in view of what the Royal Academy does best – splendid, large-scale, well-curated shows like *The Glory of Venice* or the hugely impressive *Poussin* exhibition.

Of course the other thing that makes the Royal Academy famous is its **summer show**, an almighty hodgepodge of work from important artists like Howard Hodgkin to lesser-known ones like your great aunt Tilly. Needless to say, the dubious democracy of the summer show guarantees it an enthusiastic following; in addition, all the paintings are for sale so for a very reasonable price, you can walk away with "My Cat Snuffy on a Windowsill."

A glass elevator connects the main building to the modern new **Sackler Gallery**, designed by Norman Foster and opened in 1991. The gallery also has a good cafeteria and a better gift shop.

THE SAATCHI GALLERY

98a Boundary Road, London NW8. Tel: 0171 624 8299. Thursday to Sunday, noon to 6pm. Admission £2.50 (Thursday free). Swiss Cottage tube.

Set in a massive converted warehouse in north London, this is one of the city's most spectacular (and most sought after) private gallery spaces. Group and solo shows of contemporary art are displayed in six enormous white rooms, and the people looking at the work are nearly as interesting as the stuff on the walls.

Renowned as one of the world's foremost collectors, **Charles Saatchi** still scours the degree shows for new talent, and whether you like what he shows or not, it's never dull. The room full of motor oil at the end of the gallery is stunning, and inadvertently the gallery's sole permanent exhibition – no one can figure out how to dismantle it. Before you make the trip, check with *Time Out* listings or phone to make sure the gallery is open. It closes for a number of weeks between shows for rehanging.

If you're traveling by tube, give yourself plenty of time – there's a 15 minute walk at the end. And if you're a Beatles fan, you'll notice that Boundary Road crosses Abbey Road just before you reach the gallery. Walk south down Abbey Road and in about ten minutes you'll come to the famous crossing featured on the *Abbey Road* record cover.

THE SERPENTINE GALLERY

Kensington Gardens, London W2. Tel: 0171 402 6075. Daily 10am to 6pm; November to March daily 10am to dusk. Free. Knightsbridge or Lancaster Gate tube.

We can think of no nicer way to break up a walk through Hyde Park and Kensington Gardens than with a stop at the Serpentine Gallery. Inside the large, bright rooms of this converted 1909 tea house, you'll find intelligently-curated shows of 20th century painting and sculpture, from Man Ray to Damien Hirst. The British contemporary art scene is well-represented here, both on the walls and in the flesh.

If you fancy a gape at London's current crop of talented young things, crash one of the crowded, gossipy openings – from 6pm to 8pm, the evening before a new show opens, no invitation necessary (check *Time Out* or phone the gallery for new show dates).

THE WHITECHAPEL GALLERY

Whitechapel High Street, London E1. Tel: 0171 522 7888. Tuesday to Sunday 11am to 5pm (8pm Wednesday). Admission varies according to exhibition; usually free. Aldgate East tube.

Set in the heart of London's east end, surrounded by cockney touts and the chaos of local street markets, this imposing Art Nouveau temple to art seems borrowed from another world. And in fact it was.

The gallery was commissioned by **Augustus Barnett**, a late Victorian philanthropist who moved with his wife to the east of London (think of all the worst settings in Dickens and you get an idea of what he was tackling) in order to "decrease not suffering but sin!" His theory that the poor suffered from a lack of cultural stimulation resulted in C.H. Townsend's stately design for the Whitechapel Art Gallery, which today admirably continues the tradition with its excellent mixed and solo shows of modern and contemporary art. Large, bright and attractive, it's a great place to look at art; there's also a pleasant cafe. Phone or check listings for up to date exhibition information.

ENTERTAINMENT

Zebras? Mechanical toys? Eddie Murphy in wax? Ghosts? Sometimes you've had enough Titian and just need to make faces at an ape.

CABARET MECHANICAL THEATRE

33-34 The Market, Covent Garden, London WC2. Tel: 0171 379 7961. Adults: £1.95, children: £1.20, under 5: Free. Daily 10am to 7pm, Sunday 10:30am to 7pm. Covent Garden tube.

On the underground level of the Covent Garden market, buried in among the expensive clothing and candle shops, you'll find the Cabaret Mechanical Theatre. If you haven't got any kids of your own, you might want to beg, borrow or steal one to accompany you on your pilgrimage. If you can't find one, swallow your pride and join all the other unaccompanied grown-ups gleefully pushing buttons to set these fabulous automata in motion.

The Mechanical Theatre takes an art form more or less invented by the Victorians – the mechanical toy – and catapults it into the modern day. Push a button and you set the contents of a glass box in motion: a jointed wooden dreamer lies in bed while strange creatures emerge from the closet and creep in through the windows; fish leap out of a moving sea into the mouth of a complacent cat. But if you're getting a picture of quaint, childish Victoriana, forget it. Most of these toys are made by very modern craftsmen with strange, perverse imaginations; each is a work of art in itself, and while kids do go bananas for them, we've seen all sorts of cynical grown-ups turn uncharacteristically wide-eyed and giggly in seconds. The "theatre" itself is nothing more than a room containing about 60 of these fantastical creations; set one in motion, laugh yourself silly for 30 seconds or so, then move on to the next.

Be warned that you can spend the price of admission on the ever-changing variety of toys (10-20 pence each to operate) in the front shop area. Take our advice, splash out for the full £1.95, and go forget the weather and the price of your hotel bill for one blissful half hour.

DENNIS SEVERS' HOUSE

18 Folgate Street, London E1. Tel (for information and reservations): 0171 247 4013. Liverpool Street tube.

What a strange and wonderful place this is. **Mr. Sever**, an American with a self-professed passion for British history and architecture, bought this 1724 house in east London, and has turned it into architectural performance art. Three times a week (the nights vary, phone for details), Mr. Sever conducts a walking theater piece through the house which follows an invisible 18th century family (complete with dramatic sound effects) who seem to have just left each room as you enter. It's magically, bizarrely convincing, jammed with fact and anecdote, and for once we can honestly say that there's nothing like it anywhere in the world.

The first Sunday of every month the house is open for tours (£5), and the first Monday evening of every month there's a three hour candlelight "wander" with commentary (£10) but we really do recommend you bite the bullet and shell out for the real thing (£30) which you'll remember long after the rest of your holiday has become a dim memory. Book a few weeks in advance if you can manage it, otherwise call for last minute cancellations.

MADAME TUSSAUD'S

Marylebone Road, London NW1. Tel: 0171 935 6861. Daily 10am to 5:30pm (opens 9:30am weekends; 9am during the summer. Phone to confirm opening times, they change frequently throughout the year.) Adults: £8.35; Children: £5.25. Baker Street tube.

Will someone please explain to us why Madame Tussaud's continues to thrive? Perfectly normal-looking folk from the four corners of the earth seem willing, nay, delighted, to queue for hours through cold and rain and biting wind to pay an outrageous £8.35 and gawp at a bunch of wax people. And correct us if we're wrong, but many of the above mentioned wax people don't even seem all that ... interesting. What could that group of Japanese tourists possibly find so fascinating about Viv Richards,

Captain of the West Indies cricket team? And Steve Davis, for heaven's sake? The world's most boring snooker player! Desperate for distraction, we start a mental list of people who actually look better in wax than in real life – Joan Collins, Barbara Cartland, John Major. Call us spoilsports, but for the hefty price of admission, we require more entertainment than a 70s version of Dudley Moore playing the piano to a bunch of pinkish stiffs.

Maybe it gets better, we think, ever-hopeful. And indeed, the 1765 version of Madame du Barry as Sleeping Beauty is quite interesting, even somewhat unsettling. Perhaps things are starting to look up.

Looking up, we see a wall full of disembodied heads. They are all looking down on a (you guessed it) wax statue of the great Madame Tussaud. A few feet away Jerry Hall poses, semi-naked. We stare at her for a bit, don't feel we're getting to know her any better and move on. To Napoleon, dead on a camp bed. Well, at least he's not trying to look lifelike. In the next room Timothy Dalton takes potshots at Indiana Jones. Marilyn Monroe attempts to hold her fluttering skirt down. James Dean looks sullen. Eddie Murphy laughs a mechanical version of his giggle. And, oh lord we can't go on.

We go on. Into the **Hall of English History**, where things pick up marginally. We remark on how short Richard III looks, how fierce Richard the Lionhearted looks and how totally unlike JFK, JFK looks. Yes, we feel a bit creepy making comments about these people as they look on with glazed expressions. Yes, some of them do look pretty realistic. And no, no attempt whatsoever has been made to put any of them in historical context, though Henry VIII is positioned with his six wives and a key card showing which were beheaded. Lurching ever onwards, we spy the Royal Family. Because they're placed in an awkward line, ten feet behind a velvet rope, we can't get snaps of ourselves in a clinch with the future King of England. Another fantasy shattered. Still, this is England, wouldn't do to allow the riff raff to associate with the (wax) Royal family. We wave sadly to poor piggy-faced Fergie, relegated to Siberia at the far right in a frock that makes her look like an overstuffed sofa, and move on.

To **The House of Horrors** (more cheap titillation with your basic torture scenarios, some canned screams and a model of our own American death row. Sure made us proud to be Yanks). And finally **The Spirit of London** (a £21 million ride through London history in plastic Black Cabs). This sub-Disney extravaganza gave us splitting headaches and not a smidgen of information about the city we know and love; if this is indeed the spirit of London we suggest you have your next holiday in Mongolia. We stagger out onto the sidewalk. Kiss the ground with relief.

What can we say? You might like Madame Tussaud's – thousands of people seem to. If you do, please write and tell us why.

LONDON ZOO

Regent's Park, London NW1 4RY. Tel: 0171 722 3333; fax: 0171 483 4436. Daily 10am to 5:30pm; last admission 4:30. Adults: £7; children (4 to 14): £5; family ticket (two adults, two children): £20. Camden Town tube (ten minute walk) or number 274 bus from Baker Street.

The **London Zoological Society** began in 1828 with a collection of gifts to the royal family; a hippopotamus, two giraffes, a chimpanzee, a quagga and a number of thylacines (now extinct) belonged to the original collection. Today, along with the elephants, zebra and tigers, you can see an anoa, a pudu, and an okapi, a leadbeater's possum, a zorilla (and a gorilla), two rhinos (Rosie and Jos), a tankful of regal tangs, a bird-eating spider, and a herd of oryx.

There's also a **children's zoo** where kids can pet sheep, goats, ponies and rabbits; an "animals in action" show featuring Basil the rat; camel rides; and a wonderful reptile house. The elephants are housed in architectural award-winning houses, as are the birds and the penguins.

And although we can't help having a few reservations about the whole concept of zoos, this isn't a particularly depressing one. There's a minimum of aimless, depressed pacing back and forth and the animals are obviously well-cared for and well-loved. Events are scheduled throughout the day, including pig, penguin, reptile and fish feeding, spider-breeding demonstrations (we passed), the daily elephant weigh-in and bath, and an afternoon **Meet the Keeper talk**. The majority of activities occur between 12:30pm and 3pm, so plan your trip accordingly.

A variety of cafes (pizza, fish and chips, sandwiches) are scattered around, along with de Blank's restaurant, which serves good quality hot meals at reasonable prices. There's a pretty outdoor piazza around the elephant fountain with tables for restaurant food or picnics on sunny days.

A few cautions: don't attempt the zoo on a dismal weather day, unless you're willing to see the reptiles, the fish, and go home. Don't expect really little kids to have a great time here – we went with a four and five year old, and found five a much better age in terms of stamina and attention span. And lastly, beware of the signage. It's very confusing. Stop in at the information desk when you arrive and get yourself a map. It will save all sorts of aimless depressed pacing back and forth.

LONDON BEHIND THE SCENES

This is your chance to get an insider's view – of the war effort, the government, the workings of the law. Some of our most memorable experiences have been these brushes with backstage – be it the theater or the theater of government.

CABINET WAR ROOMS

Clive Steps, King Charles Street, London SW1. Tel: 0171 930 6961. Daily 10am to 5:15pm. Adults: £4; children: £2. Westminster tube.

A spellbinding experience awaits you in the Cabinet War Rooms, which is more than anyone working and living there could claim. Built deep underground for the safety of **Winston Churchill** and his cabinet during World War II, the war rooms are one of London's most vividly evocative sites, and the sense of claustrophobia its wartime inhabitants must have felt is still palpable even to the casual visitor. From 1939 to 1945 these rooms were the center from which Churchill ran the government and directed the war effort, though he undermined at least the spirit of keeping the prime minister safe by his staunch refusal to sleep under-ground – he found it far too claustrophobic, especially after his daily bottles of scotch and champagne, and retired nightly to the Savoy.

A number of walls in the three-acre warren of rooms have been replaced with glass, so you can see into the tiny cubicles, preserved exactly as they were left in September 1945. The British love of subterfuge and spying is impossible to ignore – a toilet cubicle hung with an "engaged" sign indicated that Churchill was within, on the phone transatlantic to FDR. And this isn't all some clever recreation by the historical society, the eerie sense you get of a place abandoned in the middle of a workday is completely accurate; virtually nothing has been altered since VE day 1945. A huge world map stuck with thousands of pins indicates troop positions, a communications center filled with brightly colored 40s-style telephones still has phone messages stuck up on bulletin boards, minuscule bedrooms are neatly arranged with army-issue blankets.

The excellent audio tour that leads visitors through the maze combines real wartime broadcasts (many made by Churchill from the bunker itself) with historical narration. We emerged convinced that war is hell, and the sleeping accomodations offered during it even worse.

THE HOUSE OF COMMONS & THE HOUSE OF LORDS – THE PALACE OF WESTMINSTER

Parliament Square, London SW1. Tel: 0171 219 4272. House of Commons open Monday to Thursday 2:30pm to 10pm, Friday 9:30am to 3pm. House of Lords open Monday to Wednesday 2:30pm on; Thursday 3:30pm on. Westminster tube.

It surprises a lot of people to hear that the **Palace of Westminster** (or the **Houses of Parliament** as its more usually known) was built in the 1840s. Well it was: by Charles Barry (architect) and Augustus Pugin (interiors) after a spectacular fire burned most of the original building to the ground in 1834. The structure they created is an orgy of Victorian nostalgia for Gothic architecture – the delicate grey limestone landmark hovers aesthetically between the sublime and the ridiculous, though on a foggy day from Waterloo Bridge, or all alight on a moonless night, the sublime clearly triumphs.

Pugin's astonishing interiors incorporate mosaics, murals, frescoes and gilt throughout more than a thousand rooms – including a massive library in the Victoria Tower. And its present incarnation has not been without incident – during the second world war, the House of Commons (bombed out of their own chamber) moved into the Lords, while the House of Lords met in the grand 54 foot long Robing Room.

The original Palace of Westminster on this site was built in the 11th century, to house the king and his court in close proximity to Westminster Abbey. Virtually all that remains of that original structure is **Westminster Hall**, some of which dates from 1097 (the rest, including the ceiling, was finished in the late 14th century) and has the largest wooden hammerbeam ceiling in Europe. For six hundred years this building housed Britain's main law courts. Sir Thomas More was sentenced to death here, as was Charles I, and Guy Fawkes (for attempting to blow up the Houses of Parliament). You'll pass by it on your way into the visitors' galleries, so take a good look at the stunning old structure – the massive oak ceiling has held together for nearly five centuries without nails; it was constructed of wood beams soaked in water and then hammered together. For this reason, the hall remains unheated; if the beams were to dry out, the building would collapse.

As you face the enormous main gates to the Houses of Parliament, turn right past the statue of Oliver Cromwell (symbol of England's brief historical period as a commonwealth), walk about another 100 yards, and you come to **St. Stephen's entrance**, doorway to the House of Commons and the House of Lords. Most days you'll be alerted that you have arrived by the large queue of people waiting to be admitted and the huge bank of TV and press photographers waiting to catch MPs (Members of Parliament) on their way out for an off-the-cuff remark or two.

Depending on the season, you may have quite a wait to get into the House of Commons, so we suggest you try the shorter queue to the Lords, and once you're inside, see if you can do a bit of maneuvering. Otherwise, wait your turn patiently and enjoy the general spectacle.

One thing to remember. The fantastically vigorous shouting and jumping you see on C-Span tends only to happen during **Question Time** *(2:30-3:30pm Monday to Thursday)* and **Prime Minister's Question Time** *(3:15-3:30pm, Tuesday and Thursday)*. Amazingly, the Prime Minister and Leader of the Opposition rarely make an appearance in the House chamber for more than these 15 minutes twice a week. And the catch is, it's almost impossible for the average tourist to get a place in the visitors' gallery during these times.

If you are very intrepid, you can apply for tickets to the American Embassy in London *(5 Upper Grosvenor Street, London W1)* or in the States at least a few months before you arrive. Otherwise, resign yourself to visiting at a quieter time. The advantage of visiting at 8pm, for instance, is that you will be able to walk directly in without queuing; the disadvantage is that you may find yourself observing a mostly-empty House.

But the excitement of being there is pretty wonderful at any time of day – the building is fantastically grand, you can see for yourself the red lines on the House of Commons carpet (exactly two sword lengths apart), and there's a palpable buzz in the octagonal **Central Lobby**, created by the bustle of young aides, the clubby superiority of the MPs, and the superbly outfitted doorkeepers (in their black tailcoats and huge gold medallions) – all of whom sweep in and out with a great show of their own importance.

In short, go. It offers an unparalleled opportunity to get a look at the workings of government from the inside. And it's splendid theater.

By the way, if you happen to be wandering by late at night, look for the second light above the face of **Big Ben** – if it's lit, it means Parliament is still in session, which is not uncommon even as late as midnight or 1am. As long as they're sitting, you can visit, so take the chance and go for a quick look. The building is even more magical at night. And bring your postcards with you when you visit. You can mail them at the tiny post office in the Central Lobby where they'll be cancelled with the official House of Commons stamp.

BIG BEN EMERGING FROM THE HOUSES OF PARLIAMENT

THE NATIONAL THEATRE BACKSTAGE TOUR

Meet at the Information Desk of The National Theatre, South Bank, London SE1. Monday to Saturday 10:15am, 12:30pm and 5:30pm. Reservations necessary, tel: 0171 633 0880. Tickets: £3.50. Waterloo or Embankment tube.

What's a theater fan to do with all those empty hours between plays? Here's our suggestion: reserve yourself a place on the backstage tour at the South Bank and get acquainted with what happens behind the scenes. The week before our tour, a couple of groups were allowed to watch Arthur Miller rehearsing *Broken Glass*, so go prepared for (pleasant) surprises. We learned plenty from our voluble aspiring actor/guide – for instance:

- Laurence Olivier set up the **National Theatre Company** in 1963; Peter Hall was the first director of the new National Theatre complex when it opened at the South Bank in 1976.
- The queen ceremonially opened the **Olivier theatre** but hates it and hasn't been back since.
- The National Theatre cost £22 million to build and currently runs through a £26 million budget each year. The National is entirely non-profit; all proceeds go back into the production budget.
- Three productions run simultaneously in repertory in each theater (making a total of up to nine plays running at any one time), with the help of more than a thousand backstage hands.
- The **Olivier** theater is based on a Roman ampitheater design and seats 1,160; it has no "bad" seats.
- The **Lyttelton** is a proscenium arch theater (like most theaters you have ever visited), and seats 890 in the standard three tier system. Laurence Olivier insisted on the proscenium arch design to accommodate touring companies.
- The **Cottesloe**, an Elizabethan-style theatre, is the most popular with directors and actors because it has a large stage and a small house; it is flexible, very intimate and can seat anywhere from 250-400 depending on the production's stage configuration. Sadly, due to its size, it loses money even on sold-out runs.
- The balconies next to the stage that hold live musicians are called *ashtrays*.
- An incredible five artists make all the props, all the furniture, all the backdrops, and all the sets for all the productions. Stage props are accurate to the very last detail, even if no one will ever be close enough to appreciate it.
- A small blinking traffic light at entrance points backstage needs to be activated by an actor a few seconds before going on so the stage manager knows he or she is in position. Sometimes actors forget (being a stage manager must be the most terrifying job on earth).
- The **flytower** backstage at the Lyttelton is 115 feet high and truly awesome. It holds in storage the complete sets of the two plays not running that night.

We learned lots more than this, were privy to a wealth of behind-the-scenes secrets, and enjoyed ourselves immensely. Highly recommended.

THE OLD BAILEY (PUBLIC GALLERY)

Warwick Passage off Old Bailey, London EC4. Tel: 0171 248 3277. Weekdays 10am to 4pm, closed daily 1-2pm. (Note: NO cameras, recording equipment, packages or mobile phones allowed – and there's no place to check them.) Admission free. No one under 14 admitted. St. Paul's tube.

This is your big chance to do some eavesdropping on British justice at the **Central Criminal Court**, or the Old Bailey as it is universally known. London's main criminal courthouse, built on the foundations of the infamous (and heinous) **Newgate Gaol** has been the site of all sorts of carriages and miscarriages of justice – Oscar Wilde was convicted of homosexuality here and the Yorkshire ripper was found guilty here. Tradition lives on in the form of small bunches of flowers the judges carry on the first days of each session – a measure left over from the days when the stench of the Newgate cells demanded delicate remedial measures.

The **visitor's gallery** at the Old Bailey offers a rare opportunity to spend an utterly fascinating few hours watching British justice meted out in all its astonishingly formal m'lud-riddled, bewigged glory – all about a million miles from the wily antics of *L.A. Law* and *Perry Mason* (not to mention O.J.). Check the court schedule outside to choose your case; once you're ushered in, wardens on each landing will advise and direct you to a gallery overlooking the crime of your choice, though your selection naturally depends on who-did-what-to-whom-and-got-caught-for-it-lately. Although times are changing, the expensive, Byzantine process of becoming a barrister ensures that the Oxford and Cambridge elite continues to dominate the profession, so expect lots of imperious theatricality.

On a recent visit, the plot for a best-selling mystery unravelled itself (in the guise of a murder trial) before our very eyes. So if you keep meaning to win the academy award for best original screenplay, drop in and find your own true-life crime story. It's not an experience you're likely to forget.

THEATRE ROYAL DRURY LANE BACKSTAGE TOURS

Catherine Street, London WC2. Tel: 0171 494 5060. Tours begin in the theatre foyer weekdays at 1pm, 3pm and 5:30pm; Saturday at 11:30am and 1pm; Sunday at noon, 2pm and 3:30pm. Adults: £4; children £3. Covent Garden tube.

Every crowned monarch since 1663 has visited the Drury Lane, our tour guide told us, using the adjective "crowned" to expunge (ever-so-delicately) the memory of Edward VIII who abdicated before he was crowned King – and presumably before he had a chance to visit the Drury Lane.

You'll see some remarkable things on this tour of the world's oldest working theater, including the Waterford crystal chandeliers and 24 carat goldleaf plasterwork of the **Royal Retiring Room** in which George V knighted actor Frank Benson with a prop-room sword, and the hydraulic stage elevators bought secondhand from the Vienna State Opera in 1898.

There are frequent references to the theater's current and longest-running show, *Miss Saigon*, and the excitement of the behind-the-scenes visit comes from the sounds, smells and sights of a working theater – you'll hear singers warming up, a saxophonist practicing scales in the pit, and see stage lights running through their cues. The tour helps the theater's 332 year history come alive with anecdotes about everyone from David Garrick (the beloved 18th century actor and manager of the Drury Lane) to Noel Coward to Miss Saigon director Nicholas Hytner. Highly recommended for theater fans.

LITERARY HOMES

You've read the book, now see the living room. Some of London's most beloved literary characters have museums in their honor – they're atmospheric and replete with history; some of our favorites are listed here.

DICKENS HOUSE

48 Doughty Street, London WC1. Monday to Saturday 10am to 5pm. Closed Sunday. Adults: £3; students: £2; children: £1. Tel: 0171 405 2127. Russell Square tube.

Dickens celebrated his first wedding anniversary on April 2, 1837, and it was that same weekend that he and his growing family moved into this four-story brick townhouse in Bloomsbury. Though he lived here only three years, it was a productive time; the successes of *Oliver Twist*, *The Pickwick Papers*, and *Nicholas Nickleby* meant that by 1839 he could afford to look for a bigger house.

Ninety years later, the house of this great chronicler of Victorian England was made into a museum. Drawings, paintings, manuscripts, letters, personal effects and photographs cram every nook and cranny and just for a moment we wonder whether the whole 19th century world of London could have existed at all without Dickens to chronicle it. In the end, the sheer weight of the jumble adds up to a wonderfully atmospheric (Dickensian) whole. And who could resist pressing a curious nose against the old-fashioned display cases to try and decipher the words of Dickens' hand-penned letters?

Look for the preliminary sketches (by John Leech) for *A Christmas Carol* and compare them with the hand-painted first edition displayed just below. Equally atmospheric is *Dickens' Dream*, an unfinished painting by R.W. Buss (original illustrator of Pickwick Papers), which captures

SEEING THE SIGHTS 191

Dickens in his study, eyes closed, surrounded by swirling images from his books. Other evocative displays include numerous portraits of Dickens, his friends and family; the grafitti-covered desk Dickens used when employed as a junior clerk in Gray's Inn; and the table on which he was writing *The Mystery of Edwin Drood* the day before he died.

Souvenirs in the gift shop range from postcards and current paperback editions of the novels, to rare editions of Dickens' work.

THE FREUD MUSEUM

20 Maresfield Gardens, London NW3 5SX. Tel: 0171 435 2002. Wednesday to Sunday, noon to 5pm. Closed Monday, Tuesday and bank holidays. Admission: £2.50. Hampstead tube.

You're supposed to get shivers down your spine when you first enter The Great One's study and view The Couch. And chances are you will. The room, with its rich dense patterns of antiquities, kilims and books is, in fact, awesomely atmospheric. All those confessed compulsions! All those murderous desires!

To be strictly accurate, however, it must be said that Freud fled Nazi-occupied Vienna for Hampstead in 1938 and therefore occupied the famous study (painstakingly reconstructed from the Austrian original by his son and housekeeper) for only the last year of his life. Being (perhaps neurotically) sensitive to atmosphere, we felt his presence in the house was somewhat overshadowed by that of his daughter, the psychoanalyst **Anna Freud**, who lived here for 44 years. But that's a minor quibble. Most people come for a glimpse of the office and the couch and the requisite frisson of awe, and on that count, the Freud Museum delivers.

In an upstairs room, a video plays a series of charming Freud family home movies from the twenties and thirties, narrated by an elderly Anna. It adds personal rather than professional insight, but you can always subject the films to extensive analysis. (Bit of a family dog fixation, we thought.) The house has been left much as it was when Anna lived here, complete with the very beautiful painted Austrian country furniture. Applications for access to Freud's collection of antiquities, his library, or the archives should be made in writing.

DR. SAMUEL JOHNSON'S HOUSE

17 Gough Square (off Fleet Street), London EC4. Tel: 0171 353 3745. Monday to Saturday 10:30am to 5pm (October to April, 10:30am to 4:30pm). Adults: £3; children £1.50. Blackfriar's tube.

For those who've forgotten, or perhaps never knew, Dr. Samuel Johnson is famous for the English dictionary he published in 1755 and which represented a quantum leap over previously attempts at the form. He's also famous for saying "when a man is tired of London he is tired of life," a catchy little aphorism disproved by the thousands of Londoners who each year fly off to the Mediterranean, and, while basking semi-nude on a sunny beach, conclude that they are indeed tired of London but enjoying life immensely. Still, it's a good quote, and that's what counts in literary circles. Johnson is also famous due to Boswell's *Life of Johnson*, the biography written by his friend, literary associate, and frequent dinner companion, James Boswell.

You'll find Dr. Johnson's House down a maze of little alleys off Fleet Street, in the substantially renovated Gough Square (look for the sign on the north side of Fleet Street; when you arrive, ring the bell). The square was built around 1700; Dr. Johnson lived in the house between 1749 and 1759. He chose it for its proximity to his printer, and because the large garret room offered work space for the six clerks assisting him in the writing of the dictionary. Today the house is a bit shabby, practically devoid of fancy props and dramatic displays, but nonetheless worth a visit for the uncannily vivid atmosphere. You can almost feel the presence of former occupants; the domestic life of 18th century London seems to live on in the simple panelled rooms.

Aside from these rather abstract qualities, there are some lovely concrete ones. The comparison of Johnson's dictionary with Bailey's (the authoritative English language dictionary before Johnson) is thoroughly enjoyable. Bailey defines "bread" not entirely helpfully as "the staff of life"; "break" is explained as "to break in pieces." In contrast, Johnson's dictionary describes bread pithily as a foodstuff made of grain and risen with yeast, and uses "dull" in the sentence "to make dictionaries is dull work."

The house is full of prints, portraits of Johnson, and some rather odd displays like a silver soup-skimming spoon. Description alone can't quite explain why we like this place so much. Go and judge for yourself.

KEATS' HOUSE

Keats Grove, London NW3. Tel: 0171 435 2062. Open April to October weekdays 10am to 1pm and 2pm to 6pm; Saturday 2pm to 5pm; Sunday 1pm to 5pm. November to March weekdays 1pm to 5pm; Saturday 10am to 2pm to 5pm; Sunday 2pm to 5pm. Closed December 25-26; January 1, Good Friday, Easter Sunday and May day. Free. Hampstead tube.

Before John Keats died in 1821 at the age of 25 of pulmonary tuberculosis, he predicted that he would be remembered as one of the immortals of English poetry. And he is perhaps nowhere more evocatively and spiritedly immortalized than in this pretty house near Hampstead Heath. Adjoining that of his fiancee Fanny Brawne, the house is filled with Keats' letters (to the likes of William Wordsworth), books (his 18th century edition of Shakespeare, scrawled with notes for a poem); paintings and drawings of and by the poet, and memorabilia – Fanny's engagement ring; her lyre brooch strung with Keats' hair. The modest house has been carefully restored to the spirit (if not the letter) of the 1815 original – including the sparse basement kitchen and upstairs bedroom with canopied bed. Alas, the plum tree under which Keats was said to have composed *Ode to a Nightingale* is long gone (though it has recently been replaced with a seedling for the edification of future fans).

The house is poignant and rich with atmosphere conjured up by the young poet's own words in poetical works and letters. In a card to Fanny's mother, written from Italy just before he died, he adds a simple, heartrendingly scrawled P.S.: "Good bye Fanny, god bless you." Copies of the death mask (made in Rome, in the little house on the Spanish Steps in which he died) are also displayed.

There's nothing contrived or false about the house, and we promise you'll come away permeated with the spirit of this short-lived romantic poet, a little bit melancholy, remembering for the first time since high school English, "O what can ail thee knight at arms, so wan and palely loitering, the sedge has wither'd from the lake and no bird sings."

THE SHERLOCK HOLMES MUSEUM

221B Baker Street, London NW1 6XE, Tel: 0171 935 8866. Daily, 9:30am to 6pm (last admission 5:30pm). Adults: £5, Children: £3. Baker Street Tube.

From the fiddled address (until recently, there was no 221B Baker Street except in literature) to the quaint receipt marked "Mrs. Hudson's Lodging Rooms," this museum is a carefully contrived fiction. Appropriately enough, it was constructed using meticulous detective work – each detail in the house based on clues from **Sir Arthur Conan Doyle's** books featuring the remarkable Sherlock Holmes. The lack of encyclopedic familiarity with Sherlock Holmes makes it distinctly difficult to fully appreciate the conceit; objects that seemed to fill our fellow museumgoers with near-religious fervor left us little more than puzzled. That said, the house (restored to elaborate 19th century detail) is really quite convincing, if not strictly authentic. There's an 1893 copy of the *Times* in the newspaper rack, a cozy fire in every room (gas), Holmes' entry in a 1934 *Who's Who*, Watson's service revolver, and even Holmes' butterfly collection.

The floors, wallpaper and furniture all feel comfortably and authentically period, though the house lapses into museum on one floor and shop on another. All in all, 221B Baker Street seems rather like a contrived joke – the restored house of a totally fictional character. We suspect, however, that for serious Holmes fans a visit to the museum is mandatory and, based on the fans we observed, a very engaging experience indeed.

The shop has a wide range of Sherlock Holmes paraphernalia – bookplates, deerstalker hats, pipes, and collections of the novels. Next door, **Hudson's Victorian Dining Room** (*239 Baker Street, London NW1, 0171 935 3 1130. Lunch, 12-2:30, tea 2:30-6, dinner 6-10:30*) continues the fiction with the same slightly uneasy authentic/reproduction ambience. The room does indeed feel Victorian, and the menu offers ye olde traditional British food like Welsh Rarebit (£3.50), bubble and squeak, crumpets and cream teas (£6.50).

ROYAL LONDON

Much of the pageantry, ceremony and vast wealth of the **Royal Family** are on display to loyal subjects and curious tourists. Look carefully and you'll learn an enormous amount about history, art and architecture along the way. For the current state of Windsor family affairs, we'll have to direct you to the tabloids.

BUCKINGHAM PALACE

London, SW1. Tel: 0171 930 4832. Limited opening, first week in August until the end of September, 9am to 4:15pm daily. Exact dates change yearly, phone for details. Adults: £8.50; children (5-17): £4.50; under 5, free. Victoria, Green Park or St. James Park tube.

In order to help finance the rebuilding of Windsor Castle (severely damaged by fire in 1992), the queen opened 18 official state rooms of Buckingham Palace to visitors in 1993. These formal rooms are a symphony in red plush, gilt, huge chandeliers and royal portraits, with the occasional Rubens, Rembrandt, and Van Dyck thrown in to give a bit of depth to the proceedings. Visitors enter through the (genuine) ambassador's entrance and are shown the state dining room, the grand staircase, the throne room, a number of state drawing rooms, three picture galleries, and an expensive gift shop, exiting at last along the perimeter of the palace's private gardens, where guests are decidedly not encouraged to linger.

The queues are huge and there isn't the slightest hint of daily life among the royals, so keep a lid on your expectations. There are plans to continue with the openings until 1997; after that, it is likely that the palace will close once again to the public. There's an ever-so-slightly grudging feel about the whole experience, as if the royal family can't wait to make enough money to stop the whole unsavory business. But then, we wouldn't want thousands of members of the public tramping through our house either.

THE CHANGING OF THE GUARD

Buckingham Palace, London SW1. Tel: 0171 930 4832. Daily April to July, every other day August to March: 11:30am to 12:10pm. Victoria, Green Park or St. James Park tube.

No other single event represents London better than the traditional (since 1660) changing of the Household Division of the queen's guard, which daily accounts for the huge crowds of foreign visitors and their cameras jostling for position at the Buckingham Palace gate. Choose an overcast weekday (which reduces the crowd by half) and try to arrive by 10:30, which will give you a chance to get in position, and watch the sideshow of the splendidly attired **Horse Guards** passing by the palace (11am weekdays, 10am Sunday) on their daily trip from **Hyde Park Barracks** to the **Horse Guard Parade**. We prefer the dramatic passage of the horse guard to the main show of foot guard changing, which, after the initial dramatic arrival of the band and the new guard, slows down to a 40 minute adagio of military mumbo-jumbo while keys are exchanged, without much in the way of action. (Look for the Irish wolfhound, mascot of the Irish guard, leading his troops on parade.) Still, it's an ancient ceremony, and not one you're likely to see anywhere in the New World.

You can prolong the royal afterglow at **The Guards Museum** *(Wellington Barracks, Bird Cage Walk, London SW1; Sunday to Thursday 10am to 4pm; tel: 0171 930 4466; St. James Park tube)*, devoted to the history of the regiments of foot guards. While you're there, pay a visit to the museum's Toy Soldier Centre with its amazing selection of new and antique miniature toy soldiers from every war the English have ever fought (and circus and farm animal sets; prices £5 to £600, collectors can order by fax: 0173 4733 947).

KENSINGTON PALACE

Kensington Gardens, London W8 4PX. Tel: 0171 937 9561. Open daily 9am to 5pm (Sunday 11am to 5pm). Last admission 4:15pm. Adults: £4.50, children £3. Free guided tours conducted throughout the day. Bayswater or Queensway tube.

Fondly (or not-so-fondly) dubbed "The Aunt Heap" by King Edward VII, Kensington Palace is the only palace in Britain continuously occupied by royalty and open to the public year round. William and Mary, Queen Anne, and George II all died here. Queen Victoria was born here and occupied the house until her ascension to the throne in 1837. But since George II moved out to take up permanent residence at Buckingham Palace, it has been nicknamed the Dowagers' Dumping Ground and is generally known as home to the "B-List" royals (though most hardly qualify as minor). Today it's divided into 28 flats and eight houses, and provides primary London residence for Princess Margaret, Princess Diana, and Prince and Princess Michael of Kent among others. Princess Di is said to occupy nine rooms (compared to her estranged husband's 220 at St. James'). All this in a house originally purchased for £18,000.

William III bought what was then known as Nottingham House in the village of Kensington back in 1698, where the damp riverside location of Whitehall palace aggravated his asthma. He commissioned Christopher Wren to convert it into a palace, and the rest, as they say, is history.

Visitors enter through the garden door, decorated with an ornamental hood bearing the monogram of William and Mary. Upstairs are **Queen Mary's apartments**, including an 84 foot long Stuart-style gallery designed by Wren. Note the secret door (probably used by servants, or so say the very proper guides) in the wall next to Hanneman's portrait of William as a young man. The blue and white Chinese porcelain on the mantle is from Mary's original collection; she first introduced this style to England, along with goldfish and cocoa. Mary and William, by the way, were first cousins and had an arranged marriage for political reasons. History reports that Mary wept for two days when informed of her pending marriage, but grew to love him. Their's is the only joint rule in British history.

In Queen Mary's closet, look for the profile of Queen Anne used as a model for the coins and sovereign medals of the day; her puffy bloated face is said to be the result of gout. The portrait of the Duke of Gloucester records the only one of Queen Anne's sixteen children to survive infancy. He died a year after the portrait was painted. Over the fireplace in the intimate dining room, look for the portrait of Katherine Elliot, nanny to Queen Mary and Queen Anne. Portraits of favorite servants would have been commissioned as a symbol of royal respect and affection.

After the dark of the Queen's bedchamber, the tone of the house changes dramatically. Wren's simple, understated style wasn't grand enough for George I, so the King added a grand suite of state rooms designed by Colin Campbell and painted by William Kent. Of these, the **King's Privy Chamber** is worth noting for its showy Mars and Minerva ceiling – Mars, wearing the Order of the Garter, was intended to symbolize the king's military prowess, and Minerva, the queen's wisdom. The wool and silk Mortlake tapestries woven for Charles I and representing the four seasons are superior to any paintings in the room. The **King's Presence Chamber** is distinguished by its red, blue, and green Pompeian-style ceiling. The chair or state was made for George IV when he was Prince of Wales; the unicorn, lion and feathered crown make up the symbols of his crest.

Queen Victoria's bedroom exudes a warmth none of the others seem to manage. It's furnished with personal mementos: photographs of her beloved Prince Albert on the bed table and a portrait of her son, later King Edward VII. Her manicure set and Indian juggling clubs (for exercise) remain in the room, along with a large painting commemorating her wedding to Albert in 1840, complete with the names of the guests painted on the frame.

Kent also painted the Jupiter ceiling in the **King's drawing room**. From this room, look out at the sweeping view of **Kensington Gardens** and the **Round Pond**. In the foreground, you'll find the statue of Queen Victoria created by her daughter (one of nine children), Princess Louise, on the occasion of Victoria's 50th year of rule. In the distance you can spot the top of the American Embassy in Mayfair.

The **King's Gallery** has been recently and meticulously restored to its 18th century glory – even the white molding paint was mixed from an original formula. Van Dyck's Cupid and Sculla and two fine Tintorettos hang here, under another Kent ceiling depicting scenes from the life of Ulysses. The curiosity above the fireplace is a working wind-dial dating from 1694, and is connected to a weather vane on the palace roof. Note the frosted glass of the windows – it protects royal inhabitants from the prying eyes of the paparazzi.

The lavishly decorated **Cupola Room** was the palace's main state room, and is decorated throughout on a grand Classical theme. Fluted ionic columns support a Roman frieze; the clock that once played tunes by Handel is decorated with scenes of the four great ancient cultures (Chaldea, Persia, Macedonia, and Rome); gilded busts of Roman emperors and statues of Roman gods and goddesses complete the royal parallel. Look for the Star in the center of the ceiling; it symbolizes the Order of the Garter – the highest honor a monarch can bestow on a subject.

Don't miss the wonderful trompe-l'oeil painting of antique paparazzi along the King's staircase. And for those interested in period costumes, there's the **Royal Ceremonial Dress Collection** on the ground floor. The collection is displayed in a series of tableaux that recreate court and coronation scenes spanning three centuries. King George IV's glorious coronation robe shows the influence of Napoleonic style on the English monarchy (and the French have been leading the way in fashion ever since).

Hawksmoor designed the impressive **Orangery**, with its magnificent windows, as a greenhouse for Queen Anne in 1704. It opens from Easter to the end of September and serves morning coffee, light lunches and afternoon tea. In winter, food is served in the basement of the palace. Unless, of course, you can wrangle an invitation from one of the royal "Aunts."

(Note: Kensington Palace will be closed for renovation from September '95 to May '96. Check to confirm reopening.)

THE QUEEN'S GALLERY

Buckingham Palace, Buckingham Palace Road, London SW1. Tel: 0171 930 4832 or 0171 799 2331 (recorded information). Tuesday to Saturday, 9:30am to 4pm (last admission); Sunday 2pm to 4pm. Adults £2.50; children: £1.20. Victoria tube.

Every January, a new collection of art and objects from the extraordinary royal collection (one of the finest – public or private – in the world) is put on show at this pleasant gallery built in 1963 to replace a chapel bombed during the war. The past few years have featured Reynolds and Gainsborough and Faberge eggs; check listings for the current show. Probably the most discouraging realization you'll make when visiting this gallery is to note how superb the royal collection of old master paintings and drawings, furniture, jewelry and porcelain is, and how little of value the last few monarchs have contributed.

THE ROYAL MEWS

Buckingham Palace Road (corner of Lower Grosvenor Place), London SW1. Tel: 0171 799 2331. Open October 5 to March 28: Wednesday only, noon to 4pm; March 29 to August 4: Tuesday, Wednesday, Thursday, noon to 4pm; August 7 to September 28: Monday to Thursday, noon to 4pm. Last admission 3:30pm. Closed January 1-3. Adults: £3.50. Children under 17: £2. Victoria tube.

Attention horse-lovers: This is your chance to meet Monarch, Osprey, Mark, Susie, Laura, Barcelona, Twilight, Henrik and Iceland – and all their other handsome four-legged friends. They're a mixed group of Hungarian Greys and Cleveland Bays, they belong to the Queen (and wear horse blankets bearing the royal monogram), and are responsible for pulling a variety of ceremonial carriages, coaches, and traps. Their grooms wear ties, their stalls are cleaner than most hospitals, and they live in a stable built by the highly-esteemed **John Nash**, who designed the mews quadrangle, clock tower, coach house, stables and riding school in 1825. The groom tells us they're fed three times a day, have their own personal veterinarian, and due to their pampered lifestyle have virtually forgotten how to graze. It seems that of everyone involved with the royal family, horses have one of the best deals.

Aside from the privileged beasts, a visit to the Royal Mews offers a behind-the-scenes look at the working establishment responsible for all the Queen's horses and carriages. And what carriages! The **Royal State Coach** originally built for King George III in 1762 is entirely gold (gilded), weighs eight tons, is supported by eight gold palm trees and decorated with gold Neptunes trumpeting (on conch shells) the approach of the monarch. The chassis is adorned with Roman gods and goddesses courtesy of Florentine artist Giovanni Battista Cipriani. Among the many other carriages on display is the Cinderella-style **glass coach** (1910) that transported Queen Elizabeth, Diana, and Sarah Ferguson to their respective weddings, pony landaus belonging to various royal children, a coronation coach, an opening-of-parliament coach, and a number of marriage coaches (the way the royal family has been going lately, they might be wise to invest in a divorce coach).

Also on display are harnesses, saddles, historical photographs, and the hundreds of ribbons and trophies won by members of the royal family in riding and driving competitions.

PARKS & GARDENS

Since the great British Empire has fallen on hard times, the British have had even more time to devote to their exceptionally beautiful gardens. We think this is a good thing, and like to spend every spare moment surrounded by lilacs, roses, tulips and herbaceous borders. Nobody does gardens better than the British, and it is your duty as a tourist to spend at least an afternoon or two admiring them.

English parks are for the use of everyone – you are expected to walk on the grass and bring a picnic or a book. Do not, however, get carried away and actually pick anything; you will probably end up in jail (or lynched).

CHELSEA PHYSIC GARDEN

66 Royal Hospital Road, London SW3 4HS. Tel: 0171 352 5646. Open (April to October only) Wednesday 2pm to 5pm; Sunday 2pm to 6pm. Adults: £3.50; Children: £1.80. Sloane Square tube.

An opening in the high brick wall on **Swan Walk** tips you off that something special is afoot. And when you enter through the iron gates, you'll feel as if you've stumbled on a real life version of Frances Hodgson Burnett's *Secret Garden*. Founded in 1673 by the **Society of Apothecaries**, the Chelsea Physic Garden is one of Europe's oldest botanic gardens, and has been continuously cultivated for medicinal purposes for more than 300 years. Open to the public for the first time in 1983, its acres of sunken beds are formally arranged and neatly separated by grassy paths offering access to 7,000 species of plants.

You'll find gardens within gardens (the garden of world medicine, the folk medicine garden, the lava rock garden), rare plants and trees (Britain's largest olive tree, the unusual cork oak), useful plants (dye plants, perfume plants, poison plants) and of course a real Secret Garden. We recommend the 20p map (available at the gate) highlighting seasonal points of interest, and the twenty minute tours conducted by volunteer guides at intervals throughout the day. Medicinal cures aside, we can't think of a better place to recuperate from whatever in the modern world ails you.

The gift shop sells books, plants and botanical souvenirs; tea and homemade cakes are also available.

HAMPSTEAD HEATH

Hampstead tube.

Turn left out of the tube (the deepest in London), then left again down pretty Flask Walk, and keep walking straight until you get to Hampstead Heath. Getting there is easy, which leaves plenty of time to explore once you arrive – in good company, we might add. A hundred species of bird live on the Heath's 790 acres. Constable painted it. Keats wrote poetry in it. It is not a park; nor has it been groomed, tamed, planted and ordered. Foxes walk across it. Delicious wild mushrooms grow on it. From the top of **Parliament Hill** (to the southeast), the panoramic views of London are breathtaking; on the rare snowy day in London, it will be covered with children whizzing by on tea trays and you might have to blink once or twice to remember what century you inhabit.

Save a long afternoon for a walk across the Heath. Visit **Kenwood House** at the very top and admire the Rembrandts. Take tea in the coach house. Wander past the Highgate bathing ponds to the east. Ask directions only when you really need to, that is, when you are hopelessly lost. After all, the ability to get lost in a so beautiful a place must be one of the most perfect joys of living in London.

HIGHGATE CEMETERY

Swains Lane, London N6. Tel: 0181 340 1834. East Cemetery open April 1 to October 31, daily 10am to 5pm (11am to 5pm weekends); November 1 to March 31, daily 10am to 4pm (11am to 4pm weekends). West Cemetery open for guided tours only (£3; photo permit £1). April 1 to October 31, daily at noon, 2pm and 4pm; weekends 11am to 4pm every hour on the hour. November 1 to March 31, weekends only, every hour 11am to 3pm. Highgate or Archway tube.

Could it possibly be worthwhile coming all the way to north London for a cemetery tour? We think so. It's a great way to learn a great deal about Victorian London and its (late) inhabitants – in a remarkably beautiful setting. We recommend approaching the cemetery from the Highgate tube station, from where you'll need to walk ten minutes or so down Swain's (formerly Swine's) Lane.

On your walk, you'll pass a vista or two offering views of London that are nothing short of spectacular, so keep your eyes peeled. Stop in at the lovely **Prince of Wales pub** on your way, or take a small detour to **The**

Flask (see *Where to Drink*). The swine in question, by the way, would have been on their way to market in Highgate – the Lane provided the access to their demise.

About halfway down the hill, past any number of lovely houses, you arrive at the **East** (left hand) and **West Gates** (on your right as you descend). If you don't feel inclined to take the tour, skip it in favor of a wander through the east cemetery, where you'll find Marx (inscription: "Workers of the world unite"), Ralph Richardson, and George Eliot.

If you do join a tour, you'll learn about the history of the cemetery, which is fascinating. A quick version goes pretty much like this: the population of London was growing so fast in the early 1800s that seven private cemeteries had to be opened on the outskirts to keep up with demand, all hotly competing for "business." In 1838, 17 acres in Highgate were purchased privately, and carefully designed according to the tenets of the high picturesque – which included winding lanes, terraces, romantic paths and catacombs.

Of the 17 acres, 15 were allotted to conformists (Anglicans) and the other two to non-conformists (all newer forms of protestantism). Nineteen more acres were added in 1854, as the financial success of the cemetery burgeoned – Highgate had become not only a very fashionable place for wealthy families to be buried, but an exceedingly popular picnic and promenading spot as well. And with the average lifespan at that time a mere 38 years, there was no shortage of customers. Since then, 167,000 people have found their way to Highgate cemetery, and though the west side officially closed to new applicants over a decade ago, a mere £2,000 will still get you a nice position on the east side.

Today, though still privately owned, the **West Cemetery** is the subject of extensive charity-led conservation efforts, having been completely neglected and left to grow wild for decades. A team of volunteer gardeners tend the 200 species of wildflowers and continue to try to clear and repair some of the worst damage. The tour of the west cemetery should not be undertaken (oops!) with celeb-spotting in mind – Dickens' family is here, as is Christina Rossetti (exhumed by Dante, seven years after her death in order to retrieve the poems he impetuously buried with her). But the real stars are the more ordinary folk. Queen Victoria's royal horse slaughterer, buried with a handsome statue of a (rather cheerful, considering) horse on his grave. The Victorian sporting goods manufacturer with a cricket wicket carved onto his headstone in the "bowled out" position. Frank Hall, the 19th century portraitist, surrounded by many of his subjects (it's said he died of overwork).

George Wombwell, the menagerie owner famed for passing a rhinoceros off as a unicorn, is here with a huge sleeping lion on his tomb; so too Julius Beer, the newspaper magnate so unpopular he didn't get an *e Times* (despite – or perhaps because of – owning the rival Beer, by the way, prepared his revenge in advance by g a huge mausoleum that obscured the lovely view of London from the promenade.

Oh yes. The guides are terrific, the flowers copious and the foxes sometimes in evidence. And evening tours are available in the summer (phone for details).

THE ROYAL BOTANIC GARDENS (KEW GARDENS)

Richmond, Surrey TW9 3AB. Tel: 0181 332 5622. Adults: £4; children (5-16): £2; children under 5: free. Open 9:30am to dusk. Kew Gardens tube.

Get onto the District line headed for Richmond and when you emerge at Kew Gardens you emerge in a different world. Walk through the tiny village of **Kew** (filled with flower boxes, little shops and commuters) following the signs to the Royal Botanic Gardens and prepare to be shown exactly how seriously the English take their gardening. The 300 acres of Kew Gardens were originally laid out as a botanical research center in 1750, and included plantlife collected throughout Britain, Europe, and the new world, as well as specimens collected by Captain Cook on his voyages.

First stop has to be the glorious glass and iron **Victorian Palm House**, though cast your eyes over the pond first to admire the black swans. Inside are, of course, palms galore, not to mention coffee trees, yams (whence come vital chemicals for the production of oral contraceptives), giant bamboo (that can grow up to a meter a day), macadamia nut trees, mango trees, even a rare black ebony tree. An iron spiral staircase gives access to an upper level walkway with great bird's eye views of the proceedings. Take the staircase down for the **Marine Display**, complete with large tanks of live coral, breathtakingly beautiful cold water fish, and a bat fish in a bat fish cave (no sign of a robin fish). The star of the exhibition is supposed to be algae, but we liked the needle-nosed flat yellow square fish.

Emerging again into the less tropical climate of Kew, you'll be spoiled for choice. The **Temperate House** is to the left, where we passed a thunderstorm in perfect peace, accompanied only by a friendly little English robin, who came and perched within inches and stayed for a chat, as English robins are wont to do. Your route depends in large part on the weather and the season. In February the inside houses become magical refuges filled with singing birds and wonderful perfumes – though a million and a half (no kidding) crocuses bloom in February as well. March sees daffodils by the tens of thousands and masses of cherry blossoms; by April the magnolias and tulips are in full trumpet; and the matching lilacs and dense blankets of bluebells (head for Queen Charlotte's cottage) in May are simply staggering in their intensity. In June the Rhododendron

Dell (designed by Capability Brown) bursts into bloom. By
is a riot of color, and the **Princess of Wales Conservatory** with its ⌐
cacti, orchids, and astoundingly beautiful giant waterlily must not be
missed.

The elaborate care and planning that goes into these beds is almost
unimaginable by American standards, and while it's a remarkable experience in the spring and summer, Kew is romantic and serene on a rainy
winter day. Strangely, it's a good place to take restless kids, who can run
unhindered through the huge indoor glass houses, enjoy the warmth and
the great variety of fish, birds, flowers and trees. In fact Kew in winter or
the rain seems to be something of a haven for local mums, many of whom
pass long winter afternoons sitting and chatting in the Palm House while
the kids play exuberant games of hide and seek.

Aside from ice cream and drink kiosks, there are three main food
options at Kew – the **Orangery Restaurant**, which serves hot meals and
is particularly nice for afternoon tea; the **Pavilion**, for self-service hot
meals, sandwiches and drinks; and the **Bakery** for snacks. The Orangery
is open year round, while the other two offer limited services (weekends
or Sunday only) during the winter. On your way home, you might want
to stop for a drink at the very pleasant **Flower and Firkin** pub just by the
Kew station – it has a good selection of made-on-the-premises ales and is
a pleasant place to relax and wait for the train.

REGENT'S PARK

Regent's Park, Baker Street, Great Portland Street or Camden Town tube.
Try to imagine Regent's Park as it was in Henry VIII's day, densely
forested and filled with stags for the King's hunting pleasure. Elizabeth I
also hunted here, and it might still be filled with stags had not its 16,000
trees been chopped down, and, under Charles I, leased to tenant farmers.

In the early 1800s, the park was claimed by the **Prince Regent**, who
thought it would make a pleasant estate; he commissioned architect John
Nash to build a series of grand terraces around the edges, 26 houses in the
grounds, and a pleasure palace for himself. In the event, only the terraces
were built; they still stand, elegant monuments of grand, cream-colored
stone.

What's left is London's most beautiful park – a subjective observa-
tion, of course, but one shared by the thousands of Londoners who play
soccer and softball, who gather to feed the 25 varieties of designer ducks,
to watch Shakespeare in the Park, to sit on cold December days and warm
July days in the tea houses, to admire the exquisite rose gardens, to gaze
at the sublime flower beds, to row boats, to court, to kiss and to fall in love
there.

Queen Mary's rose gardens, the **outdoor theater** and one of the **tea houses** are all in the inner circle; the **zoo** is at the very top of the park. We like to head for the park at about 8pm on a June evening. There are still two hours of daylight, you won't get mugged, the fragrance is magical, and the atmosphere pure enchantment. Anyone who doesn't fall in love with Regent's Park has a heart of stone.

HYDE PARK & KENSINGTON GARDENS

Hyde Park Corner, Marble Arch, Knightsbridge, Notting Hill Gate, Queensway and Lancaster Gate tubes.

If it weren't for Henry VIII's great appetite for hunting, London's parks might have ended up as shopping streets and parking lots. Henry VIII established Hyde Park as a royal park back in 1536, and it has been owned and protected by the monarchy (with the exception of the Cromwell Commonwealth years) ever since. Surrounded by some of London's most fashionable real estate, it was (and is) society's place to take a bit of air, run its dogs, and show off its new frocks.

But before you imagine something terribly civilized out of a Merchant-Ivory movie, remember that until the late 18th century highwaymen still roamed the park, along with goats, sheep, cows, and the brocade-clad, kid-gloved, button-booted upper classes. In the late 17th and early 18th centuries, the **Serpentine** flowing through its center was a sewer for the growing villages of north London. In 1820 it was written of the Serpentine that "good society no longer goes there, except to drown itself." And for centuries, the area now known as **Marble Arch** was the site of myriad public floggings and hangings, some drawing crowds of more than 200,000.

Although Hyde Park and Kensington Gardens are technically and temperamentally separate (Hyde Park to the right of the Serpentine and below it; Kensington Gardens to the left), geographically they form a 620 acre rectangle in the middle of London. Within that rectangle, you'll find a very good art gallery (**The Serpentine Gallery**) and Queen Victoria's monument to her husband, **The Albert Memorial** (inlaid with semi-precious stones, and paying homage to Albert's passions: Poetry, Painting, Architecture, Sculpture, Commerce, Manufacturing, Engineering, Agriculture, Faith, Hope, Charity and Humility – among others).

You can rent paddle boats and row boats on the Serpentine, and horses on which to gallop along **Rotten Row** (from the French *route du roi* or king's road). You can hear bands playing at the **Bandstand** and orators orating at **Speaker's Corner** (the north east corner, at Marble Arch). Little boys and girls sail boats on the round pond, others feed the Serpentine geese and ducks. Tea can be drunk and lunch eaten. But whatever else the park people do, they still promenade as they did in the old days, arm in arm, child in tow or dog on lead. Hyde Park is a sociable place; Kensington Gardens more pensive and less traveled. Check your map for the precise locations of points of interest. Then, if you have time on your hands, visit them all.

GREEN PARK & SAINT JAMES PARK

Green Park, St. James Park, or Hyde Park Corner tube.

Charles II added Green Park on to St. James Park in 1660, but it has never been a very happy marriage. Although the two sit next to each other, like two diamonds attached at the points (the meeting place is Buckingham Palace), they are as different as night and day. **Green Park**, bordered by Piccadilly to the north, is a rough-and-ready patch of urban green, with banks of daffodils and tulips in no particular order. Duels were once fought here, and on a winter day, when the wind sweeps brutally across it, you can imagine them vividly. In summer, with dappled sunshine pouring through the trees, it's hard to imagine any unpleasantness ever touching it.

St. James Park, banded on two sides by **The Mall** and **Birdcage Walk**, is where English high society showed off its new 17th and 18th century fashions in elegant promenades. According to cold war legend, spies used to rendezvous here. Today, royal processions pass by on their way to Buckingham Palace and civil servants from surrounding offices come here to contemplate queen, country and the girl in accounts at lunchtime.

Beautifully manicured flower beds, a little stream and bridge, and even a tiny pastoral cottage share the 90 acres of the park with the famous St. James pelicans, whose ancestors were first presented as a gift to the court by the Russian Ambassador in the 17th century. Feeding time (fish, of course) is mid-afternoon, when the pelicans are at their most grand, flapping huge wings and looking imperious and special, which of course they are.

11. WALKING TOURS OF LONDON

When you've had enough of formal sightseeing, a walking tour of a local London neighborhood is probably just what the tour doctor ordered.

CHELSEA

For a respite from the museums, monuments and shopping a walk through one of London's prettiest village neighborhoods is in order. Start in **Sloane Square** (*Sloane Square tube*), named for Sir Hans Sloane, 18th century naturalist, antiquarian and physician. His collection, left to the nation when he died in 1758, became the nucleus of the British Museum. The **Royal Court Theatre** to the right of the station first produced George Bernard Shaw's *Major Barbara*, and John Osborne's *Look Back in Anger*; it carries on the tradition of fine theater to this day.

From the station, walk down **King's Road**, the main shopping artery of Chelsea, once the King's private road linking Whitehall to Hampton Court, and center of London's swinging sixties scene (remember Chelsea Girls?) Turn left onto Cheltenham Terrace and right again onto Leonard's Terrace. On your left is **Chelsea Royal Hospital** (Christopher Wren and John Soane, 1681-1817), home to legions of red-uniformed retired Chelsea soldiers, or Chelsea Pensioners. Royal Avenue is where Ian Fleming's famous hero James Bond lived (fictionally, of course); Bram Stoker, author of Dracula, lived at 18 Leonard's Terrace. Turn left onto Durham Place which leads to the entrance gates of the hospital grounds (*daily, 10am to noon and 2pm to 4pm*). The best way to see the Wren chapel and great hall is with a Chelsea Pensioner as your guide; there's usually one willing to provide the service.

Exit the hospital grounds at the same gate, return to Royal Hospital Road and turn left, past the **National Army Museum** (which owns Hitler's telephone switchboard and a collection of Gainsborough, Reynolds and Romney paintings). Turn left on **Tite Street** for a look at the homes of some of Chelsea's most celebrated residents: Oscar Wilde lived at 34, Augustus John at 33, John Singer Sargent at 31, and James Whistler at 13. Back on Royal Hospital Road, stop at **Foxtrot Oscar** for lunch *(79 Royal Hospital Road).*

The next stop of interest is the **Chelsea Physic Garden**, just a three minute walk from the restaurant. Founded as a teaching resource by the Royal Society of Apothecaries in 1673, the garden is open to the public only on Wednesday and Sunday (entrance on Swan Walk).

Back on Royal Hospital Road, turn left; next on the right is **Cheyne** (pronounced *chain-y*) **Walk** – one of Chelsea's best known thoroughfares. Follow it past a row of Georgian homes whose former residents include George Eliot (no. 4), Dante Gabriel Rossetti and Algernon Swinburne (no. 16), Lloyd George (no. 10). The intersection of Oakley Street and Cheyne Walk was the site of Henry VIII's Manor House, where his daughter, Princess Elizabeth (later Queen Elizabeth I) lived from 1536 to 1547; a plaque at no. 23 commemorates the site. Keith Richards of the Rolling Stones and John Paul Getty have been more recent inhabitants of the street. Look for the **statue of Thomas Carlyle** which is your cue to turn right onto Cheyne Row for a tour of his house *(no. 24, open April to October, Wednesday to Sunday 11am to 5pm, tel. 0171 352 7087).*

Back onto Cheyne Walk, you'll see the **Albert Bridge** just ahead of you; built in 1873, it is transformed at night by hundreds of white lights. Note the green wooden building to the right of the bridge – it's a cabbie shelter where licensed cab drivers can stop for a hot-cooked meal any time of day; only a few of the 61 original Victorian shelters survive. Stop in the **King's Head and Eight Bells** *(no. 50)* for a drink in its 400 year old bar.

Just ahead you'll see the clocktower of **Chelsea Old Church** *(daily 10am to 1pm and 2-5pm; Sunday 1:30-5:30pm)*, Sir Thomas More's parish church, dating from the mid-13th century; the caretakers are great sources of historical anecdote. As you leave the church, turn right onto Old Church Street. No. 46 with its charming portraits was the site of the Old Chelsea Dairy; no. 66 was designed by Walter Gropius in 1936.

Rejoin King's Road, and turn back towards Sloane Square, stopping for a piece of homemade poppyseed strudel at **E. Bovis** *(no. 251)*. **L.K. Bennett** *(no. 239)* is worth a stop for its elegant English and French designer dresses, hats and knits. Pass **Chelsea Town Hall**, the stairs of which have been the scene of many a trendy wedding photo, and continue along to **Antiquarius** *(no. 135-141)*, a warehouse of antiques worth at least half an hour of browsing. If your feet are starting to go, sit down at the rear cafe for a glass of wine, cup of tea, or one of the best potato fritatas in London. Cross over at Marks & Spencer, and follow Markham Street to a small square of grass known as **Chelsea Common** or **Chelsea Green**. This living-room-sized patch of green is all that's left of a thirty acre pasture dating back to the 17th century. To this day, it retains its traditional grazing rights, so feel free to tether your goat.

Follow **Cale Street** for its good traditional shops, including Jane Asher's **Bakery and Tea Shop** (Britain's answer to Martha Stewart). Retrace your steps back to King's Road, where you might want to make one final detour before you reach Sloane Square (and the tube) – for **J. Sandoe Books** *on Blacklands Terrace*.

Diehard walkers can turn left at Sloane Square onto Sloane Street, taking in the **General Trading Company**, or continue down Sloane Street to Hans Street where another left turn takes you to the back entrance of **Harrods**. If that doesn't finish you off, nothing will.

FLEET STREET TO ST. PAUL'S

This tour must be done on a weekday (the City virtually shuts down at weekends), and begins at Waterloo tube station, though you can cheat and begin on the Strand. If you begin at Waterloo, walk over Waterloo Bridge, stopping in the middle to admire London's best views of St. Paul's cathedral (our destination) to your right and the Houses of Parliament and Big Ben to your left. Turn right off the bridge on to the Strand (in the 18th century, this theater district strip would have been teeming with jugglers, pickpockets, prostitutes, gentlemen and worst of all, actors). From here, our walking tour is virtually a straight line due east, ending with St. Paul's Cathedral, and with a short detour or two on the way.

THE LADIES' BRIDGE

The original Waterloo Bridge was opened in 1817, and its graceful granite arches and Doric columns were deemed so beautiful, it was described as "the noblest bridge in the world." Sadly, it had begun to settle so badly by the 1920s that it had to be demolished. Its far more prosaic replacement, designed by Sir Giles Scott, was built between 1937 and 1942 – a period during which most of the available workforce was at war. Thus, the bridge was built by a team of laborers made up almost entirely of women, a fact which is responsible for its Cockney nickname "The Ladies' Bridge."

The first stop is for art-lovers only, the **Courtauld Institute** (*Somerset House, Strand, London WC2. Tel: 0171 873 2526. Monday to Saturday, 10am to 6pm; Sunday 2pm to 6pm*) with its exceptional collection of paintings. From there, head east down the Strand; stop in at the **Twinings** shop (*216 Strand*), which has been selling loose tea at this location since 1716. Note the two Mandarin figures above the entrance door – they have stood guarding the shop since it first opened. Tea experts will scoop loose tea from large tins, offering advice on flavor and brewing; treat yourself to the Earl Grey marmalade made with bergamot. Take a moment to visit the tiny museum at the rear of the store.

Back to the Strand, which soon turns into **Fleet Street**, famed worldwide as the center of Britain's newspaper industry (though most of London's newspapers have moved to cheaper real estate elsewhere). At *number 37 Fleet Street* is **C. Hoare & Co. Bank**, whose customers since its inception in 1672 have included Lord Byron, Jane Austen, and Samuel Pepys. All statements and ledgers were written by hand until 1962, and to this day, the bank tellers wear swallowtail coats. The decor is superb (burnished wood, old leaded windowpanes), but don't try and open an account, you'll need a sponsor and references, if you please.

Continue down Fleet Street until you come to **Middle Temple Lane** on your right. The Temple is a snaking maze of lanes home to the most exclusive of London's **Inns of Court** (or barristers' chambers) including the chambers of *Rumpole of the Bailey* author John Mortimer in Dr. Johnson's Buildings (named after its famous 18th century occupant). Take particular note of the **Inner Temple Gateway** *on Fleet Street*, one of the most imposing and complete Tudor half-timbered buildings to survive the 1666 Great Fire of London, and to survive the intervening 330 years of development.

Turn down the Lane and get a feel for the area; although bombed heavily during the Blitz, it has been beautifully restored. Seek out **Temple Church**, the lawyers' private chapel which is open to the public. Consecrated in 1185, it is one of London's oldest churches, and one of only five surviving round churches in England. Stylistically it is a bit of a mishmash, combining the simple beauty of the Romanesque with the more elaborate Gothic, including a stunning, rib-vaulted ceiling.

Emerging from the Temple, if you're ready for lunch, try **Ye Olde Cock Tavern**, *22 Fleet Street*, established 1554. It serves good ploughman's lunches, steak and mushroom pie, sandwiches, and to drink, our favorite Theaxton XB and Old Peculier (only for those with a good tolerance for alcohol) and wines by the bottle and glass *(closed Sundays, open Saturday 11-4pm)*.

If you're not ready for lunch, continue on to **Dr. Johnson's House** *(daily 11am to 5pm, closed Sunday)* on Johnson's Court, off the north side of Fleet Street. Then head back out onto Fleet Street via Wine Office Court, where you will find the venerable **Ye Olde Cheshire Cheese** public house. The Cheshire Cheese is a tourist pub, but very well-used by locals too, and so historical and with such good traditional food, it would be a shame to pass it by. If the Cheshire Cheese doesn't appeal, try **The Tipperary** ("The Smallest Pub on Fleet Street") just across Fleet Street, for a jumbo Abbot Ale sausage or ploughman's, followed by treacle sponge, or the mysterious Tipperary pie. The tiny sliver of a pub has a comfortable panelled room upstairs overlooking Fleet Street, perfect for the solitary traveler with a newspaper or book.

Next stop is **St. Bride's Church**, the journalists' church, rebuilt by Christopher Wren after it burned to the ground during the Great Fire – along with 87 other City churches. Wren's church was seriously bombed during the Blitz, but has since been rebuilt according to Wren's original plans. St. Bride's is most famous for its steeple, which, in the late 1700s, inspired a local baker to create the first white tiered wedding cake based on its design. The good little museum in the crypt has displays of relics found in and around the site, ranging from Roman coins to 19th century cutlery, and is definitely worth a visit. Lunchtime concerts are held here at 1:15 and 1:45pm Tuesday, Wednesday and Friday.

In front of St. Brides, the 17th century **Olde Bell Tavern** was built by Wren as a hostel for the St. Bride's workmen. At risk of turning this into a pub crawl, we'll mention one or two other possible stops. The **Punch Tavern** next to the Olde Bell, is a beautifully tiled and restored high Victorian pub, well-attended by local journalists until the newspapers moved out of the neighborhood. Turning right down New Bridge Road, walk toward Blackfriar's Bridge until you see, on the left, **The Blackfriar**, which gets our vote for the most rare and wonderfully beautiful pub in London. Stop in for a look, if not a drink *(closed weekends)*. Back on Fleet Street there's the **Old Bank of England Ale and Pie House**, another wonderful choice for food and drink.

Tearing yourself away from the beer, stop in at **St. Martin-within-Ludgate** church, another Wren church rebuilt after the Great Fire. It's also famed for it's beautiful spire, designed by Wren as a counterpoint to the huge dome of St. Paul's a few hundred feet away. Inside, a substantial amount of the dark wood carving is the work of Grinling Gibbons, whose trademark open peapod (which he used as a signature) can be seen among the wooden fruit and flowers. William Penn, the founding father of Pennsylvania was married here in 1643.

And as we approach the end of the walking tour, you now have a dilemma as to how to finish. A visit to the public gallery of the **Old Bailey** (*Warwick Passage off Old Bailey, weekdays 10-4pm, closed 1-2pm, no children under 14, no cameras – and no place to check them*) is the restful option. You can sit in the visitor's gallery and watch British justice in action. Or, continue on to **St. Paul's** – not for the weary or the half-hour tour. If it's nearly 4pm by this time, it's really too late to do either one. So have a good look at St. Paul's and go home, saving both for another day.

GREENWICH

Follow the Thames about five miles southeast, and you come – round the great twisting bend of the Isle of Dogs – to the once-great port city of **Greenwich**. Vikings anchored here, the Romans built a fort here, but it began to thrive in earnest in the 15th century as home to the Tudor court of Henry VIII. Henry was born in Greenwich, as were his daughters Mary (later Queen of Scots) and Elizabeth (later Queen Elizabeth I), and it housed the favorite of his many palaces. Henry VIII had good reason to keep his court in Greenwich – convenient to the Royal Dock in Deptford (home of the Royal Navy), it was also an exceedingly beautiful rural location for hunting, shooting, and frolicking.

It wasn't until the next king, James I, hired Inigo Jones to build the **Queen's House** for his wife (Anne of Denmark) that the Greenwich we recognize today began to take shape. The Palladian villa Jones built was of exceedingly radical design for England in 1635, far more Italian Renaissance than Tudor half-timber. Anne died before the house was finished, and James' son, Charles I, turned it over to his wife, who decorated Jones' Queen's House to a legendary standard of magnificence.

Cromwell turned the house into a prison during the commonwealth years; after the monarchy was restored, Charles II hired France's Andre Le Notre, designer of the gardens of Versailles, to make **Greenwich Park** the finest in England. Little remains of Le Notre's formal French design, except the grand chestnut-lined avenues and the faint remnants of a magnificent grass staircase that can still be seen (just) to the left and below the statue of Nelson.

Finding Greenwich far too damp, William and Mary finally moved the court back to Kensington (see Kensington Palace) and hired Christopher Wren to turn Charles II's palace into a Royal Hospital; since 1873 it has housed the **Royal Naval College**.

The nicest way to get to Greenwich is by boat, various companies run year round from **Westminster** or **Charing Cross Pier** (*Westminster or Charing Cross tube, trip time 45-60 minutes; £3.25*). The scenic trip usually comes with a colorful Cockney commentary pointing out monuments, celebrity houses and pirate pubs; they also usually stop at the Tower of London. Otherwise, catch a British Rail train from Charing Cross (frequent service; 20 minute journey) to Greenwich Station.

If you arrive by river, take a few minutes to admire the lovely tea clipper, the *Cutty Sark* by the dock. Built in 1869 for the tea trade with India and China, it was the fastest transport in the world – the 19th century equivalent of Concorde – and it made the journey from China to England in 107 days. You can pay £3.25 to go on board, but note that the ship has been gutted, leaving a series of educational exhibitions that give no true sense of life on board. Still, there's an excellent collection of figureheads on the lower level (including Abraham Lincoln, Gladstone, Disraeli, Cleopatra, Florence Nightingale and Hiawatha, as well as the usual variety of lovely ladies) that helps make a visit worthwhile. Take another moment to admire the *Gypsy Moth IV*, the 53 foot ketch sailed around the world singlehanded by Sir Francis Chichester (at the age of 65); then head into town.

If you're ready for lunch, stroll around **Church Street** where you'll be spoiled for choice. **Ye Olde Pie House** *(45 Church Street)* has been doing the traditional British steak and kidney thing since 1890; **Taste of India** *(57 Church St.)* serves up excellent Indian food; you can have fish and chips at **Beachcomber** *(34 Church St.)*; more good Indian at **Mogul** *(10 Church St.)*; or continue round the corner for **Pistachio's** deli, **Treasure of China**, **Bar du Musee**, or **Saigon**. You might also want to take some time to explore the excellent nautical antique shops on Church Street (specializing in boat models and maps and prints), and visit the central market specializing in new crafts (weekends only).

Next stop is the **National Maritime Museum** and the **Queen's House** *(daily 10am to 5pm; Adults: £5.50, children: £3; tel: 0181 858 4422; one comprehensive ticket also admits you to the Royal Observatory at the top of the hill)*. The Maritime Museum is heaven for kids, who might want to skip through the excellent 15th and 16th century seafaring paintings and head straight through the models room to the **All Hands Gallery** *(open daily after 2:30pm, and all day weekends)* a new interactive gallery designed for kids up to 15.

But the hero of the museum is the **Neptune Gallery**, a massive hangar of a space filled with full-sized ships – from royal barges to Chinese junks to an enormous 1930 paddle tug, *The Reliant*, with glass cut-away sections revealing the control rooms and cabins. The 17th and 18th century royal barges are also wonderfully impressive, dramatically lit, covered with elaborate carving and gilding, and seemingly better suited to Cleopatra than Queen Mary. Next stop is the **20th Century Seapower** gallery, with lots of hands-on computer navigation demonstrations and good wartime newsreel footage. Pause for a cup of tea or a sandwich at the **Bosun's Whistle Cafe**; get a table outdoors overlooking the park if it's a nice day.

A hand-held audio guide walks you through the **Queen's House** (Inigo Jones, 1614-1660) giving historical detail throughout; what it won't tell you is the story of the controversial millions spent on reproducing the original silk damask wall-hangings and hand-woven velvet. The house has a beautiful cantilevered staircase, some good paintings, and superb views of the park from the pretty balcony.

Now make the steep ascent to Christopher Wren's lovely **Observatory**. (If the climb is too much for you, a shuttle bus runs from the *Cutty*

Sark to the top of the hill.) It was built in 1675 for John Flamsteed, astronomer to Charles II, and used by successive royal astronomers until 1948. Today, it houses an impressive display of quadrants, sextants, spyglasses and telescopes, and best of all, the beautiful octagonal room designed by Wren to house Flamsteed's late 17th century state-of-the-art telescope. It is one of the few intact Wren interiors in existence, and the radiant purity of its design hints at the architect's genuine passion for astronomy.

In the observatory itself, pause for a look at the world's 7th largest refracting telescope – built, astonishingly, in 1893. Next door, a daily planetarium show begins at 2:30pm. And before you leave, straddle the **Greenwich meridian line**, get a picture of yourself with one foot in the eastern and one in the western hemisphere, and set your watch by the most accurate clock in the world.

THE THAMES: FROM FOUL FACTORIES TO FAIR FISHING

From the 11th to the 19th centuries, the Thames was filled with sewage and the waste from tanneries and slaughterhouses; by the late 19th century, the stench got so bad that sheets soaked in chloride of lime were hung in the Houses of Parliament to try and improve the air quality.

During this time, the Thames docks were villainous, unsavory places populated with "devil's taverns," famed for their pirates, scoundrels, and press-gangs. If a sailor indulged in one pint too many, he often woke with a headache on board a ship bound for China, or found himself press-ganged into the Royal Navy (not as salubrious a job as it might sound). Alternately, he might have a shilling dropped secretly into his beer; if he drank to the bottom, he was considered to have accepted the "commission" for many miserable months at sea.

Today, the Thames may look dirty but it has become one of the cleanest rivers in Europe – though the silt never settles due to the force of the tides. Salmon swim upstream yearly to spawn (a 17 pound salmon was caught here last year); trout, bass herring, flounder and Dover sole (and another 100 species) thrive in its waters. Cormorants, eating their weight in fish daily, can be seen skimming across the surface, and otters and seal have returned to the northern reaches of the river.

Depending on the state of your feet, we suggest you sit for a minute and examine the stunning view of London from the **Horatio Nelson statue**, then turn round and walk back toward the tea house for a cup of tea and a wander in the very beautiful flower gardens; or, facing the river, head down the hill towards the little pond near the bottom right hand corner of the park. When you emerge (on the corner of Park Vista and

Park Row), cross Trafalgar Road and continue down Park Row towards the Thames. Stop in the **Trafalgar pub** for a riverside drink (diehards can turn right by the Trafalgar and walk another 10 minutes to the historic **Cutty Sark pub**, est. 1695); then turn left and follow the riverwalk back to the dock and your boat home.

HAMPSTEAD

This day out requires – if not sunshine – at least an absence of downpour, as much of it will be spent walking on **Hampstead Heath**. It takes the form of a large circle; bring your map with you, the walk is simple but the Heath can be endlessly confusing.

Start your day on the Northern Line to Hampstead tube station. Once you arrive, turn left down Hampstead High Street (stopping for coffee at the **Dome**) and window-shop your way through Hampstead's delightful shops until you reach Downshire Hill. Turn left, and then right onto Keat's Grove; your first stop is an hour or so at the very delightful **Keats' House** (*Wentworth Place, Keat's Grove, London NW3, tel: 0171 435 2062, open Monday to Saturday 10am to 1pm; Sunday 2pm to 5pm*).

Return to Downshire Hill after your tour and turn right. Stop at the **Freemason's Arms** for a pint in the lovely garden (or lunch if you're hungry). Continue into Hampstead Heath, and head due north, keeping the bathing ponds to your right. You are heading for **Kenwood House**, and will need to ask directions frequently; there's plenty of time to get lost, however, so enjoy a leisurely meander across the Heath.

At Kenwood, spend some time looking at the grand house and its excellent picture collection, then retire to Kenwood's coach house for tea and cakes. If you still have any energy left, continue back westward along the top of the Heath, telling anyone you meet that you are heading for the **Spaniard's Inn** on Spaniards Road. Directions from locals are essential, unless you are an exceptional navigator. Settle down for a few pints at The Spaniard's (Keats often did), and then head back along Heath Street to the tube station (you will be aproaching it from the north).

If you are a serious pub aficionado (or have merely worked up a thirst on your walk) make a quick detour across from the tube station, up Holly Hill to Holly Mount, for a last pint at the lovely **Holly Bush pub**. This day trip is our idea of heaven, but unsuitable for those who dislike poetry, art, walking, and beer.

ST. JAMES & PICCADILLY

St. James is a neighborhood of lords and ladies, kings and queens, airs and graces. Its monuments boast of deeds and victories of an empire that still exists in the minds of its inhabitants; its shops cater to a clientele that prefers the bespoke (custom-made) – and can afford to pay for it. The grand tradition of old-fashioned service, virtually extinct in most other parts of Britain, persists in the extraordinary deference of the local shopkeepers. We suppose you expect a fair amount of deference if you're paying £1500 for a pair of shoes.

For walkers, St. James is a treasure trove of tradition; the neighborhood is filled with hidden passageways, historical pubs and invisible courtyards. Do bring your credit cards, just in case you suddenly can't figure out how you ever lived without a custom made suit, pair of boots, fedora, or umbrella.

Exit the Green Park tube station and turn left onto **Piccadilly**, which gets its name from the "picadil," a stiff , ruffled collar worn by courtiers of the 17th century; the tailor who made his fortune selling this fashion item built a mansion here and named it Piccadilly Hall. Walk to the **Burlington Arcade** *(51 Piccadilly)*, an enclosed 18th century passage lined on both sides with mahogany-fronted shops. It was designed in 1817 by Sam Ware for Lord George Cavendish, who wanted to shop in an area protected from the mud and bustle of the main road. The top-hatted beadles patrolling the arcade make up the smallest police force in the world, and continue to enforce 180 year-old laws forbidding shoppers to whistle, sing, carry an open umbrella – or hurry. How very civilized.

At the north end of the arcade, you'll see the **Museum of Mankind** *(6 Burlington Gardens)*, an Italianate building built in 1866 for London University. It now houses the Ethnographic Department of the British Museum and is an engaging small museum with a first-rate cafe.

Exit the museum and turn right towards **Saville Row**, a street synonymous with fine tailoring since 1785 when Gieves & Hawkes first opened its doors to outfit Horatio Nelson, Wellington, and Livingston and Stanley (we presume). Turn right at the next corner into **Sackville Street**, all restrained symmetry and Georgian elegance. Nip into **Henry Sotheran** with its rows of antique books and good selection of prints *(2 Sackville Street)*.

At the end of the street, turn right again (we're back on Piccadilly) and before you cross the street, note the mechanical clock that crowns the entrance to **Fortnum & Mason**, the department store founded in 1701 by George Fortnum, a footman in the household of King George III. The clock, added in 1964, puts on an hourly show of Mr. Fortnum and Mr. Mason greeting each other. Cross over onto Duke Street and walk straight past Jermyn Street and past the Cavendish Hotel. Duke Street is filled with exclusive art galleries, for those with extra wall space. Look for **King Street**, the next large intersection, turn right and head for **Christie's**, the world-famous auction house *(8 King Street)*. The viewing galleries are free and open weekdays – go in and see what's for sale next (anything from old master paintings to Beatles memorabilia).

Across King Street, the **Golden Lion** is a perfect spot for a good pub lunch *(weekdays noon to 2:30pm)*. Cozy and inviting, its dark wood walls are lined with theater posters, playbills and prints, evoking the bygone days of the St. James Theatre that stood next door until 1957 and staged the first production of Oscar Wilde's *Lady Windermere's Fan* and *The Importance of Being Earnest* (a campaign led by Laurence Olivier and Vivien Leigh failed to save the theater).

Turn left out of the pub and pass through Rose and Crown Yard to **Pall Mall**. This broad boulevard (named after the royal game of Pall Mall, not unlike French boules) boasts many of the most exclusive gentlemen's clubs in the city, if not the world; their only concession to the outside world, a discreet street number to satisfy the post office. The **United Oxford and Cambridge University Club** (founded 1830) *is at number 71*; the friezes above its main windows depict literary greats including Homer, Shakespeare, Virgil and Bacon. *At number 89*, there's the **Royal Automobile Club**, founded in 1897 for the "Protection, Encouragement and Development of Automobilism." This is the newest club on the block and contains a swimming pool, Turkish bath, solarium and rifle range.

The **Travellers Club** *(number 106)* was founded in 1819; applicants for membership were required to have travelled at least 500 miles from London. This is the only club that will open its doors for a behind-the-scenes tour *(phone weekdays 0171 930 8688 for an appointment)*. Next is the **Athenaeum** *(number 107)* founded in 1823 as a club for "scientific and literary men and artists" by Sir Humphrey Davy, (president of the Royal Society), Lord Aberdeen (Prime Minister 1852-55), and Sir Thomas Lawrence (president of the Royal Academy). The building features a frieze copied from the Parthenon. Its entrance, marked by a gilt statue of Athena is around the corner on Waterloo Place.

Several other notable statues stand at this junction. The group that commemorates the Crimean War (1854-55) was built in 1867 and funded by public subscription. In its center is the **Guards' Monument** with three guardsmen, Florence Nightingale and Lord Herbert of Lea, the Secretary of War at the time. To the right is the equestrian statue of Edward VII, and beyond, the **Duke of York's Column** in Tuscan granite, standing 124 feet high, designed by Benjamin Wyatt and erected in 1834. It commemorates the Duke of York, second son of Geroge III, who commanded the British Army from 1795 to 1827.

At the top of the Duke of York steps, underneath the maple tree to the right, you'll notice a small tombstone with the name "Giro" carved at the top. Beneath it, a German epitaph translates as "A true friend!" The beloved Giro was a pet terrier belonging to Leopold von Hoesch, the German ambassador to Britain in the 30s.

To conclude your walk, continue down the steps and walk through **St. James Park** (straight ahead). Or turn left at the bottom of the stairs and visit the **ICA Gallery** (Institute of Contemporary Art) with its good bar and cafeteria. Or continue walking left along the Mall to reach **Trafalgar Square** and the **National Gallery**. Or retrace your steps and walk back along Waterloo Place, towards **Piccadilly Circus**. This street becomes **Regent Street** and leads directly to the Piccadilly Circus tube station.

For a shopping diversion, turn left onto **Jermyn Street** and investigate the cheesemonger, hatter and parfumier, all of which date from the mid-18th century.

12. CULTURE

The rich mix and cherished tradition of fine theater, music, dance, and film is no doubt one of the reasons you decided to come to London in the first place, and a wise decision it was, too. You could live here for years without ever tiring of the extraordinary panoply of offerings on the various London stages. And we ought to know. After a decade or so, we've shown no signs of flagging.

THEATER

As we mentioned in the *Planning Your Trip* chapter, we highly recommend booking theater tickets before you arrive, especially in high season. However, it's almost always possible to get tickets for something good once you arrive. We're not big fans of the mega-hit Andrew Lloyd Webber-style musical, but even tickets to the sold-out shows can usually be had through ticket agencies – at a price, often a steep one.

If you're more our sort of theatergoer (Alan Rickman, Ralph Fiennes, Ian McKellan, and Helen Mirren in anything), here are a few helpful guidelines. The **National Theatre** *at the Southbank* is consistently reliable for superb productions, playwrights, and acting. The other dependable is the **Royal Shakespeare Company** (**RSC**) *at the Barbican Centre* (or at Stratford-upon-Avon, which is a must for theater buffs, never mind the tourists), where your chances are better than even of seeing a play you'll never forget. And notwithstanding the name, the RSC doesn't just do Shakespeare; check listings for the current schedule.

The **Old Vic** (thanks to director Jonathan Miller) and **The Royal Court** are other theaters to keep an eye on. For fringe, particularly look at the **Hampstead Theatre**, **The Almeida**, **Riverside Studios**, and the **Donmar Warehouse**. And for reviews, you can generally trust *Time Out*. We tend to agree with their intelligent theatre reviews far more often than we disagree, and at least it offers a weekly update and a who's-in-what guide.

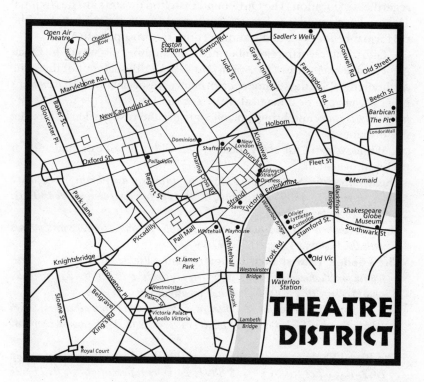

The **Leicester Square Ticket Booth** (*no phone, Leicester Square tube*) on the south side of Leicester Square offers half-price tickets the day of the performance. You won't get the very top shows here, but there are often bargains for the National Theatre, long-running hits and matinees. Matinee tickets go on sale at noon (for 2pm performances – there are matinees weekdays and Saturday, sometimes with a second-string cast, check for specific shows); evening tickets are on sale from 2:30-6:30pm. In season, the lines are long but move quickly; cash only is accepted; maximum four tickets per person; a £1.50 booking fee per ticket is added. Be sure to ask where the tickets are – we've been offered front row extreme left with the assurance that "they're very good seats."

When booking tickets directly with the box office, phone with your credit card and be sure to specify seat location. The tickets will either be sent to your hotel, or can be picked up (with your credit card) at the box office half an hour before the curtain. There are numerous options for cheap last minute tickets: queue at the box office 90 minutes before a performance and you are offered unsold Barbican tickets for £10 each, regardless of location. The Olivier and Lyttelton theaters at The National Theatre have a similar policy, offering unsold seats two hours before the performance for £6-8, and standing room for most plays at £3.

One theater worth remembering in the summer months is the **Open Air Theatre** *at the Inner Circle in Regent's Park.* Although not of the same quality as the RSC, the summer performances (especially of *A Midsummer's Night Dream*) can be a magical treat. *Tel: 0171 486 2431 for schedule and ticket information,* and bring a picnic to eat in the rose garden before the performance.

While we can't list every theater, herewith a list of essential and/or useful information:

- **Theatreline** *(information about plays and daily seat availability) Telephone for plays: 0836 430959; musicals, 0836 430960; comedies, 0836 430961; children's: 0836 430963.*
- **Firstcall** *(the centralized 24-hour booking service for plays, concerts and movies with the lowest fee) Tel: 0171 497 9977.*
- **The London Tourist Board Theatre Lines Plays**: *0891 505475. Telephone for Shakespeare: 0891 505474; musicals: 0891 505 473; comedies and thrillers: 0891 505472; fringe theatres: 0891 505476.*
- **The National Theatre** *(for the Cottesloe, Lyttelton and Olivier theaters) South Bank, London SE1. Box office tel: 0171 928 2252. Waterloo or Embankment tube.*
- **The Royal Shakespeare Company at the Barbican**, *Barbican, London EC2. Box office tel: 0171 638 8891; 24 hour information tel: 0171 628 2295. Barbican tube.*
- **The Royal Shakespeare Company at Stratford**, *Stratford-upon-Avon, Warwickshire. Box office tel: 0789 295623.*

FILM

By the time most films get to Britain, they've usually already passed through suburban Nebraska, so we can't imagine most Americans wanting to spend a lot of time in London at the cinema. To further discourage you, ticket prices in central London start at £6.50 and go up to £9 (though most cinemas offer cheap Monday night tickets); you need to book popular films by credit card in advance; and there's a 15-20 minute program of ads and coming attractions before the film starts.

On the plus side, if you come from suburban Nebraska, you'll probably find the variety of films stunning (about 250 per week), and most cinemas have a bar where you can get beer, wine and hard liquor in addition to ice cream, coffee and coke. For those of you who can't live without your fix, check *Time Out* for listings, make sure to book by credit card at least a few hours in advance and avoid the Leicester Square cinemas if expensive tickets and huge milling crowds aren't your thing (though our resident fanatic assures us that the **Warner Leicester Square** has the best popcorn in London – available, American-style in large, extra-large and jumbo sizes).

For lovers of revivals and art films, check listings for the repertory cinemas in *Time Out*: the **ICA**, the **National Film Theatre**, and the **Everyman** are our favorites.

OPERA, MUSIC, & DANCE

They take their music seriously in Britain, whether it's Verdi, the Pet Shop Boys or Stravinsky at the ballet. Opera and ballet fans should take note that plans are afoot to close both the English National Opera and the Royal Opera (and Royal Ballet) at Covent Garden over the next couple of years (1996-97) for extensive building renovation. Alternative venues are being planned; check up-to-date listings.

Main Venues

No trip to London would be complete without a ticket to one or two of these venerable arenas – at which the audience (and the architecture) can be almost as riveting as what's on stage. Book well-ahead if you possibly can; they're the locals' favorites as well.

• **The Barbican**, *Barbican Centre, Silk Street, London EC2. Tel: 0171 638 8891. Box office open Monday to Sunday 9am to 8pm. Major credit cards.* In the heart of the City, the Barbican houses the Royal Shakespeare Company, three cinemas, two theaters, two galleries and a concert hall. The Barbican is also home to The London Symphony Orchestra and features a huge range of guest performers. Free foyer performances, recitals and exhibitions complete the offerings of this full-service cultural center. The difficulty in navigating around the center is the butt of endless (justified) jokes. Tickets £10-40.

• **English National Opera**, *The London Coliseum, St. Martin's Lane, London WC2. Tel: 0171 632 8300; fax: 0171 379 1264. Box office open Monday to Saturday, 9:30am to 8:30pm. Major credit cards. Charing Cross or Leicester Square tube.* With prices at the Royal Opera becoming ludicrously inflated due to expense account booking and lack of government funding, The English National Opera has begun coming into its own. Productions here are entirely in English, and tend to be far more innovative, less stuffy and self-important than at the Royal Opera, though Covent Garden still gets the big names. Tickets are easier to come by, and cost £9 to £48.

• **Royal Albert Hall**, *Kensington Gore, London SW7. Tel: 0171 589 8212. Box office open Monday to Sunday 9am to 9pm. Major credit cards. Gloucester Road or South Kensington tube.* Built by money raised from the Great Exhibition of 1851 with the aim to promote the arts and sciences, the

Royal Albert Hall hosts pop aand classical concerts as well as sporting events – everything from Eric Clapton to Pavarotti to sumo wrestling. Tickets £7 to £30.

• **Royal Opera House**, *Bow Street, London WC2. Tel: 0171 304 4000; fax: 0171 497 1256. Box office open Monday to Saturday, 10am to 8pm. Major credit cards. Covent Garden tube.* Dating back to 1732, the 2,000 seat Royal Opera is still one of the world's most impressive venues, renowned these days for its elaborate productions (with subtitles), huge stars and grandiose prices. Each year it presents nearly 300 performances of the Royal Opera, the Royal Ballet and the Birmingham Royal Ballet. Tickets sell out quickly; it's best to call when you book your flight. The box office can put you on hold for 10 minutes or so, so we suggest you fax your request for a brochure (which will arrive about a week later by mail), and then fax your ticket request. Schedules are produced every two and a half months and they will put Americans on the mailing list. Ticket prices range from £20 to £200.

• **South Bank Centre**, *South Bank, London SE1. Tel: 0171 928 8800. Box office open Monday to Sunday 10am to 9pm. Major credit cards. Waterloo tube.* This grand cement arts center is home to The London Philharmonic and houses three concert venues – the Royal Festival Hall, Queen Elizabeth Hall and the Purcell Room. Free foyer performances, recitals and exhibitions complete the offerings. Tickets, £5 to £25.

More Intimate Venues

This is by no means a complete list of good places to go for music and dance, but it does include some of London's most popular and most visited smaller stages:

• **Chisenhale Dance Space**, *64-84 Chisenhale Road, London E3. Tel: 0181 981 6617. Box office open Monday to Friday 9:30am to 6pm. No credit cards. Bethnal Green tube.* A small 70-seat theater dedicated to performance at the experimental end of dance, mixed-media and physical theater. A recent program featured Japanese butoh. Tickets £6.50.

• **The Place**, *17 Duke's Road, London WC1. Tel: 0171 387 0031. Box office open Monday to Saturday noon to 6pm. Major credit cards. Euston tube.* The lobby of this small venue is a studio for the London Contemporary Dance School by day; by night the theater presents some of the most innovative dance performances in Europe. Tickets £4-£12.

• **Sadler's Wells**, *Rosebery Avenue, London EC1. Tel: 0171 713 6000. Box office open Monday to Saturday 10am to 6m. Major credit cards. Angel tube.* Sadler's Wells offers London's best contemporary dance, opera, performance art and theater – from flamenco to Glyndebourne's touring company – and has been doing so for more than 300 years. It's an intimate theater, with tickets priced £5-30.

• **St. John Smith's Square**, *Smith Square, London SW1. Tel: 0171 222 1061. Box office open Monday to Friday 10am to 5pm. Visa only. Westminster tube.* This church (circa 1728) is home to some of London's best chamber music, and a weekly Monday and alternate Thursday lunchtime series of classical music from the BBC Radio Orchestra (Monday's performances are broadcast live on BBC Radio 3). Tickets £6 to £20.

• **St. Martin-in-the-Fields**, *Trafalgar Square, London WC2. Tel: 0171 839 8362. Box office open Monday to Friday, 10am to 4pm. Visa and Mastercard only. Charing Cross tube.* Good lunchtime concerts two or three times a week (free) and candlelit evening concerts (Thursday, Friday and Saturday) take place throughout the year. Featured composers include Vivaldi, Bach, Pergolesi, Pachelbel and Mozart.

• **Wigmore Hall**, *Wigmore Street, London W1H 0BP. Tel: 0171 935 2141. Box office open Monday to Saturday, 10am to 7pm. Major credit cards. Bond Street tube.* The intimate atmosphere and fine acoustics of this hall combine to make it an outstanding venue for early and medieval music, the classical repertoire and solo recitals. Concerts are held every evening and Sunday mornings (with coffee), the concert season runs from September to the end of July.

13. NIGHTLIFE & PUBLIFE

These days, you'll have plenty of company in London if you're the sort who likes to stay out till 4am, especially in Soho and especially if you're under 30. But the pubs still close at 11pm, and London still isn't a stylish late night city; noisy bars with admission charges and door policies rule.

Here are some of the more permanent (and tolerable) ones. Best to phone and check before you hit the clubs, as this sort of venue tends to come and go. (And don't expect us to wait up.) If you're looking to experience a bit of traditional London, skip ahead a few pages and go straight to our section on *Pubs*.

FOOD & DRINK

- **Bar Italia**, *22 Frith Street, London W1. Daily, 24 hours. Tel: 0171 437 4520. Leicester Square tube*. Probably London's favorite place to hang out on the street or at the bar, drink espresso and watch Italian football with the rest of the Soho all-nighters. You'll no doubt run into someone you know (or wish you knew).

- **Brick Lane Beigel Bake**, *159 Brick Lane, London E1. Tel: 0171 729 0616. Daily, 24 hours. Aldgate East tube*. In the old days, this was the last resort of hungry night owls. A favorite of cabbies, you might have to queue at 4am, but it's worth it. Divine old fashioned bagels (doughy, and only available in one flavor) with a variety of fillings including chopped herring like you wish mom used to make and cream cheese and smoked salmon for 85pence. Oy vey!

- **Cafe Boheme**, *13 Old Compton Street, London W1. Tel: 0171 734 0623. Daily 8am to 3am; Sunday 10am to 11pm. Leicester Square tube*. Reasonably attractive brasserie with tables on the street; drinks served till closing with moderately priced food.

- **Costa Dorada**, *47-55 Hanway Street, London W1. Tel: 0171 636 7139. Daily (except Sunday) 7pm to 3am. Tottenham Court Road tube.* Combination tapas bar, bar and restaurant with a tiny stage for flamenco; you might find yourself culturally confused but not bored. Admission is £3.50 after 10:30pm, but the drinks are very reasonably priced. Spanish food runs about £30 a head with drink. We just hang around at the bar on tiptoe and watch the flamenco.
- **Dionysus**, *14 Tottenham Court Road, London W1. Tel: 0171 637 5917. Daily 11:30am till 2am (4am Friday and Saturday).* No alcohol after 11, but this is lots of people's favorite place to sit down or take away a desperate late night kebab or fish and chips. Tacky atmosphere is just the thing at 3am.
- **Harry's Bar**, *19 Kingly Street, London W1. Tel: 0171 4343 0309. Daily (except Sunday) noon to 6am.* Thai food metamorphoses into big English breakfasts and fry ups as the evening draws on. Popular with clubbers.
- **Maroush II**, *38 Beauchamp Place, London SW3. Tel: 0171 581 5434. Daily noon to 3am. Knightsbridge tube.* Good Lebanese food in this posh neighborhood for about £20 a head. Drinks until 1am.
- **Mayflower**, *68-70 Shaftesbury Avenue, London W1. Tel: 0171 734 9207. Daily 5pm to 4am. Piccadilly Circus tube.* Good Chinese food long after the rest of Chinatown has gone to bed. The specials are usually the best bet; £15 per person.
- **Soho Soho**, *11 Frith Street, London W1. Tel: 0171 494 3491. Daily (except Sunday) noon to 1am. Tottenham Court Road tube.* Lively Mediterranean-style rotisserie with an appealing, varied menu.
- **Yung's**, *23 Wardour Street, London W1. Tel: 0171 437 4986. Daily noon to 4:30am. Leicester Square tube.* Big menu, big portions, good food, reasonably priced.

MUSIC & ENTERTAINMENT

Admission prices vary, so phone for up-to-date information.
- **Camden Palace**, *1A Camden High Street, London NW1. Tel: 0171 387 0428. Camden Town tube.* A huge, popular Indie/rock club with live music beginning at midnight. Young crowd, loud music.
- **The Comedy Store**, *Haymarket House, Oxendon Street, London SW1. Tel: 0142 691 4433. Tuesday to Sunday 8pm (doors open 6:30pm); late shows Friday and Saturday at midnight (doors open 11pm). Admission £8-10. Food available. Piccadilly Circus tube.* The foremost new wave comedy club in Britain attracts hot new acts and some big (local) names. Expect crowds on weekends and get there early.
- **Heaven**, *Under the Arches, Villiers Street, London WC2. Tel: 0171 839 3852. Charing Cross or Embankment tube.* A licensed disco with two dance

floors that's still hot and happening in its second decade. It starts grooving after 11pm; for a quieter mood, try the Happy House, a sitting area where the ambience is a little softer.

- **HQ West Yard**, *Camden Lock, London NW1. Tel: 0171 485 6044. Camden Town tube.* Latin dance classes on Saturday evenings at 8pm set the stage for very late nights of live Latin jazz and salsa.
- **Ministry of Sound**, *103 Gaunt Street, London SE1. Tel: 0171 378 6528. Elephant and Castle tube.* This is it, clubber's heaven. Garage, house and club music weekends only 11pm to 9am. Huge queues and serious door policy; if you have to ask whether you're hip enough to get in, you're probably not.
- **100 Club**, *100 Oxford Street, London W1. Tel: 0171 636 0933. Tottenham Court Road tube.* Jazz, blues and swing bands live on Friday nights until 3am at this classic jazz venue; still going strong after all these years.
- **606 Club**, *990 Lots Road, London SW10. Tel: 0171 352 5953. Fulham Broadway tube.* Live jazz every night at 9:30pm and 11:30pm, later Thursday to Saturday. Alcohol served only with food. Reservations recommended.
- **Ronnie Scotts**, *47 Frith Street, London W1V. Tel: 0171 439 0747. 8:30pm to 3am. Leicester Square or Tottenham Court Road tube.* London's most important, most famous, best-loved jazz club. Reservations suggested.

PUBS

Let's start by telling you where we stand. We love pubs. And beer. Particularly the warm stuff, the bitter stuff, the real hand-pulled strong dark British stuff. Which means that our recommendations will not include specific mention of fizzy lagers and bottles of Budweiser (though it's worth knowing that the Bud brewed in the UK is stronger and tastier than the American equivalent, and the Budvar Budweiser from Czechoslovakia is wonderful).

The other thing to mention is that we're enthusiasts rather than experts, and if you're the sort of person who'll travel miles for a pint of Hops Back Summer Lightning, get yourself the *Campaign For Real Ale's Good Beer Guide* and set off on your pilgrimage.

Beer Basics

A couple of basics. **Lager** is the pale gold fizzy stuff you're used to drinking in America in cans, and in most pubs there's a cheap lager that's cold, fizzy, not very tasty and not too alcoholic (usually Skol or Carlsberg). One of the best lagers is Stella Artois, which is French, fairly strong, delicious, and full of character. After lager, things get more interesting. **Bitter** is the medium brown, warm, flat beer you hear so much about, and though a bit of an acquired taste, it's a taste worth acquiring. Young's and Adnams bitters are particularly fine.

Best Bitters are a step up in terms of price, alcohol content and quality; London Pride is an excellent Best Bitter. After Bests come **Strong Bitters**, like Theakston's XB, Ruddle's County, or Adnam's Broadside. These taste even more delightful and have a high alcohol content, so beware.

Old Ales are halfway between bitter and stout (typical stouts are Guinness and Beamish), quite dark, quite strong, quite superb and particularly popular in winter when there seems to be some justification for fortifying oneself. Young's Winter Warmer and Theakston Old Peculier are very good examples indeed.

And last, there's **Stout**, which is black with a smooth white head, can sometimes taste a bit medicinal to the uninitiated, and is the acknowledged fuel behind generations of sublime Irish literature. A couple of pints of Guinness and you'll be writing great poetry too. Or at least you'll think it's great, which will do fine.

Beer can be ordered in **pints** or **half-pints** (or bottles); if you just say "a half of lager" or "a half of bitter," you'll be given the cheapest of the beers on offer. So if you see something that looks nice, specify by saying "a half of Flowers, please." And if someone asks you what you're drinking, look pleased and let them buy you another. The tradition in pubs is to take turns buying rounds – it's bad form to offer your £2 if someone buys you a drink, and even worse form not to return the favor at the next round.

We tend to recommend a few beers repeatedly, and that's because they're our favorites. Once you develop your own favorites, you can adopt a superior air and treat our advice with contempt. When developing your own favorites, you can always try asking the barman for a good recommendation, but this only works sometimes.

Another technique that's entertaining (though unscientific) is to go for the strangest name. Hall and Woodhouse Badger Best Bitter is a very nice beer, as is Coach House Blunderbus Old Porter.

If you order a pint of Flowers or Old Speckled Hen in one pub and can't figure out why it tastes so much better than it did the other day, you're not imagining things. Storage and pumping methods seriously affect the taste and quality of beer. Aficionados swear by hand-pumped beer, and after a while you really can taste the difference.

Do try and remember, however, that pubs aren't beer museums; you go for a good chat and as nice a drink as possible, and if all you end up doing is talking about the beer, you're probably missing the point.

Hard liquor is doled out in ludicrously tiny and expensive measures, so splurge on a double Blackbush after a long day sightseeing – but otherwise stick to beer as a basic drink. Although there are vague stirrings of change, wine in all but the new-wave-good-food pubs borders on the undrinkable.

Finally, this doesn't pretend to be a definitive list of London pubs. We've put together a few that we like and think you might like too. And don't forget the good news: no tipping – ever – in pubs.

A note of caution about opening hours: As we go to press, traditional pub hours (11am to 11pm Monday to Saturday; noon to 3pm and 7pm to 10:30pm Sundays) are changing to allow uninterrupted noon to 10:30pm openings on Sunday and summer openings till midnight – with even further changes afoot. "Regular pub hours" assumes the current status quo.

BLOOMSBURY & HOLBORN

THE ENTERPRISE, *38 Red Lion Street, London WC1. Tel: 0171 242 8040. Regular pub hours; closed Sunday. Holborn tube.*

For the information of dedicated pub crawlers, this attractive pub forms a convenient trilogy with two other very good, very close-at-hand pubs – the Lamb and the Sun on Lamb's Conduit Street (just across the way). The Enterprise has wooden floors, a very pleasant atmosphere, and a serious dedication to real (and really unusual) ales, most of which we'd never heard of, nearly all of which were terrifically good. The selection changes frequently.

THE LAMB, *94 Lamb's Conduit Street, London WC1. Tel: 0171 405 0713. Regular pub hours. Holborn tube.*

This has to be one of London's more popular pubs, and one of its most handsome and most comfortable. Although it was built in the early 18th century, it has somewhere along the way been renovated into a perfect example of high Victorian chic, with its scallop-shaped configuration of banquettes and the fantastically picturesque etched glass "snob screens" designed to shield pubgoers from the prying eyes of the bartender (and each other). Literary groupies might like to know that the Bloomsbury group used to meet here; the very good beer includes **Young's Special Bitter** and the aptly named and avidly sought **Winter Warmer**.

THE MUSEUM TAVERN, *49 Great Russell Street, London WC1. Tel: 0171 242 8987. Regular pub hours. Bar food noon to 10pm. Tottenham Court Road tube.*

Probably the best thing about this pretty Victorian pub, aside from its high ceiling, big mirrors, etched glass and expansive bar, is its location – directly across from the British Museum. It's a genteel pub, polite, clean, polished and mannerly, which means it tends to attract a similarly mannerly crowd that combines museum types and tourist types. Airy, comfortable and civilized, it also happens to serve very good ales and decent lunches, which makes it a good refuge from all the ancient civilizations across the street. Beware of the height of the tourist season, however, when getting a good position at the bar is harder than getting a good look at the Rosetta Stone.

THE SEVEN STARS, *53 Carey Street, London WC2. Tel: 0171 242 8521. Monday to Friday 11am to 9:30pm. Closed weekends and bank holidays. Food served 11am to 7pm. Holborn tube.*

On a shortcut from Lincoln's Inn (and the John Soane's Museum) to the Strand one day, we happened upon this tiny little pub, stopped for "just one drink" and stayed till closing. Wedged in on a tiny lane amidst the Gothic majesty of the lawcourts, the Seven Stars sits, twice as pretty as a picture, endearingly ancient (it was established in 1602), and perfectly unpretentious.

Its original patrons were Dutch sailors – the name refers to the seven provinces of the Netherlands – but today its hours and location indicate that its sole purpose it to cater to local lawyers. It's only a few minutes walk from the Strand, however, and worth ferreting out for the lovely facade, the untouristy atmosphere, and the good **Courage Best.**

CHOOSING A PUB

What about choosing a pub? There are about a zillion pubs in London, and half the fun is finding a great one on your own. Avoid pubs with loud music, fruit machines, lots of big signs advertising Trivial Pursuit nights (or anything else for that matter) and huge crowds of people who look much younger and more skimpily attired than you (unless you're into that sort of thing). Wood floors are good. So is real architectural detail. A crowd that looks like your sort of people is even better.

Don't be afraid to walk into a pub, change your mind and walk out again; we do it all the time. And once you do push your way to the bar, catch the barman's eye. If it's crowded, this will usually guarantee that you've been added to an invisible queue. But if you don't seem to be making any headway, by all means mention with the utmost politeness that, actually, you think you were next.

THE SUN, *63 Lamb's Conduit Street, London WC1. Tel: 0171 405 8278. Regular pub hours. Food served noon to 2:30pm and 6pm to 10pm. Russell Square or Holborn tube.*

Forget your etched glass and your padded banquettes. The Sun specializes in bare wooden floors, minimal decorations – and fabulous beer. Strangely, the new fashion in pubs is to imitate what The Sun does without trying – i.e., get back to bare design and good beer. And somehow, despite (or perhaps because of) the sparseness and simple wood tables, the atmosphere is always just right for a beer and a chat –

though lately the music has had a tendency to turn a chat into a shout. And what beer ... thanks to a maze of storage vaults under the pub, there are always between 10 and 20 real ales (all hand pumped) on offer, ranging from the sublime to the ridiculously good. You might have to try the **Tanglefoot** just because it sounds so nice (it is). If **Broadside** is on offer, try it – but be careful, its name is a good description of exactly how it will knock you.

Rumor has it that the manager can be prevailed upon to take serious beer fans down for a tour of the catacombs. If you fit that description, ask.

CHELSEA & SOUTH KENSINGTON

THE ANTELOPE, *22 Eaton Terrace, London SW1. Tel: 0171 730 7781. Regular pub hours. Sloane Square tube.*

This pretty pub around the corner from Sloane Square dates from the late 18th century, though its history as a coaching inn goes back much longer. Today it's a really pleasant, up-market, welcoming place to drop in for a drink (use either of the two doors – they used to separate the posh servants who drank there from the common ones), though we regret to add that the ubiquitous fruit machines have somehow managed to install themselves here. It's a mixed neighborhood crowd with lots of women, and gets a good overflow from the Royal Court Theatre. There's an unusually wide variety of real ale; we also recommend the **Adnams**. Food is simple (old-style chops, sausages and mash) and good.

THE FOX AND HOUNDS, *29 Passmore Street, London SW1W 8HR. Tel: 0171 730 6367. Regular pub hours. Sloane Square tube.*

This small family-owned neighborhood pub has survived virtually intact since 1860 – particularly in relation to its pub license. Due to a limited "working man's clause" that deemed hard liquor a dangerous indulgence, the pub still serves only beer to its motley crew of customers: priests from St. Mary's church, actors from the Royal Court Theatre, and Chelsea Pensioners (retired soldiers resident at the Chelsea Hospital – recognizable by their red or blue uniforms). The walls are covered with the family's collection of old neighborhood photographs and paintings of foxes and hounds; the real ales are real tasty. The Fox and Hounds is an exceedingly congenial place to drink.

THE KING'S HEAD AND EIGHT BELLS, *50 Cheyne Walk, London SW3 5LR. Tel: 0171 352 1820. Regular pub hours. Sloane Square tube.*

You'll have to imagine this pub as it was 400 years ago – smaller, rougher and actually on the riverside. The landfill of the Embankment brought all that to an end (it now overlooks a busy road with the river beyond), but the "Established circa 1580" sign, gas lights, etched glass windows, tin ceiling and dark wooden bar still give you a good sense of the grand history of the place. Whistler and Turner drank here, and when it became a swinging hangout in the '60s, Keith Richards, inhabitant of nearby Cheyne Walk, used to wander down for a pint.

Today, this tiny neighborhood enclave holds much of architectural interest, including the pretty 18th century houses (writer Thomas Carlyle's home at 24 Cheyne Row, tel: 0171 352 7087, is open to the public) and Chelsea Old Church, founded in the 12th century and parish church of Sir Thomas More. Try the **Wethered's** and **Flowers** bitter, then stroll along the Embankment for a better look at the handsome Prince Albert bridge.

THE CITY & EAST LONDON

THE BLACKFRIAR, *174 Queen Victoria Street, London EC4. Tel: 0171 236 5650. Monday and Tuesday 11:30am to 10pm; Wednesday to Friday 11:30am to 11pm; closed weekends and bank holidays. Blackfriars tube.*

What a wonderful place this is. In fact, if we had to recommend one pub in London worth making a detour for, this would have to win (or at least tie for first place with The Spaniard's). The Blackfriar is a glorious glittering art nouveau jewel of a pub, set on the site of an old Dominican monastery.

The ceilings are gold mosaic, the fireplaces copper and tile and the furniture arts and crafts oak. There's a huge sweep of a marble horseshoe bar, wondrous bronze reliefs of monks, and a lovely, loony variety of inscriptions throughout: "A good thing is soon snatched up," "Industry is all," "Haste is slow," "Finery is foolery." Exactly who is indulging in foolery isn't completely clear, but the architect and sculptor are suspect (H. Fuller Clarke and Henry Poole). The crowd couldn't be nicer, a mix of down-to-earth beer drinkers, City folk and aesthetes drawn by the decor. Try the **Adnams**, **Tetley**, or **Wadworth**.

THE FOX & ANCHOR, *115 Charterhouse Street, London EC1. Tel: 0171 253 4838. Open Monday to Friday 7am to 9pm; Saturday 8am to noon. Closed Sunday. Food served 7am to 10:30am and noon to 2:15pm. Farringdon or Barbican tube.*

Since 1898, this gorgeous pub has been serving massive English breakfasts to the Smithfield meat market butchers who start work at 4am. And though the market, sadly, is due for redevelopment (causing the butchers to go elsewhere), the glorious breakfast goes on, in glorious surroundings. The pub itself has a patterned tin ceiling, wooden booths with etched glass dividers, William Morris wallpaper and a lovely mahogany bar that runs the length of the establishment. Breakfast costs £6.50, and these days you probably should reserve to make sure you get a place among all the City traders and company directors washing down their sausage, bacon, eggs, black pudding, toast, fried bread, beans and tomato (seconds, anyone?) with champagne.

If all that sounds a bit much first thing in the morning, the Scottish fillet steak is the light option, and please, please don't ask for coffee, much less decaf. You haven't come all the way here to miss a crack-of-dawn pint of **Tetley**, **Nicholson's**, **Adnams Broadside**, or **Guinness**. The dining room in the back is divided into a series of wood-panelled snugs holding a single table each; we can't imagine a more atmospheric place for breakfast or lunch. This is still one of the few pubs in London with an early morning licence (for the meat market) so drink up.

THE OLD BANK OF ENGLAND ALE AND PIE HOUSE, *194 Fleet Street, London. Tel: 0171 430 2255. Monday to Friday, 11am to 11pm, closed weekends. Food served noon to 8:30pm. Temple tube.*

The Old Bank of England isn't actually very old. Under a year, to be precise. It's not really a cheat, however, because this wonderful public house with 20 foot ceilings and giant windows is actually a conversion from the 19th century Law Court branch of the Old Bank of England. The decor is so grand and distinguished that it feels more like a private club than a bar; dining and club rooms with leather Chesterfield chairs, a selection of newspapers, and Victorian photographs and prints on the walls suggest a scene from a previous century. The extensive lunch and dinner menu includes bangers and mash, pasta, fish, and a vegetarian dish of the day. Wine, champagne, and port are served, along with espresso and cappuccino. Okay, so it hasn't been a pub since Hector was a pup. We like it anyway.

YE OLDE CHESHIRE CHEESE, *Wine Office Court, London EC4. Tel: 0171 353 6170. Regular pub hours, closed bank holidays. Food served noon to 3pm and 6pm to 9:30pm daily; Sunday noon to 3pm (bar food only). Blackfriar's tube.*

Ignore the sign that says "Gentlemen only served in this bar." Like the rest of the pub, it's a venerable antique. Sixteen kings and queens have sat on the throne while the Cheshire Cheese has served beer, and until renovations five years ago to stop it falling down, not much had changed since 1667 (if the date rings a bell, 1666 was the great fire of London). Although it's one of London's few remaining 17th century chop houses, a lot of people come here to dine on the atmosphere alone.

Working fireplaces, leatherbound books, and dark wood panelling spread throughout six bars and three restaurants means there's plenty of room for locals, tourists and the ghosts of Samuel Johnson, Oliver Goldsmith, and Charles Dickens. The last three regularly drank and dined here, and their table is commemorated in the restaurant.

For a quick sandwich or hot meal, head for the Courtyard Bar. But the original Chop Room, with its tables tucked into wooden bays and high-backed church pews, is the place for good, hearty, traditional meals. It's a popular venue and worth reserving before you set off. Above the fireplace, look for the painting of William Simpson, an early 19th century waiter. The portrait was commissioned by his customers (he must have been some waiter) and donated to Mr. Dolamore, the landlord. It has since become the pub heirloom, passed down from generation to generation and from landlord to landlord. The attractive, clubby private rooms upstairs can be reserved for lunch or dinner.

THE PROSPECT OF WHITBY, *57 Wapping Wall, London E1. Tel: 0171 481 1095. Open daily 11:30am to 3pm and 5:30pm to 11pm; Sunday noon to 3pm and 7pm to 10:30pm. Wapping tube.*

Wapping isn't exactly convenient to Harrods or the Savoy (or anything else for that matter), but somehow everyone (including Dickens, Whistler, and Turner) finds his or her way to the Prospect of Whitby eventually. It's a charming, historic pub perched on the edge of the Thames in the middle of what used to be serious dockyards, filled with seriously dangerous characters. If it's London history you're after, you won't find more of it anywhere – the history of scoundrels, rogues and criminals, that is.

The original tavern on the site was called The Devil's Tavern (1520), and it was famous for its public and frequent hangings, including that of Captain Kidd who, in 1701, was (falsely some say) accused of turning from pirate hunter to pirate. The pub that replaced the tavern was named after a ship (the eponymous Prospect) and the pub has a nautical feel – real nautical, not theme park nautical. In any case, as London's oldest and most esteemed riverside pub, The Prospect is popular and bustling, with tables on the river in the summer, fish and chips and shepherd's pie at the bar, and a rather serious restaurant upstairs. History aside, it's an exceptionally pleasant place to spend a summer afternoon or evening.

COVENT GARDEN

THE CROSS KEYS, *31 Endell Street, London WC2. Tel: 0171 836 5185. Regular pub hours. Food served noon to 2:30. Covent Garden tube.*

The Cross Keys is a favorite with the Covent Garden lunch crowd, and in summer, the wooden picnic tables out front are crowded with happy drinkers. The very attractive pub itself is covered with dense ivy outside and a plethora of brass decorations inside; the bar is long, narrow, rustic, cozy and comfortable. As it's just up the road from Emporio Armani in Covent Garden, it's an excellent place to retire for a pint of real ale while you talk yourself out of spending hundreds of pounds on something in taupe. You'll spot it from Armani by its year-round strings of colored lights.

THE LAMB AND FLAG, *33 Rose Street, London WC2. Tel: 0171 497 9504. Regular pub hours. Bar food noon to 5pm Monday to Saturday. Covent Garden tube.*

Bare floors, wood tables and centuries of Covent Garden history identify the Lamb and Flag, which can be reached up an alley from Longacre or down an alley and under a low arch from Floral Street. It's nearly always crowded after work and at lunchtime, but if you sneak in mid-afternoon, you're in for a peaceful, wonderfully pleasant time in the least touristy pub around. In the summer, the cheerful overflow runs out onto tiny narrow Rose Street, and some of our fondest memories have more to do with the sidewalk than the pub itself. There's decent barfood upstairs in the Dryden room and we recommend a pint of **Director's**, **Beamish**, or **John Smiths** to go with it.

THE SALISBURY, *90 St. Martin's Lane, London WC2. Tel: 0171 836 5863. Regular pub hours. Leicester Square tube.*

This is a wonderfully beautiful pub in a wonderfully convenient location. And like most pubs that fit that description, it has a tendency to be crowded in the most unwonderful way. So take the usual advice, and go at an off hour – 3:30 in the afternoon would be about perfect – in order to give yourself a chance to breath, have a peaceful drink, and admire the stunning art nouveau decor. Of which there's plenty: Bronze sculptures of lissome ladies, little scallops of banquettes, that strange breed of drippy art nouveau flora and fauna, and everywhere mirrors and more mirrors. Until recently, the Salisbury was a well-known gay pub, but the atmosphere seems to have shifted with a management change. Try the **Theakston** or the **Tetley** and crawl to safety before the marauding hordes start their evening smokathon.

GREENWICH

THE CUTTY SARK, *Ballast Quay, London SE10. Tel: 0181 858 3146. Regular pub hours. Bar food daily noon to 2:30 and Tuesday to Friday, 6pm to 9:30pm.*

We don't list a tube station for The Cutty Sark because it doesn't really have one. Stranded on the once bustling strip north of Greenwich, it has been serving drinks to sailors and dockworkers since 1804 – and now to locals and loyal visitors. The way to get to it is to turn your back to the Cutty Sark ship in Greenwich and walk north along the river (past the Naval Academy away from London). It's not too far and worth the pretty walk for its genuine salty charm and river views.

Downstairs you can drink pints of **Bass** or **Flowers** and eat sausages or fish and chips (by the fire in winter), upstairs a "proper" restaurant with lovely river views serves substantial Sunday lunch; across the path, picnic tables overlooking the Thames are jam-packed on anything resembling a pretty evening.

THE TRAFALGAR TAVERN, *Park Row, London SE10. Tel: 0181 858 2437. Regular pub hours.*

The Trafalgar is a must for anyone spending the day in Greenwich – it's a big grand dignified pub, recently redecorated, with civilized food, big fish dinners, good bar snacks, and a charming, cozy little upstairs bar with sparklingly pretty views of the Thames. Downstairs the huge windows give you an unimpeded view of the rowers at the next door Curlew rowing club as they set off for their battles with the Thames. Portraits of Horatio Nelson line the walls and the atmosphere is altogether too stately to make the Trafalgar anything but the biggest, most important riverside pub in Greenwich. Try the **Ruddles**.

PRIMROSE HILL, HAMPSTEAD, & HIGHGATE

THE FREEMASON'S ARMS, *32 Downshire Hill, London NW3. Tel: 0171 435 4498. Regular pub hours. Bar food daily, noon to 10pm. Hampstead tube.*

If it's summer it has to be the Freemason's. Built in the 30s, this isn't one of your thatched roof low beamed ye olde kind of pubs; it's big and pretty and comfortable and historical – and a one minute walk from the south west parking lot of Hampstead Heath. But that's not what's best about it. It has an absolutely wonderful rose garden with a fountain that seats 200 and on a nice day it almost always does.

Inside, the pub has a pool table and a darts board but its weirdest attribute is the skittles alley in the basement where, on Tuesday, Thursday and Saturday nights, grown men hurl 12 pound "cheeses" at the skittles in order to knock them over. Ok, we've never witnessed it but we bet it's true. Still, skittles or not, there can be nothing finer than a long, sociable, crowded summer evening with a pint of **Bass** or **London Pride** among the roses. Ah, bliss.

THE FLASK, *14 Flask Walk, London NW3. Tel: 0171 435 4580. Regular pub hours. Bar food daily noon to 3pm and 6 to 10pm; Saturday, 11am to 11pm Sunday, noon to 3pm and 7 to 10pm. Hampstead tube.*

Not to be confused with The Flask across the heath in Highgate, this pretty Victorian pub (named for it's 18th century bottled waters) makes a good stopping point on a tour of Hampstead. It's just off the main drag, has tables outside in the summer, and as a Young's pub has some great beers – try **Young's Special**, **Bitter** or **Oatmeal Stout**. Food is served in the conservatory.

THE FLASK, *77 Highgate West Hill, London N6. Tel: 0181 340 7260. Regular pub hours. Bar food daily noon to 9pm. Highgate tube.*

If you don't believe London is still made up of villages, spend a few hours at The Flask. You certainly won't believe you're only a couple miles from the center of one of the world's biggest cities in this rural idyll of a drinking spot. The Flask is one of London's most popular drinking spots and at lunchtime, after work or at weekends it's harder to get seats here than at the opera. Which can sometimes be inconvenient, because the food is substantial and good, and runs to roasts and two veg with steamed puddings and custard.

In good weather (and on milder winter days too) the crowd spreads outdoors, but it's the meandering irregular rooms, low beams, old photographs and books that give The Flask its considerable charm. The average pubgoer here on a Saturday night tends to be young, with blonde hair and a successful daddy; the average beer well above average. This is another good Young's pub – try the rich, dark **Winter Warmer** (when they have it) or **Young's Special** ("a pint of special" is the way to ask for it).

THE HOLLY BUSH, *22 Holly Mount, London NW3. Tel: 0171 435 2892. Daily 11am to 3pm and 5:30 to 11pm. Saturday, 11am to 4pm and 6pm to 11pm; Sunday noon to 3pm and 7pm to 10:30pm. Bar food always available. Hampstead tube.*

The problem with Hampstead is that it's just too damn picturesque, and you're spoilt for choice when it comes to pubs. However this is the one you should choose. First of all, it's very close to the tube station, and convenience is important when you plan to do any serious drinking. Second, it's astonishingly pretty. And third – well, after a couple pints of **Benskins Best** we can't remember what third was.

Check your trusty *A to Z* before you set off, there's a confusing maze of streets all similarly named (The Mount, Holly Bush, Holly Hill), but if you cross the street from the tube and walk up Holly Hill, you'll find Holly Mount without a problem. The pub was built in the mid-17th century, and reputedly had panoramic views of London; now the views are of the neighborhood's lovely cottages, which doesn't seem such a bad result of 350 years of progress. And we've even had good reports on the shepherd's pie.

THE QUEENS, *49 Regent's Park Road, London NW1. Tel: 0171 586 0408. Regular pub hours (closed 3-5pm weekdays). Food served daily noon to 2:30pm. Chalk Farm tube.*

Popular, attractive, clubby, upmarket – this pretty arts and crafts/art nouveau pub is the center of life in Primrose Hill, and a required stop on any visit. The windows are leaded stained glass, the decor William Morris, the furniture quartersawn oak, the mirrors large and the crowd classy and local. And the beer couldn't be nicer – **Young's Bitter**, **Special** and **Oatmeal Stout**.

Start your day with a walk in Regent's Park, cross over to Primrose Hill, stop in at the Queens, explore the lovely small shops, and retire to dinner at one of the village's terrific restaurants. We can't think of a nicer way to spend the day.

PUBS TO WRITE HOME ABOUT

There's a certain something about a certain few pubs that causes us to think back on our lost hours there and sigh. In our book, that's what pubs are for. Here are a few of the evenings we'll never forget.

THE SEVEN STARS, *53 Carey Street, London WC2. Tel: 0171 242 8521. Monday to Friday 11am to 9:30pm. Closed weekends and bank holidays. Food served 11am to 7pm. Holborn tube.*

THE BLACKFRIAR, *174 Queen Victoria Street, London EC4. Tel: 0171 236 5650. Monday and Tuesday 11:30am to 10pm; Wednesday to Friday 11:30am to 11pm; closed weekends and bank holidays. Blackfriars tube.*

THE FOX & ANCHOR, *115 Charterhouse Street, London EC1. Tel: 0171 253 4838. Open Monday to Friday 7am to 9pm; Saturday 8am to noon. Closed Sunday. Food served 7am to 10:30am and noon to 2:15pm. Farringdon or Barbican tube.*

THE LAMB AND FLAG, *33 Rose Street, London WC2. Tel: 0171 497 9504. Regular pub hours. Bar food noon to 5pm Monday to Saturday. Covent Garden tube.*

THE FLASK, *77 Highgate West Hill, London N6. Tel: 081 340 7260. Regular pub hours. Bar food daily noon to 9pm. Highgate tube.*

THE HOLLY BUSH, *22 Holly Mount, London NW3. Tel: 0171 435 2892. Daily 11am to 3pm and 5:30 to 11pm. Saturday, 11am to 4pm and 6pm to 11pm; Sunday noon to 3pm and 7pm to 10:30pm. Bar food always available. Hampstead tube.*

THE ALBION, *10 Thornhill Road, N1. Tel: 0171 607 7450. Daily, standard pub hours. Angel or Highbury and Islington tube.*

THE NAG'S HEAD, *53 Kinnerton Street, London SW1. Tel: 0171 235 1135. Regular pub hours. Bar food noon to 10pm. Knightsbridge or Hyde Park Corner tube.*

THE GUINEA, *30 Bruton Place, London W1. Tel: 0171 409 1728. Regular pub hours. Closed Sunday. Bar food noon to 2:30pm and 6:30pm to 10:30pm. Restaurant food daily noon to 2:30pm (except Saturday) and 6pm to closing. Green Park or Bond Street tube.*

THE SPANIARD'S INN, *Spaniard's Road, Hampstead, London NW3. Tel: 0181 455 3276. Regular pub hours. Food served noon to 2:30pm and 6pm to 9:30pm weekdays; noon to 9:30pm weekends. Hampstead tube.*

People tend to fall into a kind of boozy rapture when talking about The Spaniard's and we're no exception. It's pretty much everyone's platonic ideal of a pub, and therefore worth the extra effort of getting there (more than half a mile walk from Kenwood House, just under a mile from the Hampstead tube; if you're not a walker, take a cab). Built in 1585, legend says it was once the residence of the Spanish Ambassador to King James I (hence the name), though no one can quite explain what the ambassador would have been doing living so far from court.

You can reach the pub on a lovely walk across Hampstead Heath, but do make sure to ask directions often – it's possible to get insanely lost. You'll know you've arrived by the traffic jams in all directions. Originally called The Inn at the Old Gate, the pub guarded the toll gate into London, and the narrow bottleneck with drivers lunging for a opening still exists today (beware of getting mown down as you try to bolt across the road). Just about everyone makes it to The Spaniard's at some point or another, including (over its 400 year history) Charles Lamb, Dickens, Keats, Shelley, Byron, and Joshua Reynolds. Dick Turpin, the famous highwayman, is reputed to have holed out from the law in the mazes of tunnels and passageways underneath the Inn; it's one of the many place Keats reportedly wrote *Ode on a Nightingale*.

In summer, head straight for the lovely rose-filled garden (featured in Dickens' *Pickwick Papers*), and bring the kids to cavort and twitter with the flock of budgies in the aviary. In winter, various cozy fires in copper fireplaces roar away in the oak panelled rooms, and once you've got your pint of **London Pride** or **Adnams Extra**, you might find yourself too happy to live. The food is on the good side of decent, and ranges from the usual salads, sandwiches and shepherd's pie to leek and parsnip soup, chicken chasseur and plum crumble.

ISLINGTON, CLERKENWELL, & KING'S CROSS

THE ALBION, *10 Thornhill Road, N1. Tel: 0171 607 7450. Daily, standard pub hours. Angel or Highbury and Islington tube.*

Sadly for tourists, but perhaps luckily for locals, The Albion isn't really close to any public transportation, but it's definitely worth a walk or a taxi ride – especially in summer when the big pleasant beer garden out back is filled with honeysuckle, wisteria and happy drinkers. The Albion started life as a coaching inn, has been serving beer for the better part of two centuries, and isn't short on customers or charm. Old saddlery and horsey prints abound and there's an eclectic mix of wooden tables and comfortable chairs.

In winter, roaring fireplaces warm the cozy recesses of the back rooms (one is non-smoking) and in good weather just about everyone hangs around outside – either at the few tables in front or the many in back. The Albion is at its best during the day when it's quiet and full of character – and before the smoky evening crowds arrive. Lunches are hearty, substantial and well above average pub fare. The hero of the place, however, is the **Theakston XB**. A couple of pints and you'll find yourself munching happily on the honeysuckle till closing.

THE EAGLE, *159 Farringdon Road, London EC1. Tel: 0171 837 1353. Monday to Friday, noon to 11pm. Closed bank holidays. Food available 12:30 to 2:30pm and 6:30 to 10:30pm. Farringdon tube.*

We weren't sure whether to include The Eagle as a pub or a restaurant, so we did the only sensible thing and included it as both. Extremely popular with artists, architects, journalists from The Guardian next door and City types, the Eagle is nearly always jammed, lively (or riotous) and fun. The floors are bare wood, ditto the tables, and there are frequently a couple of huge dogs lying around underfoot. The food, as described in the restaurant section, is exceptionally good Italian country cooking. If the noise and crowd get too much for you, try O'Hanlon's just a short jog up Rosebery Avenue.

O'HANLONS, *18 Tysoe Street, London EC1. Tel: 0171 837 4112. Regular pub hours. Food served noon to 2:30pm and 6pm to 9pm. Farringdon Road tube.*

We discovered O'Hanlon's when the bartender at our local reported that it served the best **Guinness** in London – we took his kind advice and haven't been back to his place since. The Guinness is imported from Dublin (not brewed in England as is customary), tastes sublimely smooth and rich and has a head so thick and creamy you could shave with it. You can't rush pumping it however, so pay up and go hum along with the Irish music for the 6 minutes or so it takes to get it right. Lately we've developed a taste for the flavorful **Kilkenny** ale that's been on offer. It's made by Guinness and just proves that those Irish are very clever people indeed. The pub itself has developed a bit of a reputation lately, and tends to be crowded, so anti-smoking lobbyists beware. The food is Irish, hearty, and good – and it's the real thing, prepared by Mr. O'Hanlon's dear old darlin' mum, imported from Ireland (his mum, that is, along with her recipe for Guinness pie).

THE WATERSIDE INN, *82 York Way, London N1. Tel: 0171 837 7118. Regular pub hours. Food served noon to 3pm and 6pm to 9pm. King's Cross tube.*

Now here's a weird one – a tudor pub in a ten year-old building. But it's a useful one if you happen to find yourself in the rather unsavory King's Cross neighborhood in search of a beer, as it's only a 5 minute walk around the back of the station. And it's an exceedingly pleasant one as well. You feel a bit like you've entered a time-warp as you walk through the door; apparently an entire country pub was purchased and transferred beams, boards and bar to this new brick development behind the station. In summer (or any marginally warmish day) the back door is flung open and the drinkers pour out onto the sparkling canalside. When the sun is shining, it's a delightful place to sit (or at least to try and jockey for a seat) and watch the houseboats, the ducks and the water glinting off Battlebridge Basin.

THE CAMDEN HEAD, *Camden Walk, London N1. Tel: 0171 359 0851. Regular opening hours. Food served 11am to 3pm. Angel tube.*

This pretty pub reigns supreme over the Camden Passage antique market, and it's easy to see why – all the mirrors and elaborately pretty etched glass of the late 19th century make you feel as if you're sitting inside a piece of sparkling Waterford Crystal. It's a great place to stop for a pause and a pint of **Theakstons**, and you won't even have to leave the main market drag to do it.

NOTTING HILL

THE WINDSOR CASTLE, *114 Campden Hill Road, London W8. Tel: 0171 727 8491. Regular pub hours. Bar food always available when pub is open. Notting Hill Gate tube.*

On a pretty road, in a gorgeous neighborhood exactly between Kensington Palace and Holland Park, you'll find this popular, exuberant pub. It's famed as the Notting Hill meeting place and it's easy to see why, especially in summer when the large, lovely garden is open and every well-to-do young actor and barrister in London seems to be outside drinking pints of **Young's** or sherry and tomato juice. The Windsor Castle is one of those superb London pubs (like the Flask in Highgate or The Hand in Hand in Wimbledon) that reminds you how recent all this dense city development is – try and imagine the fields that surrounded it, and the straight view all the way to Windsor Castle. Not exactly easy.

A friend of ours is one of the many young cooks in this pub, and considering what a madhouse the kitchen is on a busy day, is pleased when the food gets raves – and it does. The traditional Sunday lunch of beef and Yorkshire pudding is unusually good; get there early because it's first come first served. The rest of the menu might include couscous, fish cakes, beef and Guinness pie, stir fried vegetables, steamed mussels, raw oysters and of course chips. (The chef recommends the fish cakes.)

KNIGHTSBRIDGE & BELGRAVIA

THE BUNCH OF GRAPES, *207 Brompton Road, London SW3. Tel: 0171 589 4944. Regular pub hours. Food available 11am to 8pm. Knightsbridge or South Kensington tube.*

The Bunch of Grapes is the grand old lady of Knightsbridge pubs. Big, Victorian, comfortable, and popular, it boasts lots of etched glass, wood panelling, and a handsome carved mahogany grape vine in case you forget where you are. The food leans heavily towards roast beef and two veg; like everything else in this pub, grand tradition is all. It's a polite, attractive, civilized place to meet, with lots of banquettes with tables and nooks and crannies so you can enjoy your pint of **John Smith's** and steak and kidney pie with a bit of privacy on the side.

THE GRENADIER, *18 Wilton Row, London SW1. Tel: 0171 235 3074. Daily noon to 3pm and 7pm to 11pm (10:30pm Sunday). Knightsbridge or Hyde Park Corner tube.*

The Duke of Wellington and his officers used to use this small, attractive pub (circa 1827) as a general eating, gambling and drinking place, and the feeling of God and country still features strongly in everything from the pewter bar and the creaking floors and to the military artifacts collected and displayed throughout.

There's a really good cozy little pub restaurant at the back, and the bartender is famous for his Bloody Marys which are guaranteed to assuage homesickness. If you're not homesick, do as the natives do and "Take Courage" (the beer, that is).

THE GROUSE AND CLARET, *14-15 Little Chester Street, London SW1X 7AP. Tel: 0171 235 3438 (pub); 0171 245 1224 (restaurant). Regular pub hours, closed Sundays. Victoria Station tube.*

Velvet everywhere, potted flowers everywhere else – the Grouse has lots of wood panelling, an uppercrust, businessy sort of crowd, and perhaps most surprisingly, a Swedish restaurant upstairs. Window seats and tables in the bar are discreetly partitioned with handsome wood dividers for the utmost privacy. The beers are picturesquely named and excellent: **Old Speckled Hen**, **Hard Tackle**, and **Tangle Foot** are among our favorites. There's a wine bar in the basement; Schillerstrom's, the stylish Swedish restaurant, is upstairs; and hot and cold lunches are served at the bar.

THE NAG'S HEAD, *53 Kinnerton Street, London SW1. Tel: 0171 235 1135. Regular pub hours. Bar food noon to 10pm. Knightsbridge or Hyde Park Corner tube.*

This very charming tiny pub on this charming little street is so quintessentially English and intimate, you might find that everyone goes quiet for ten seconds or so as you walk in. But the pause indicates curiosity rather than hostility, and though decidedly not the place to confess to your partner that you think you're pregnant by someone else (unless you're looking for general advice, which would no doubt be forthcoming), it is a thoroughly friendly place to drink and eavesdrop over a pint of very, very good beer.

Try the **Benskins**, **Young's**, or our perennial fave, **Adnams**. Or stop in on your way home for a whiskey nightcap. In winter the fireplace is blazing, in summer the crowd spills out into the mews. As its name would suggest, The Nag's Head started life as a horsey pub – in 1820, Kinnerton Street housed the stables for Wilton Place, and the pub's habitues were grooms and stable boys to the rich folk of Knightsbridge.

THE SWAG AND TAILS, *10-11 Fairholt Street, London SW1. Tel: 0171 584 6926. Regular pub hours weekdays; 11am to 3pm Saturday, closed Sunday.*

Bar food available noon to 2pm weekdays; noon to 3pm Saturday. Knightsbridge or Sloane Square tube.

This is a pretty, upmarket, flashy little pub with lots of pale wood and a very ambitious menu. It's the sort of place that people who aren't really comfortable in smoky old-fashioned pubs will enjoy; on the other hand, don't go looking for low beams and lots of authenticity. The beer includes **John Smiths**, **Directors**, and **Pedigree**; the food tends towards soft shelled crab, chargrilled tuna steak, braised oxtail, and venison pie (all around £7). There's an unusually good variety of wines by the glass, a nice fireplace, and a well-dressed conservative Knightsbridge crowd. Tucked behind Sloane Street in a tiny little maze of mews, it's a bit tricky to find, so do what we did and ask directions (repeatedly).

MAYFAIR & ST JAMES

THE CLARENCE, *53 Whitehall, London SW1. Tel: 0171 930 4808. Regular pub hours. Restaurant food daily 11am to 9pm. Charing Cross tube.*

The Clarence is a rather touristy pub, but it can't help that, given its location near Downing Street and Trafalgar Square. But it's a nice pub for all that – with lots of dark wood, timbered ceilings, gas lamps, leaded glass, and best of all, a most untouristy selection of real ales. You're going to have to taste for yourself, but we're partial to **Ruddles County**, **Theakston**, and **Abbot**. By the time you've made up your mind, you will probably forget what you were testing.

YE GRAPES, *16 Shepherd Market, London W1. Tel: 0171 499 1563. Regular pub hours. Food served 11:30am to 10:30pm. Green Park tube.*

If you haven't ever visited Shepherd Market in the scenic heart of Mayfair, here's your excuse. It's a charming chaos of nice restaurants and smart shops in a small area famed for the call-girls who have dominated its streets for upward of a century. Happily (or sadly, depending on your needs), the girls have moved on, or at least are no longer in evidence, but the nice restaurants and popular pub remain.

Ye Grapes (Ye Gods would be more appropriate given the crush) is a good old-fashioned eccentric masterpiece of a pub, chock full of stuff like fish, guns and deer heads on the walls, that somehow manages to maintain an air of dignity and elegance nonetheless. It's a handsome drinking establishment with a quite stunning selection of beverages including **Old Speckled Hen**, **Wethered**, and **Brakspear**. On a pleasant summer evening, be prepared to battle your way to the bar and drink as the natives do, lounging in voluble groups outdoors.

THE GUINEA, *30 Bruton Place, London W1. Tel: 0171 409 1728. Regular pub hours. Closed Sunday. Bar food noon to 2:30pm and 6:30 to 10:30pm. Restaurant food daily noon to 2:30pm (except Saturday) and 6pm to closing. Green Park or Bond Street tube.*

What a gorgeous little pub. This is the sort of place that gives pubs a good name, and makes you forget all the horrors of fruit machines, mail-order horse brasses and swirly red carpeting. First of all it's in Mayfair, which indicates superior breeding even when it comes to the lowly public house, second it's a Young's pub, which means the beer is far better than average, and third, it boasts a really impressively good restaurant.

Start with a drink in the handsome, panelled bar (there's been a pub here since the early 15th century but not exactly this one), then move on to the restaurant, even if it means reserving ahead and fighting through the crowds, as The Guinea tends to be incredibly popular at meal time. Which is no surprise, given that the food is far superior to your usual pub grub, and not in the newfangled way of risotto and bruschetta either.

Meat reigns supreme both in the elegant restaurant to the rear and in the bar: Scottish beef, steak and kidney pies, and mixed grills the likes of which you'll remember long after you're back to Lean Cuisine and turkey dogs. The bar food is reasonably priced and delicious (in 1991 The Guinea won the award for the best steak and kidney pie, though we're not exactly sure who gives out such an award); the restaurant is fairly expensive – and worth every penny. It offers a set price lunch which, with a pint or two, means you might escape for around £20. Try the **Young's Special**, **Oatmeal Stout**, or **Winter Warmer** (in season).

THE RED LION, *23 Crown Passage, London SW1. Tel: 0171 930 4141. Open daily 11am to 11pm; Saturday 11am to 4pm; closed Sunday. Food served noon to 2:30pm. Green Park tube.*

The pubs of Mayfair and St. James can not be compared to the pubs of Bloomsbury or Covent Garden. For one thing, they tend to be older, and for another, well, classier. Lovely panelled bars and an atmosphere of clubby restraint prevail. The Red Lion, for instance. Set across from St. James Palace in a tiny old-fashioned passage, the pub is located exactly in the heart of London – but definitely an earlier London than we inhabit today.

All those Tudor beams and the antique lamps and leaded glass are real; the pub is one of London's oldest, dating from the late 1500s, and its cellar is said to have been the starting point for Charles II's mistress Nell Gwynn's nightly sojourns to his bed. What's happened to the tunnel we don't know, but there's still a good variety of beer (they serve **Old Speckled Hen** if you haven't tried it yet) and a journey back in time to be had at The Old Red Lion. ·

NORTH OF OXFORD STREET

THE BARLEY MOW, *8 Dorset Street, London W1. Tel: 0171 935 7318. Regular pub hours. Food served noon to 3:30pm. Closed Sunday. Baker Street tube.*

The Barley Mow is one of those London pubs that everyone knows and everyone likes. It's loaded with authentic detail (as opposed to the sort of decor lots of pubs buy mail order) like 19th century price lists engraved in brass on the bar, and private wooden booths for four built so pawnbrokers could conduct their business undisturbed. If you manage to find a free one, grab it (and your drinks), jump in and close the door. They're fantastically intimate and a great place to hang around if you're feeling anti-social, or just want to pretend you lived in another era.

The Barley Mow was supposedly a farmers' pub and a few years after the farmers left for greener pastures, the Beatles occasionally dropped by.

THE PRINCE ALFRED, *118 Marylebone Lane, London W1M 5FX. Teíl: 0171 486 0828. Regular pub hours (open to 11:30pm Monday and Wednesday). Closed Sundays. Oxford Street tube.*

This dark, wood-panelled, Victorian ale house has a lovely tin ceiling, nice glass lamps and a resident jazz band providing live entertainment every Monday and Wednesday, 9pm to 11:30pm. All the food is home-made on the premises, and includes traditional fare along the lines of meat pies, chili, sausage and mash, and a daily vegetarian dish. Tipples include **Thomas Hardy Country**, and a series of good guest ales that change every fortnight.

SOUTHWEST LONDON (RICHMOND, WIMBLEDON, KEW)

THE HAND IN HAND, *6 Crooked Billet, London SW19. Tel: 0181 946 5720. Regular pub hours. Food served noon to 2:30pm and 7pm to 10pm. Wimbledon tube.*

If you've managed to get all the way to Wimbledon for the tennis, why not walk an extra 15 minutes or so and pay a visit to The Hand and Hand. We'd even go so far as to say that the summer afternoon or evening you spend here will probably prove more memorable than the tennis.

Because this is one of those delightful but rare London pubs that will make you feel as if you've been transported to a charming village in the Cotswolds. In tandem with The Crooked Billet nearly next door (another exceedingly engaging establishment), The Hand and Hand has a large and loyal following of locals who come for the simple rustic atmosphere, the gorgeous flowers hanging everywhere, the good food and the **Young's** beers.

The pub is pretty as a picture, and on those long, beautiful summer evenings, you'll find the patrons arranged, according to precepts of the rural picturesque, on the lovely little green in front of the pub. Now doesn't that sound nicer than a lot of guys out of Nike advertisements trying to murder each other with fuzzy balls?

THE WHITE CROSS HOTEL, *Riverside, Richmond, Surrey TW9 1TH. Tel: 0181 940 6844. Regular pub hours. Food served noon to 8pm. Richmond tube.*

Follow Water Lane down to the Thames in Richmond and you'll find yourself on a pretty little riverfront parade complete with floating restaurant, boatmakers plying their trade, and a most wonderfully attractive pub, confusingly named The White Cross Hotel. Confusingly, that is, because it's not a hotel at all, but no less charming a pub for that. There are tables outdoors for soaking up the sun while watching the action on the riverside; in winter there's a sparkling view of the river and the seagulls from the glassed-in room by the bar. The good food combines Italian-style pastas and Neapolitan sausage with traditional sandwiches and savory pies. As a Young's pub, it offers the usual range of superb **Young's Bitter**, **Special** and **Winter Warmer**.

THE WHITE SWAN, *25-26 Old Palace Lane, Richmond, Surrey TW9 1TH. Tel: 0181 940 0959. Open daily 11am to 3:30pm and 5:30pm to 11pm. Sunday, noon to 3pm and 7pm to 10:30pm. Food always available. Richmond tube.*

This lovely old pub is situated on a pretty lane leading down to the Thames, just a few minutes walk from The White Cross Hotel, for those of you interested in a double feature. Where The White Cross is riverside and sunny, the Swan is cozy, dark and picturesque. It dates from the 16th century and shows its age most charmingly – all wood panelling, cozy spaces and roaring fires. There's a pretty little garden, its atmosphere of perfect peace marred only somewhat by the commuter trains that occasionally roar past. Try the **Courage** beers, or compare **Beamish** to **Guinness**, as this pub – unusually – carries both.

SOHO

THE DOG & DUCK, *18 Bateman Street, London W1. Tel: 0171 437 3478. Regular pub hours. Tottenham Court Road tube.*

The Dog and Duck is so popular with advertising and film people that it's pretty near useless trying to get to the bar at lunchtime or after work. But in the middle of the afternoon when the crowd has gone back to work, it become quiet, nearly empty, and a very pleasant place for a drink. Lots of dark wood, etched glass and brass, combined with a good roaring fire in the back that burns all winter, makes this tiny corner sliver of a pub cozy and charming (when it's not jam-packed and screamingly loud).

THE FRENCH HOUSE, *49 Dean Street, London W1. Tel: 0171 437 2799. Regular pub hours. Leicester Square tube.*

The French is something of a London landmark. Until recently, it was owned and run by Gaston Berlement, who, since the 40s, made it a meeting point for anything and everything French – legend has it that members of the French underground used to drink here, though we're not entirely sure what they were doing in Soho. Those famous Frenchmen Brendan Behan and Dylan Thomas could usually be found here in the '40s, and today it has something of a feeling of being stuck in time.

It's one of the most hardcore of the hardcore Soho pubs – in terms of tradition (lots of wine, and beer only offered in half-pints) and its permanent 11am to 11pm habituees. Have a peek in on your way upstairs to the very fine French House restaurant. Although not the most obvious place for a tourist to feel at home, if you're the sort to whom lifting a pint is more natural than breathing, you'll be welcomed with only the slightest of sidelong glances.

THE THREE GREYHOUNDS, *25 Greek Street, London W1. Tel: 0171 734 8799. Regular pub hours. Food served noon to 7:30pm. Leicester Square tube.*

The Greyhounds has recently turned from a rough and rowdy misery of a pub to a completely revamped, civilized, pleasant place for a pint of **Adnams**, **Young's**, or a bottle of beer and half a dozen oysters. Its mock-Tudor decor dates from the early part of this century (though it's genuinely 200 years old), it serves good cafe food all day, and it's one of the few pubs worth recommending around the Soho area that's not either too clique-y or too horrible to consider.

SOUTH LONDON

THE GEORGE INN, *77 Borough High Street, London SE1. Tel: 0171 407 2056. Regular pub hours. Food served noon to 2:30pm. London Bridge tube.*

A block or two south and across the road from Southwark Cathedral, not far from the original Globe Theatre, just down from London Bridge station, through a little narrow court with an iron gate, you'll find The George. It's incredibly famous (did Shakespeare drink at The George? legend says yes) and rightly so, one of the few remaining pubs of the sort that Falstaff frequented, Dickens wrote about, Hogarth and Rowlandson drew and everyone dreams about, but that barely exist anymore. A coaching inn has been on this spot for centuries, with galleried walls wrapped round a courtyard – only one of the galleried walls still stands today, but given the number of fires, bombings and architectural redevelopments, that's pretty good going.

Inside, The George wanders around corners, through passageways, by fireplaces, into little hidden bars and out again. It's a meandering kind of place with only the squeaking floorboards to record your progress. There's good bar food and a restaurant with "proper" food. And the ales? "Belly, god send thee good ale enough," exhorted Shakespeare, and with **Abbot**, **Boddingtons**, **London Pride**, **Flowers** and **Castle Eden**, The George continues to provide good ale enough. And then some.

14. SHOPPING

In the early to mid-eighties, you'd save the price of a plane ticket on a shopping trip to London. Sadly, the relative weakness of the dollar has reversed that trend, and the only people who find the transatlantic shopping trip worthwhile are the Brits.

There are, however, one or two things still worth buying in London. Shoes, for instance. Keep a look out for the many branches of **Pied a Terre** (for trendy men and women) and **Church's** (for men).

And do not, under any circumstances, turn up your nose at **Marks & Spencer**. According to the most reliable sources (film wardrobe people and stylists), M & S has cornered the European fashion markets by virtue of sheer buying power. They've lured lingerie designers from Italy's posh La Perla and made use of the same fabrics and manufacturers as expensive Joseph and G Gigli. For simple t-shirts, linen shirts, men's denim shirts and wool sweaters, bathing suits, exercise and underwear, and now even shoes, there are all sorts of bargains to be had. The branch at Marble Arch has the best selection.

Aside from Marks, there's only one place really worth trashing the limit on your credit card – **Liberty**. Avoid the billions of tourists clawing through all those traditional prints (though you can still get an overpriced washbag for your Aunt Lillian), skip the ubiquitous Liberty scarves unless you're genuinely into such things, and head for the jewelry (costume and otherwise), bags and luggage, clothes, shoes, hats, stationery, linen, fabrics, books, kitchenware, ethnic, and needlepoint departments. Liberty's buyers are wonderful, and if you're going to spend too much money on something in London, it may as well be something fabulous in a fabulous mock-tudor building.

Did we forget to mention **Harrods**? Harrods is, by its own admission, the greatest department store in the world. You can purchase a Ferrari at Harrods, an Elephant (does madam prefer Indian or African?) or a house on the Cote d'Azur. You can also buy perfectly ordinary things like microwaves, hairdryers, and pantyhose. The food halls, as everyone knows by now, are museum quality. The clothing is glamorous. The selection of goods superb. Princess Diana shops here. In fact, the only reason we don't buy everything at Harrods is the prices, which are as grand as the rest of the store.

Fortnum & Mason is another must-see, and a good place to buy expensive little gifts like Lapsang Suchong jelly. The staff still wear morning dress, the tea room is exceedingly civilized, and lots of Londoners do their daily grocery shopping here. They tend, however, to be Londoners like Michael Caine, who have millions to spend on a pound of butter and a bunch of carrots.

Where else should you look? Sloane Street, Knightsbridge, Fulham Road, South Molton Street and St. Christopher's Place, Covent Garden, and Hampstead High Street for fashion clothes and shoes. Oxford Street and Knightsbridge for the big department stores. Mayfair and St. James for traditional high-quality British products, Bloomsbury and Charing Cross Road for books. Remember that many, if not most of the good mid-priced clothing shops are chains. That means you'll find anywhere from two to twenty outlets in London alone, not to mention on the high street of every town in England.

Clothing

Of the chains, **Jigsaw** is every London girl's staple for this season's leggings, t-shirts, sweaters, colored jeans, silk shirts and suits. A big step up is **Nicole Farhi**, with flattering, chic, professional clothing and accessories in nice fabrics for the sort of woman who doesn't much care what things cost. Ditto **Joseph**, famed for its outrageous sweaters and well-tailored jackets. **Margaret Howell** has crept into a lead position with her heavy silk and linen shirts and good tailoring. **Whistles** is another London staple featuring slightly offbeat classics at fairly serious prices. **Monsoon** combines acres of ethnic with raw silk ballgowns (go figure); the famed **Butler & Wilson** is a treasure trove of over-the-top costume jewelry.

One-offs include **Jones**, perfect for that backless, sideless vinyl and foil day dress you can't live without. **Browns** is offbeat designer heaven (Vivienne Westwood to Donna Karan by way of Romeo Gigli) and should be avoided at all costs unless you're serious about clothes that cost lots of money (**Browns' Own Label** shop on South Molton Street is much more reasonable and worth a look). **Space NK** is one of our favorites for men and women's clothing, make-up and accessories. **Egg** is a one-of-a-kind establishment for clothing and home furnishings and is just plain special.

Make your decisions carefully. The only place that takes returns without question is Marks & Spencer; everyone else will give you a store credit (if you're lucky).

Antiques

Certain market antiques and collectibles are also worth pursuing in earnest – though we recommend not losing your heart to a twelve foot Irish pine dresser unless you own a shipping company. Look for serious bargains on heavy, silver-plated Georgian and Victorian flatware and bone-handled knives; old, handcarved bread boards; bronze and brass doorknobs; 19th century wooden tools; enamelled kitchenware from the forties and fifties; and best of all prints.

Hand-colored eighteenth century English caricatures can be found for as little as £150; good quality black and white publisher's proofs from the same period (lithographs, usually printed on both sides) for about £20. Don't forget to make sure the coloring is contemporary with the print and not done last year.

And we'll say it now and repeat it later: when at the markets, bargain. The usual rules apply. Ask if there's a discount for cash or offer a price 15-20% below what's being charged. Be polite. Be willing to walk away. And if the seller agrees to your price, don't start to dither, pay up. It's bad manners to do otherwise.

Sales

And now the subject you've all been waiting for, the sales. London's sales are legendary, mainly because the populace is so starved for a bargain that they're willing to queue for hours to snatch up a chartreuse Versace loincloth for £250 off the original hilarious price. But if you happen to land in London during January or July, you may as well give it a go.

Here's our pocket guide to the sales. Buy *Time Out* for a complete listing of places and prices. The first and last days of any establishment's sale are when the serious bargains can be had – a crystal pitcher with an invisible chip marked down from £30 to £2; a sample cashmere coat for £80; a discontinued line of Italian dinner plates for 50% off. The rest of the time is potluck, and if we had access to Loehmann's, T.J. Maxx, or the continual sale rack at Bloomingdale's, we'd probably skip the whole chaotic mess.

Not all sales start the same day; most winter sales start December 27th; Harrods about a week later. Do we think it's worth queuing all night to be the first one into Harrods? Not for all the discounts in China. But we do think the **Harrods** and **Liberty** sales are two of the best in town. Skip the first hysterical days, and have a leisurely browse when the feeding frenzy has died down. And skip the Versace loincloth. That chic toga party you might need it for just ain't gonna happen.

BIG & CLASSIC STORES

These are the shopping venues for which London is famous. And if there are a few you've never heard of, ask that rather chic Frenchman or Italian to direct you.

- **Burberry**, *165 Regent Street, London W1. Tel: 0171 734 4060. Piccadilly or Oxford Circus tube.* You know about the raincoats, but how about the Burberry tartan print shirts now appearing at every hip club in London? Very good quality, traditional British clothing. So conservative it's funky.
- **The Conran Shop**, *Michelin House, 81 Fulham Road, London SW3. Tel: 0171 589 7401. South Kensington tube.* Sir Terence Conran's flagship store and not to be confused with his chain of the same name in the U.S. Flashy, expensive, beautiful kitchen and houseware, furniture, dishes, linen, etc. The Michelin Building is a work of art in its own right.
- **Designers Guild**, *267 and 277 King's Road, London SW3. Tel: 0171 351 5775. South Kensington tube.* A wonderfully modern, elegant, expensive take on classic home style – luminous colors and contemporary patterns prevail in everything from fabric to furniture to kitchenware. Just about anything we admire in decor magazines and at friends' homes turns out to have come from here.
- **Fortnum and Mason**, *181 Piccadilly, London W1. Tel: 0171 734 8040. Piccadilly tube.* Groceries for the very rich and the very old fashioned. A good place for gifts and people-watching, the windows are always beautifully designed (especially at Christmas) and the one-of-a-kind mechanical clock over the entrance is a must-see when it strikes on the hour.
- **Harrods**, *87-135 Brompton Road, Knightsbridge, SW1. Tel: 0171 730 1234. Knightsbridge tube.* Everything you've ever dreamed of and then some, spread over 4.5 opulent acres. Conservative, expensive and comprehensive. And of the 35,000 customers per day, only one in four is a tourist.
- **Harvey Nichols**, *109 Knightsbridge, London SW1. Tel: 0171 235 5000. Knightsbridge tube.* Patsy and Edina of Absolutely Fabulous shop here, but that shouldn't discourage you. The boutique and designer clothes are divine, younger and more chic than Harrods. Not for the faint of purse.
- **Heals**, *196 Tottenham Court Road, London W1. Tel: 0171 636 1666. Goodge Street tube.* London's favorite home furnishings store for more than a century, now updated in high style. Glittering selection of designer kitchenware and home accessories as well as furniture, linen and gifts.
- **John Lewis**, *277-306 Oxford Street, London W1. Tel: 0171 629 7711. Oxford Circus tube.* The best, old-fashioned, all-purpose department store in

London which carries everything from clothes to kitchenware but excels in the sort of thing American department stores no longer carry, like fabrics (huge selection), sewing accessories, and needlepoint supplies. John Lewis is legendary for the lowest prices in town – and has an exceptionally fine button department. Don't go expecting the flash and glamour of Bloomingdale's.

- **Liberty**, *Regent Street, London W1. Tel: 0171 734 1234. Oxford Circus tube.* Our favorite place to browse and buy everything from shoes to little black dresses to men's suits to jewelry to stationery to kitchenware to soap.

- **Marks & Spencer**, *Oxford Street at Marble Arch, W1 (and branches). Tel: 0171 935 4422. Marble Arch tube.* Don't turn up your nose – good quality, low prices, legendary underwear (and we're not talking cotton bloomers) and some amazing fashion bargains for men and women.

VERY ENGLISH, VERY QUAINT

Just about everything can be found in American shops these days – a few of the notable exceptions are listed below:

- **The Burlington Arcade**, *51 Piccadilly, London W1. Piccadilly Circus tube.* Fisher cashmere, Penhaligons, the Irish Linen Company, Michael Rose (handmade wedding and engagement rings) and a variety of other traditional shops line this attractive arcade. Built in 1819 to provide a retreat for the gentry from the mud-splashing carriages of Piccadilly, it still performs that service admirably. The top-hatted beadles on patrol were originally hired to protect well-heeled citizens from pickpockets and knavery; today they enforce the arcade rules: no running, singing, whistling, or carrying of open umbrellas.

- **Colefax & Fowler**, *39 Brook Street, London W1. Bond Street tube. And 110 Fulham Road, London SW3.* South Kensington tube. Traditional, beautiful, expensive fabrics, wallpapers, wool throws, cushions, etc.

- **Czech & Speake**, *39C Jermyn Street, London SW1. Green Park tube. Or 125 Fulham Road, London SW3. South Kensington tube.* Traditional, excellent quality 19th century-style chrome and brass bathroom accessories: shaving mirrors, taps, shower fittings, toiletries, towel rails, etc.

- **Droopy & Browns**, *99 St. Martin's Lane, London WC2. Leicester Square tube.* Old fashioned silk ball gowns, tweed hacking jackets with velvet collars, and wonderful hats predominate in this strange shop that feels more like a theatrical costumer than a modern clothing store. Prices aren't frightening.

- **Floris of London**, *89 Jermyn Street, London SW1. Piccadilly Circus or Green Park tube.* Juan Famenias Floris left his native island of Minorca in 1730 and the fashionable Mayfair shop he established has been selling perfumes, essences and soaps to fashionable Londoners ever since. The gleaming Spanish mahogany showcases beautifully packaged toiletry items for men and women.

- **James Lock & Co.**, *6 St. James Street, London SW1.* The finest men's hats in London – since 1759. Lock & Co. made the plumed hat Wellington wore at Waterloo when he defeated Napoleon.
- **James Smith & Sons Umbrellas**, *Hazelwood House, 53 New Oxford Street, London WC1. Tel: 0171 836 4731. Tottenham Court Road tube.* Est. 1830 and virtually unchanged to this day. Visit for the superb Victorian shopfront graphics as much as for the umbrellas. Three hundred styles of walking sticks and umbrellas ranging from £10 to £1,250.
- **Neal's Yard Dairy**, *17 Shorts Gardens, London WC2. Tel: 0171 379 7646. Covent Garden tube.* A sliver of a shop crammed floor to ceiling with the new wave of traditional British farmhouse cheeses, much of it unpasteurized, none of it short of perfection. "Please taste before you buy" is their generous (and delicious) motto. If you happen to be there as the hour strikes, nip outside to look at the whimsical water clock.
- **Penhaligons**, *41 Wellington Street, London WC2. Covent Garden tube. (And 16 Burlington Arcade, London W1.)* Beautifully scented soaps and colognes in an atmosphere of 19th century opulence. The shop itself is a museumpiece; all rich wood, brass and etched glass.
- **Smythson of Bond Street**, *44 New Bond Street, London W1. Bond Street tube. And 135 Sloane Street, London SW1. Sloane Square tube.* The Queen, the Queen Mother, and the Prince of Wales shop here for fine stationery and notecards, not to mention one of the most handsome collection of leatherbound albums, diaries and address books in the world. Priced accordingly.
- **W. & H. Gidden**, *15D Clifford Street, London W1. Piccadilly tube.* "Upstairs for people, downstairs for horses" you're told as you enter. Silk scarves, beautiful leather boots, jockey silks, hunt jackets, wallets and bags share the premises with saddles, bits, bridles, and horse blankets. Very chic equestrian outfitter to the queen.

WOMEN'S FASHIONS

English clothes (and English women) are cut skimpier than American, so choose a size at least one if not two up from your normal (an American size 8 would be a 10 or even 12 here).

And remember – don't expect to get your money back if you've made a mistake.

- **Ally Capellino**, *95 Wardour Street, London W1. Leicester Square tube.* Wonderfully relaxed English designer clothes (suits, jackets, shirts, dresses, coats, jewelry, hats, accessories) for working women with spirit and style, plus a more reasonably priced diffusion line, Hearts of Oak.

- **Browns**, *23-27 South Molton Street, London SW1. Bond Street tube.* Romeo Gigli, Vivienne Westwood, Patrick Cox, Donna Karan; the list is impressive, the prices even more so.
- **Butler & Wilson**, *20 South Molton Street, W1. Bond Street tube. And 189 Fulham Road, SW3. South Kensington tube.* Everyone who's anyone buys glitzy chunky sparkly fashionable costume jewelry from Butler & Wilson.
- **Georgina von Elsdorf**, *149 Sloane Street, London SW1. Sloane Square tube.* Exquisite English-made, hand-printed silk, devoree velvet, and linen scarves, neckties and vests.
- **Joseph**, *26 Sloane Street, London SW1. Sloane Square tube. And 77 Fulham Road, SW3. South Kensington Tube. (And branches.)* Famous for their big bold sweaters, beautifully tailored, cutting-edge suits and funky separates. Pricey.
- **Janet Fitch**, *25a Old Compton Street, London W1. Leicester Square tube. And 37 Neal Street, London WC2. Covent Garden tube.* A constantly changing showcase for talented young jewelry designers. Mainly earrings and pendants, moderately priced and always tempting.
- **Jigsaw**, *21 Longacre, London WC2. Covent Garden tube. And 31 Brompton Road SW3. Knightsbridge tube. (And branches.)* Working girls' paradise – basic, fashionable wool, linen, silk and cotton suits, separates, denim and lycra jeans, mohair sweaters. If it's in this season, it's at Jigsaw at a really reasonable price.
- **Jones**, *15 Floral Street, London WC1. Covent Garden tube.* Very avant-garde, very designer, very strange, very expensive. Lots of fun to browse.
- **Laura Ashley**, *256 Regent Street, London W1 (and branches). Oxford Circus tube.* Pretty sprigged daywear, party dresses and home furnishings for women and children.
- **Margaret Howell**, *29 Beauchamp Place, London SW1. Knightsbridge or South Kensington tube. (And branches.)* Beautifully tailored updated classics in wool, heavy silk, linen and cotton.
- **Monsoon**, *264 Oxford Street, London W1. Oxford Circus tube. (And branches.)* Lots of modern indian-print, easy, fairly inexpensive clothes combined with handknit sweaters, jackets and (strangely) raw silk eveningwear.
- **Nicole Farhi**, *11 Floral Street, London WC2. Covent Garden tube. And 193 Sloane Street, London SW1. Knightsbridge tube. And 25 St. Christopher's Place, London W1. (And branches.)* Beautiful, simple, superbly cut, but less face it, overpriced clothing. Every professional woman in London owns at least one or two pieces (often bought in the sale).

- **Pringle**, *93 New Bond Street, London W1. Bond Street tube.* Traditional lambswool and cashmere for men and women.
- **Space NK**, *Thomas Neals, 41 Earlham Street, London WC1. Tel: 0171 379 7030. Covent Garden tube.* The dominant force in this pretty new mall, Space NK features chic modern clothes for real women (and men), cosmetics, jewelry, accessories and an espresso bar.
- **Westaway & Westaway**, *62-65 Great Russell Street, London WC1. Tottenham Court Road tube.* Cashmere and shetland sweaters, shawls and scarves for men and women at some of the most reasonable prices in London.
- **Whistles**, *12-14 St. Christopher Place, London W1. Bond Street tube. And 27 Sloane Square, London SW1. Sloane Square tube. And 14 Beauchamp Place, London SW1. Knightsbridge or South Kensington tube. (And branches.)* Eclectic, individualistic, up-to-the-minute clothing for women with creative lifestyles and reasonably well-padded wallets.

SIZES

Women's Dresses & Skirts

American	6	8	10	12	14
English	8	10	12	14	16

Women's Shoes

American	6	7	8	9	10	11	12
English	4	5	6	7	8	9	10
European	34	35	36	37	38	39	40

Women's Underwear*

American	5	6	7
English	7	8	9

(bra sizes are the same)

Men's suits, shirts and trousers are the same sizes in England as in America, but beware of shirt cuffs which are often designed for cufflinks rather than buttons.

Men's Shoes

American	6	7	8	9	10	11	12
English	5	6	7	8	9	10	11

MEN'S FASHIONS

British tailoring and designerwear tends to be slimmer and more snugly cut than its American equivalent. Alterations are widely available, however, so ask.

- **Bates the Hatter**, *21A Jermyn Street, London W1. Piccadilly Circus or Green Park tube.* This tiny shop is slim as a magazine and crammed with felt fedoras and wonderful straw Panamas that look equally smart on Fifth Avenue or the French Riviera. Prices are reasonable and the quality superb. Lots of women cross the gender barrier and make wonderful finds here.

- **Duffer of St. George**, *29 Shorts Gardens, London WC2. Covent Garden tube.* The very very most up-to-the-minute men's fashion, club and street styles. On the expensive side but an image this hip doesn't come cheap.
- **Hackett**, *137 Sloane Street, London SW1. Sloane Square tube. (And branches.)* Hackett offers the essential British kit for men. Start with a haircut upstairs before or after being fitted for a made-to-order suit (from £475) or waistcoat (from £155). Conservative tastes will like the lovely tweeds and corduroys, silk ascots and the whimsical collection of cufflinks.
- **Jaeger**, *96 Brompton Road, 145 King's Road, 184 Kensington High Street. (And branches.)* Conservative, quality fashions for men (and women).
- **Jigsaw Menswear**, *14 James Street, London W1. Bond Street tube. (And branches.)* Moderately-priced, well-designed menswear from the famed women's chain.
- **Les 2 Zebres**, *38 Tavistock Street, London WC1. Covent Garden tube.* Fashionable beautifully cut French clothes for creative dressers.
- **Moss Bros.**, *27 King Street, London WC2. Tel: 0171 240 4567. Covent Garden tube.* Do as the natives do and pronounce the name "Moss Bross." Converted from a 19th century firehouse, it still specializes in emergencies, only nowadays they're of the haberdashery sort. Everyone in London rents tuxes and morning suits here for weddings, Ascot, Glyndeborne opera, etc. Top designer labels too, and great original plasterwork.
- **Paul Smith**, *41-44 Floral Street, London WC2. Covent Garden tube.* Nouveau traditional, trendy, well-tailored men's clothes, shoes and accessories; trendy (high) prices to match.
- **Turnbull & Asser**, *71-72 Jermyn Street, London SW1. Green Park tube.* The very famous, very traditional, very swanky place to buy your suits, ties and shirts – made to order or off the rack.
- **Westaway & Westaway**, *62-65 Great Russell Street, London WC1. Tottenham Court Road tube.* Cashmere and shetland sweaters for men and women and some of the best prices in London.

SHOES

We continue to maintain that this is the fashion purchase to make in London. Avoid the American biggies (like Joan & David and DKNY) and go for the quality locals – there are very good prices to be had on very well-made English and Italian shoes.

Virtually every shop in London will translate competently from American sizes.

- **Bally**, *71 and 197 Brompton Road, 92 King's Road, 246 and 472 Oxford Street, 260 and 152 Regent street. (And branches.)* Beautiful, well-made, and a bargain compared to New York City prices.
- **Church's**, *112 Jermyn Street, 143 Brompton Road, 436 Strand, 163 New Bond Street. (And branches.)* Beautifully made traditional men's shoes that last forever. Much cheaper than in the States.
- **Dr. Martens**, *1-4 King Street, London WC2. Covent Garden tube.* A five floor department store full of Doc Martens shoes, boots, clothes and miscellaneous accessories.
- **Lobb's**, *9 St. James Street, London SW1. Green Park tube.* Not for the timid of heart, foot or pocketbook. Made to measure shoes (starting at about £1200 for a pair of calf brogues). No appointment necessary; expect to wait six months for delivery.
- **Patrick Cox Shoes and Antiques**, *8 Symons Street, London SW3.* White patent leather faux snakeskin (for men or women) anyone? The hottest fashion in town, his designs are cloned by nearly every wannabe shoe store in London; people actually queue to get into this small eccentric shop. Moderate to expensive.
- **Pied a Terre**, *19 South Molton Street, 33 King's Road, 5 Garrick Street, 14 Sloane Street. (And branches.)* Good quality, fashionable shoes for men and women at very reasonable prices (Sloane Street shop is the flagship – it carries their high fashion line at higher prices).
- **Plumline**, *55 Neal Street, Covent Garden WC1.* Covent Garden tube. Very up-to-date foot fashions for men and women.

BOOKS

London is famous for the quality and variety of its bookshops – old and new. For antiquarian and second-hand bookshops the best hunting grounds can be found all along **Museum Street** (across from the British Museum) and the **Leicester Square** end of Charing Cross Road (between and along Great Newport and Litchfield Streets). **Skoob Books** on the pedestrian mall Sicilian Avenue (Holborn Tube) is also worth a look-in if you're in the neighborhood. The following are browsers' paradise for new books:

- **Books Etc.**, *120 Charing Cross Road, London WC2. Tottenham Court Road tube. (And branches.)* Big, comprehensive, helpful – large fiction, travel, children's sections (etc.) This branch has a nice cafe attached.
- **Daunt Books**, *83 Marylebone High Street, London W1. Bond Street tube.* One of our very favorites. Daunt specializes in travel books, and with its dramatic skylights and mahogany fittings, is a wonderfully attractive place to browse.

- **Dillons**, *82 Gower Street, London WC1. Goodge Street tube. (And branches.)* Huge, modern and accessible.
- **Hatchards**, *187 Piccadilly, London W1. Piccadilly tube.* Very pretty, very traditional Mayfair book emporium on numerous levels. Huge children's section.
- **Waterstones**, *121-125 Charing Cross Road, London WC1. Tottenham Court Road tube. (And branches.)* One of the big quality standards with lots of branches.
- **W.H. Smith**, *36 Sloane Square, London SW1. Sloane Square tube. (And branches.)* Another of the big quality standards.
- **Zwemmers**, *80 Charing Cross Road, London WC2; 26 Litchfield Street, London WC2. Leicester Square tube.* Two tiny, jam-packed shops offering the city's finest collection of art, design and photography books.

ANTIQUE MARKETS

A lot more people have been decorating their homes for a lot longer over here, which explains why there are so many more antiques for sale. And it shows in the prices – which are generally considerably lower in London than in the States. Some items (like prints and old kitchenware) are real bargains.

- **Antiquarius**, *Antique Centre 135 King's Road, London SW3. Monday to Saturday 10am to 6pm. Sloane Square tube.* More than 120 dealers are packed into this one building, selling everything from cameos and clocks to porcelain, prints and lace. A "no pressure to buy" atmosphere makes it particularly pleasant for browsers. Snack bar.
- **Bermondsey Market**, *Bermondsey Square (south of Tower Bridge), London SE1. Friday, 4:30am to 2pm. London Bridge tube.* Sadly for the criminals, the ancient "market ouvert" law that allowed stolen goods to be bought and sold here before dawn has recently been changed. It lasted long enough, however, for a very lucky buyer to pay £35 for an original (stolen) Gainsborough. He is still fighting for possession in court. This is where all the professional dealers shop, reselling their goods in antique shops around Britain and Europe. Just about anything changes hands here, including silver, jewelry, glassware, prints, china and, of course, paintings.
- **Brick Lane Market**, *Brick Lane, London E1. Sunday, 5am to 2pm. Aldgate East tube.* Head to the north end of Brick Lane where the highest density of stalls are, but don't expect to head home laden with treasures. Dickensian is the word most often associated with Brick Lane, junk is the other. Great finds can be found, but they're likely to be at the more eccentric end of taste. Go for the atmosphere and the great 24-hour bagel shops; if you find something worth buying it's a bonus.

- **Camden Lock and Camden Stables**, *Camden High Street to Chalk Farm Road. Saturday and Sunday, 8am to 5pm. Camden Town or Chalk Farm tube.* Part flea market, part crafts market, part street festival, Camden Lock specializes in just about everything. Crafts, jewelry (mostly new), cast offs, toys, Indian furniture, food, textiles, clothing, lots of old things that don't quite qualify as antiques – we couldn't even begin to describe the chaos. Camden Lock is teen heaven, but if you can handle the crowds, an hour or so can be tolerated by people over 30. Afterwards walk along the canal to Regent's Park and the Zoo, or take a canal trip on a passenger boat.

- **Camden Passage**, *Camden Passage, London N1. Wednesday and Saturday 7am to 3pm. Angel tube.* This high-quality antiques market has turned Islington into London's fifth most popular tourist spot. Stalls sell the cheaper goods (china, knickknacks, flatware, jewelry) while the surrounding shops deal in serious prints, furniture, china, antique games, clothing and lamps. Everything from enamel kitchenware to deco jewelry to dolls – and lots of bargains – can be found here. Come early enough to really explore, along with all the French and Italians in their expensive furs.

- **Chenil Galleries**, *181-183 King's Road, London SW3. Monday to Saturday 10am to 6pm. Sloane Square tube.* Specialists in art nouveau, deco furniture and jewelry, Chenil's more serious prices favor the more serious antique shopper.

- **Chelsea Antiques Market**, *253 King's Road, London SW3. Monday to Saturday 10am to 6pm. Sloane Square tube.* A flea market atmosphere with a huge variety of eccentric items.

- **Gray's Antique Markets**, *58 Davies Street and 17 Davies Mews, London W1. Monday to Friday 10am to 6pm. Bond Street tube.* About 200 stalls selling antiques and antiquities from around the world, conveniently placed at the end of South Moulton Street. The atmosphere manages to be both serious and seedy at once; prices don't look so bad if you've just spent half an hour shopping for clothes at Browns.

- **Furniture Cave**, *533 King's Road, London SW9. Monday to Saturday, 10am to 6pm. Sunday 11am to 4pm. Sloane Square tube.* The largest selection of antique furniture under one roof in London. Fifteen dealers on three floors. Porcelain, prints, and other items as well.

- **Portobello Road**, *(Chepstow Villas end) Saturday, 7am to 5pm. Notting Hill Gate tube.* Join the exuberant neighborhood crowd searching for hidden treasure, bargains or just a pretty old teapot. Portobello Road consists of stalls, arcades and antique and junk shops – it's packed and fun and runs all the way up to Goldbourne Road, but the merchandise takes on a distinctly seedy air the further north you head. Lots of good cafes and pubs to retire to with your spoils.

MISCELLANEOUS

Just a few of our favorites to round up your American Express bill:

• **Egg**, *36 Kinnerton Street, London SW1. Knightsbridge or Hyde Park Corner tube.* "The ordinary invested with particular charm" just begins to capture the spirit of this magical shop. Balls of tarred string from the Faroe Islands, Irish linen sheets, wooden nesting bowls made by Indian monks, delicate stitched and dyed pillows, quilts and silk shirts, fisherman's sweaters handknit by fishermen.

• **Jerry's Home Store**, *163-167 Fulham Road, London SW3. Tel: 0171 225 2246. South Kensington tube.* Two floors of practical and beautiful kitchenware with a traditional country English and French bent: earthenware, patterned dishes, beautiful pots and pans. Very reasonable prices – bet you don't leave empty-handed.

• **The Kasbah**, *8 Southampton Street, London WC2. Tel: 0171 379 5230. Covent Garden tube.* Unusual ceramics, pillows, clothing, tiles and other Moroccobilia.

• **Muji**, *26 Great Marlborough Street, London W1. (And branches.) Tel: 0171 494 1197. Oxford Circus tube.* Japanese minimalist design – clothing to stationery to food to linen to housewares.

• **David & Charles Wainwright**, *251 Portobello Road, London W11. Tel: 0171 792 1988. Notting Hill Gate tube.* Home accessories from glass balls to silver jewelry to furniture to Indian movie posters, all from Rajasthan in northern India. Famous for its literary/stage celebrity clientele.

15. AFTERNOON TEA

Once upon a time, when life was active and lunch for the country gentry included half a ham, a brace of grouse, and a haunch of venison, high tea was necessary to tide over 4pm hunger pangs. In working class families, tea is often still the preferred word for supper, and indicates a light meal in the early evening.

And to the vast majority of British people in the 1990s, afternoon tea consists of a mug of tea and a chocolate biscuit. So it's mainly tourists who think it's a good idea to consume a couple of thousand calories before dinner – and as long as you don't do it every day, we wholeheartedly agree.

Most hotel teas consist of three courses, served in sequence or all at once: **sandwiches** (with the crusts cut off, usually smoked salmon, cucumber, ham, cream cheese and chive, or tuna paste); **scones** (with or without *sultanas* – raisins, that is) served with jam and clotted cream; and **pastries** (fruit tarts, custard horns, eclairs and the like).

You'll be offered a selection of teas – our favorites are **Earl Grey** (a blend of China and Indian, weak and fragrant with Bergamot); **Assam** (from India; rich, strong and flavorful, perfect for breakfast or a pick-me-up); and **Lapsang Suchong** (from China; smoky, mysterious and fragrant).

If your sole experience with tea is Lipton or red zinger, try a cup of Assam, brewed strong, with milk. It's deliciously fortifying and completely addictive; after a week or two you'll wonder what you ever saw in coffee.

AFTERNOON TEA CLASSICS

BASIL STREET HOTEL, *8 Basil Street, London SW3 1AH. Tel: 0171 581 3311. Daily 3:30pm to 5:30pm. Knightsbridge tube.*

All the charm of an Edwardian sitting room, but the tea is served without much aplomb and without the silver trays, fine china, linen, and the other accessories of ritual. There is, however, a good reason to come here for tea, and that is the convenient, comfortable surroundings. A predominantly English crowd uses the Basil Street Hotel as a Knightsbridge retreat from the office and shopping; we occasionally follow suit. If you get tired of people-watching, there are plenty of magazines and newspapers to browse through. Full cream tea is £8.30; two scones, clotted cream and jam, £5.30.

THE BERKELEY, *Wilton Place, London SW1X 7RL. Tel: 0171 235 6000. Daily 3pm to 6pm. Hyde Park Corner or Knightsbridge tube.*

This deluxe Knightsbridge hotel offers a splendid high tea (with particularly nice smoked salmon sandwiches) in comfortable, traditional surroundings. Scones and pastries are baked half-size, so you can enjoy a taste of everything without ruining your appetite. The Berkeley is probably not the ideal place for a cranky two year old; the atmosphere is one of quiet wealth and restraint. The full tea is £12 per person; you can also order a la carte.

BROWN'S HOTEL, *Albemarle Street and Dover Street, London W1A 4SW. Tel: 0171 493 6020. Daily 3pm to 6pm, although reservations can only be made for 3pm. Green Park tube.*

This is one of the most pleasant and most famous places in London to take tea, without the touristy, impersonal service that plagues many of the larger hotels. The quintessentially English sitting room with its dark wood-panelling and soft chintz sofas offers quiet, tucked-away corners for intimate chats and a rest from all that shopping and sightseeing. The tea is beautifully presented by formally dressed waiters, the flatware heavy silverplate, and the food fresh, delicate and delicious. Brown's is popular with Londoners too, and it's advisable to reserve, especially in high season and the hectic shopping weeks before Christmas. Full cream tea: £14.95.

CHELSEA PHYSIC GARDEN, *Swan Walk, London SW3. Tel: 0171 352 5646. Wednesday 2pm to 4:45pm; Sunday 2pm to 5:45pm. Sloane Square tube.*

From April to October on two days a week only, you can enjoy a simple pot of tea served in pretty blue and white crockery, and a selection of traditional homemade cakes (lemon, carrot, Victorian sponge and coffee cakes – all excellent) on an oilcloth-covered table at this lovely, informal garden setting. Not exactly the Connaught, but on a sunny summer day, much nicer.

FORTNUM & MASON, *The St. James Restaurant, Piccadilly, London SW1. Tel: 0171 734 8040, ext. 241. Monday to Saturday 3pm to 5:30pm. Closed Sundays. Piccadilly Circus tube.*

Avoid the obvious Fountain Restaurant on the first floor of Fortnum's, it's low on atmosphere and not much fun. Head instead to the fifth floor and follow the sound of chamber music until you come to the St. James Restaurant. The softly-lit, spacious room is formal yet welcoming, with a wonderful away-from-the-crowd feeling. If the full high tea seems a bit overwhelming, you might try a pot of tea and anchovy toast or a cheese and chive sandwich. The restaurant also offers champagne by the bottle or the glass. Minimum charge: £5.

THE SAVOY, *The Strand, London WC2R OEU. Tel: 0171 836 4343. Open Monday to Friday noon to midnight; Saturday 5pm to midnight; closed Sunday. Charing Cross tube.*

Skip the afternoon high tea that's served in the gaudy, marble-pillared Thames Foyer; it's impersonal and touristy. Instead, head upstairs to "Upstairs at the Savoy," an informal cafe and oyster bar overlooking the bustling Savoy courtyard. There, at a romantic table for two (or a comfortable table for one), you can watch all the comings and goings of this world famous hotel while you drink tea, champagne, and wine by the glass or order from the cafe menu specializing in seafood dishes like grilled cod with white bean stew, salmon kedgeree and monkfish with wild rice.

THE STAFFORD, *St. James Place, London SW1A 1NJ. Tel: 0171 493 0111. Daily 3pm to 6pm. Green Park tube.*

The cheery sitting room of this small, hidden hotel is our favorite place for afternoon tea. In the winter it's cozy, comfortable and warm; in summer, pleasant and welcoming. Prepare yourself for the graceful attentions of the knowledgeable staff, who serve each course separately and pour the tea for you; the slow, relaxed pace and appreciation of ritual are primary elements of The Stafford's success. Scones are freshly baked and available plain, with almonds, or sultanas, often still warm from the oven. If the full tea is more than you can handle, try ordering a la carte tea, scones, sandwiches or pastries. The price is £10 for the full tea.

THE WALDORF, *Aldwych, London WC2B 4DD. Tel: 0171 836 2400. Daily 3:30pm to 6pm. Covent Garden tube.*

At the heart of this turn-of-the-century hotel is the Palm Court, a grand marble-floored circular room with two huge palm trees. Afternoon tea is served here every afternoon, one course at a time, by friendly staff. The entire atmosphere is redolent of the gone-but-not-forgotten "Tango Teas" of the 20s and 30s. The atmosphere is nostalgic, the pace leisurely, and the pastries and eclairs particularly delicate.

For the ballroom dancers among you, the tea dances are back: every weekend from 3:30pm to 6pm there's tea, a live band and dancing. Full cream tea: £13.25 (a la carte service available); weekend dancing: £20.50, reservations required.

16. CHILD'S PLAY

It's a lucky child indeed who manages to wrangle a trip to London. There are any number of fantastic (cheap) pleasures like the mummies at the **British Museum**, the changing of the guard and a ride on the top of a double-decker bus, not to mention one or two expensive ones (beg mom and dad to take you to the **Blue Elephant** for Sunday lunch). Future theater-lovers have a huge variety of entertainment from which to choose, from puppet shows to *Cats*.

Although England still clings to something of a "children should be seen and not heard" attitude, reasonably well-behaved kids are welcome pretty much anywhere, and there are lots of parks to run around in, ducks to feed, and men in silly uniforms to gawp at. Children are generally welcome in the gardens of pubs (in summer), but not in the pubs themselves. Buses and taxis are in general very helpful for parents with strollers (conveniently, stroller and baby can roll right into black cabs).

Kidsline is a telephone information service which offers help finding and choosing entertainment of all sorts: movies, exhibitions, courses, workshops and sports – and best of all, you get to talk to a knowledgeable, friendly, helpful human on the other end. It's a great resource for anyone with children to entertain. *Phone 0171 222 8010 Monday to Friday, 4pm to 6pm.*

BABYSITTING

From the land that practically invented nannies, a few of the best services:

BABYSITTERS UNLIMITED, *Tel: 0181 892 8888 (reservations, daily 10am to 5pm).*

A London-wide service that can provide qualified babysitters for infants to 10 year olds with 24 hours notice. Judy Thomas, a mother herself, has operated the business since 1978 and says she can usually provide a sitter even if you call the same day. Rates for a 4-hour minimum range from £3.25-£4 an hour, depending on the time of day, plus a £6 booking fee and carfare home for the sitter. For the minimum four hours, expect to pay about £23.

BRILLIANT BABYSITTERS, *22a Campden Grove, London W8. Tel: 0171 938 2006.*

Experienced nannies and au pairs available by the day, evening or weekend; they will also organize children's parties to order.

AT LAST, A CHILDREN'S HOTEL!

PIPPA'S POP-IN, *430 Fulham Road, London SW6. Tel: 0171 385 2458; fax: 0171 385 5706. Rates (including dinner, breakfast and VAT): £25 per night Monday to Thursday; £30 Friday to Sunday. Fulham Broadway tube.*

This big yellow Georgian house with a white picket fence has been turned into the world's first children's hotel, and has proved a great success with kids and parents alike. Children's artwork adorns the walls, and the playroom has teddy bears on chairs, toys, and games galore. The child-friendly atmosphere is competent, warm and friendly – in the three years the hotel has been running, no parent has ever had to come collect a child before the stay was up.

Children can be brought in any time after 4:30pm and are served a home-cooked supper (vegetables optional) before going to look for the fairies and the pet rabbits that live in the garden. Magic bubble baths for younger kids are followed by bedtime stories and a cup of hot chocolate. There are two pretty bedrooms, the Clown Room and the Bunny Room (divided by age), each with four single beds (maximum number of guests is 8). The overnight staff consists of two qualified, experienced nannies; one of whom is on "wide awake" duty all night.

On weekends there are games and 8pm midnight feasts. The atmosphere is geared towards pure pleasure and treats, and if the repeat-visit rate is anything to go by, it seems to work. In the morning the children have breakfast; get dressed and ready to go, and (if they're not staying for the day) can be delivered back to their parents, or picked up by 11am.

There's a maximum three night stay, and a daytime playschool for kids staying more than just the night; reservations should be made at least a week in advance.

UNIVERSAL AUNTS, *Tel: 0171 738 8937 (reservations weekdays 10am to 5pm).*

This agency has been providing Londoners with childcare for more than 50 years, making it the longest established in the city. In addition to babysitting, they can provide someone to escort children to and from the airport, see them to the hotel or chaperone them around London until parents arrive. Twenty-four hours notice is advisable for all bookings.

Rates (3-hour minimum) range from £4.25 to £4.50 per hour plus a £13 agency fee.

MUSEUMS

The majority of London's museums cater to children – with printed "trails" handed out at the information desk. These trails provide a treasure hunt of things to find, recognize and record, and help give kids an accessible structure for exploring.

BRITISH MUSEUM, *Great Russell Street, London WC1. Tel: 0171 636 1555. Tottenham Court Road tube.*

Kids particularly love the mummies in rooms 60 and 61; Children's trails are available at the information desk.

CABARET MECHANICAL THEATRE, *33-34 The Market, Covent Garden, London WC2. Tel: 0171 379 7961. Adults: £1.95, children: £1.20, under 5: Free. Daily 10am-7pm, Sunday 10:30am-7pm. Covent Garden tube.*

Though not exactly a museum, the Mechanical Theatre offers an exhibition of upward of 60 mechanical toys that operate by pushbutton and are guaranteed to entertain grown-ups and children equally. On the lower level of the Covent Garden market – don't miss it.

IMPERIAL WAR MUSEUM, *Lambeth Road, London SE1. Tel: 0171 416 5000. Lambeth North tube.*

Planes, the Blitz and Trench experiences, the chance to be a passenger in a (simulated) RAF plane over Germany. Highly recommended for kids and adults. Children's quiz at reception.

LONDON TRANSPORT MUSEUM, *The Piazza, Covent Garden, London WC2. Tel: 0171 379 6344. Covent Garden tube.*

Buses, trams, and the chance to drive your own Underground train make the Transport Museum kiddy heaven. Actors in period dress help bring the exhibits alive. Ask at the cloak room for children's activities.

MUSEUM OF LONDON, *London Wall, London EC2. Tel: 0171 600 3699. Barbican tube.*

The story of London from the Ice Age to the present – there's tons for kids to enjoy here, including a vast recreation of Victorian shops, and the Great Fire experience. Trails available at the gift shop.

MUSEUM OF THE MOVING IMAGE, *South Bank, London SE1. Tel: 0171 928 3535. Waterloo or Embankment tube.*

From Chinese puppets to Superman, via a kids' animation workshop, kid-height monitors and lots of interactive displays, MOMI is mandatory for rainy days with kids. A special children's trail is marked out by Sesame Street's Oscar.

NATIONAL MARITIME MUSEUM, *Romney Road, Greenwich SE10. Tel: 0181 858 4422. Greenwich British Rail or boat from Charing Cross or Westminster pier.*

A special new gallery just for kids and huge boats in the Neptune Gallery make this a great day out. There's also all of Greenwich park to explore (including a playground with boat-shaped jungle gyms just behind the museum) and of course the wonderful boat ride that gets you to Greenwich. Family trails at the information desk.

NATURAL HISTORY MUSEUM, *Cromwell Road, London SW7. Tel: 0171 938 9123. South Kensington tube.*

From the animatronic dinosaurs to the creepy crawlies to a huge section of interactive displays, if you make just one stop with the kids, make it this one. Activity sheets at the information desk.

SCIENCE MUSEUM, *Exhibition Road, London SW7. Tel: 0171 938 8000. South Kensington tube.*

The oldest locomotive in the world, the Apollo 10 launch module, an airplane hangar full of airplanes and The Launch Pad – a vastly entertaining series of interactive displays – not to mention the best kid's gift shop in London.

PARKS, PLAYGROUNDS, & THE ZOO

One of the best reasons to come to London is the parks – they're great all year round, but of course best in spring and summer. Children will find themselves in good company, as every park in London is loaded with mums and nannies with prams. And it's a good excuse to get the grown-ups to the rose gardens.

CHELSEA ADVENTURE PLAYGROUND, *Royal Hospital Grounds, Royal Hospital Road, London SW3. Sloane Square tube.*

This playground is specially designed for children with physical disabilities. It's equipped with a soft-play area and outdoor site with sandbox, swing boats, climbing structure with musical chimes, tricycles, and in the summer, a wading pool. The site is staffed with full-time playworkers, and arts activities are available free every day. All children 5-15 are welcome.

BATTERSEA PARK, *Albert Bridge Road, London SW11. Sloane Square tube plus bus 19 or 137.*

This 200 acre park is a very popular family destination with a lovely Thames frontage. There's an art gallery, herb garden, deer enclosure, and London's largest adventure playground for 5-16 year olds. Maps of the park and tree and nature trails are available from the park office to the left of the Albert Bridge entrance.

CORAM'S FIELDS, *Russell Square tube.*

Set on the grounds of the renowned 18th century foundling hospital (now demolished), this seven acre garden allows entrance only to adults accompanied by a child, and includes a little farm with sheep and goats.

Princes William and Harry used to play here, probably one of the few times the royal family ventured into Bloomsbury.

HOLLAND PARK, *High Street Kensington or Holland Park tube.*

Behind the busy high street shops, this beautiful park boasts secluded lawns, gardens and woodland containing 3,000 species of trees and plants, squirrels, rabbits, and peacocks. There's an adventure playpark for children 5-15, and an under-8s area.

The pretty **Belvedere** restaurant is open May to October and there are lots of places to buy ice cream.

HYDE PARK, *Knightsbridge, Marble Arch or Hyde Park Corner tube.*

Hyde Park is kiddie-heaven, simply head for the Serpentine with a bag of bread – and try to keep your child from being eaten by swans! The duck-feeding is famous, and the variety of ducks and geese delightful. In the spring and summer, paddle boats and row boats can be rented on the Serpentine (£6 an hour, £5 deposit).

KIDSTOP, *Edgware Road (junction of Colindale Avenue) London NW9. Tel: 0181 201 3580. Monday to Friday 11:30am to 6:30pm; Saturday and Sunday, 10am to 6:30pm. Admission £3-5.50. Colindale tube.*

This multi-level 6,000 square foot indoor play arena in north London is jammed with activities including slides, climbing ropes, ladders, a giant climbing frame, and a bouncy castle for children 2 to 12. There's also a roller-skating rink (skate, helmet and pad rental available) and a special area for under-4s.

KENSINGTON GARDENS, *Lancaster Gate, Queensway or Bayswater tube.*

This lovely park (attached by an invisible border to the west side of Hyde Park) has large grassy areas and The Round Pond for sailing toy-boats. A well-equipped children's playground is located by the top of Broad Walk, near Queensway tube station. It has swings, rocking animals, a playhouse, jungle gym, and a sandpit, and benches and tables for picnics.

Near the playground is the **Fairy Oak**, a fossilized oak tree carved with whimsical birds and animals. The swings were donated to the park by J.M. Barrie, author of *Peter Pan*.

REGENT'S PARK, *Camden Town tube.*

The best of all possible parks has a playground near Gloucester gate, the best selection of exotic ducks to feed on the bridge near the open air theater, and of course **London Zoo**. If you're not up for the whole zoo experience, walk along the perimeter of the zoo in the park – on Broad Walk you'll see the wolves, and around the corner there's a decent view of camels, elephants and giraffes.

ST. LUKE'S GARDENS, *Sydney Street, London SW3. Sloane Square tube.*

Adjoining the grounds of St. Luke's Cathedral is an enclosed play area with swings, animal rockers, a small adventure play structure, and slide with safety tiles. Also, benches and toilets.

ST. JAMES PARK, *Victoria or St. James tube.*

Within view of Buckingham Palace is the Park's playground, an enclosed area with swings, sandbox, seesaws and slide. It's not far from the lake where ducks, geese and swans await stale bread with enthusiasm. Benches, covered table and toilets are available; there's a snack kiosk just outside the gate.

KID-FRIENDLY RESTAURANTS

As well as the selection here, it's worth noting that most museums feature special children's menus at their on-site cafes.

THE BLUE ELEPHANT, *4-6 Fulham Broadway, London SW6. Tel: 0171 385 6595. Open daily, noon to 2:30pm and 7pm to 12:30am (10:30pm Sunday). Closed Saturday lunch. Major credit cards. Fulham Broadway tube.*

This highly-acclaimed Thai restaurant offers an excellent all-you-can-eat **Sunday brunch buffet** (£14.50 for adults) and charges children under 4 foot tall at £2 per foot. There's always a good variety of child-friendly food like noodles and rice, and the Thai village atmosphere of waterfalls and fishponds is pure film-set magic.

Clowns entertain while you eat at the Sunday buffet. Reservations are essential.

DEALS HARBOUR YARD, *Chelsea Harbour, London SW3. Tel: 0171 352 5887. Monday to Thursday, noon to 11pm; Friday and Saturday, noon to 11:30pm; Sunday noon to 10pm. Major credit cards. Earl's Court tube and then C3 bus to the harbour.*

Sunday is family day at Deals, which means from 1pm to 4pm a magician and face painter are on hand to entertain. The standard children's menu (available every day) includes burgers, fish fingers and French fries, and is priced at about £3.50. Grown-ups can count on spending £15-20 for three courses with service and a drink. Sundays are very popular, make sure to book.

GEALES FISH RESTAURANT, *2 Farmer Street, London W8. Tel: 0171 727 7969. Open Tuesday to Saturday noon to 3pm and 6pm to 11pm. Closed Sunday and Monday. Visa and Mastercard only. Notting Hill Gate tube.*

A classic fish and chips restaurant for the whole family that, after 50 years, is still considered one of the best in London. They serve a large selection of fresh fish, all bought daily from Billingsgate Market, mainly fried (but some are available grilled). The chips (French fries to you) are delicious.

Children's portions at a reduced rate are available on request. High chairs and booster chairs provided.

PIZZA ON THE PARK, *11 Knightsbridge, London SW1. Tel: 0171 235 5273. Open daily 8:15am (9:30am weekends) to midnight. Knightsbridge or Hyde Park Corner tube.*

This very attractive, rather up-market member of the Pizza Express chain with its expanses of glass and pale wood is primarily a grown-up's restaurant, but you wouldn't know it from the number of families scattered about at any one time. This particular branch is equally famous for its very good pizzas and excellent evening cabaret shows, but if you've brought the kids, skip the show (downstairs) and do what the other families do: order pizza (or sandwiches or salads) and don't worry overly about making a mess or a fuss – the nice staff seem to take it in stride.

ROCK ISLAND DINER, *2nd floor, London Pavilion, Piccadilly, London W1. Tel: 0171 287 5500. Open daily noon to 11:30pm (11pm Sunday). No reservations except parties of eight or more. Major credit cards. Piccadilly Circus tube.*

This English version of a 50s American diner comes complete with dancing waitresses, and – in the evening and at weekends – a live DJ. The menu features all the things your kids might miss like mad about home: grilled sandwiches, burgers, hot dogs, salads and chocolate brownies with ice cream.

From noon to 5pm daily, a special children's menu is available, and on weekends kids eat free when accompanied by an adult ordering a main course.

Fast Food

When all else fails, there's always the familiar and friendly (and universal). We've listed below a few convenient fast food locations that might come in handy.

All branches have high chairs and most will take bookings for children's parties.

• **McDonald's**, *57 Haymarket, London SW1. Tel: 0171 930 9302. Piccadilly Circus tube; 108-110 Kensington High Street, London W8. Tel: 0171 937 3705. Kensington High Street tube; 35 Strand, London WC2. Tel: 0171 930 7530. Charing Cross tube; 155 Victoria Street, London SW1. Tel: 0171 828 6911. Victoria tube; 8-10 Oxford Street, London W1. Tel: 0171 636 4350. Tottenham Court Road tube.*

• **Pizza Hut**, *3 Cambridge Circus, London WC2 (and branches). Tel: 0171 379 4655. Open Daily noon to midnight (Saturday 11am to midnight). Visa and Mastercard. Leicester Square tube.* Ok, so it's not Le Gavroche, but it does have branches throughout London, a children's menu, free toys and playpacks, and an all-you-can-eat buffet. Sometimes that's just what we all need.

SHOPPING

BOOTS *(Branches throughout London).*

Britain's largest chain of drugstores will help if you run out of formula, diapers (ask for "*nappies*"), bibs, pacifiers (ask for a "*dummy*") or children's aspirin.

CHILDREN'S BOOK CENTRE, *237 High Street Kensington, London W8. Tel: 0171 937 7497. Monday to Saturday 9:30am to 6:30pm (6pm Tuesday, 7pm Thursday). Sundays (summer months only) noon to 6pm. High Street Kensington tube.*

This is the largest children's bookshop in Britain with more than 20,000 titles for babies up to teenagers. They also sell videos and toys, and during school holidays there are storytelling sessions.

COVENT GARDEN BOOKSHOP, *10 Covent Garden Market, London WC2. Tel: 0171 379 7650. Monday to Saturday 10am to 8pm; Sunday, 11am to 5pm. Covent Garden tube.*

This big new bookstore offers a good collection of children's books, including an extensive range of Puffins, the child's imprint of Penguin.

THE DOLL'S HOUSE, *29 The Market, Covent Garden WC1. Tel: 0171 240 8681. Covent Garden tube.*

Elaborate handmade period doll houses including such architectural feats as a 10 room Georgian house (£1,400) and Victorian townhouse (£1,100). Period room furnishings (including chandeliers, stuffed chairs, miniature Chippendale furniture, and sets of dishes) are also on sale in this cluttered, Victorian-style shop.

EARLY LEARNING CENTRE, *36 King's Road, London SW3. Tel: 0171 581 5764. Monday to Saturday, 9am to 6pm (7pm Wednesday). Sloane Square tube.*

Toys that make learning fun is the theme of this attractive chain of stores. That means a wonderful selection of games, building sets, books and puzzles for children up to 8 years old. A train set and pedal car keep young shoppers happily engaged while their parents shop; the helpful and knowledgeable staff hold free drop-in activities (mask-making, Easter egg decorating, clay modelling, etc.) every Wednesday from 9:30 to 11am for children 18 months to 5 years. Activities take place everyday during holiday breaks and midterm.

FORBIDDEN PLANET, *71 New Oxford Street, London WC2. Tel: 0171 379 6465. Monday to Saturday 10am to 6:pm. Tottenham Court Road tube.*

This book and toy store specializes in the world of science fiction, super-heros, fantasy and horror. There's a huge selection of comic books (including British and European underground comics), videos, and models of all the latest action heros.

JACADI, *48 Brompton Road, London SW3 1BW. Tel: 0171 584 3478. Monday to Friday 9:30am to 6pm. Knightsbridge tube.*

Gorgeous, expensive French clothes for children up to 12. Printed cotton creepers, sweatshirt infant jumpsuits in wonderful colors and patterns, hand-smocked dresses, etc. We buy all our baby presents here, preferably in the 50% off (or more) sales during January and July.

MOTHERCARE, *461 Oxford Street, London W1R 1DB (and branches). Tel: 0171 629 6621. Monday to Saturday, 9am to 5pm. Marble Arch tube.*

Forgotten the rain coats? Mysteriously lost your baby's left shoe? Need safety covers for your hotel sockets? Mothercare will fix it. A big, comprehensive selection of clothes, carriages, baby furniture, car seats, and safety accessories – for children up to 11.

POLLOCKS TOY THEATRES, *44 The Market, Covent Garden, London WC1. Tel: 0171 379 7866. Covent Garden tube.*

Wonderful Victorian toy theaters and theater accessories including puppets, masks, marionettes, old fashioned toys, pop guns, toy soldiers, pop-up books, etc.

TROTTERS, *34 King's Road, London SW3. Tel: 0171 259 9620. Monday to Saturday 9am to 6:30pm. Sloane Square tube and 127 Kensington High Street, London W8. Tel: 0171 259 9620. Hours as above. High Street Kensington tube.*

An extensive selection of good-looking, very well-made sporty clothing and shoes for real kids – infants up to 9 years. The shop also features a juice bar and children-only haircutting (£8.50 up to 3 years; £9.50 ages 3 to 12) by appointment only.

Department Stores with Special Facilities for Mothers and Children

FORTNUM & MASON, *181 Piccadilly, London W1. Tel: 0171 734 8040. Green Park tube.* If you get caught short in this neighborhood, the baby-changing room is on the second floor.

HAMLEYS, *188-196 Regent Street, London W1. Tel: 0171 734 3161. Oxford Circus tube.* London's biggest toy store is chaotic and packed with toys – heaven for children, hell to just about everyone else. The mother and child's room is on the fourth floor.

HARRODS, *87-135 Brompton Road, London SW1X 7XL. Tel: 0171 730 1234, Knightsbridge tube.* Don't bother shopping for children's clothing here unless you're trying to dispose of a huge inheritance. The adjacent book department, however, is worth a visit. The mother and child's room on the fourth floor is clean, roomy, and welcoming.

JOHN LEWIS, *Oxford Street, London W1. Tel: 0171 629 7711. Oxford Circus tube.* London's most reasonably priced department store is a good place to shop for children's clothes and accessories. Nothing fancy, just good quality, basic baby and kids' stuff. Mother and baby's room is on the third floor.

PETER JONES, *Sloane Square, London SW1W 8EL. Tel: 0171 730 3434. Sloane Square tube.* Part of the very sensible John Lewis chain of department stores. Mother and baby's room is on the third floor.

SELFRIDGES, *400 Oxford Street, London W1A 1AB. Tel: 0171 629 1234. Bond Street or Marble Arch tube.* Huge, modern, bustling, with a good department of kids' clothes. Baby-changing facility is on the third floor.

CHILDREN'S THEATER

Not surprisingly, London has a variety of theaters that specialize in children's productions, or produce seasonal children's programs at Christmas and during school breaks.

COVENT GARDEN STREET THEATRE, *The Market at Covent Garden, London WC2. Covent Garden tube.*

Covent Garden has to be the cheapest, happiest place in London to entertain kids. From April to October the marketplace plays host to excellent jugglers, musicians, unicyclists, dancers and fire-eaters – more often than not mixed with comedy. Audience participation is encouraged, and one three-year old we know participated so engagingly, he left London £5 richer!

THE NATIONAL THEATRE, *South Bank, London SE1. Tel: 0171 928 2252. Embankment or Waterloo tube.*

The National offers some of London's best theater for adults and children. At any one time there are up to nine productions in repertory and at least one is usually geared to children or a general family audience. Educational packs are available for every production, in addition to workshops, backstage tours and lectures.

PUPPET THEATRE BARGE, *(bookings and details from) 78 Middleton Road, London E8. Tel: 0171 249 6876.*

An outdoor marionette theatre in a converted barge which has regular moorings at Little Venice (in Maida Vale) from September to May. Performances Saturday and Sunday during school term and Monday through Sunday during school holidays.

TRICYCLE THEATRE, *269 Kilburn High Road, London NW6. Tel: 0171 328 1000. Admission: £2.75 (adults and children). Kilburn Park tube.*

Hour-long children's shows every Saturday at 11:30am and 2pm change weekly and include music, puppetry, theater and storytelling. Children under 7 must be accompanied by an adult. There is wheelchair access, and an induction loop for deaf children is available.

UNICORN THEATRE FOR CHILDREN, *6-7 Great Newport Street., London WC2. Tel: 0171 836 3334. Leicester Square tube.*

London's most established children's theater presents plays (often specially written for the Unicorn) and other entertainment for ages 4 to 12.

17. SPORTS & RECREATION

Let it be said, in a burst of radical understatement, that the English are not a fitness-obsessed race. Most of our English friends consider lifting a pint glass and lighting a cigarette exhausting enough; wearing shiny clothes and galloping about on a treadmill is tantamount to dementia. The good news is that lots of Americans live in London, thus providing a reasonable demand for high-quality fitness facilities.

And we have noticed that as the numbers of such facilities increase, so too has the number of Brits wandering in tentatively to enquire about toning their torsos. We'll have them drinking Bud Light and eating dairy-free cheese yet.

For information on where to find a personal trainer, aerobics class or tennis court, phone the **Sportsline** on *0171 222 8000, Monday to Friday 10am to 6pm.*

GYMS, SPAS, & WORKOUT CLUBS

• **Chelsea Sports Centre**, *Chelsea Manor Street, London SW3. Tel: 0171 352 6985. Sloane Square tube.* Daily aerobic, body conditioning and step classes, 7:30am to 9pm. Fee: £3.15-£3.30 per class. Swimming, Monday to Friday 7:30am to 10pm (last admission 9:15pm); Sunday 8am to 5:45pm. Fee: £2.

• **Jubilee Hall**, *30 The Piazza, Covent Garden, London WC2. Tel: 0171 836 4007/4835. Monday to Friday 6:30am to 10pm; Saturday and Sunday 10am to 5pm. Fee (classes): £5; (gym) £6. Covent Garden tube.* This is London's largest fitness center, located in the old Covent Garden flower market, now beautifully converted. A wide range of classes are offered, including step, circuit training, fat burner, jazz, gymnastics and self-defence. Other facilities include a 5,000 square foot fully-equipped gym with lifecycles, rowing machines, stairmasters, nautilus and free weights. Children's classes include karate, gymnastics and football (soccer). Osteopathy, shiatsu and massage treatments are also available seven days a week. The attached cafe serves hot dishes, soups, sandwiches, salads, hot and cold beverages.

- **Portchester Spa**, *225 Queensway, London W2 5HS. Tel: 0171 792 3980. Bayswater tube. Open 10am to 10pm (last entry, 8pm). Women admitted Tuesday and Thursday only; Men admitted Monday, Wednesday and Saturday. All day admission: £15.40 (includes the use of swimming pool).* This traditional Turkish steam bath and sauna is a wonderful place to get away from it all. There are lounge chairs for reading or napping between your water treatments; light snacks can be purchased. Massage and body scrubs are available by appointment for £17 (half hour) and £26 (hour)
- **Queen Mother Sports Centre**, *223 Vauxhall Bridge Road, London SW1. Tel: 0171 798 2125. Open daily 6:30am to 10pm. Pool open Monday to Friday, 6:30am to 7:30pm; weekends 8am to 8pm. Admission £1.80. Phone for class schedule. Victoria tube.* A good-quality council-owned sports center just behind Victoria Station with three swimming pools (a lap pool, children's and beginner's pool), badminton and basketball courts and lunchtime and evening aerobics, step, yoga and boxercise classes. Massage and beauty treatments are also available.
- **The Sanctuary**, *12 Floral Street, London WC2E 9DH. Tel: 0171 240 9635. Open Saturday to Tuesday, 10am to 6pm; Wednesday to Friday, 10am to 10pm. Admission (day): £39.50, (evening) £27.50. Covent Garden tube.* London media trendies hang out at this ultimate health and beauty spa for women only. Its lush tropical decor provides the perfect setting for a unique range of treatments from massage to facials to the Ultimate Aromatherapy Experience. The last consists of two hours of massage, body brushing and a detoxifying mask, accompanied by lots of relaxing aromas. The rather steep admission fee entitles you to the use of the whirlpool, sauna, steam room, unlimited towels, robe and sunbed. All other treatments are extra and require as much advanced booking as you can manage, preferably a week or two. Food is offered at a poolside bar and a restaurant stocked with California-style healthy delicacies.
- **The Gym at The Sanctuary**, *11 Floral Street, London WC2E 9DH. Tel: 0171 240 0695. Open Monday to Friday 7:30am to 8:30pm (Wednesday 9:30pm); Saturday and Sunday 10am to 5pm. Admission: £12.50 for pool, gym and sauna. Covent Garden tube.)* This attractive women-only gym, sauna and swimming pool is connected with the spa next door and also offers daily scheduled aerobic classes for an extra £1 per class.
- **Seymour Leisure Centre**, *Seymour Place, London W1H 5TJ. Tel: 0171 723 8019. Edgware Road tube. Daily classes 7:15am to 9pm. Fee: £3.60-£3.70 per class. Swimming, Monday to Saturday 7am to 8pm; Sunday 8am to 8pm (last entry 1/2 hour before closing). Fee: £1.70.* The Centre's Move It, Fitness Workout, and Aerobic Classes offer step, yoga, fat-burner workout, circuit training and stretch classes, taught by an enthusiastic

team of certified teachers throughout the day *(tel: 0171 402 5795, class information only)*. Levels from beginner to advanced.

HORSEBACK RIDING

- **Hyde Park Riding Stables**, *63 Bathurst Mews, London W2. Tel: 0171 723 2813 (phone for reservations). Lancaster Gate tube.* London's most popular riding stable caters to adults and children; five is the minimum age for supervised hour-long pony or horseback riding in Hyde Park. Safety helmets are provided, comfortable clothes and hard boots are recommended. Rates are £25 per hour; £50 for a private one-hour lesson. Reservations are required, credit card payment is made at booking.

- **Roehampton Riding Stables**, *Priory Lane, London SW15. Tel: 0181 876 7089. Putney Bridge tube plus bus 74 to Danebury Avenue.* Adults and children six and older can ride through beautiful Richmond Park for £19 an hour weekdays, £20 weekends. Lessons are £13 for a half hour, £24 per hour, with an extra £2 fee for (mandatory) safety helmets. Reservations are required; no credit cards.

- **Ross Nye's Riding Establishment**, *8 Bathurst Mews, London W2. Tel: 0171 262 3791. Lancaster Gate tube.* Supervised riding for adults and children seven and over, safety hats and boots are provided. Rates: £25 an hour, no credit cards.

SWIMMING, TENNIS, & GOLF

- **Hampstead Mixed Bathing Pond**, *East Heath Road, Hampstead Heath, London NW3. Tel: 0171 485 4491. Hampstead tube*; and **Highgate Men's Pond and Kenwood Ladies' Pond**, *Millfield Lane, London N6. Tel: 0171 485 4491. Highgate tube.* These outdoor swimming ponds on Hampstead Heath are open year round, are great fun and they're also free. Just show up with your swimsuit and a towel and jump in. As they are very deep, young children are generally not allowed in, though the lifeguards will give older kids a proficiency swim test and if they qualify they're welcome. Hours vary, so check, but a general guide is 7:30am to 9pm during the summer; 7am to 3:30pm during the winter, and 7am to 7pm the rest of the year.

- **Leaside Golf**, *Picketts Lock Centre, London N9. Tel: 0181 803 3611. Edmonton Green British Rail station.* Golf for non-members is available daily, 8am to 6:30pm. Fee: £9 weekdays, £12 weekends for 18 holes. Reserve a few days ahead; weekend reservations are taken on Wednesday.

- **Hyde Park** and **Regents Park** both have public tennis courts, but as there are no telephone reservations, you have to show up and take potluck. You can reserve an indoor or outdoor court at the **Islington**

Tennis Centre *(Market Road, London N7, tel: 0171 700 1370; Caledonian Road tube)* during their less busy daytime hours, for £5 (outdoor), £9 (indoor). Or try the **Westbourne Green Sports Complex** *(Torquay Street, London W2, tel: 0171 798 3707; Royal Oak tube)* for just £3.80 an hour.

SNOOKER

The English equivalent of pool, and a favorite late night pastime. The tables are bigger and the balls all one color, but pool sharks will soon get the hang of it.

• **Centre Point Snooker Club**, *New Oxford Street, London WC1. Tel: 0171 240 6886. Daily, 11am to 6am. Guest membership: £2; tables £4.25 per hour. Tottenham Court Road tube.* Look for signs for this underground den of iniquity at the subway entrances. Atmospheric as hell, or should we say heaven.

• **King's Cross Snooker Club**, *275 Pentonville Road, London N1. Tel: 0171 278 7079. Daily, 24 hours. Annual membership: £8; tables £2.10 per hour (£3.50 before midnight).* A favorite with serious players. You wouldn't take your mother here, but then you probably wouldn't want to.

MAJOR SPORTS & SPORTING EVENTS

Cricket

Ah, the sound of willow on leather (say that a lot and people will think you understand the incomprehensible rules of cricket). The cricket season runs from April to September and on a sunny day, it's the quintessential British experience – though be warned it takes a lot longer than baseball (and a lot less happens). Bring a hat, champagne or beer, sandwiches and sunscreen. Although tickets to the international test matches are hard to come by *(phone Keith Prowse Hospitality on 0181 795 2222 if the grounds are sold out)*, county cricket looks pretty much the same to non-aficionados, and perfectly good tickets start at just £6 (to £40).

Lord's, by the way, is the architectural award-winning cricket ground to the upper classes; the Oval is more democratic and less stuffy: **Lord's Cricket Ground**, *St. John's Wood Road, London NW8. Tel: 0171 289 1300 (test match tickets: 0171 289 8979). St. John's Wood tube*; and **The Oval Cricket Ground**, *Kennington, London SE11. Tel: 0171 582 6660. Oval tube.*

Horseracing at Ascot

For followers of royalty, hats, and even horseraces, you can't beat the four days of **The Royal Meeting at Ascot** in June (remember Eliza Doolittle's auspicious debut?) The Royal Procession occurs daily at 2pm as the Royal Party enters the course; the whole event offers some of the finest people-watching on earth.

If you have a hat (in the Royal Enclosure, morning suit and top hat is required of gentlemen; ladies must wear a dress and hat "covering the crown of the head"; grandstand dress is less formal but still Sunday best) and wish to attend, you can apply to your embassy for Royal Enclosure tickets, *or phone 01344 876 456 for Grandstand ticket credit card booking, after January 1 of the year you wish to attend.*

As of this writing, grandstand tickets run £10-25. Frequent trains depart from Waterloo to Ascot station with a 7 minute walk at the other end. Race meetings (with far easier ticket access) take place all year round, phone for a schedule or more information.

Soccer (football)

The British football season runs from August to May, and tickets are obtainable directly from the clubs. It's usually not difficult to get tickets unless a big traditional rivalry is being played out, or the playoffs are approaching. Reserved seat tickets start at about £12.

Telephone numbers for London's **Premier League Teams** are as follows:

- **Chelsea**, *0171 385 5545*
- **Arsenal**, *0171 226 0304*
- **Tottenham**, *0181 365 5050*
- **Queens Park Rangers**, *0181 743 0262*
- **West Ham**, *0181 472 2740*
- **Wimbledon**, *0181 771 2233*
- **Crystal Palace**, *0181 653 1000.*

Tennis at Wimbledon

All England Lawn Tennis Club, Church Road, Wimbledon SW19 5AE. Tel: 0181 944 1066. Wimbledon tube.

Every year during the last week of June and the first week in July, tennis aficionados talk and think of nothing else. Here's the usual way to apply for tickets: Send a self addressed stamped envelope enclosing a 60 pence international postal coupon to: **The All England Lawn Tennis Club**, *P.O. Box 98, Wimbledon SW19 5AE*, requesting an application for the **Public Ballot**. You must file your ballot between August and December the year prior to the match you wish to attend. Names are chosen by lottery at the end of January, and you will be notified in March.

If your name is chosen, you are entitled to two tickets for Centre Court or Court 1 on the day you chose on your ballot (ticket prices £20-50). Although this may sound arduous, the only real pain is the 60 pence postal coupon, and you will save literally hundreds of pounds if your application is successful.

Otherwise, you can buy a hospitality package from your travel agent in the U.S., or from **Keith Prowse Hospitality** *(0181 795 2222)* or

Sportsworld Group *(01235 555844)*. Their full-day (11:30am to 6pm) VIP packages include one ticket on Centre Court or Court 1, champagne reception, four-course lunch, open bar, afternoon tea of strawberries and cream, souvenir program, valet parking and close-circuit TV coverage of all the courts. Prices per person range from £389 to £1500, depending on the day and court; top prices are for men's finals.

The third and cheapest option is to turn up on the day you wish to attend, and simply queue for a **Grand Pass** which gives access to courts 3-17 (unreserved seating). Much is made of the huge lines, but in our experience they move quickly (you will be inundated with free newspapers and visors while you wait), and you shouldn't have to wait more than a very pleasant, sociable 45 minutes.

Ticket prices are just £7-8, and though you probably won't get to see the glamour matches, you do get to soak up the atmosphere, catch glimpses of lots of celebs (players and spectators), and watch the up-and-coming stars.

18. EXCURSIONS & DAY TRIPS

We've mixed the obvious with the not-so-obvious in this section, recognizing that there are lesser-known destinations within easy reach of London that will give you a sense of what's most attractive about Britain – its arrestingly pretty, historical villages, country houses and gardens. Do double check all train information, and make sure you note the time of the last train back.

And while you're making plans, don't forget the ultimate day trip from London – the three-hour **Eurostar** train to Paris *(for reservations phone Eurostar on 01233 617 575 or Rail Shop booking on 0345 300 003).*

BRIGHTON

A day in **Brighton** makes a good, manageable escape from London, and allows you to get acquainted with that strange atmosphere of faded grandeur that permeates English seaside towns.

ARRIVALS & DEPARTURES

This is not a daytrip to contemplate by car; getting out of London via the south is a lengthy process that can easily result in a three or four hour trip. The pleasant train, on the other hand, takes a mere 55 minutes, leaves Victoria Station twice an hour, and travels through lots of pretty countryside. As for all these trips, try and venture forth on a sunny day.

SEEING THE SIGHTS

Brighton doesn't have a particularly interesting history until the Prince Regent (the future George IV) moved in with his mistress, and proceeded to erect what is probably England's largest and most elaborately gilded and embellished folly: **Brighton's Royal Pavilion**. In 1815 he hired the most fashionable architect of the day, **John Nash** (see also the lovely cream-colored terraces around Regent's Park, and Regent Street in London) to build a palace dedicated to luxury and pleasure.

Nash's creation beggars description; you really have to see it yourself to believe it. Suffice it to say, however, that its influences are Chinese and Indian in the main, and there's a superabundance of palm trees, lacquer, bamboo, monkeys, golden dragons and parrots. The music room, recently restored, must be one of the most fantastic (in the true sense of the word) ever built; the Pavilion itself went on to become a kind of early template for Regency style. The huge kitchens have been decked out in so lifelike a manner, you feel as if the legions of cooks have just stepped out.

Don't miss the entertainingly insulting collection of caricatures of the Prince Regent – it makes what politicians go through today at the hands of the press seem positively affectionate. *(The Royal Pavilion, open daily 10am to 6pm June to September; 10am to 5pm October to May. On arrival at the train station, walk down Queens Road towards the sea, turn left onto Church Street and right onto Pavilion Parade.)*

After the Royal Pavilion, continue down Pavilion Parade, turning right onto North Street. Between North Street and the sea, you'll find yourself in **The Lanes** — a wonderfully convoluted series of pedestrian-only streets that represent the original layout of the fishing village Brighton once was. Within the maze are a vast assortment of antique shops, mixed in with clothing shops, junk shops, bars and restaurants.

If you're too hungry to browse, head for East Street just below The Lanes. There you'll find **English's Oyster Bar** *(29-31 East Street)*, a charming, very attractive seafood restaurant that's been around as long as anyone can remember. Although on the pricey side, those in search of a bargain can take advantage of the good set-price lunch menu in effect weekdays, or simply sit at the oyster bar, and order a big bowl of clam chowder and a glass of white wine.

When you've seen enough of The Lanes, head down to the waterfront. On a nice day, you'll find all sorts of activity centering around the consumption of ice cream and fish and chips. Turn right along the coast and a 10 minute walk will take you to **Hove**, Brighton's sister-town, with its grand Nash-designed squares.

Finish your day with a walk on **Brighton Pier**. It's particularly beautiful at twilight when the gaudy lights begin to come on and you can imagine yourself part of the slightly tawdry tradition of dirty weekends in Brighton. Depending on your stamina and age, the fun fair at the end of the pier is great ... fun. Skip the arcades unless you like penny bets and video games.

DIVORCE ENGLISH-STYLE

In the '30s and '40s, the seedy seaside hotels of Brighton made it popular both with couples out for a bit of fun and those seeking divorce. The only way to obtain a quick divorce was to produce a valid, documented episode of adultery; a set procedure required that the divorce-seeking husband spend the night in a hotel room with a (hired) "other woman." A (hired) witness would observe and document the husband and other woman emerging from the hotel room in the morning, thus validating grounds.

HAMPTON COURT PALACE

Hampton Court, East Molesey, Surrey. Tel: 0181 781 9500. Open daily (mid-March to mid-October) 9:30am (10:15am Monday) to 6pm; daily (mid-October to mid-March) 9:30am to 4:30pm. Adults (including maze): £7.50; children (5-15): £4.90.

ARRIVALS & DEPARTURES

During the summer months, the trip to **Hampton Court** starts with a delightful 15 mile boat ride down the Thames *(river boat service from Westminster Pier 10:30am, 11:15am and noon, phone 0171 930 2062 for more information)*. If you're making the trip during the rest of the year, take one of the frequent British Rail trains from Waterloo Station.

SEEING THE SIGHTS

At any time of year, Hampton Court is one of England's grandest royal and historical sites. Generations of British monarchs since Henry VIII have made it their country home and hunting ground, walked the beautiful grounds, and filled the massive Tudor edifice with priceless furniture and paintings. Thomas Wolsey (later cardinal and Lord Chancellor) bought the site in 1514 and presented it to Henry VIII in 1525. Four years later, when he failed to arrange Henry's divorce from Catherine of Aragon, Wolsey was ousted from the palace and his lands were declared forfeit to the king.

Henry VIII enlarged the palace and replaced the cardinal's **Great Hall** with his own, designed to impress and intimidate; you feel dwarfed and humbled here – as Henry intended visitors should. Sixty foot walls are covered in silk Flemish tapestries (1540) depicting the history of Abraham from the Old Testament, an appropriate subject for Henry who, as self-appointed head of the Church of England, fancied himself a similar brand of leader of a similarly Chosen People. Above the tapestries, stained glass windows seem to support the famous fan-vault ceiling. In this hall, 600 men ate two meals daily (at 10:30am and 4pm); if there was a bed shortage, they slept here too.

Food was prepared in the **Great Kitchen**, an apartment of ten rooms described in Henry VIII's time by a visiting Spanish dignitary as a "veritable hell." Built in 1542 and now wonderfully restored, they are the oldest surviving palace kitchens in Europe and a treat to explore. Hot, smokey, and wet, they would have been crammed with a staff of 230 men, women and children carrying out kitchen duties: boiling, baking, butchering, roasting, stuffing and saucing.

Meat made up 75% of the daily 5,000 calorie diet and in one year, the cooks prepared and the courtiers consumed 1,240 oxen, 8,200 sheep, 2,300 deer, and 53 wild boar. Bundled herbs line the walls; a giant mortar and pestle carved from the trunk of a tree stands in the corner; an immense basket of bay leaves stands on the floor. The copper-lined cauldron has its own room above the fires used to heat it. Day in and day out, cooks prepared soup stock for the potage, a staple of the 16th century diet, made of garlic, leeks, oats and herbs.

In another room, a fire crackles in a fireplace large enough to hold seven spits of roasting wild boar. Little boys (strictly instructed not to "relieve themselves" in the fire) were enlisted to turn the blazingly hot spits hour after hour. The 17th century brought clay skillets and charcoal burners into use, on which cremes and custard sauces were prepared. Enormous baskets of almonds and eggs stand on the floor; pewter platters are filled with (artificial) feasts – venison and whole baked carp in prune sauce.

More complicated dishes like roast peacock were prepared in smaller rooms off the kitchen; in these hatches, peacocks were skinned and roasted, then re-dressed in their feathers and plumes, their beaks gilded with real gold. Marzipan (a paste of almonds and sugar) would have been sculpted into great castles and forts. The **Tudor Kitchen Shop** carries an impressive stock of kitchen utensils, pewter and stoneware, herbs and spices, wine, cookbooks and chutneys.

Next is the **wine cellar**, a brick vaulted crypt lined with wooden kegs. Yearly beverage consumption in the 16th century would have averaged 600,000 gallons.

If all that food has made you hungry, head for **Queen Elizabeth's Privy Kitchen** for a cafeteria snack. Sandwiches, soups, good desserts and drinks are available (but no roast peacock). The **Garden Cafe** serves hot and cold meals year round. And the **Tiltyard Restaurant** (also in the gardens) provides lunch and afternoon tea.

The **Royal Chapel** (weekly Sunday services open to the public) is the third major area that remains intact from Tudor days. The stunning

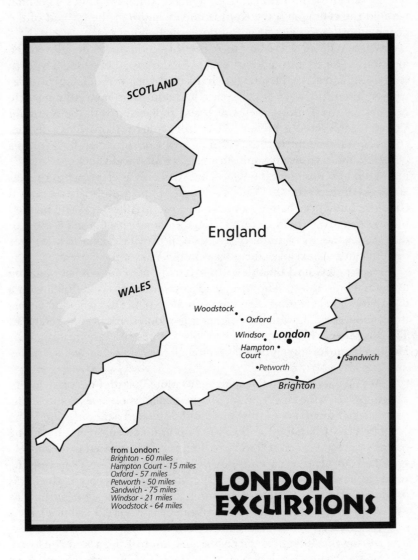

from London:
Brighton - 60 miles
Hampton Court - 15 miles
Oxford - 57 miles
Petworth - 50 miles
Sandwich - 75 miles
Windsor - 21 miles
Woodstock - 64 miles

LONDON EXCURSIONS

turquoise and gilt fan-vaulted ceiling is best viewed from the **Royal Pew** upstairs. Christopher Wren designed and Grinling Gibbons carved the reredo screen behind the altar for Queen Anne; Sir James Thornhill painted the ceiling and the trompe l'oeil window at the far end of the chapel in order to mask a view of domestic buildings.

When William and Mary took the throne in 1689, they loved the location but hated the buildings; except for the cost, they would have torn it all down and started from scratch. Instead, they commissioned Christopher Wren to "beautify" the place and add some new buildings. He demolished the Tudor Green Court and replaced it with the **Fountain Court**. Wren's serene, refined 17th century courtyard provides a distinct contrast to the cobbled 16th century **Clock Court** (named for Wolsey's beautiful and technically sophisticated **Astronomical Clock**).

Wren also designed the King's and Queen's apartments to the left and right of the Fountain Court, each with its own grand staircase, guard chamber, audience chamber and drawing room. Antonio Verrio painted the staircase frescoes with scenes from the *Satire of the Caesars*. A Roman tale of Alexander's triumph over Caesar, it provides classical metaphor for William's victory over the Stuarts in the War of the Roses.

The king's **Guard Chamber** would have housed 40 yeoman watching over the king's safety. The room is decorated as it was in 1699, with a display of 3,000 arms arranged in decorative patterns – the don't-even-think-about-messing-with-the-king message comes across loud and clear. The **Presence Chamber** holds two lovely tapestries commissioned by Henry VIII and originally hung at Whitehall Palace: *The Labours of Hercules* and *The Triumph of Bacchus*.

As you pass through the apartments, note that they decrease in size as you approach the king. Entrance to the smaller rooms was granted only to privileged members of the household or invited heads of state.

The **Privy Chamber** was the most important ceremonial room in the palace (and the Privy Gardens were designed to be viewed from above – so poke your head out the window). Not even the grooms carrying the royal clothes were allowed to enter the King's dressing room, which was presided over by the Groom of the Stool (the stool in question, by the way, was not a three-legged piece of furniture). The Verrio ceiling depicts Endymion asleep in the arms of Morpheus. Note the rock crystal chandelier. During the 1986 fire, the ceiling and floor of this room collapsed, leaving the chandelier completely shattered. Using transparent glue, restorers put the entire fixture together again without a trace of breakage.

Downstairs you'll find the **Orangery** where William grew orange and bay trees. Fossils can be spotted in the original marble floors. The last room on the ground floor was built as William's private dining room; a more intimate contrast to Henry's Great Hall. The silver and gold plate displayed on the buffet table was never actually used, its purpose solely to display the king's wealth.

After William and Mary's deaths, Queen Anne used the **King's Apartments** while the **Queen's Apartments** were completed. Georges I and II spent vacations at Hampton Court but since 1730 no monarch has lived in the royal apartments. Queen Victoria opened the palace to the public in 1838.

Take a break and stroll through the gardens. The sixty acres include the **Fountain Garden**, **Elizabethan Knot Garden** (planted with kitchen and medicinal herbs), **Pond Garden** (once stocked with freshwater fish for Henry VIII's kitchens) and the **Wilderness** in which you'll find the **Maze**. Designed by David Moreau in 1689 for William II, the English yew hedge stands seven feet tall and is clipped annually in August. The design hasn't been altered except for a slight enlargement of the center; in the 1960s the entire hedge was replanted. Getting lost in it is mandatory, though taking every possible right turn is said to lead you out eventually.

The most famous plant in the garden is the **Great Vine**, the world's oldest and longest. It was planted in 1768 for George II by Capability Brown and today is housed in its own greenhouse and tended by the royal **Vine Keeper** who is responsible for keeping it healthy and harvesting its annual 600 pound crop of Black Hamburg grapes. In the fall, the grapes are sold in the palace gift shops.

Along the east front of the gardens you'll find the entrance to the **Close Tennis Court** built for Henry VIII in 1532; history reports that he was playing tennis when word came of Anne Boleyn's execution. Enthusiasts still use the court to play Real Tennis, the original version of the game.

And finally, to the **Renaissance Picture Gallery**. Henry used the gallery for royal PR, employing English and foreign artists to enhance the reputation and glory of the monarchy. By 1640, one thousand five hundred paintings had been acquired for the collection. Highlights include the Holbein portraits, Titian's *Portrait of a Man* (presented to Charles II); Mabuse's haunting *Children of Christian II of Denmark* (all dressed in mourning); Raphael's self-portrait (his name is written on the buttons of the shirt); and Brueghel's terrifying *Massacre of the Innocents*. Examine the Brueghel closely and you'll see ghost images of massacred babies showing through under the farmyard animals – restorers discovered the original during cleaning.

The **Georgian Rooms** house William II's **Cartoon Gallery** and 18th century copies of Raphael's cartoons (originals in the Victoria & Albert Museum). The **Banqueting House** was built in 1700 and features Verrio ceilings. And last, but assuredly not least, the **Lower Orangery** houses Mantegna's magnificent series of nine *Triumphs of Julius Caesar*. Commissioned in 1474 by Mantua's Ludovico Gonzaga, they were bought by Charles I in 1629 for £10,500 and have been recently restored. They make an extraordinary high on which to finish your visit; don't miss them.

Finish your day at Hampton Court with an ice cream and a quiet half hour on the banks of the Thames. Chances are you'll be far too tired for anything else.

OXFORD & WOODSTOCK

This is the quintessential tourist trip, and although Oxford is a wonderful place to spend a day (or a weekend) it's actually quite a busy, complicated town. If you have the time, we strongly suggest that you make your trip a weekend, adding **Woodstock** to your day in Oxford.

ARRIVALS & DEPARTURES

Oxford is one hour and seven minutes by train from Paddington, and anywhere from one to two hours (depending on traffic jams) on the coaches which are cheaper: Oxford Tube *(0186 572 2250)* and City Link *(0186 524 8190)*, which leave every 20 minutes from Marble Arch.

By car, follow Marylebone road west to the M40 and get off at the Oxford exit.

To get to **Woodstock**, take the Chipping Norton Thames transit bus from Oxford (from the bus station, or in front of the Cornmarket Street HMV Record store, every thirty minutes). Get off at the stop after the Blenheim gates and turn left into the town.

Driving, take the M40 to the J9 exit and follow the brown heritage signs to Blenheim. Woodstock is on the A34, and is about a 1 1/2 hour drive from London.

SEEING THE SIGHTS: OXFORD

Whether you come in to Oxford by car, at the train, or the bus station, ask directions to **Gloucester Green** and the tourist information center. There you can get a map, and join one of the informative **tours of the colleges** *(at 11am and 2pm during the winter, more frequently in spring and summer)*.

If you'd rather strike out on your own, head first for the **Radcliffe Camera** (behind the University Church off the High Street). It's a camera in the Latin sense, that is, a room – in this case, a rather beautiful round reading room. Built in 1737 by James Gibbs, it is a classic of the kind of Italianate style that you'll see in a much grander form in the architecture of Vanbrugh's Blenheim Palace in Woodstock. The Radcliffe Camera is impossible to miss, and a good place to start your tour.

From Radcliffe Camera, return to the High Street and turn right and then left on St. Aldates till you come to **Christ Church College** (*open daily 10:30-1pm and 2-4:30pm; closed Sunday morning*). Founded by Thomas Wolsey in 1525, Christ Church was taken over by Henry VIII (after Wolsey proved unable to obtain papal permission for Henry's divorce); it is traditionally the most aristocratic of the colleges, has the most snob appeal, and certainly lays claim to the best bell – **Great Tom**, in Christopher Wren's Tom Tower. Don't leave without a visit to the **Christ Church Picture Gallery**, with its astonishing collection of Renaissance paintings (Michelangelo, Tintoretto and Leonardo among others), and the tiny cathedral with its pre-Raphaelite stained glass windows by Burne Jones.

A COLLECTION OF COLLEGES

*Oxford University was founded by Henry I in the early 12th century with **University** and **Balliol Colleges**. Today it is made up of 35 colleges, each a separate entity. Students apply to, are accepted by, and taught at the individual colleges (each of which is noted for a particular academic strength) while the University as a whole has only an administrative function.*

Plan to explore the beautiful college courtyards, gardens, and chapels in the afternoon, when they are most likely to be open to the public.

The other mandatory visit is **Magdalen College** (pronounced *maudlin*) on High Street near the **River Cherwell** (pronounced *char-well*). *It's open daily, noon to 6pm with a £1 admission.* The thirteenth century tower is considered Oxford's most beautiful, and the chapel contains a Renaissance copy of Leonardo da Vinci's *Last Supper* that was used as a guide to restore the original in Milan. Look for the spectacularly grotesque stone gargoyles in the cloister, then, if it's a nice day, cross the bridge and do a turn round **Addison's Walk** which is completely covered with flowers in April and May.

You can rent a **punt** at Magdalen Bridge for £7 an hour with a £20 deposit, and while exceedingly tricky for beginners, it will at the very least provide your passengers with much amusement.

Other recommended visits include Britain's oldest **botanical gardens** (across from Magdalen College), the **Ashmolean Museum** on Beaumont Street, **University College** where President Bill Clinton studied as a Rhodes Scholar, and the **Bodleian Library** on Broad Street with its five and a half million books. One of Europe's oldest libraries, *there are tours at 10:30, 11:30, 2 and 3pm (closed weekend afternoons) for £3.*

For lunch, try the very old, very venerable **Turf Tavern** off Holywell Street on Bath Place; **Browns** (*5-11 Woodstock Road*) for fisherman's pie, sandwiches and salads; or the delightful, more upmarket **Gees**, for fresh, modern, elegant cooking in a lovely conservatory setting (*61a Banbury Road; noon-2:30pm and 6-11pm; tel: 01865 53540*).

If you decide to make a weekend of this area, try the lovely **Old Parsonage** hotel *(tel: 01865 310210)* or stay in Woodstock for prettier, more reasonably priced hotels.

SEEING THE SIGHTS: WOODSTOCK

Now let's talk about **Woodstock** (*tourist information on Hensington Road: turn right off Oxford Street at the entrance to the village*). This beautiful little stone village just seven miles from Oxford is quite simply one of the nicest places in England.

Through nearly a thousand years of association with kings, it has a prosperous, elegant air, and although it can get pretty overrun with tourists at the height of a summer weekend, it somehow manages to retain its unspoiled, low-key charm in spite of the crowd. Aside from being very pretty, it is also home to **Blenheim Palace**, the enormous Italianate residence of the current Duke of Marlborough and birthplace of Winston Churchill (who is buried in the nearby village of Bladon). These days, the Duke of Marlborough is mainly famous for having disinherited his criminally reprobate son, a legal precedent achieved only after a long and difficult court battle.

Woodstock has a number of pretty antique shops, some good pubs (a drink at the 13th century coaching inn, **The Bear**, is mandatory) and makes a wonderful place to spend Christmas. If your budget possibly allows, don't stay anywhere other than the very beautiful, very romantic **Feathers Hotel** (*Market Street, Woodstock, Oxfordshire tel: 019 9381 2291, fax: 019 9381 3158. Double room, £99-145 including VAT and breakfast*).

For your day in Woodstock, we highly recommend that you book **The Feathers** for lunch – there's an elegant main dining room, but we prefer the very charming **Winchat Bar** with its lovely open fireplaces and comfortable chairs. In summer, the bar lunches extend out into the pretty, honeysuckle-filled garden. This isn't your ordinary pub food either – chicken liver parfait with sweet onion marmalade, chargrilled salmon with saffron mayonnaise, game terrine, and suckling pig with apple crisps are the sort of fare to expect (£15-20 per person with a glass of wine and coffee). The main restaurant serves two excellent courses for £17.50 and three for £22.50, but unless you're planning to stay overnight, you probably want to get on with your tour.

After lunch, walk along the main village road (past The Bear, with decent pub lunches and afternoon tea at the bar) to the huge gates of **Blenheim**, Britain's largest private home. Designed by John Vanbrugh in the early 18th century Italian Baroque style, it's really more impressive than comely, but what it lacks in grace is more than made up for by its sheer size and the breathtaking beauty of its grounds, laid out and designed by Capability Brown. With Vanbrugh's perfect Italian bridge over the man-made lake as a focal point, the grounds of Blenheim are nothing short of exquisite. It's hard to put your finger on exactly what makes them so lovely, they quite simply are – in the way beautiful faces and paintings by Raphael are — although the overall impression of bucolic bliss isn't hurt by the sheep scattered everywhere, the ducks on the pond, and the small herd of auburn cows on the footpaths.

The real magic of Blenheim emerges when all the tourists have gone home, at 8pm on a summer evening as twilight starts to color the park violet, and you begin to imagine what it was like to live in the 18th century on the grounds of such a place.

Depending on your inclination (you can tell what ours is), you can spend the afternoon walking around the grounds, or opt for a tour of the **Palace** *(open Easter to October, 10:30am to 5:30pm; admission £6)*. The tour takes under an hour, and the interior of the house is suitably impressive, filled with goldleaf and elaborate marble carving, portraits, priceless furniture, rare tapestries and a good deal of Churchill memorabilia. But we still prefer the park.

If you're lucky enough to have a car and another day, make sure to visit nearby **Rousham House** *(off the A4260 from Oxford; daily 10am to 4:30pm April to September, no young children)*, a 1635 mansion with 20 acres of one of the most beautiful gardens in Britain – designed by William Kent in the high Romantic style and featuring Greek follies, an elaborate monument to an otterhound (read the wonderful poem in his memory), pergolas, separate white, blue and pink walled gardens, century-old espaliered fruit trees, an 18th century dovecote, etc.

PETWORTH

You've probably guessed by now that we're big fans of **Capability Brown**. You might have noticed that we're partial to paintings. We've also been accused of having something of a weakness for antiques. In fact, this trip contains three of our very favorite things – a 2,000 acre Capability Brown park, a magnificent stately home filled with the world's largest private collection of Turners, and a pretty country village packed with antique shops.

Petworth is best in spring and summer, and it's best to avoid visiting it on Monday, Friday, and Sunday if you want access both to Petworth House and to the antique shops. The current Lord Egremont, his wife, and four chilren still live in the house, so if it is the house that interests you most, visit on a weekday when more rooms are likely to be open.

ARRIVALS & DEPARTURES

The pretty market town of Petworth is 50 miles from London in Sussex county, a bedroom commuter county which gets increasingly rural the further from London you stray. If you're going by car, take the A3 to the A283, or the M23 to the A264 to the A272 (a map is a must).

By train, there's an hourly service (two minutes past each hour, one hour and 10 minutes to Pulborough; £10 day-return ticket) from Victoria station to Pulborough, then travel the six miles to Petworth by taxi (taxi stand at station, approximately £8-9). The numbers 1 and 1a buses also travel between Pulborough and Petworth Square *(bus information: 01903 237 661)*.

SEEING THE SIGHTS

The town retains some Tudor buildings but today is mainly 18th century, and remarkably unchanged since that time. Petworth has a distinct air of prosperity, due in part to its being a market town, but also to the presence of its very grand stately home, **Petworth House** *(tel: 01798 342 476; open April to October, Tuesday, Wednesday, Thursday, Saturday and Sunday, 1pm to 5pm, closed Monday, Friday and bank holidays; Adults: £4.50; park open daily till dusk year round).* The manor provided work and a geographical focal point to the area, and attracted artists from throughout Britain who enjoyed the hospitality of the house.

Today, signs in the tourist information center (on the market square) proclaim that Petworth is "The Antique Centre of the South," which could well be true, based on the number and quality of the many shops. The **market arcade** on **East Street** houses upward of 40 dealers of furniture, prints, bric-a-brac and china; other good quality shops are spread throughout the town. **Lombard Street** is the prettiest in town, still cobbled as it was 300 years ago when it was the main route to Petworth House.

Start your tour with a walk around Petworth's grounds, considered to be one of the most beautiful parks ever designed by Capability Brown. Its untamed, rolling expanse and sprawling deer park provide a good contrast to the more orderly beauty of our other favorite Capability Brown design, the grounds of Blenheim Palace in Oxfordshire.

The bucolic idyll is enhanced by a large herd of deer (a sign on entering the park reads "Do not pick up the Antlers"), grazing sheep, and the occasional horse and rider cantering across your vista. The entire park consists of more than 2,000 acres; of which 750 are owned and kept up by the National Trust.

The best view of the house can be had from across the lake, where its rather formal, imposing French facade is shown to best advantage – though be warned the house is far superior from the inside. Petworth House was commissioned in the late 1700s by Charles Seymour, the sixth

Duke of Somerset; the architect, though unknown, is presumed to be French. A later occupant, the Third Earl of Egremont, was a great collector of art; he encouraged contemporary painters to enjoy his hospitality and use the house and lovely grounds as a base from which to paint.

Petworth's superb collection of Claude, Rembrandt, Van der Weyden, Bosch and Van Dyck (among others) inspired such later painters as Turner, Lely and Reynolds. Turner was commissioned to paint four views of Petworth to decorate one of the grand public rooms and today the house contains 20 of his paintings, the largest collection in the world outside the Tate Gallery. He worked in the huge studio over the chapel, currently closed to the public (look for the large arched window).

A tour of the house takes in the superb public rooms, the **Grand Staircase** with its wacky frescoes, the 13th century chapel, and the thoroughly wonderful 200-year-old kitchens, exquisitely restored with all their beautiful 18th century cooking and baking paraphernalia intact. The impressive **Carved Room** is crammed with the work of court carver Grinling Gibbons and the galleries play host to hundreds of paintings (Lely, Gainborough, Reynolds, Millet, Ruisdael) Greek and Roman marbles and a large collection of Victorian sculpture.

Lunch or tea can be had in the lovely, high ceilinged **Petworth Cafe** in the old kitchen complex; alternately, walk the two minutes into town to one of the pretty tea shops, or drive or catch a cab to **Tillington** (about a mile away) to the **Horse Guards Inn**; the most attractive old pub in the area with seriously good quality, inexpensive pub food (between noon and 2:30pm). The Horse Guards also has three pretty rooms and a self-catering cottage at £50 per night for those who want to stay over. *Reserve in advance, tel: 01798 342332.*

If you've started your trip with lunch in Tillington, it's a comfortable mile walk to Petworth House through the deerpark: turn left out of the pub, walk uphill past the cricket ground until you come to Park Hill House (1/4 mile). Turn right, go through the gate, and follow the main wide dirt path along to the right – it will take you straight to the house – about a 15 minute walk.

When you're ready to return to Pulborough, phone *Silverline Taxis on 874 007 or 874 321* (you'll find a phone booth in the old market square).

SANDWICH

Like Petworth, **Sandwich** is most decidedly off the beaten tourist track. One of the medieval **Cinque Ports** (Dover, Hythe, New Romney and Hastings were the other four), Sandwich was chosen by Edward the Confessor to help ensure safe passage of royal fleets through the Channel.

Each of the five ports was duty-bound to provide troops and ships in case of attack or invasion. In return, each was granted special economic protection by the king, and grew prosperous as a result. Sandwich featured in Mallory's *Morte d'Arthur*; Thomas a Becket came through the town in 1170; Henry VIII came to inspect his fleet; and Samuel Pepys (the famed London diarist) stayed at the **Bell** – still the town's biggest and most famous hotel.

ARRIVALS & DEPARTURES

The trip starts at Charing Cross station, where trains leave hourly for Sandwich, on the coast of Kent, 75 miles south east of London. The trip takes two hours and lands you in one of the most intact medieval towns in England. This is a good trip to take anytime of year (though obviously nicest in good weather), but don't do it on a Sunday – everything will be closed.

SEEING THE SIGHTS

Today Sandwich has retained virtually all of its medieval charm, most of its medieval buildings, and is unruined by tourism or development. The one concession to its rich history and proximity to London is the discreet information boards in front of important buildings. Although now close to a mile inland, it sits on a pretty quay surrounded by medieval ramparts. The nearby PGA golf courses account for what tourism there is, but most of the year it is simply a lovely, quiet, very handsome, very old town to explore. Shoppers take note: Sandwich has an abundance of antique shops (many featuring nautical antiques of the region) whose prices reflect it's non-mainstream location.

The town meanders and wanders in labyrinthine disorder, as medieval towns do (**Chain Street** measures exactly one medieval chain – 20 meters – long). For lunch, seek out the toll bridge; just to its left is the excellent **Fisherman's Wharf** seafood restaurant with pretty views over the quay. There's a charming mile and a half walk to the very rocky beach, that begins through arbors of trees and ends up with half a mile on public footbaths through the middle of a golf course.

But the nicest walk is the five mile walk to **Deal** along the coast. Deal, another of the Cinque Ports, was famous as a smugglers town, and to this day caches of stolen and smuggled 16th to 18th century French goods are being discovered behind hidden panels in the walls of old houses. Deal has a number of lovely pubs on the waterfront with tables outside, meals served under big umbrellas and on clear days, a good view of France. (Keep walking past the rundown part of town until you get to the pretty center.) Get a taxi back to the train station at Sandwich (last train back to Charing Cross – as of this writing, do check – is at 9:30pm).

If you decide to spend the night, we highly recommend the very attractive **St. Crispin Inn** *(The Street, Worth, tel: 01304 612 081)* in **Worth**, a tiny hamlet between Deal and Sandwich, and a cheap cab ride from either. The St. Crispin won Kent's Pub of the Year last year, has clean, comfortable rooms for about £50 a night and a popular restaurant with a superb selection of cask ales. Make reservations as much ahead of time as you can, it has a loyal following.

WINDSOR CASTLE

As you follow the Thames 15 miles southwest towards Heathrow Airport, you come to a most dramatic sight indeed – the huge, fairytale castle of Windsor with its medieval tower rising majestically above the busy little town. Set in nearly 5,000 acres of lovely parkland, it is the weekend home of the queen, crammed with priceless works of art and 900 years of royal history.

The first castle on the site was a wooden structure erected by William the Conqueror as a defense outpost of London. The year was 1068; it was named Windsor after the Saxon village Windlesora.

WINDSOR INFO

Tel (recorded information): 0175 383 1118; tel (further information): 0175 386 8286. Daily 10am to 5pm (last admissions 4pm). Adults: £8; children under 17: £4; family ticket (two adults, two children): £18 (£1 extra on all tickets for admission to Queen Mary's dollhouse). Changing of the guard daily (except Sunday) at 11am.

The state apartments are closed at Easter and during June and December when the queen is in residence, and during special state occasions; there is virtually no other access to the interior of the castle, so we highly recommend phoning ahead before you make the trip.

ARRIVALS & DEPARTURES

Trains every half hour from Waterloo Station (approximately £5 round trip) to Windsor-Eton Riverside station. The journey takes 50 minutes.

SEEING THE SIGHTS

The oldest part of the castle is the **round tower**, built in the 12th century by Henry II on the site of the original defense outpost. Its height made it strategically ideal for scouting and defense, it offered unimpeded vistas for 10-15 miles in all directions. The fortunes of the castle are closely linked with the **Order of the Garter**, a chivalrous order founded in 1387, when (legend has it) a lady's garter fell off in front of an audience of tittering courtiers, and King Edward III, reaching to pick it up, admonished them with the words (now the motto of the Order): *Honi soit qui mal y pense*. Literally, the phrase means "evil to him who thinks evil," though perhaps more in the spirit of "shame on you, dirty-minded brigands."

WHAT'S IN A NAME?

One of the strangest facts about Windsor is that the royal family was actually named after the castle – and quite recently at that. In 1917, **King George V** *adopted the surname Windsor and declared that it would remain the official name of the royal family for his descendants as well.*

Exactly how this charming skirmish led to the establishment of The Order of the Garter is left somewhat unclear in history books, but there have been a mere 900 knights of the order since the 14th century (just 24 at any one time), and to this day it is the highest personal honor the queen (or king) can bestow, only open to those who have offered the highest standard of service to the crown, and then only to replace a knight who has died during the previous year. Eyebrows were raised in 1995 when the queen awarded the honor to ex-prime minister Margaret Thatcher with whom her relationship had been traditionally frosty.

The castle had its biggest bout of publicity in years when a 1992 fire (reputedly set by a palace employee with a grudge, a fact that is not widely publicized) gutted one hundred rooms on five floors. Not a single work of art was lost in the fire, but centuries-old panelling, furniture and decoration were irretrievably damaged. Renovation and rebuilding is proceeding apace, and is reflected in the high entrance fees, and lack of even the most basic free guide to the castle; visitors are required to spend an additional £3-5 on guidebooks of that particularly bland, official sort.

Our advice is to skip the glossy brochures, and instead ask the many superbly informed guards as many questions as you can think up. You'll find your questions answered with a wealth of fascinating detail and anecdote – we wish one of the charmingly voluble guards had written the official guide.

Enter the castle by the main entrance up **Castle Hill**. Once inside, head for **Queen Mary's Dollhouse** (the queue moves quickly), a delightful royal folly of the first order. Built by architect Edwin Lutyens in 1920 for the current Queen Elizabeth II's grandmother (she was obviously no longer a child), it is five feet tall (1/12 scale) and includes marble floors, cut crystal chandeliers, miniature books bound in Moroccan leather (every page readable), tiny toilets that actually flush, a gramophone that plays twelve records, complete suits of armor, jewellry made by the royal jeweller, six working Rolls Royces, gas lamps, copper pots in the kitchen ... you get the idea. If the thought of all this royal privilege proves irksome, it may help to know that the separate admission fee to the dollhouse is donated to children's charities.

Continuing along (past the 3-foot antique dolls with their fur coats, embroidered kid gloves and tiaras), you come to the **armory rooms**, containing an elaborately engraved suit of armor that once belonged to Henry VIII, as well as a huge variety of swords and weapons. The rooms were originally open courtyard, but were enclosed by George IV in 1820, who, as Prince Regent, commissioned the outrageous pleasure palace, Brighton Pavilion. Echoes of George's over-the-top taste can be see in the ceiling design of elaborate plasterwork and bright green flowers.

The **Waterloo Chamber** is next, with its banquet table for 175 and portrait of George III looking (for fans of the recent movie *The Madness of King George*) not entirely unlike Nigel Hawthorne. Look for the *Honi soit qui mal y pense* Order of the Garter slogan carved throughout.

The **Kings Drawing Room**, or **Rubens room** as it is known, begins to give you an idea of the range and value of the Queen's art collection. Three huge Rubens dominate, though a loopy portrait of the young George III shooting an arrow through a red parrot (signs of future madness, perhaps?) deserves an appreciative squint. The view from the window frames **Eton College Chapel** – a large Gothic church that looks more like a small cathedral.

BEAUTIFUL WINDSOR CASTLE, AS SEEN FROM THE THAMES RIVER

Past the King's bedroom with its very kingly purple, gold, and green embroidered silk canopy (topped with ostrich feathers), the **King's Dressing Room** boasts one of the most famous paintings in the castle, the triple portrait of Charles I by Van Dyck. There's also a Memling, a Durer, two Rembrandts and a Rubens self portrait. And this is one of the castle's smaller rooms.

Later rooms reveal a superb collection of Holbeins, a lovely portrait of Princess Mary with bow and arrow (by English painter Peter Lely), and in **Charles II's dining room** (17th century), elaborate limewood carving by Grinling Gibbons and a banquet of the gods (swan is on the menu) painted Verrio ceiling. Seven Van Dycks grace the **Queen's ballroom**, as well as two hideously ornate silver tables and mirrors, one presented to Charles II, the other to William III as a wedding present from the people of London. Eighteenth century French Gobelin tapestries grace **Queen Catherine of Braganza's audience chambers**, along with another Verrio ceiling.

Emerging from the state apartments, the pretty green just ahead of you looks across to the Queen's rooms. The last time we visited, we saw Princes William and Henry arriving for lunch.

Continue down the hill towards **St. George's Chapel**, and at the bottom you'll notice a series of lovely timber and brick Tudor houses. Built in the 15th century, the **Horseshoe Cloister** today provides housing for the members of the chapel choir. If you time your visit to the chapel to coincide with the evensong (5pm) service, you have a good chance of hearing them sing. Visitors to Windsor who wish to avoid the hefty entrance fee are admitted free to the chapel for services (you must queue outside the chapel gates at 5pm weekdays or 10:45am Sundays, though entrance is not guaranteed), and can afterward walk around the castle courtyards (Sunday only), but there is no admission to the state apartments except by ticket.

A number of historical grandees are buried in **St. George's Chapel**, including Jane Seymour (1537), Henry VIII (1547) and Charles I (1648). Edward IV began the chapel for the Order of the Garter in 1475, but by the time it was finished nearly 50 years later, the Renaissance was in full swing and the Gothic style was considered out of date. We have no such qualms today, and are content to admire the stained glass window that covers the entire end wall, the elaborate choir carved out of Windsor oak, and the crest and flags of the members of the Order of the Garter. (Any member of the Order who falls into disgrace, we are told, has his crest thrown into the Thames. It hasn't happened lately.)

Next door, the flamboyantly ornamented **Albert Chapel** (built in 1240 by Henry III and dedicated to Edward the Confessor) was reclaimed from disrepair by Queen Victoria and redecorated to honor the memory of her beloved husband. Etched and inlaid marble depicts scenes from the Old Testament with particular relevance to Albert's life; marble relief heads of each of their nine children (plus one daughter-in-law for symmetry) line the walls.

A variety of very touristy cream teas are offered throughout Windsor; we preferred the very good coffee and decent sandwiches at **Importers** (*11 Peascod Street, nearly across from Marks & Spencer*). But to escape the tourist madness of Windsor, walk just across the bridge over the Thames into the village of **Eton**, home of the most exclusive boy's school in the world (founded 1440). This pretty village a mere two minutes walk from Windsor is much less spoiled, you'll get a good look at the boys in their formal morning coats, and there are a variety of tea houses and restaurants (try the **Eton Wine Bar**, *82-83 High Street*) with a considerably more authentic air. Be careful not to postpone lunch too long – as in most rural villages, pubs and restaurants in Eton tend to close as early as 2 or 2:30pm. The **Eton College Chapel** with its medieval frescoes is worth a visit (*open Easter to October from 10am to 4:30pm daily*).

Spend the rest of your day walking along the towpaths at the side of the Thames; or take one of the many half-hour boat trips offered on this lovely stretch of river. The swans (most of which officially belong to the queen) are numerous, lovely, and aggressive when defending their nests in early spring. Springtime's legions of huge, fluffy gray cygnets are a sight to behold.

THE QUEEN'S GUARDS - HOW DO THEY DO IT?

Surely the most distinctive symbol of Royal Britain at Windsor are the red-uniformed guards in bearskin hats standing perfectly still for hours on end. They're the **Queen's Guards***, theirs is a primarily decorative function, and they are required to stand absolutely, perfectly still for the duration of their two hour shifts.*

How do they do it? In order to prevent muscle cramps, and fainting due to blood pooling in the lower extremities, they pass the time on duty invisibly flexing and relaxing each separate muscle in their arms, legs, back and stomach. Sounds boring – but apparently it isn't. An ex-guard told us that he had to empty his boots after every shift, as they were full of young women's phone numbers and hotel room keys. Something about a man in uniform we suppose.

INDEX

Afternoon tea, 260
Airlines, 32
Airports: transportation to and from, 37-38, 40
Albert Memorial, 204
Ascot races, 276

Banks, 41-42
Banqueting House, 159
Beefeaters, 148
Blenheim Palace, 286, 288
Boat trips, 56-57
Brighton, 279; Royal Pavilion, 279
British history, 19-31
British Museum, 134
British Tourist Authority, 33
Brown, Capability, 203, 285, 289
Buckingham Palace, 194
Burlington Arcade, 215, 251
Bus tours, 58
Buses, 37-38, 57-58
Business hours, 42-43

Cabaret Mechanical Theatre, 180
Cabinet War Rooms, 184
Carlyle, Thomas (house), 207, 231
Cars: car rental, 38-39; driving in London , 43, 59-60
Central Criminal Court (see Old Bailey)
Changing money, 41-42
Changing of the Guard, 195
Chelsea (walking tour), 206
Chelsea Old Church, 207
Chelsea Physic Garden, 199
Chelsea Royal Hospital, 206
Chelsea Town Hall, 207

Cheyne Walk, 207
Children (263-272): babysitting, 263; children's hotel, 264; Kidsline, 263; playgrounds, 266; restaurants, 268; shopping with, 270; theater, 272
Christies, 215
Churches (services), 49
Churchill, Winston, 184-185, 288
Climate: weather, 34; when to visit, 35
Clothing: English sizes, 252, 254; sales, 249; shopping for, 247-256; what to pack, 34
Courtauld Institute, 161, 208
Credit cards, 42
Cricket, 276
Crown Jewels, 150-151
Currency, 43-44
Customs and Immigration, 33

Dance, 221-222
Day trips, 18, 279-297
Dennis Severs' House, 181
Dental emergencies, 46
Design Museum, 162; Blue Print Cafe, 129, 163
Dickens House, 190
Dinosaurs, 141
Disraeli, Benjamin, 161
Doctors, 45
Drug stores, 46
Dulwich Picture Gallery, 163

Electricity, 44
Emergencies, 54
Etiquette, 44-45

Eurostar, 61

Film (see also Museum of the Moving Image), 220-221
Fleet Street, 208-209
Fortnum & Mason, 215, 248, 250
Freud Museum, 191

Gatwick Airport: transportation to and from, 37-38; Gatwick Express, 37
Geffrye Museum, 163; cafe, 164
Gibbons, Grinling, 144, 210, 284, 291, 296
Golf, 275
Green Park, 205
Greenwich (walking tour), 211; restaurants, 212
Greenwich meridian line, 213
Greenwich park, 211
Gropius, Walter, 207

Hampstead Heath, 200
Hampton Court Palace, 281; cafe and restaurants, 282
Handicapped travelers, 45
Harrods, 208, 247, 250
Hawksmoor, 156, 197
Hayward Gallery, 177
Health, 45-46
Health clubs, 273-275
Heathrow Airport: transportation to and from, 37-38, 40
Highgate bathing ponds, 200, 275
Highgate cemetery, 200
Holidays, 41
Holmes, Sherlock (see Sherlock Holmes Museum)
Horseback riding, 275
Horseracing, 276
Hotels: "Best" recommendations, 70; Booking ahead, 36; Booking services, 39; "Budget" recommendations, 89; map, 66-67
Hotels, list (63-89):
Abbey Court, 82
The Ascott, 64

The Basil Street Hotel, 69
Bloom's Hotel, 78
Brown's Hotel, 64
The Cadogan, 71
The Capital Hotel, 71
The Cheshire, 79
The Diplomat Hotel, 72
Dorset Square Hotel, 85
Dukes Hotel, 65
Durrants Hotel, 86
Embassy House Hotel, 72
The Executive, 72
The Feathers, 288
The Fenja, 73
Fielding:, 79
The Franklin Hotel, 73
La Gaffe, 88
The Gate Hotel, 83
The Gore, 74
The Halkin, 74
Hazlitt's, 80
The Holland Park Hotel, 83
Horse Guards Inn, 291
L'Hotel, 75
James House, 75
John Howard Hotel, 75
The Lanesborough, 68
Lime Tree Hotel, 76
The Marlborough, 80
Montague Park Hotel, 81
The Morgan, 81
Number Sixteen, 76
The Pavilion Hotel, 86
The Pembridge Court Hotel, 84
The Portobello Hotel, 84
Regents Park Hotel, 87
St. Crispin Inn, 293
The Sloane Hotel, 77
Tophams Ebury Court, 77
22 Jermyn Street, 65
The Sandringham Hotel, 88
The Stafford Hotel, 68
The Wilbraham Hotel, 78
Willet Hotel, 78
House of Commons, 185
House of Lords, 185
Houses of Parliament, 185

Hyde Park, 204

Imperial War Museum, 164; cafe,
    165
Inns of Court, 209
Institute of Contemporary Arts;
    (ICA), 178, 217
Introduction, 13
Iveagh Bequest (see Kenwood House)

Jetlag, 40
Johnson, Dr. Samuel (house), 192,
    209
Jones, Inigo, 160, 211, 212

Keats' House, 192, 214
Kensington Gardens, 204
Kensington Palace, 195; Orangery
    restaurant, 197
Kenwood House, 165, 200, 214; cafe,
    166
Kew Gardens, 202; cafes, 203
Kings and Queens of Britain (list), 29-
    31
King's Road, 206
Knightsbridge, 16

Le Notre, Andre, 211
Leighton House, 166
Liberty, 247, 251
London Transport Museum, 170
London Zoo, 183, 204
Lost & found, 47

Madame Tussaud's, 181
Maps of London (about), 55-56
Marble Arch, 204
Marks & Spencer, 247, 251
Marx, Karl, 201
Medical emergencies, +45-46
Money, 41-42, 43-44
Mummies (Egyptian), 136
Museum of London, 166
Museum of Mankind, 169, 215
Museum of the Moving Image, 169
Music, 221-223

Nash, John, 198, 203, 279-280
National Army Museum, 206
National Gallery, 136, 217; Brasserie,
    137
National Maritime Museum, 212
National Portrait Gallery, 140
National Theatre backstage tour, 187
Natural History Museum, 141
Newspapers and magazines, 48

Old Bailey (Public Gallery), 189, 210
Opera, 221, 223
Oxford, 286

Palace of Westminster (see House of
Commons or House of Lords)
Parks and Gardens, 199-205
Parliament Hill, 200
Passports, 33
Pelicans (in St. James Park), 205
Petworth, 289
Petworth House, 289-291
Post offices, 49
Pubs: "best" pubs, 237; choosing a
    pub, 229
Pubs, list (226-246):
    Albion, 238
    Antelope, 230
    Barley Mow, 243-24ç4
    Bear, 288
    Blackfriar, 210, 231
    Bunch of Grapes, 240
    Camden Head, 240
    Clarence, 242
    Cross Keys, 233
    Cutty Sark, 214, 234
    Dog & Duck, 245
    Eagle, 239
    Enterprise, 228
    Flask (Hampstead), 235
    Flask (Highgate), 235
    Flower and Firkin, 203
    Fox & Anchor, 231
    Fox and Hounds, 230
    Freemason's Arms, 214, 235
    French House, 245-246
    Golden Lion, 216

George Inn, 246
Grenadier, 241
Grouse and Claret, 241
Guinea, 242-243
Hand in Hand, 244
Holly Bush, 214, 236
Horse Guards Inn, 291
King's Head and Eight Bells, 207, 230
Lamb, 228
Lamb and Flag, 233
Museum Tavern, 228
Nag's Head, 241
O'Hanlons, 239
Old Bank of England Ale and Pie House, 210, 232
Olde Bell Tavern, 210
Prince Alfred, 244
Prospect of Whitby, 233
Punch Tavern, 210
Queens, 236
Red Lion, 243
Salisbury, 234
Seven Stars, 229
Spaniard's Inn, 214, 237
Sun, 229
Swag and Tails, 241-242
Three Greyhounds, 246
Tipperary, 209
Trafalgar, 214, 234-235
Waterside Inn, 239
White Cross Hotel, 245
White Swan, 245
Windsor Castle, 240
Ye Grapes, 242
Ye Olde Cheshire Cheese, 209, 232
Ye Olde Cock Tavern, 209

Queen Mary's rose garden, 204
Queen's House (Greenwich), 211
Queen's Gallery, 198

Radio, 52
Regent's Park, 203
Restaurants: budget bests, 104; expensive bests, 133; map, 96-97

Restaurants, list (90-133):
Alastair Little, 121
Alfred, 91
Andrew Edmunds, 122
The Arts Theatre Cafe, 101
Bar Central, 129
Belgo Centraal, 102
Bistrot 190, 109
Blue Elephant, 109
Blue Print Cafe, 129
Browns (Oxford), 287
Casale Franco, 107
Chelsea Kitchen, 110
Chez Gerard, 122
Chiaroscuro, 91
China China, 93
Chuen Cheng Ku, 93
The Coffee Gallery, 92
Como Lario, 110
The Crusting Pipe, 102
La Delizia, 111
Diwana Bel-Poori House, 107
The Eagle, 98
Emporio Armani Express, 111
English's Oyster Bar, 280
The Enterprise, 111
Est, 127
F. Cooke & Sons, 106
La Famiglia, 113
The Fifth Floor at Harvey Nichols, 113
The Fire Station, 130
Fisherman's Wharf, 292
Foxtrot Oscar, 112
Freedom, 123
The French House Dining Room, 123
Fung Shing, 94
Gees, 287
Gopal's of Soho, 124
The Greenhouse, 118
The Halkin, 114
H.R. Higgins, 119
Hudson's Victorian Dining Room, 194
Ikkyu, 95
The Ivy, 103

Joe Allen, 105
Ju-Jiro, 124
Kensington Place, 95
Kettners, 126
King's Cross Tandoori, 108
King's Road Cafe, 114
Lemonia, 120
The Lexington, 125
Made In Italy, 115
Maison Bertaux, 125
Le Metro, 115
New World, 93
Odette's, 121
Ognisko, 115
Le Palais du Jardin, 105
Patisserie Valerie, 126
Pearl Restaurant, 116
The Peasant, 99
The People's Palace, 131
Pizza Express (Bloomsbury), 92
Pizza Express (Covent Garden), 105
Quaglino's, 119
The Quality Chop House, 99
Ravi Shankar, 108
Saigon, 128
St. John, 100
Sofra, 120
Soho Soho, 127
Singapore Garden, 117
Tate Gallery Restaurant, 131
Villandry Dining Room, 117
Wagamama, 93
Rosetta Stone, 135
Rotten Row, 204
Rousham House, 289
Royal Academy of Art, 178
Royal Botanic Gardens, Kew, 202
Royal London, 194-199
Royal Mews, 198
Royal Naval College, 211
Royal Observatory, 212-213
Royal Opera, 221
Royal Shakespeare Company, 220
Rumpole of the Bailey, 209

Saatchi Gallery, 179
Saint Bartholomew The Great
    Church, 174

Saint Bride's Church, 210
Saint James (walking tour), 214
Saint James Park, 205, 217
Saint Martin-within-Ludgate Church,
210
Saint Paul's Cathedral, 142, 208, 210
Sandwich, 291-293
Saville Row, 215
Science Museum, 146
Serpentine Gallery, 179, 204
Sherlock Holmes Museum, 193;
    Hudson's Victorian Dining Room,
    194
Shopping (247-259): antiques, 248-
    249, 257-258; books, 256; clothing
    sizes, 254; sales, 249; shoes, 255-
    256; VAT refunds, 50
Sir John Soane, 172, 206
Sir John Soane's Museum, 172
Snooker, 276
Soccer, 277
Speaker's Corner, 204
Spencer House, 173
Sports, 273
Strand, 209
Swimming, 275
Synagogue, Bevis Marks, 160
Synagogues (services), 49

Tate Gallery, 147; restaurant, 148
Taxis, 37, 51, 60
Tea (see Afternoon Tea)
Telephones, 51-52
Television, 52
Temple Church, 209
Tennis courts, 275
Theater: Barbican, 218; booking
    tickets, 219-220; booking tickets in
    advance, 33, 219-220; half-price
    tickets, 219; National Theatre,
    218; Open Air Theatre, 220; Royal
    Shakespeare Company, 218;
    Theatre Museum, 171; Theatre
    Royal Drury Lane (backstage
    tours), 189
Tickets:London Transport, 56;
    Theater tickets (see Theater)
Tillington, 291

Time, 53
Time Out, 48
Tipping, 53
Toilets, 47
Tower of London, 148, 211
Trafalgar Square, 217
Transportation:
  at train stations, 39
  buses, 37-38, 57-58
  cars, 38-39, 43, 59-60
  Eurostar, 61
  taxis, 37, 51, 60
  to and from airports, 37-38, 40
  trains (British Rail), 37, 61
  tubes (London Underground), 38, 60
Turner, J.M.W., 148, 289, 291

Victoria & Albert Museum, 152;
  restaurant, 155

Visas, 33

Walking, 61
Walking tours, 61-62, 206-217
Wallace Collection, 175
Water, 53
Waterloo Bridge, 208
Weights and measures, 53
Westminster Abbey, 155; evensong, 159
Whitechapel Art Gallery, 180
Wimbledon, 277-278
Windsor Castle, 293
Woodstock, 286
Wren, Christopher, 144, 145, 156, 196, 206, 210, 211, 212-213, 284, 287

Zoo (see London Zoo)

FROM THE PUBLISHER

Our goal is to provide you with a guide book that is second to none. Please remember, however, that things do change: phone numbers, prices, addresses, quality of food served, value, etc. Should you come across any new information, we'd appreciate hearing from you. No item is too small, so if you have any recommendations or suggested changes, please write to us.

Have a great trip!

Open Road Publishing
P.O. Box 20226
Columbus Circle Station
New York, NY 10023